PERFORMING POWER

Performing Power

Cultural Hegemony, Identity, and Resistance in Colonial Indonesia

Arnout van der Meer

SOUTHEAST ASIA PROGRAM PUBLICATIONS

AN IMPRINT OF CORNELL UNIVERSITY PRESS

ITHACA AND LONDON

First published 2020 by Cornell University Press

Library of Congress Cataloging-in-Publication Data
Names: Meer, Arnout van der, 1980– author.
Title: Performing power: cultural hegemony, identity, and resistance in colonial Indonesia / Arnout van der Meer.
Description: Ithaca, [New York]: Southeast Asia Program Publications, an imprint of Cornell University Press, 2020. | Includes bibliographical references and index.
Identifiers: LCCN 2020046264 (print) | LCCN 2020046265 (ebook) | ISBN 9781501758577 (hardcover) | ISBN 9781501758584 (paperback) | ISBN 9781501758591 (epub) | ISBN 9781501758607 (pdf)
Subjects: LCSH: Politics and culture—Indonesia—Java—History—19th century. | Politics and culture—Indonesia—Java—History—20th century. | Group identity—Indonesia—Java—History—19th century. | Group identity—Indonesia—Java—History—20th century. | Indonesia—Politics and government—1798–1942. | Java (Indonesia)—Social life and customs—19th century. | Java (Indonesia)—Social life and customs—20th century.
Classification: LCC DS625.M44 2020 (print) | LCC DS625 (ebook) | DDC 959.8/20223—dc23
LC record available at https://lccn.loc.gov/2020046264
LC ebook record available at https://lccn.loc.gov/2020046265

Cover image: Resident P. Sijthoff of Semarang with his servant holding his gilded *payung*, 1904. Source: Leiden University Library, Royal Netherlands Institute for Southeast Asian and Caribbean Studies 2603.

S | H **The Sustainable History Monograph Pilot**
M | P Opening up the Past, Publishing for the Future

For Amelie and Sofie

CONTENTS

FIGURES

ACKNOWLEDGMENTS

The process of writing a first book is like a play. It consists of distinct acts, beginning with formulating a research topic and question in graduate school, conducting research in libraries and archives, working through challenges, and honing the narrative and arguments until it finally all comes together in published form. Unlike a play, however, the reader only sees the result of this laborious journey. I am therefore excited for the opportunity to recognize and thank the many people who have offered me instruction, support, friendship, and insightful feedback along the way. Without their help, this book simply could not have been written.

This book began at Rutgers University, where I was lucky to work with some of the most amazing scholars and teachers I know. I am especially grateful for the enduring guidance and friendship of Michael Adas, whose questions about photographs depicting Dutch colonial officials surrounded by Javanese status symbols prompted my interest in the interplay between culture and power many years ago. I treasure our conversations over coffee on cultural hegemony, agency, and material culture just as much as those on contemporary politics, baseball, and life. Bonnie Smith is among the most inspiring people I have ever met. She taught me numerous invaluable skills, but her most important lesson is one that I consistently convey to my own students: when writing, make sure it is interesting. I also profited tremendously from my conversations with Matt Matsuda about culture and power and am forever inspired by his exemplary energy in the classroom. To this day, I feel privileged to have had Eric Tagliacozzo as my outside reader, as he encouraged me to expand the scope of my project and always provided me with invaluable advice.

Throughout researching and writing the manuscript, I received vital support from friends I made in graduate school, especially Kris Alexanderson, Stephen Allen, Alejandro Gomez-del Moral, Annie Kinkel-De Vries, Kathryn Mahaney, Elizabeth Churchich, and Adam Zalma. During my research trips and conferences, I met many inspiring people who each in their own way helped me to develop my project, including Tom van den Berge, Marieke Bloembergen, Kees van Dijk, Liesbeth Ouwehand, Remco Raben, Pauline K. M. van Roosmalen, and

Abdul Wahid. I benefited from the help and friendship of Hazel Hahn, whose invitation to participate in a project on cultural exchange between Southeast Asia and Europe and her insightful commentary on my writing positively shaped my project. Similarly, Henk Schulte Nordholt's challenge to develop a collaborative study with Tom Hoogervorst and Dafna Ruppin significantly impacted my own understanding of my research. No less inspiring was my teamwork with Bart Luttikhuis, whose sharp mind and pen were a great help in articulating social change in colonial Indonesia. And finally, I'd like to thank my colleagues at Colby College, who made me feel right at home and were always supportive of my research agenda. I especially appreciate the support and feedback provided by Sarah Duff, Noa Gutow-Ellis, Elizabeth LaCouture, Mary Beth Mills, and John Turner.

Throughout my years of work on this project, I have received generous financial support that enabled research trips in Europe and Indonesia, language instruction, editing services, and much-needed time for writing. I am especially grateful for my Fulbright Fellowship from the Netherlands America Commission for Educational Exchange; the substantial support of the Department of History, School of Graduate Studies, and the Rutgers Center for Historical Analysis at Rutgers University; various fellowships and grants from the Andrew W. Mellon Foundation; an Affiliated Fellowship at the Royal Institute for Southeast Asian and Caribbean Studies (KITLV); and my Colby College Start-Up Funds as well as several Colby College Social Science Division Grants. Without a doubt, the help and guidance of librarians and archivists enhanced my research tremendously, especially at the former library and collections of the KITLV, Leiden University Library's Special Collections, and the National Archives in The Hague.

My editor, Sarah Elizabeth Mary Grossman, has been supportive of—and patient with—my book project since I first pitched it at the Association for Asian Studies' annual meeting in Toronto in 2017. I thank her for her encouragement and persistence in seeing this project come together. I am also very much obliged to the two anonymous readers whose thoughtful suggestions have undoubtedly improved this book. And I owe special thanks to Alix Genter, my fellow Rutgers graduate, whose assistance in editing my manuscript was essential in honing my writing and clarifying my thoughts. Finally, I am truly grateful for the generous support of the Andrew W. Mellon Foundation's Sustainable History Monograph Pilot program, which greatly expands the reach of my scholarship.

My own understanding of this project developed as I sharpened my thoughts and approach through research fellowships, talks, conference presentations, and of course publications. All of these experiences come together in this book. Parts of chapters 2 and 3 originally appeared in "Rituals and Power: Cross-Cultural Exchange and the Contestation of Colonial Hegemony in Indonesia," in *Cross-Cultural Exchange and the Colonial Imaginary: Global Encounters via Southeast Asia*, edited by Hazel Hahn (Singapore: NUS Press, 2019), 75–103; and "Igniting Change in Colonial Indonesia: Soemarsono's Contestation of Colonial Hegemony in a Global Context," *Journal of World History* 30, no. 4 (2019): 501–32. Small portions of chapters 3 and 4 can be found in an article I wrote with Bart Luttikhuis: "1913 in Indonesian History: Demanding Equality, Changing Mentality," *TRaNS: Trans-Regional and-National Studies of Southeast Asia* 8, no. 2 (2020): 115–33. A version of chapter 6 was first published as "Performing Colonial Modernity: Fairs, Consumerism, and the Emergence of the Indonesian Middle Classes," *Bijdragen tot de Taal-, Land-en Volkenkunde* 173, no. 4 (2017): 503–38.

It was my mother's fascination with colonial literature that introduced me to the history of Indonesia, although my parents always encouraged an interest in the past more broadly. Their greatest accomplishment is creating a warm and supportive family that allowed my sisters and me to chase our dreams, knowing that we could always count on one another. The fulfillment of this particular dream of mine is therefore also their achievement. Joke, my wife, has supported this project from the very beginning and is thrilled with its completion. Her kindness, courage in life, and ceaseless passion for academic work and our family inspire me every day. And finally, I thank our daughters, Amelie and Sofie. This project has been intertwined with their whole lives, and these last few months they have been increasingly asking if it is finally finished. To my great joy and relief, the next time they ask I can tell them that yes, it is done. This is for them.

A NOTE ON SPELLING AND TERMS

This book deals with a dynamic period in Indonesian history during which identities and languages were in constant flux. My decisions about language reflect my hope to assist in further research, to honor the ethnic and national identities of the indigenous peoples of colonial Indonesia, and to make the text as clear and comprehensible as possible.

To enable others to locate and identify people, associations, unions, and political parties in the historical record, these names appear in their original spelling as found in archives and publications. For instance, I use *Soemarsono* instead of *Sumarsono* and *Boedi Oetomo* instead of *Budi Utomo*. Place names, however, appear in their contemporary spelling to make it easier for readers to identify and locate these places on a map (see figure 1). Thus, I use *Purwakarta* instead of *Poerwakarta*. The exception to this rule is when a particular place had a Dutch name in the colonial era, like Batavia, which was renamed Jakarta following Indonesian independence. In addition, both historians and contemporaries have referred to the former Dutch colonial empire in the Indonesian archipelago by a great diversity of names, the most common being the Dutch East Indies, Dutch Indies, Netherlands East Indies, and the Netherlands Indies. In this study I use *Netherlands Indies* and also employ the term *colonial Indonesia* to emphasize the colonial character of the state and identify it as the precursor to modern Indonesia.

Since the Dutch referred to themselves as both Dutch and European interchangeably in publications and official and private documents, I do the same. In addition, this book is primarily focused on Java, which is home to several large ethnic groups, the primary ones being the Javanese, Sundanese, Madurese, and Betawi (Malay). The term *Javanese* can refer to inhabitants of the island of Java as well as ethnic Javanese. Moreover, this volume documents a period during which people from throughout the archipelago developed a national consciousness and created a collective Indonesian identity. Through this process, often referred to as the national awakening, Javanese, Sundanese, Sumatrans, Balinese, and many others began to also consider themselves Indonesians. In other words, a person could be ethnically Sundanese, an inhabitant of Java (Javanese), and identify as

Indonesian. I have tried to make these different designators as straightforward and context-dependent as possible.

Finally, I have included Indonesian terms in their modern spellings, especially those for which there is not a satisfactory translation; for example, *hormat* (customary ways of showing respect) and *sembah* (a gesture of respect in which a person brings their hands together in front of their face). Similarly, I have maintained modern spellings for Indonesian classifications and titles, i.e., *bupati* (regency head) instead of *boepati*. Unless otherwise indicated, all English translations from Indonesian and Dutch are my own.

PERFORMING POWER

Introduction

The Performance of Power

FOLLOWING A SUCCESSFUL PERIOD working in the colonial capital
of Batavia (Jakarta), Prawiradinata, a young and ambitious clerk in the
indigenous civil service, was transferred to a new post in Purwakarta,
a small town in Java's interior. His enthusiasm about his career advancement
quickly evaporated when he discovered that beyond the capital, conservative
attitudes pervaded the colonial administration. In December 1912, Prawiradinata was summoned by his Dutch superior, Assistant Subdistrict Administrator
A. A. C. Linck, who, in a confrontational tone, accused the clerk of not submit-
ting his paperwork on time. Startled by the rebuke, Prawiradinata responded in
Dutch rather than Javanese—a signal that he was not only Western-educated
but also unwilling to offer traditional deference to his supervisor. At the time,
it was still customary for Javanese subordinates to adhere to a strict colonial
language hierarchy, addressing superiors in high Javanese while they in turn
answered in a lower form of the language. This deviation from bureaucratic practice infuriated Linck, who bellowed that he would "not be lied to by a native."
Declaring that everyone in the civil service complained about Prawiradinata's
sluggish work ethic, Linck clearly attempted to reassert his authority over an
insolent colonial subject by invoking the trope of the lazy native.[1] In the ensuing
battle of wills, Prawiradinata persisted and vowed—still in Dutch—that he was
neither lazy nor a liar. Linck dismissed Prawiradinata but immediately filed an
official complaint with the local *bupati*, the Javanese district head. Tellingly,
when Prawiradinata later appeared before the bupati, he was not questioned
about the missing paperwork but rather about his alleged impolite and boorish
behavior in addressing his superior.

This seemingly minor encounter illustrates the importance of the everyday
staging and performance of power in colonial Indonesia and in colonial societies
more broadly. The palpable anxiety surrounding Linck and Prawiradinata's confrontation stemmed from competing assumptions about the proper social and
cultural norms that structured all interactions between colonizer and colonized.
The Dutch administrator expected to receive traditional Javanese deference as
validation of his authority, whereas the Javanese clerk adopted Western etiquette
to signify his education and modernity. Linck's attitude and expectations of how

the encounter and its aftermath would unfold reveal the manner in which colonial hegemony was communicated through language, manners, material status symbols, and even physical gestures and posture. Through this scripted performance of power, authorities sought to affirm, uphold, and strengthen colonial hierarchies of race, class, and gender, which the Dutch overlords proclaimed were natural and enduring. But as Prawiradinata's actions show, the colonized were not merely extras in the colonial play. By the early twentieth century, reliance on these nineteenth-century tropes was starting to give way, and many Javanese began to assert their agency through subversive responses to the script. Their actions enabled them to negotiate and contest colonial hegemony, which, as Prawiradinata and Linck's confrontation reflects, resulted in mounting tensions between proponents of tradition and modernity in colonial society.

Encounters like the one between Prawiradinata and Linck are central to this book, which focuses on the changing history of colonial hegemony and its contestation through everyday interactions in nineteenth-and early-twentieth-century colonial Indonesia. Though histories of economic exploitation and political movements provide essential context for studying systems of hegemonic control, my analysis focuses on culture, the performance of power, everyday experiences, and the steady development of Indonesian agency. The study of the performance of power in colonial Indonesia reveals a new understanding of the Indonesian national awakening, one rooted not in the founding of political movements and organizations but in the proliferation of everyday discursive acts that challenged colonial hegemony and strategies of domination.

Javanization, Hegemony, and Resistance

In the seventeenth century, the lucrative spice trade drew the Dutch to the Indonesian archipelago, where they established a colonial foothold on the island of Java that lasted until Indonesian independence in 1949.[2] By the nineteenth century, the Dutch had created a colonial state that oversaw the production of cash crops, labor exploitation, and resource extraction through a combination of ruthless subjugation and cunning diplomacy and trade. As with many colonizing powers, rather than relying solely on the "right of conquest," the legitimacy of Dutch authority on Java depended on preserving the traditional indigenous elite—in this case, the *priyayi*, a class of Javanese nobles and aristo-bureaucrats. While the institution of indirect rule in colonial Indonesia, including Dutch colonizers' essential collaboration with the priyayi, has been the subject of excellent historiographical studies, the actual exercise of colonial power has received scant scholarly attention.[3] This is surprising because their collaboration required significant cultural accommodations, and the Dutch adopted Javanese deference etiquette, symbols of power, sartorial hierarchies, lifestyles, and architecture to legitimize their colonial authority. In historical scholarship, this process of acculturation is often treated as a byproduct of centuries of cultural and racial mixing due to the immigration and conjugal policies of the Dutch East India Company (Vereenigde Oostindische Compagnie, VOC).[4] Benedict Anderson, for example, describes the "Javanization" of the Dutch as a cultural osmosis resulting from the influences exerted by Europeans' Asian wives or concubines.[5] Such an interpretation obfuscates the deliberate nature of Dutch institutions designed to maintain control over increasing numbers of colonial subjects. In this book, I employ the term "Javanization" to designate a conscious policy of cultural appropriation to legitimize colonial rule.

The Javanization of colonial power in the nineteenth century can be traced back to cultural practices and concepts of authority in the Javanese Hindu-Buddhist past. It was as part of the so-called Indianization of Southeast Asia that complex bureaucracies and increased social stratification first emerged in Java from the eighth century onward. These early precolonial states were characterized by low population-to-land ratios, weak administrative organization, and interelite rivalries. As a consequence, a powerful ruler was someone who could gather and retain the largest following, not the largest territory. To that end, rulers relied on devotional state cults inspired by Indic cosmology that emphasized their prowess and elaborate networks of patron-client relations to maintain social and political order. These vertical relationships, extending throughout social rankings from the court to the village, were expressed through appearance, etiquette, language, and status symbols.[6] These outward forms of social communication developed in conjunction with a traditional Javanese political philosophy that emphasized, in Anderson's words, "the signs of Power's concentration, not the demonstration of its exercise or use."[7] Thus, Java's precolonial states were prime examples of what Clifford Geertz famously dubbed "theatre states," polities where displays of power—through spectacle, ceremonies, and rituals—were essential in upholding authority. According to Geertz, "Power served pomp, not pomp power."[8]

The Dutch adoption of Javanese deference rituals and symbols alongside the construction of the colonial state did not, however, result in a theatre state. On the contrary, I argue that the colonial Javanese state illustrates some of the limitations of this concept, especially for the colonial period. While appealing, the idea of a theatre state is rather static and ahistorical, and does not satisfactorily allow for change over time. By prioritizing cultural and symbolic power over domination by force, the theory disregards rulers' need for political and economic authority to orchestrate, shape, and direct the theatrical staging of power. Similarly, there is little room for agency, as one is left to assume that all play their assigned roles without contestation or mediation. Consequently, the framework of the theatre state does not explain historical transitions and social transformations.[9] For instance, the Dutch adoption of Javanese symbols of power and etiquette during the first decades of the nineteenth century did not result in widespread acquiescence to their rule. On the contrary, coercive measures were necessary to meet the challenges of large-scale revolts, everyday avoidance protest, and messianic movements.[10] These forms of resistance underscore the fact that theatre states require political and coercive power in order to be imposed and maintained.

John Pemberton similarly argues that power in colonial and postcolonial Indonesia was not simply enforced from above but was a pervasive cultural effect produced through the performance of tradition. Crucially, he shows that while the Dutch assumed Javanese culture was static and enduring, it was precisely through the colonial encounter that the Javanese elite articulated a "traditional" identity, expressed through language, dress, and etiquette, in contradistinction to the Dutch. In this way, the colonial encounter itself produced a more fixed construction of Javanese culture. The Dutch attempt to legitimize power through cultural appropriation and the crystallization of Javanese cultural identity demonstrates that power and tradition are fluid and malleable concepts.[11] Thus, a more expansive analysis beyond the theatre state is essential to understand the relationship between culture and power in colonial Indonesia.

The concept of cultural hegemony offers a more dynamic and historical perspective that, significantly, emphasizes agency as a key component of the interplay between culture and power. Although formulated by the Italian Marxist and activist Antonio Gramsci to explain and contest the rise of fascism in early-twentieth-century Italy, cultural hegemony offers scholars valuable insights into the relationship between culture and power in colonial societies as well. Cultural hegemony refers to the continuous process through which a dominant group—in this case, the colonizer—tries to attain and maintain the consent of the great majority of the people it rules—here, the colonized. This was accomplished through the manipulation of cultural values, norms, beliefs, and traditions in an attempt to validate the ruling group's worldview and make it appear favorable to all. In this way, the hegemonic discourse of the ruling group rationalized the social, racial, political, and economic inequalities of colonial society and sought to inculcate a sense that those inequalities were enduring and inevitable. In theory, a successful ruling group could rely less on domination by force and the coercive apparatus of the state and more on the majority of the population's passive resignation. But hegemony is never static or absolute. It is inherently contested, thus enabling subordinate groups to negotiate and sometimes defy the terms of hegemonic discourse. Managing such negotiations and counterhegemonic challenges requires that the dominant group constantly renew and adjust its approach. In other words, hegemony involves continual cultural struggle, as ruling groups seek to legitimize their authority while inevitably leaving openings for subordinate groups to contest it.[12]

Cultural hegemony thus offers an insightful approach to the study of Dutch dominance in Indonesia and its contestation at the subaltern level. This is especially apt given the importance and pervasiveness of ritual display and highly refined rules for social interaction in Javanese society, particularly in political intercourse. Although there are numerous studies on the ways in which cultural hegemony has been applied to the colonial context in South Asia in particular, the concept is conspicuously absent from studies on colonial Indonesia.[13] In part this can be explained by the association of colonialism with violence and oppression, which is reflected in numerous studies on moments of upheaval, revolt, and organized political movements. As Jan Breman has shown, this has too often resulted in the problematic assumption that between moments of outright confrontation, the endemic oppression and exploitation of colonialism were passively endured in everyday life.[14] This is where the explanatory value of cultural hegemony lies; maintaining hegemony requires a balance of coercion and consent, with domination by force at one end of the spectrum and consensus and negotiation at the other.[15] Although cultural hegemony was never fully attained in the colonial context—Ranajit Guha fittingly described colonial rule as "dominance without hegemony"—the concept enables historians to explore the myriad ways in which power was continuously communicated and contested in colonial systems of dominance.[16] This approach also illuminates why, when, and how colonial power could be made to seem natural and legitimate rather than alien and oppressive.

As historical methodology, cultural hegemony offers a way to understand how the Dutch, and colonizers in general, were able to impose an exploitative socioeconomic and repressive political order that most officials could justify as a civilizing enterprise. Their alliances with, and ability to incorporate the interests of, indigenous elites and bureaucrats were an essential prerequisite to sustained control.[17] The Dutch partnership with the priyayi, for instance, was based on a notion of parallel elites: Dutch officials and Javanese priyayi were supposedly equal in administering their own constituencies. In return for their allegiance to the Dutch, the priyayi were rewarded with hereditary rights, economic incentives, and the retention of their pomp and ceremony.[18] In a similar vein, the Dutch granted far-reaching economic, legal, and political privileges to Chinese merchants, shopkeepers, and moneylenders, who were indispensable as middlemen in the colonial economy.[19] And last but not least, indigenous mercenary soldiers filled the ranks of the colonial army, which was essential to the coercive apparatus of the state.[20]

Because a large majority of the population consisted of illiterate peasants, conveying hegemonic ideas and ideology posed a significant challenge for Dutch colonizers. Their strategies made it imperative that my research move beyond the realm of official reports, legal proceedings, ordinances, popular periodicals, and other written forms of communication that scholars deploying Gramsci's approach to cultural hegemony generally analyze. Thus, in addition to these standard textual sources, I emphasize the ways in which the hegemonic discourse was communicated through a complex array of social performances and material culture. In what I will refer to throughout this book as the performance of power, the Dutch announced their hegemonic discourse through etiquette, material symbols, language, clothing, architecture, urban planning, and lifestyle. These sociocultural practices created an experiential reality in which colonizers and colonized actively performed power and status during everyday encounters. These encounters took place within the civil service, on plantations, in the streets, and in households, trains, stores, and offices.[21] It was through these prescribed interactions that the Dutch and their Javanese allies sought to normalize colonial hierarchies and instill a sense of compliance throughout the colonized populace. When effective, these modes of imposing hegemony bolstered acceptance of foreign domination through the manipulation of indigenous culture and rendered it more difficult—but not impossible—to reject or resist the colonizers' demands. The deliberate Javanization of colonial authority is the topic of the first chapter.

The performance of colonial power was, however, like hegemony itself, not a one-way imposition of public and social behavior but an interactive encounter between colonizer and colonized. Although performance was instrumental in expressing the hegemonic discourse, a degree of defiance was always possible. Focusing on this tension, James Scott describes interactions between colonizer and colonized as reflecting a public transcript—the hegemonic discourse. He cautions against overestimating the acquiescence of the colonized and argues that they critiqued the colonial relationship offstage, a practice he characterizes as fashioning hidden transcripts.[22] According to Scott, it is through these hidden transcripts that we can explore the everyday struggles of subordinate groups. In this book, however, I focus on encounters and instances in which this everyday resistance manifests onstage, in the face of power. Acts of symbolic defiance took various forms, from feigned ignorance to outright insubordination, such as Prawiradinata's refusal to offer traditional deference to his superior. This approach draws attention to Indonesian agency in everyday colonial encounters, as opposed to limiting active resistance to direct political opposition or rebellion. By tracing the development and evolution of the performance of power, a dynamic and engaging history emerges that reveals the modes and sites of Indonesian defiance as well as the ways in which the Dutch continually worked to legitimize their authority.

The primary geographic focus of this book lies on Java (see figure 1), but the histories it explores more broadly illustrate how the performance of power shaped emergent Indonesian cultural narratives and identities. After establishing Batavia in 1619 (present-day Jakarta), the island of Java was at the center of the Dutch colonial project in Asia. Following the bankruptcy of the VOC at the turn of the nineteenth century, the Dutch transformed the trade empire's dispersed possessions into a Java-centered colonial state known as the Netherlands Indies. Through a series of brutal wars—such as the infamous Aceh War (1873–1904)—and diplomatic coercion, the vast Indonesian archipelago was effectively consolidated under Dutch control by the twentieth century. Java remained the administrative, political, and economic bedrock of this modern colonial state, and the island's major cities became meeting grounds where people from throughout the archipelago discovered, discussed, and contested their shared colonial subjecthood. Java was home to the majority of Western-style schools, institutions of higher education, political and cultural associations, and vernacular newspapers and periodicals. As Robert Elson asserts, "the cities of Java were the fulcrum of intellectual life" where the "idea of Indonesia" was not only embraced but also began to flourish during the final decades of colonial rule.[23] Analyzing the performance of power in these locations, this book offers an original perspective on the transition from a Javanese identity to an Indonesian one.

Tracing how Indonesians viewed and experienced this cultural hegemonic struggle is quite a challenge for historians. The task is complicated by the nature of the colonial archives, which reflect and confirm the Dutch colonizer's hegemonic worldview. There are limited sources that shed light on the Indonesian

FIGURE I. Java, ca. 1900–1942

perspective in the nineteenth century, in particular.[24] It is possible to read the
archival record against the grain and decipher modes of hegemonic protest in
the form of foot-dragging, flight, vandalism, and millenarianism.[25] There is also
linguistic evidence of such everyday resistance, eternalized, for instance, in the
nineteenth-century Dutch proverb that someone is "East Indian deaf," referring
to situations in which a person pretends not to hear a question or a command.
Rooted in the colonial trope of the lazy native, the saying is associated with
indolence to this day but also with colonial officials who were indifferent to
the concerns of the colonized.[26] However, from the late nineteenth century onward, the Indonesian experience comes more sharply into focus through the
increasing availability of sources penned by the colonized themselves, such as
vernacular newspapers and periodicals, pamphlets, correspondence, novels, and
biographies. By drawing extensively on these sources, I reconstruct and analyze
the interactive hegemonic struggle between colonizer and colonized.

The private correspondence of Indonesian national heroine Raden Adjeng
Kartini, an early advocate for women's rights and education, offers an instructive
example of how Indonesians perceived the colonial performance of power. In a
letter to a Dutch friend, Stella Zeehandelaar, in January 1900, Kartini wrote that
she detested offering traditional Javanese deference to Europeans. She confided
that she could not suppress a smile and had to bite her lips to prevent herself
from laughing outright at the manner in which Dutch officials emphasized their
prestige over the Javanese. Obviously, Kartini did not buy into the "ridiculous

spectacle" that Dutch colonizers maintained was crucial to legitimizing their authority to the Javanese population. She even went so far as to call Dutch prestige "imaginary," in essence undermining the cultural grounds on which colonial rule was constructed. Significantly, Kartini also suggested that she was not alone in her views. For instance, she described how humble crowds respectfully retreated before an assistant resident under the shade of his gilded *payung*—a Javanese ceremonial parasol—only to burst out laughing once he turned his back.[27] Although Kartini's letters do not constitute evidence of direct hegemonic contestation, they do shed light on the Indonesian mentality in the colonial encounter. Due to her privileged position as a woman of noble birth, Kartini was able to critique the Dutch as long as her views did not spread too widely throughout the population—yet. Although Kartini was ahead of her time, her letters indicate that the times were changing. Only a few years later, the colonized would increasingly declare and perform such private sentiments of resistance directly to Dutch officials.

The turn of the twentieth century was a tumultuous period of social and cultural change in colonial Indonesia and the world more broadly.[28] Characterized by rapid technological innovation, demographic growth, and urbanization, the era saw the increased mobility of people, goods, and ideas. The nature of colonialism itself was also changing, due to the social application of evolutionary science as well as the privatization of the colonial economy and its incorporation into global trade networks. In addition, the rise of imperial Japan and the American colonization of the Philippines shifted the regional balance of power and created a growing self-awareness among the colonized.[29] Under these circumstances, it became increasingly difficult to legitimize the Dutch colonial project through the Javanization of power. The inevitable adjustment to these transformations occurred in 1901 with the proclamation of the Ethical Policy. The Dutch equivalent of the civilizing mission, the Ethical Policy was based on the premise that Dutch superiority, rooted in scientific and technological prowess, created a moral obligation to "civilize" the supposedly backward colonized peoples. The new policy resulted in educational, agricultural, and administrative reforms—all topics of previous historical inquiry—and, crucially, in a new hegemonic script for the performance of colonial power.[30] As representatives of European civilization and modernity, the Dutch could no longer rely on cultural accommodation without losing their credibility. Colonial officials and civil servants were thus instructed to replace Javanese deference traditions with modern Western etiquette. These instructions set the tone for a comprehensive overhaul of the appearance of colonial power reflected in language, social norms, architecture, public spaces, and consumer culture.

The implementation of this ethical discourse was far from straightforward, however. Like all civilizing ideologies, the Ethical Policy was based on a contradictory premise. While the Dutch publicly proclaimed a moral responsibility to civilize the indigenous population, Social Darwinist beliefs about racial difference suggested that the colonized could never *be* civilized; that is, could never match the colonizer's level of evolutionary development.[31] Predictably, the Ethical Policy divided colonial officials, administrators, and civil servants with regards to its feasibility and desirability. Policymakers and officials in the colonial government sought to employ Dutch tutelage and Western examples to advance Java and its inhabitants toward limited political participation. However, the majority of Dutch colonial civil servants maintained that due to intrinsic differences between colonizer and colonized, it would be more effective to uphold Javanese traditions as the basis of colonial rule. In their opposition to the Ethical Policy, Dutch civil servants found support among conservative members of the priyayi, who similarly feared a loss of power and prestige with the implementation of "ethical" protocol. I explore this discrepancy between emancipatory theory and conservative practice in the performance of colonial power in chapter 2.

1913: From Everyday Resistance to National Awakening

Where colonial authorities were unable to bridge the gap between discursive theory and practice during the first decade of the twentieth century, an emerging generation of Indonesians succeeded in 1913. As civil servants like Assistant Resident Linck continued to insist on receiving Javanese deference, young Indonesians like Prawiradinata grew more outspoken, self-confident, and vocal. It was this modern, educated generation that eventually demanded equality and respect by disturbing the colonial performance. In April 1914, the official newspaper of the Sarekat Islam, Indonesia's first political movement, published an article titled "Freedom" (*kemerdekaan*).[32] Contrary to what the modern reader might expect, the author did not refer to a desire for political or national independence but rather to the struggle for freedom from the oppressive, humiliating, and belittling attitude of Dutch officials within colonial society. The article described how in previous months, many young Indonesians changed their attitudes and behaviors in the colonial encounter by refusing to cower for the colonizer, demanding to sit on chairs instead of on the floor, withholding traditional gestures of respect, ignoring the Javanese language hierarchy, and addressing officials by their position rather than by an undeserving aristocratic title. Through these disturbances of the colonial performance, the author argued, the colonized could force colonial officials to treat them with more respect and dignity and finally live up to their so-called ethical promises. He therefore implored readers to follow this example. This article was not the only call to action. From mid-1913 onward, the vernacular press was filled with articles that describe how, through acts of defiance in the face of power, a new generation of Indonesians subverted Dutch expectations and demanded to be treated as human beings and as equals. Their actions drastically altered the performance of power in the everyday colonial encounter.

The sudden proliferation in 1913 of everyday discursive challenges to the colonial performance of power signaled a broad social transformation and change in mentality that has been largely overlooked in the scholarly literature. Historians of the Indonesian national awakening have primarily focused on explicit political defiance and protest—such as associations, political parties, rallies, unions, strikes, and a critical press—as indicators and drivers of broad social change. This preoccupation with political resistance obscures everyday forms of resistance that were not overtly political, ideological, or organized, and yet sought to negotiate and alleviate colonial inequalities. I suggest that instead of focusing on political events as hinges of historical change, everyday discursive acts—changes in language, attitude, and appearance—reveal a more pervasive moment of social transformation.

Evidence of everyday forms of resistance is hard to find in the archives, which reflect colonial authorities' fixation on political resistance. However, by critically examining a series of Dutch circulars that prescribed the etiquette of the colonial encounter—specifically, those addressing attire and *hormat* (customary ways of showing respect)—I am able to trace the growth and pervasiveness of everyday discursive acts in the early twentieth century. This history challenges the prevailing notion that this was an era of relative "peace and order" (to use a deceptive colonial catchphrase) without much anticolonial resistance. It also suggests that a broader and more conscious challenge to the colonial order of things grew out of these everyday struggles. This book therefore offers an important revision to the prevailing narrative of the Indonesian national awakening, demonstrating that it was not just a movement that a small political elite incited from the top-down but also one that grew out of a large social transformation from below.

As I have argued with Bart Luttikhuis, the manifestation of everyday resistance and demands for equality indicate a broad change in mentality in 1913 that constitute a turning point in Indonesian history.[33] These events are best understood as the outcome of long-term developments that converged in 1913 to decisively move Indonesian society in a new direction. My focus on every-day forms of resistance as indicators of social change complements and contex-tualizes more familiar benchmarks in colonial Indonesian history. Many have been the subject of previous studies, such as the impact of the Ethical Policy, the growing availability of Western education, and young Indonesians' subsequent embrace of modernity, specifically science, technology, and consumerism.[34] In addition, Indonesians increasingly displayed a new global consciousness inspired by the rise of Japan as an imperial power, the British Indian nationalist move-ment, Chinese nationalists' victory in 1911, and the international Islamic mod-ernist movement, originating in Egypt.[35] In part encouraged by these crusades, this new political consciousness was reflected in the creation of Indonesia's first cultural, religious, and political organizations, foremost among them Boedi Oetomo and Sarekat Islam, founded in 1908 and 1911, respectively.[36] Finally, there was the development of a critical vernacular press in which Indonesians expressed themselves and debated their place in the world.[37] On their own, these events did not amount to instantaneous and broad social change, but their for-tuitous culmination in 1913 created the circumstances under which Indone-sians began to actively demand respect and dignity by challenging the colonial performance.

Chapter 3 examines this moment in 1913, detailing the ways in which a gener-ation of assertive, educated, professionally employed, and well-informed young Indonesians contested Dutch colonial hegemony. It demonstrates how minor confrontations over appropriate etiquette quickly ballooned into more pervasive social activism. Of pivotal importance to this history is the release of a hormat circular in August 1913, a government decree prohibiting colonial officials from demanding traditional deference from the colonized.[38] The circular was written in response to the escalation of a conflict between a Javanese public prosecutor who refused to sit on the floor and wear traditional Javanese clothing and his European superior who insisted on submissive behavior from a colonial sub-ject. What set this particular confrontation apart was both actors' persistence in their respective performances of power, which eventually brought the incident to the attention of high colonial officials in Batavia. Fearing that civil servants' lofty attitudes alienated young Indonesians and undermined colonial peace and order, the government issued the hormat circular to forcibly align its perfor-mance of authority with the ethical discourse it espoused. This was a remarkable piece of colonial legislation, as it recognized that traditional deference rituals were humiliating for the colonized, publicly condemned the attitude of colonial civil servants, and pledged betterment on the part of the colonizer. The circular also led the colonial government to increasingly support the nascent nationalist movement. This seemingly contradictory consequence illustrates that times were indeed changing.[39]

The hormat circular of 1913 played an important but often overlooked role in energizing the Indonesian nationalist movement. The vernacular press widely and publicly reviewed the implications of the circular, and the Sarekat Islam, with the colonial government's support, publicized and interpreted it at rallies and meetings. These discussions instilled in the colonized an increased sense of confidence and justice that encouraged them to *perform* truth to power by refusing to submit to traditional deference customs. Decisions about how to present oneself became empowering acts of hegemonic contestation. In response to these challenges, conservative colonial officials as well as Javanese aristocrats condemned young Indonesians and Dutch supporters of ethical ideals, accusing the progressive coalition of destabilizing colonial society and destroying indigenous culture. This resulted in a fierce public debate over the nature and form of the colonial encounter. Although the reactionary conservatives regained control over the government in the 1920s, Pandora's box had been opened. It proved impossible to reimpose nineteenth-century colonial hegemony, as discussions about what constituted proper etiquette expanded into larger conversations about Indonesian culture and identity.

The social transformations of 1913 were reinforced by a deliberate change in attire. Chapter 4 takes a closer look at this particular aspect of indigenous demands for equality and respect, demonstrating that clothes were an important instrument and site of hegemonic contestation. The timing of what effectively constituted a sartorial revolution was certainly no coincidence. Beginning in September 1913, in the wake of the hormat circular, many young Indonesian professionals, such as teachers, clerks, and railroad personnel, suddenly and swiftly replaced their traditional sarong and headscarf with trousers, a jacket, and tie. By donning Western attire, Indonesians visually expressed that they considered themselves modern and equal to Europeans. In the process, they asserted that they would no longer cower and humiliate themselves in front of colonial officials. While this was not a political revolution, the sartorial transformation was an unmistakable statement directed toward both European colonizers and the conservative Javanese priyayi. The new generation's abrupt change in clothes reverberated throughout colonial society, visually signifying the dawn of a new era in the colonial encounter.

Indonesians' adoption of Western clothing undermined nineteenth-century sartorial regulations that prescribed ethnic dress for all inhabitants of the

Netherlands Indies—policies that enabled the colonizer to create and maintain
ethnic stereotypes. The only group to transgress this imposed sartorial hierarchy
was the Dutch themselves, who donned indigenously inspired clothing, like the
sarong, batik trousers, and *kebaya* (a long-sleeved blouse) as leisure wear in the
semiprivate spheres of their homes and neighborhoods. When Indonesians put
on trousers to signal their modernity in the early twentieth century, the Dutch,
suddenly at risk of appearing unrefined themselves, could no longer wear what
seemed like indigenous garb. In an attempt to reassert their dominance in colonial society, the Dutch increased their own sense of sartorial correctness by
dressing "up" in the latest European fashions while simultaneously ridiculing
Javanese attempts to appear modern and civilized. For Indonesians, the sartorial
revolution was both empowering and disruptive, as it raised questions about
how one's appearance reflected one's ethnic, religious, and national identities.
Thus, through changes in appearance, both colonizer and colonized actively experimented with and performed new identities in the early twentieth century.
These experiments and discussions ultimately led to the emergence of an explicit
Indonesian national costume and identity.[40]

Competing Modern Identities:
The Final Act in the Colonial Performance

In 1929, the Dutch Kuyck family visited Batavia's annual Pasar Gambir (Gambir
Fair) with their young son, whom they took to a popular attraction: a wooden
submarine with a periscope. When it was their turn to peek through the periscope, one of the Indonesians in line suggested—in fluent Dutch—that Mrs.
Kuyck lift up her son, as he was not tall enough to reach the device. While protecting her son's face with a handkerchief, another Indonesian complimented
her wisdom in presuming that the periscope's glass was probably dirty from continuous usage. Mrs. Kuyck was initially taken aback; in the not so distant past
"it would not have crossed the mind of a native to address a European woman."
In spite of this, rather than appearing hostile or rude, the Indonesians at the
Pasar Gambir struck her as neat and civilized. Seemingly for the first time, she
realized that "many of them consider themselves completely equal to the Europeans."[41] At first glance, the encounter Mrs. Kuyck described was rather different
from the one discussed at the beginning of this introduction, but in both cases,
identity and status were communicated and performed through language, appearance, and etiquette. Mrs. Kuyck's prejudicial assumptions about Indonesian
behavior exemplify the ways in which Indonesians subverted expectations by

speaking a different language, taking liberties where they previously had not, changing their attire, and sharing modern concerns—in this case, regarding hygiene. It was through these sorts of performances that Indonesians successfully contested and negotiated colonial hegemony, signaled their equality, and created new and distinct identities.

In response to the profound social transformations around 1913, the colonial performance of power changed in character and appearance. No longer was colonial authority supported by the Javanization of power, but gradually—and begrudgingly, in the case of some officials—it became rooted in a notion of Dutch or even global modernity.[42] The script of this new performance reflected the Dutch belief that they were harbingers of progress and could claim any Indonesian enactment of modernity as their own.[43] The Dutch had, according to this hegemonic narrative, introduced modernity to colonial Indonesia, evidenced by trains, cars, steamships, electricity, engineering projects, department stores, cinemas, and fairs, as well as medical science, education, and the modern state. The narrative juxtaposed this Dutch sense of being modern with local customs and practices that allegedly illustrated the backwardness of the colonized, for whom modernity was to be aspirational but always out of reach. However, as Mrs. Kuyck's experience shows, the colonized did not passively accept the roles assigned to them; they created their own modern identities and imaginings.[44] This encounter reveals the importance of colonial modernity as a discursive site in colonial society, especially in light of the repressive turn in colonial policy following the national awakening.[45] By the end of the 1910s and into the 1920s, authorities implemented strict censorship guidelines and began interning political dissidents.[46] While these measures stymied outright political protests—especially following failed communist uprisings in 1926 and 1927—the everyday performance of new modern identities continued to challenge the colonial hegemonic worldview.

These new modern identities were not just imagined conceptually but communicated and experienced in the everyday colonial encounter, as both colonizer and colonized continued to perform and negotiate colonial hierarchies of race, class, and gender. Although Europeans and Indonesians increasingly distinguished themselves from one another and even began to reject racial and cultural mixing, their reinterpretations of their identities were very much interdependent, constructed in conversation with and against each other. The apparent omnipresence of the modern colonial state played an important part in instilling a sense of shared subjecthood among the colonized. This consciousness sprouted from Batavia's classrooms, where students from throughout the archipelago discovered that they faced a similar predicament. This became the foundation for the articulation of a new Indonesian identity.[47] However, as there was no consensus among the colonized over what it meant to be Indonesian beyond rejecting Dutch colonial subjecthood, this identity was not homogenous. Colonizer and colonized alike thus questioned what it meant to be modern, resulting in elaborate discussions about lifestyle, morality, and identity. As a consequence, modes of individual comportment and social interaction—including changes in social customs, sexual norms, culinary preferences, and consumer behavior—became sites in which to contest and negotiate the colonial hegemonic project.

As Indonesians increasingly demanded respect and expressed their own modernity through new clothes, language, manners, and attitudes, the inevitable question arose: did being modern require mimicking Western ways? At stake was whether westernization was a necessary means to an end in the hegemonic struggle, or on the contrary, an undesirable development that would result in an irreparable loss of self. Discussions about the merits and dangers of westernization led many Indonesians, depending on their political, religious, and social outlook, to reject what they viewed as the negative influences of Western modernity. This was often expressed in efforts to fashion modern lifestyles according to what they considered to be more respectable indigenous practices. While there was certainly no consensus among Indonesians as to what was virtuous, there was a clear understanding that unbridled Western modernity—free interaction between the sexes, dancing, and consumerism, for example—was not. As chapter 5 shows, these concerns came to the fore in discussions over mixed marriages, a topic that has not previously been considered from the Indonesian perspective.[48] During the last decades of colonial rule, Indonesians came to consider mixed unions as dangerous and degenerative, eventually invoking the same racist rhetoric espoused by the colonizer. In the process, conversations ensued about ethnic identities, such as Javanese, Sundanese, and Madurese, as well as about what it meant to be a colonial subject, and Indonesians began to articulate local, modern identities that were specifically non-Western and non-Dutch.

The colonial Dutch were largely taken aback by these sudden and widespread changes. Having relied on the Javanization of colonial authority and indigenous influences on their everyday lifestyles, they were now unexpectedly faced with colonial subjects who embraced modernity. In response, the Dutch forcefully asserted their own European modernity, contrasting their approach with the alleged backwardness of the colonized in an attempt to maintain their authority. Although it was Indonesian emancipation that prompted the Dutch to redefine their colonial identity, they rooted this transformation firmly within the civilizing mission discourse and developments in Western science, especially the fields of evolutionary biology and climatology. Whereas nineteenth-century theories of acclimatization suggested that Europeans could adjust to tropical environments through cultural accommodation and even racial mixing, in the twentieth century these solutions were thought to cause racial and cultural degeneration.[49] In an effort to purify colonial culture from such degenerative influences, colonial society saw increased attempts at Europeanization. This disentangling of Eastern and Western culture was the cause of much anxiety, especially given the large Eurasian population in the colony. The Dutch suddenly considered the tropical climate, indigenous culture, and the colonized themselves to be dangerous. This was reflected in the propagation of a more European lifestyle, facilitated by the immigration of European women, advances in transportation and communication technologies, medical developments, and the creation of leisure spaces, like mountain resorts, where Europeans could seek protection from the tropical heat. But perhaps most importantly, these pseudoscientific beliefs about degeneration meant that the Dutch sought to minimize close contact with the allegedly less-developed indigenous population, especially household servants, and to no longer conform to Javanese hygienic practices, social customs, and diet.[50] Chapter 5 argues that all of these ideas influenced the colonial encounter dramatically—in ways that exclusively political narratives do not capture.

As a consequence of increased European immigration and the emergence of an Indonesian middle class and larger educated elite, the colonial encounter became more frequent in the early twentieth century. These meetings between colonized and colonizer were especially pervasive and visible in spaces associated with modernity, such as offices, train stations, stores, restaurants, movie theatres, and public streets, squares, and parks. It was in public spaces like these that the performance of new identities accrued meaning; they were the stages of the hegemonic struggle.[51] Perhaps the most illustrative space of the modern colonial encounter was the fairground. Late-colonial Indonesia witnessed the proliferation of annual fairs and exhibitions that attracted hundreds of thousands of visitors from all ethnic backgrounds and walks of life.[52] Chapter 6 argues that Dutch colonizers organized these fairs as part of a larger hegemonic attempt to legitimize colonial authority within a new cultural context. At the fairgrounds, special exhibits demonstrated the benevolence of colonial governance, while staging modernity to emphasize Western cultural, technological, and scientific superiority. Visitors were invited to consume Western products and associated lifestyles and worldviews. These fairs were mainly directed toward the nascent Indonesian middle classes, which became increasingly central to maintaining colonial rule. However, I demonstrate that fairs were sites of interaction, discursive spaces where the middle classes did not simply buy into colonial discourse but negotiated and challenged Western modernity to create a distinctly Indonesian middle-class lifestyle and culture. Moreover, the fairs were sites in which they could perform their new identities through the way they dressed, consumed, socialized, and engaged in entertainment. Colonial fairgrounds thus offer an intriguing case study of the late-colonial encounter, as Indonesians critically embraced modernity, subverted colonial stereotypes, and created new identities as they moved toward emancipation from Dutch rule.[53]

During the final decades of Dutch colonial rule, but especially after 1913, Indonesians took center stage in the colonial performance of power. As they became more assertive in articulating their desires and experimented with new modern identities, the colonial discourse that legitimized Dutch authority became less effective. As a result, the colonial government increasingly resorted to repression and coercion to maintain its hold on power, censoring and exiling those it deemed political extremists. However, everyday resistance persisted in the form of performing new identities, and Indonesians steadily subverted the colonial worldview and its associated hierarchies. In the process, they created space for the articulation of a modern Indonesian identity. That identity remains the most enduring legacy of the performance of power. When the Japanese conquest of colonial Indonesia definitively closed the curtain on the colonial performance in 1942, most of the audience had already left.

CHAPTER I

Setting the Stage

The Javanization of Colonial Authority in the Nineteenth Century

I N JANUARY OF 1900, Raden Adjeng Kartini, a vocal Indonesian advocate for women's rights, wrote an elaborate response to Stella Zeehandelaar, a Dutch friend who questioned whether the general "condition" of the Javanese people had improved since the abolition of the Cultivation System. The repressive forced cultivation of cash crops had characterized colonial Indonesia from 1830 to 1870. Kartini replied that while there were many indications that the government now cared for the welfare of the Javanese, colonial officials, who acted as Javanese aristocrats, maintained their sense of superiority. As an example, Kartini related the experience of a young Indonesian man who attended a European high school and graduated first in his class. At school, he was accustomed to conversing in Dutch and interacting freely with Europeans. On returning to his parents' hometown to join the colonial civil service, he therefore assumed that he could address the local resident (colonial administrator) in Dutch. This was a crucial mistake, Kartini wrote, as the next morning he was assigned the position of clerk to a lowly European official in a mountain town. To make matters worse, his Dutch superior was eventually replaced by one of the man's former classmates—a European of inferior intellectual capacity for whom he had to crouch, sit on the floor, and address solely in high Javanese. According to Kartini, the young official learned a life lesson in Java's mountains: the best way to serve European officials was by groveling in the dust and never speaking Dutch. For good measure, Kartini offered several additional examples of Dutch mimicry of the Javanese elite, such as demanding to be addressed as "great lord" (*kanjeng*), to receive a knee kiss (*sungkem*), and the right to walk under a gilded parasol (*payung*). She sarcastically added that she had always thought only the "backward Javanese" loved all this pomp and circumstance but learned that "civilized and educated" Westerners craved it, as well.[1]

Kartini sketches an intriguing portrait of the late-nineteenth-century Dutch performance of colonial authority. Although her letter conveys that the colonial appropriation of Javanese forms of etiquette and deference was adopted during the Cultivation System, the Dutch had been experimenting with employing local rituals and symbolism as a means of regulating contact between colonizer and colonized for much longer. This approach can be traced back to the seventeenth century, when the Dutch East India Company (VOC) first established a permanent presence in Java. However, Kartini was correct in that it was during the nineteenth century that the Javanization of colonial authority was institutionalized and made into a pillar of colonial rule.[2] This was not a straightforward process, but it was a deliberate policy of cultural appropriation through which the Dutch tried to communicate and justify their dominance in recognizable terms. The Dutch thus created hegemonic standards of public conduct that provided at least the outward impression of conformity to racial and social hierarchies and helped reify difference in colonial society. This chapter explores in detail the conscious development of a Javanized colonial performance, encapsulated in meticulous regulations regarding etiquette, dress, status symbols, architecture, and even culinary culture, and acted out according to a hegemonic script. Crucially, the Dutch were more than the directors of this colonial performance; they played the leading roles.

The Javanization of the performance of colonial authority has received scant attention in the historiography of colonial Indonesia. Most studies dealing with nineteenth-century Java have focused on the political economy, primarily the material exploitation of the Javanese, and discourses justifying colonialism, including analyses of race and gender. In these studies, cultural appropriation is often considered a byproduct of these other aspects of colonialism.[3] What has been published on culture and power is often limited to specific cultural elements in isolation, such as dress, rather than as significant parts of a larger system of cultural domination.[4] This is a missed opportunity, as hegemonic discourse was communicated through everyday cultural performances to rationalize colonial inequality and exploitation. It is therefore necessary to consider the regulation of etiquette, classificatory schemes, rituals, and the appearance of power as integral components of the system of colonial governance. Doing so offers a cultural layer to scholarship about the institution of indirect rule, its reliance on a dualistic civil service, the comprehensive system of racial stratification, and the politics of sex.[5]

The Dutch East India Company: Profitability and Cultural Exchange

The Dutch East India Company established a foothold on the northwest coast of Java in an attempt to control the seventeenth-century spice trade. In 1619, the VOC destroyed the town of Jayakarta and constructed Batavia (present-day Jakarta) on its ruins, creating the center of its Asian maritime trade empire. While the company had operated trading posts in Java since 1603, it was establishing Batavia that marked the Dutch's permanent presence on the island, thus requiring the formulation of settlement and colonization policies. As the first multinational corporation in world history, these policies were informed by cost efficiency and profit maximization but had significant effects on the intricacies of Dutch colonial culture in Java for centuries. In a way, it was the VOC's obsession with the bottom line that created the circumstances out of which colonial officials in Kartini's time emerged.[6]

In order to transform Batavia into a dominant center of intra-Asian trade, the VOC sought to create a stable settlement population as the basis of its strength. Rather than relying on settler colonialism (unlikely in a densely populated area resistant to European diseases—instead Europeans were at risk of tropical diseases), the company enforced strict regulations on immigration and conjugal relations. Only high-ranking officials were allowed to bring European wives to Batavia, while lower officials and company personnel were actively encouraged to cohabitate with or marry local women. As Jean Gelman Taylor meticulously shows, the Eurasian offspring from these unions quickly became the bedrock of Batavia's social world, where they grew up in predominantly Asian households, conversed in Malay, consumed indigenous cuisine, and wore locally inspired clothing. Cultural exchanges in these Eurasian households further shaped gender relations, spiritual beliefs, deference behavior, hierarchical rituals, and material markers of social status. The VOC had intended that their settlement policies restrict private trading interests while at the same time create a small settler community to supply cheap Eurasian manpower for lower rank positions. But by the mid-seventeenth century, their regulations had also resulted in an autonomous colonial society with a culture that could no longer be characterized as either Dutch or Asian but as Eurasian. Through this particular colonial society, the Dutch gleaned valuable knowledge about local culture that would become instrumental for the Javanization of colonial authority in the nineteenth century.[7]

The Dutch East India Company initially had no intention of pursuing a land-based empire in Java, content with its settlement in Batavia and its status as a vassal of the largest kingdom on the island. However, to protect and expand its mercantile interests, the company was gradually drawn into internal Javanese politics. Between 1677 and 1749, the VOC increasingly gained sovereignty beyond Batavia by exploiting the indigenous kingdoms' rivalries and internal weaknesses. This process culminated in 1755–57 with the division of the once-powerful sultanate of Mataram into three princely states, of which Surakarta and Yogyakarta were the largest and most important.[8] Within a century, the VOC thus acquired control over most of the island save the newly formed principalities. On paper the Javanese rulers retained sovereignty over their much-reduced territories, although the company exercised significant influence at the princely courts through company representatives. The resulting situation left room for competing views on the relationship between the Dutch and the Javanese rulers.[9]

The VOC's territorial expansion from its base in Batavia forced the trading company to consider how to rule its colonial possessions. Due to a preference for an indirect system of governance, also informed by economic concerns, the company's administrative structure was predominantly Javanese in personnel, organization, and ideology. The VOC relied on collaborations with the Javanese bureaucratic elite, the *priyayi*, a social group consisting of nobility, officials, and administrators. In practice, this meant that the highest members of the priyayi, the traditional Javanese regency heads known as *bupati*, were allowed a large degree of independence as long as they remained loyal to the VOC, abstained from relations with foreign powers, guaranteed peace within their districts, and promptly collected and delivered the required tribute.[10] Often their power even increased from their service to Javanese courts, since supporting the Dutch allowed them to transgress the norms of the indigenous social system.[11] A noticeable exception to this rule was the administration of the Priangan, the mountainous region immediately south of Batavia, where in the latter decades of the eighteenth century the VOC made the bupati subservient to company officials in order to directly oversee the forced cultivation of coffee beans.[12] This incorporation of bupati into the colonial administration of the Priangan provided the company, according to Heather Sutherland, with "the methods of establishing, maintaining, and legitimizing authority which had developed in Java over the centuries."[13]

As they extended their control over Java, the Dutch acquainted themselves with the intricacies of a Javanese system of social and political organization. With origins in the Hindu-Buddhist period of the island's history (between the eighth and fifteenth centuries), a distinctly Javanese political order developed, characterized by bureaucratization, social stratification, and a style of rulership inspired by Indic cosmology. An abstract concept of social hierarchy known as *kawula-gusti* (servant-master or patron-client) outlined the relationship between the king and his subjects, and also applied more generally to relationships between social superiors and inferiors. This hierarchy governed chains of patron-client clusters that extended from the royal courts to local officials and beyond. In theory, the kawula-gusti relationship was based on mutual respect and reciprocal responsibility through which the master protects and the servant pledges devotion in return. This vertical relationship was intricately expressed in sartorial etiquette, language hierarchies, demonstrations of social deference, status symbols, and cultural performances, such as *wayang*, a form of (shadow) puppet theatre, and gamelan, a traditional Javanese percussion ensemble.[14] These forms of social communication were more than just trappings of power; they were theatrical rituals that, according to Clifford Geertz, "were not mere aesthetic embellishments, celebrations of a domination independently existing: they were the thing itself."[15] These theatrical displays of power would become essential to legitimizing and preserving Dutch colonial authority in Java.

The Dutch East India Company's colonization policies—limited immigration, unions between European men and Asian women, and indirect rule—created a colonial society that was highly attuned to Javanese social and cultural traditions. By the late seventeenth century, Javanese status symbols and deference rituals were employed to differentiate between various social classes and ethno-religious groups living within Batavia, as well as between company officials and the Javanese priyayi who facilitated the system of indirect rule. The Dutch preoccupation with these Javanese manifestations of power even inspired the promulgation of various sumptuary laws and deference regulations. For instance, in 1719 it was decided that on encountering the governor general on the road, Europeans and Eurasians were required to dismount their horses or carriages and bow, whereas a Javanese was expected to squat on the spot as a gesture of deference. This squatting as well as the custom to approach a superior in a crouching-walk were known as *jongkok* and were an appropriation of customs previously reserved for Javanese royalty and aristocrats.[16]

One of the colonial Dutch's more intriguing and popular adoptions was that of the Javanese payung, a ceremonial parasol that, through its colors, bore the distinctions of its owner's rank. Most likely introduced in Java as a status symbol during the Hindu-Buddhist period, the payung was one of the most revered symbols among the Javanese aristocracy. A servant carried the payung while following the bearer of authority either on foot or in his carriage, or while sitting close to him on the ground.[17] Both in precolonial and colonial Java, there were two elite hierarchies: that of the noble families who had the right to carry a payung from birth, and that of the Javanese priyayi who had the right to carry the payung by virtue of their office.

Europeans and Eurasians living under the auspices of the VOC were quick to adopt the payung as a status symbol. Its growing popularity in the seventeenth century warranted clear regulations on who had the right to a servant with a payung and who had to carry his own parasol. These regulations were first introduced in 1647 and somewhat relaxed in 1729, 1733, and 1754, but still only junior merchants and those higher up in the company's hierarchy were allowed the privilege of having a servant carry their payung. However, the payung employed by Dutch merchants were not part of an institutionalized payung hierarchy with designated color schemes, as was the case in Javanese society. They were simply copies of Javanese status symbols detached from their traditional usage.[18]

Such experiments with Javanese semiotics and rituals were central components of VOC governance with lasting impact on Dutch colonial rule in Java. Although the many sumptuary and deference laws were retracted in 1795 when the company went bankrupt, that did not mean that these symbols and rituals were forgotten.[19] The ensuing period, characterized by political unrest and shifting colonial regimes, would nonetheless preserve elements of Javanese cultural appropriation to justify colonial power.

The Birth of the Colonial State

The decline of the Dutch East India Company marked the beginning of a prolonged transition period in Java during which a trade empire was transformed into a colonial state.[20] It took considerable time for the Dutch state to establish sovereignty over the VOC's former possessions and implement new ideas about how to govern a colonial empire. The process of colonial state formation was complicated by the loss of Dutch independence in Europe, as the small nation was caught between France and Britain during the French Revolution and the Napoleonic Wars. This new geopolitical reality was reflected in consecutive regime changes in Java accompanied by ongoing political instability. Nominal control of the island passed from the merchant company to the Batavian Republic (1795–1806), the French puppet state the Kingdom of Holland (1806–11), England (1811–14), and finally the Kingdom of the Netherlands (1814–1942). Even so, this tumultuous period laid the foundations for the eventual formation of the Dutch colonial state.

Following the demise of the VOC, it took over a decade, due to the global war triggered by the French Revolution, before colonial governance in Java could be resumed and reinvented. In 1808, King Louis Napoléon Bonaparte of Holland ordered Dutch politician Herman Willem Daendels to assume sovereign control over Java and reorganize its administration. Daendels was tasked with breaking through a British blockade, protecting Java from British invasion, and establishing Franco-Dutch sovereignty over the island. Although the VOC had gained de facto dominion over Java in 1749 with the fall of Mataram, in practice the company's relationship with Mataram's successor states, Yogyakarta and Surakarta, had continued as one between equals. This inconsistency was an issue that required Daendels's immediate attention. Rather than resorting to outright force to impose Dutch control, he issued the Edict on Ceremonial and Etiquette in July 1808—a statute altering the symbolic display of colonial power.[21] As predicted, Daendels's edict shocked the Javanese principalities, as it directly challenged the Javanese hierarchical worldview, and, in the words of historian Peter Carey, "struck at the heart of the Javanese understanding of the Dutch presence in Java."[22] Reactions to the Edict on Ceremonial and Etiquette ultimately became so contentious that they resulted in an attempted Javanese rebellion in 1810, instigated by an official in Sultan Hamengkubuwana II's court in Yogyakarta. Daendels squashed the attempt with a show of force, returning with three thousand soldiers and coercing the sultan to abdicate the throne in favor of his son. One of the new sultan's first acts was to accept Daendels's Edict on Ceremonial and Etiquette and with it, Franco-Dutch sovereignty.[23]

Daendels could not revel in his victory for long, however, as he was soon recalled to Europe right before a British invasion terminated Franco-Dutch rule over Java in 1811. For Hamengkubuwana II, the arrival of a competing European colonial power provided a window of opportunity during which he overturned Daendels's edict and reinstated himself as sultan of Yogyakarta. But his return to power was short-lived. British statesman Thomas Stamford Raffles assumed leadership in Java and, like Daendels before him, responded to the sultan's claims to authority with force. On June 20, 1812, Raffles arrived in Yogyakarta with a small army, and sacked, burned, and looted the palace (*kraton*) in an event that contemporaries likened to the British victory at Plassey in 1757. As with Daendels's triumph in 1810, Raffles's assault was an utterly humiliating experience that instilled a broad sense of discontent and frustration among the Javanese elite.[24] Moreover, the skirmish solidified an unmistakable new order in Java—one characterized by colonial sovereignty.

State Formation, Colonial Power, and Culture Wars

Javanese dissatisfaction had been mounting since the VOC's exit from the island, with colonial policies and performances regarding issues like etiquette and status symbols driving the conflicts outlined above. While the aforementioned succession of regimes made it difficult for either Daendels or Raffles to execute a coherent and sustained colonial policy, the main objective of these competing regimes was remarkably similar: to establish sovereignty over the island and concurrently create a modern state with fixed territorial boundaries, a centralized bureaucracy, the right to levy taxes, and an economic relationship with the metropolis that was characterized by free trade and labor instead of mercantilist monopolies and systems of forced cultivation of cash crops. Ostensibly inspired by European enlightened idealism, they sought to break with the illiberal and oppressive VOC-era and its reliance on and maintenance of traditional, or as they saw it "feudal," Javanese administrators. In order to achieve these goals, a more direct form of colonial administration was considered necessary, resulting in the formation of a European colonial civil service.[25] Simultaneously, and as part of this process, the power and influence of Javanese administrators, foremost the bupati, was significantly reduced. As hereditary prestige and other aristocratic privileges were revoked, members of the Javanese elite were transformed into salaried officials of the colonial state. Crucially, this new colonial reality was communicated through changes in the hegemonic appearance of colonial authority, captured in detailed regulations regarding deference rituals, dress codes, and the right to status symbols. These disruptions to Javanese social and cultural order caused substantial tension with colonial authorities during Daendels's and Raffles's tenures on the island.[26]

Daendels's 1808 Edict on Ceremonial and Etiquette—the first colonial policy enacted after the fall of the VOC—directly addressed questions of etiquette and displays of power, as its title implies. At that time, colonial representatives still performed VOC-era ceremonial functions at the Javanese courts, which Daendels viewed as inappropriate and degrading. For instance, residents, as the company's representatives were called, participated in court ceremonies without a payung to signal their status and with their heads uncovered. They were expected to bow three times when greeting Javanese rulers, and to serve them in a menial fashion, offering wine, betel nuts, and cleansing water.[27] To communicate colonial officials' freshly elevated status as representatives of the king of Holland, Daendels decorated them with the title of "minister," a new official costume of state, a considerable military escort, and most importantly, a large gilded and light blue payung emblazoned with the arms of Louis Napoléon. The edict further dictated that a minister not remove his hat when approaching a Javanese monarch but instead wait for the ruler to rise, welcome him, and offer him a seat at the left-hand side of the throne, at the monarch's level. In addition, the edict explicitly prohibited ministers from serving the ruler wine or betel nuts. Ministers were further instructed to escort Javanese rulers during public ceremonies, walking arm-in-arm in a highly gendered manner that implied a feminine reliance on a colonial paternal figure. The edict even dealt with proper forms of salutation outside the *kraton* (palace). For instance, when riding in his carriage, a minister was no longer expected to yield to Javanese monarchs when crossing paths on public roads.[28] The edict thus signified the beginning of Dutch attempts to control the appearance and performance of colonial authority as a means of legitimizing its power.

Such stipulations in the Edict of Ceremonial and Etiquette were directly responsible for ongoing conflicts between Daendels and the Javanese monarchs. While the sunan of Surakarta begrudgingly accepted Daendels's proposed changes, the more outspoken sultan of Yogyakarta protested them fiercely. Sultan Hamengkubuwana II was particularly bothered by the Dutch appropriation of deferential honors that he believed were the sole privilege of the Javanese courts, such as a gilded payung, which, as Daendels was acutely aware, symbolically placed Dutch ministers on equal footing with the sultan and his family.[29] Sultan Hamengkubuwana II officially objected to the edict in a letter to Daendels, clearly signaling that he did not accept colonial sovereignty within his court or over the whole of Java. In addition to addressing the offensive payung, the sultan asserted that he would prohibit any Dutch official from sitting at his level at court and would send his travel itineraries to Daendels's office in advance in order to avoid any situation in which he would be required to yield to the minister's coach in public.[30]

The Edict of Ceremonial and Etiquette and ensuing clashes over court protocols grew so contentious that they ultimately prompted the 1810 rebellion, Daendels's decision to forcibly remove Hamengkubuwana II, and the coerced acceptance of Dutch rule.[31] Although Raffles and the British soon replaced Daendels and the Dutch on the island, perceived breaches in etiquette continued to generate conflict over power and hierarchy. In an attempt to reestablish his authority, Hamengkubuwana II repeatedly snubbed British colonial officials at court through seating practices, placing his throne on a wooden bench to ensure that he sat higher than them. Like Daendels before him, Raffles grew tired of the old sultan's behavior and led an attack on the palace (*kraton*) so brutal that

British sovereignty over Java was unmistakable. As both violent responses to these conflicts demonstrate, the performance of colonial power was ultimately enhanced by its forceful execution.[32]

Just as Daendels and Raffles compelled the central Javanese courts to acknowledge colonial sovereignty, they sought to exert greater control over the priyayi. During the VOC's tenure on the island, Company representatives were diplomats rather than administrators, partaking in a system of indirect rule. But following instructions to reorganize the system of colonial administration, Daendels and Raffles's combined policies are best characterized as attempts at direct colonial rule, at the Javanese aristocracy's expense. The two governors converted residents into powerful provincial administrators who supervised the bupati and lower-ranking indigenous civil servants.[33] For the bupati, this was a clear demotion, as they were reduced from aristocratic lords to the highest-ranking indigenous officials in the newly created colonial civil service. For instance, in August 1808, Daendels informed the bupati on Java's northern coast that they would now receive a fixed salary, lose their right to demand labor services and crop deliveries as well as their appanage holdings, and that their position would no longer be hereditary. These were considerable changes from VOC policies, ultimately centralizing all power in the governor general's office.

Analogous to his issuance of the Edict on Ceremonial and Etiquette to communicate a changing colonial relationship with Javanese monarchs, Daendels issued new regulations on retinue and status to signal the bupati's demotion within the colonial administration. In the eighteenth century, the bupati mustered substantial retinues as evidence of their rank and status. These entourages consisted of hundreds of servants carrying symbols of power, such as payung, lances, guns, kris (spiritual daggers), and golden betel boxes, with countless household workers in tow. In 1808, Daendels meticulously limited and prescribed the size of these retinues. For instance, high-ranking bupati on Java's northern coast were allowed to gather retinues of "only" 168 servants, while lower-ranking bupati were allotted retinues of 134 or even a mere 70 servants.[34] In a letter to the minister of commerce and colonial affairs, he explained that while he had "sufficiently preserved the outward authority of the indigenous bupati in the eyes of the ordinary Javanese," they nonetheless had become "completely subservient to the objectives of the government."[35] In other words, Daendels transferred administrative and executive control to European civil servants, while leaving the Javanese aristocracy with some symbolic vestiges of authority.[36]

Raffles went much further than Daendels in his assault on the status of the traditional Javanese elite, stripping the bupati of administrative and executive

authority and leaving them with very little real power.[37] He also focused much
of his efforts on modifying cultural rituals. On his arrival in Java, Raffles was
struck by the extreme deference and respect that the Javanese showed toward
their superiors. Acquainting himself with Javanese culture and society (which
eventually resulted in his famous two-volume work, *The History of Java*), he
learned that in Java, "each delegated authority exacts the same marks of obei-
sance so that no one dares to stand in the presence of a superior."[38] To his surprise, the Javanese always squatted in front of their superiors, approached them
while "closing his hands and raising them to his forehead, in token of respect"
(*sembah*), and never addressed them in the same language.[39] Raffles viewed
these customs as incredibly humiliating for the Javanese. While Daendels had
curtailed such customs to an extent, Raffles prohibited many deference rituals
in order "to raise the lower orders, as much as was prudent, from the state of
degradation to which their chiefs, aided by the Dutch authority, had subjected
them."[40] Yet out of political expediency, Raffles did not dare cut the Javanese
bureaucratic elite entirely out of the colonial administration. Maintaining the
bupati, he reasoned, was a "political mode of employing many persons of influence" who would otherwise be disgruntled over their removal from office. He
therefore opted to profoundly restrict but not "abolish the rank, title, or state of
the present native chiefs."[41]

For now, the Javanese aristocracy, and the bupati in particular, were incorporated into the hierarchy of the colonial civil service, albeit with much-reduced
power and status. Although the Dutch and British believed that maintaining
this sort of shared authority, even superficially, was a vestige of feudal power,
they reasoned that doing so would be temporary, lasting only until a complete
transition to a system of direct rule could be implemented. However, the ongoing
manipulation of Javanese cultural traditions had irrevocably soured relations between colonial rulers and their indigenous subjects. Java passed back into Dutch
possession in 1814, but Daendels's and Raffles's legacy of cultural approaches to
governance would continue to influence diplomatic affairs on the island.

Colonial Experiments with Cultural Accommodation

The end of the Napoleonic Wars initiated, much to Raffles's chagrin, a transfer
of most of the VOC's former Southeast Asian colonies to the newly established
United Kingdom of the Netherlands.[42] Although the agreement was signed
in 1814, it was not until 1816 that a three-person commission, including new
Governor General Baron van der Capellen, arrived in Java to resume Dutch

governance. The main challenge for the commissioners was how to handle
Daendels's and Raffles's legacies; should the colony be governed directly by a
centralized European civil service, or indirectly through either a modernized or
a traditional Javanese bureaucracy? Initially, the commissioners decided to continue their predecessors' work, further strengthening the residents' position and
reducing the bupati and priyayi's influence. However, rising discontent among
the Javanese aristocracy, a shortage of European civil servants, and a lack of coercive force would lead Van der Capellen to reconsider these policies within a
few years.[43]

During a tour of Java in 1819, Governor General Van der Capellen was confronted with the unforeseen consequences of Daendels and Raffles's preparation
for direct colonial rule. In a letter to the minister of public education, national
industry, and colonial affairs, he related his distress on witnessing his residents'
"most detrimental" attitude toward the bupati. The colonial civil servants treated
Javanese administrators with contempt, excluded them almost completely from
governance, and seemed to regard them as redundant cogs in the colonial administration's modern machinery. Considering that the bupati's administrative
and judicial powers had been transferred to the residents, this attitude was not
entirely illogical. Van der Capellen observed that the bupati appeared disgruntled and humiliated; the residents' behavior had clearly alienated them from the
colonial administration. This worried him tremendously, as the general populace
was not susceptible to direct rule by outsiders and the depth of the government's
coercive apparatus was limited. Maintaining the support of the bupati, who still
exerted great influence over the ordinary Javanese, was essential.[44] European
civil servants lacked precisely what the bupati had to offer, namely, in Van der
Capellen's words:

> [A] powerful and honored influence, which with the utterance of a single
> word, and without the use of force, moves or halts thousands, and steers
> their labor in the public's interest [which is that of the colonial govern-
> ment], and can only be obtained and maintained by a perfect symmetry in
> language, religion, color, virtues and customs, and appears therefore never
> to become the exclusive domain of the European civil servant, who governs
> a district, to which he has no ties other than his temporary appointment.[45]

Van der Capellen's observations during his tour of Java instilled a certain prag-
matism in his policies. He realized that a stable, effective, and profitable colonial
regime was impossible without the support of the Javanese bureaucratic elite. He
therefore resolved to appease the bupati by restoring some of their administrative

authority and responsibilities as well as some of the traditional distinctions of power that they had lost in previous years. But Van der Capellen did more than simply overturn a number of Daendels's and Raffles's policies. Significantly, he also proposed the systematic and calculated implementation of the bupati's traditional status and influence to legitimize Dutch colonial authority.

Inspired by his firsthand observations, Van der Capellen initiated policies to more fully incorporate the bupati, and the priyayi in general, into the colonial administration. In 1820, he issued new regulations that modified the bupati's position within the colonial government as well as their titles and ranks, designated symbols of power, and the size of their retinues.[46] The regulations described the bupati as the "first persons" among the indigenous population, only subservient to European residents, whom they were expected to provide with counsel. In return, residents should treat the bupati as "younger brothers." This designation was a colonial reinterpretation of the kawula-gusti relationship essential in Javanese social hierarchies. The term priyayi itself denotes "younger brother of the king," a clear reference to the Javanese bureaucratic hierarchy before the arrival of the Dutch. Under Van der Capellen, this familiar social structure was applied to the colonial administration. He also strengthened the bupati's position by restoring some of the office's traditional responsibilities, such as overseeing the cultivation of cash crops, the maintenance and construction of infrastructure, local police, administration, education, religious matters, and corvée labor. They were not, however, allowed to be involved in tax collection or the management of government warehouses nor were they permitted to engage in any kind of trade or industry. Van der Capellen's regulations can be regarded as the foundation of a dual civil service consisting of two branches: one European and one Javanese.[47]

Perhaps the most significant insight that Van der Capellen gained during his tour of the island was the extent of the bupati's "honored authority" in the eyes of the ordinary Javanese, communicated through language, etiquette, deference, dress, and status symbols. It was this realization that prompted Van der Capellen to officially appropriate these outward representations of power to legitimize colonial authority. This strategy contrasted with his predecessors' policies. Daendels had initiated an incremental reduction of the right to deference and retinues to signal the Javanese bureaucratic elite's subservient position to his government. Both he and Raffles sought to decrease these "feudal" representations of power over time to create a truly modern bureaucracy. Van der Capellen, however, was convinced that colonial rule actually benefited from retaining these influences. He believed that reinstating some of the bupati's former pomp would assuage fears of further social decline and lead them to encourage the Javanese to accept Dutch colonial rule.[48]

Van der Capellen used his knowledge of Javanese symbols and rituals to officially integrate the Javanese bureaucratic elite into the colonial administration. In 1824, he declared the bupati and all other indigenous administrators above the village level to be civil servants of the colonial administration, and, in accordance with the strict social hierarchies within Javanese culture, assigned each of them a distinct title, rank, and right to traditional insignia of power. This was best illustrated, figuratively and literally, in an elaborate payung hierarchy that mimicked those of the Javanese principalities.[49] But in contrast to the principalities' aristocracies, which had separate payung hierarchies for members of the royal family and civil servants, the colonial government's payung hierarchy was primarily a bureaucratic one. Under Van der Capellen, each payung's colors and decorations reflected the rank and office of its owner. In descending order, the most prestige was associated with the colors gold, yellow, white, green, blue, dark brown, gray-black, and light red. For instance, a public prosecutor (*jaksa*) received a payung with a green top, blue bottom, and three gilded circles, while subdistrict administrators (*wedana*) carried ones with blue tops, dark brown bottoms, and three golden circles. This payung hierarchy expanded throughout the nineteenth century to incorporate new professions within the civil service, such as teachers, doctors, and even pawnshop personnel.[50]

The decision to embrace rather than phase out Javanese social etiquette, deference rituals, and insignias of power also affected European civil servants. Daendels and Raffles deliberately used status symbols like the payung to provoke the Javanese principalities. By asserting the right to assign a gilded payung to their representatives, they signified in unmistakable terms the colonial claim to sovereignty. Since Daendels assigned a semi-gilded payung to his representatives at the Javanese courts in 1808, colonial officials came to regard the payung as part of their office insignia. Under Raffles's administration, residents used a fully gilded payung to signify their status as representatives of the governor general, while assistant residents were given a payung with a white top and gilded bottom. For both "enlightened" governor generals, the adoption of the payung, which they considered a "feudal" relic, was foremost born out of practical considerations, and once colonial sovereignty was firmly established these symbols were to be discarded. Van der Capellen, however, decided differently. He opted to allow colonial officials to claim Javanese deferential practices and institutionalized the employ of powerful symbols such as the payung. As the representative of the king of the United Kingdom of the Netherlands, Van der Capellen, for instance, claimed the right to a gilded payung, previously the sole privilege of Javanese monarchs. This moment marked the beginning of the Javanization of colonial authority, as the Dutch government relied more and more on Javanese etiquette and symbols of power to legitimize their rule. Within decades, the gilded payung was no longer linked with Javanese monarchs and instead strongly associated with colonial power.[51]

In hindsight, Van der Capellen's reconciliation with the Javanese bureaucratic elite was timely, as it occurred on the eve of the outbreak of the Java War (1825–30). The rebellion was the final act in the struggle over sovereignty between the colonial government and the Javanese principalities (especially the court of Yogyakarta) that had begun with Daendels and Raffles's coercive interventions. Having experienced forced abdication, new mandatory court etiquette, loss of territory, imposed economic reorganization, and the plunder of Yogyakarta's palace, the principalities harbored a great deal of shame and resentment. These grievances, heightened by a cholera epidemic in 1821, the eruption of Mount Merapi in 1822, and soaring rice prices, sparked a millenarian movement around Prince Diponegoro of Yogyakarta. The June 1825 uprising took the Dutch by surprise, and spread like wildfire over central, east, and northeast Java, developing into a serious threat to colonial rule.

For Prince Diponegoro and his followers, the Java War was as much about the preservation of Javanese honor and cultural values as it was about economic grievances and millenarian hopes. They intended to purge the island of detrimental European cultural influences.[52] As the oldest son of Sultan Hamengkubuwana III and one of his secondary wives, Diponegoro grew up at the Yogyakarta court and witnessed firsthand his people's humiliating subjugation to colonial interests under Daendels and Raffles. He took great pride in Javanese history and mythology, valued Javanese court etiquette and deference traditions, and was deeply troubled by the growth of European influence over court society. It appears that the 1823 arrival of Dutch resident Anthonie Hendrik Smissaert set the prince on the path toward rebellion. The new colonial representative could only speak Malay in court society—an offense to propriety that rendered useless the subtle Javanese language hierarchy. To show his discontent, Diponegoro traded insults by replying to the Dutch representatives in low Javanese. The prince was also bothered by Smissaert's appropriation of a gilded payung, traditionally imbued with deep symbolic and spiritual power.[53] These offensive breaches in etiquette prompted Diponegoro to action.

In his masterful study of Diponegoro, Peter Carey argues that the prince's rebellion can be interpreted as the old order's final stand in defense of Javanese sartorial, linguistic, and cultural codes.[54] Indeed, during the Java War, the prince's preoccupation with cultural values manifested in various ways, as he employed precisely those symbols and traditions that he felt were most threatened by colonialism to validate his cause. For instance, to demonstrate his royal claim to the throne, he adopted a gilded payung and brought it into battle to boost morale.[55] He even "deployed" his ceremonial parasol to rally his forces in distant villages while he was active elsewhere. But while Diponegoro's payung legitimized his claim in the eyes of his followers, to Dutch observers his use of the parasol demonstrated the importance of controlling and employing Javanese status symbols and deference rituals to express colonial authority.[56]

Moreover, and most importantly, throughout the five-year conflict the colonial authorities were assured of the bupati and priyayi's support in the territories that remained under their control. This was a real testament to Van der Capellen's foresight in incorporating the Javanese bureaucratic elite into the colonial administration and assigning them traditional insignias of power. To maintain their support and convince the bupati that their interests were best served by the Dutch rather than the Javanese courts, the colonial government promised them even greater responsibilities and hereditary positions at the end of the conflict. With this goal in mind, Dutch residents were also instructed to treat the Javanese bureaucratic elite with respect and distinction.[57] In this way, the Java War firmly cemented an increasingly interdependent partnership between the Javanese bureaucratic elite and the Dutch.

After five years of suffering, colonial forces ended the war by luring Diponegoro to the negotiating table and arresting him. It was the last major challenge to colonial rule until the Second World War and marks a crucial turning point in Indonesian colonial history. The Java War forced the Dutch to reexamine the character and appearance of their colonial administration. They realized that attempts to establish direct rule with a European style of colonial governance had backfired, as they had generated widespread discontent under Daendels and Raffles, and ultimately motivated Diponegoro to rebel. The war made it clear that, in Van der Capellen's words, the Dutch lacked the "perfect symmetry in language, religion, color, virtues and customs" with the local populace required to rule them directly.[58] Understanding that a profitable and stable system of colonial rule depended on the cooperation of the Javanese bureaucratic elite, the colonial government strengthened the bupati's position politically, economically, and symbolically in the years following the Java War. Moreover, the Dutch implemented a system of indirect rule that deliberately attempted to bridge the social and cultural distance between colonial officials and their subjects. Appropriating Javanese cultural elements, such as language hierarchies, etiquette, deference rituals, symbols of power, architecture, and dress, the Dutch sought to legitimize their domination through the "Javanization" of colonial authority.[59]

The Cultivation System and
the Javanization of Colonial Authority

The Javanization of colonial authority corresponded with the introduction of a new system of colonial exploitation known as the Cultivation System. The Cultivation System allowed for the extensive appropriation of Javanese labor, cash crops, and services—measures regarded as necessary to make the colonial endeavor profitable. One year prior to the end of the Java War, Van der Capellen's eventual successor, Governor General Johannes van den Bosch, wrote a spirited appeal to the Dutch king, Willem I, arguing that the only way for the colony to turn a profit was through the use of forced labor. He stated that the Javanese were "innately lazy" people who without proper direction could barely cultivate sufficient rice for their own sustenance. He therefore rejected the policies of his predecessors, who had sought to create a system of colonial exploitation based on relatively free labor, market production, and taxation. Instead, Van den Bosch proposed to revert to the VOC's earlier, more "successful" system of forced cultivation of cash crops—a form of colonial exploitation hinging on the principle that as the sovereign of Java, the Dutch king had the right to extract corvée labor and a portion of the country's crops. Just as under the VOC, the new Cultivation System required the support of the Javanese bureaucratic elite and their aristocratic culture.[60]

Experiences during the Java War had confirmed the importance and potential of having the Javanese priyayi as collaborators in the colonial administration. Like Van der Capellen a decade earlier, Van den Bosch believed that the Javanese bureaucratic elite was uniquely qualified to employ its traditional authority to administer and oversee the cultivation of cash crops, and in doing so, help fill colonial coffers. Once in office, Van den Bosch fulfilled promises made during the war and increased the bupati's stature and power, granting them hereditary succession and reinstating their right to private landholdings. These and other government regulations cemented the bupati's position as intermediaries between the colonial government and the Javanese people.[61] In addition, Van den Bosch designed a financial incentive for the bupati to collaborate with the Dutch, rewarding them with a share of the proceeds (*kultuurprocenten*) from the cash crops that their regencies delivered to the government. Through these measures, Van den Bosch reasoned that "the most prominent class among the Javanese [can] be tied closer to [the colonial government]. Consequently, they would have nothing to gain and everything to lose from a change in circumstances."[62] Moreover, by administering Java through the bupati—and thus according to Javanese customs and institutions—European civil servants retreated from direct interference with the ordinary Javanese. Their main task became to supervise the Javanese aristocracy and protect the ordinary man against possible mistreatment and abuse by its native chiefs.[63]

But although the colonial administration encouraged Javanese customs, their adoption most certainly did not signify a restoration of the precolonial order under the VOC. With the help of the Javanese elite, the colonial government executed a process of modern state formation and agro-industrial exploitation that made far more extractive demands on the labor and services of the ordinary Javanese than ever before. The tension between a traditional façade and modern colonial administration was also reflected in the bupati's new position. Under the Cultivation System, the bupati's prestige and wealth increased considerably, but they gained their new power without retaining much autonomy; as civil servants in the colonial administration, they remained under European supervision. For instance, it was as civil servants that the bupati achieved hereditary succession, which had eluded them in the precolonial Javanese world.[64] There was thus an inherent contradiction within their position as both "native chief" *and* colonial civil servant. As a consequence, the traditional relationship between the Javanese bureaucratic elite and the ordinary Javanese changed. The bupati no longer derived their power from the traditional kawula-gusti relationship, in which devotion for the patron was exchanged for protection of the client. Now their power came directly through supporting Dutch rule. This meant that the bupati could exploit their subjects without consequence—for instance, increase their percentage shares of cash crop cultivation—as long as they enjoyed the support and military backing of the Dutch.[65] While this was not necessarily evident at the time, this practice manipulated and corrupted the principle of kawula-gusti, causing tensions between the traditional elite and the ordinary Javanese that would simmer under the Cultivation System and eventually boil over in the twentieth century.

As part of reconceiving the colonial administration, Dutch authorities sought to justify their dominance by appropriating Javanese social customs, deference rituals, and etiquette to regulate public interactions with their colonized subjects. In a way, this too was a return to the more pragmatic practices of the VOC rather than the failed attempts at direct European rule in the previous decades. The Dutch were well aware of the value of manipulating social etiquette and status symbols, as they had already used this tactic to undermine the Javanese monarchies and gain the bupati's support. At Van der Capellen's behest, colonial officials claimed the right to forms of deference traditionally reserved for the Javanese royal houses, as representatives of a sovereign power. By continuing to insert themselves, as it were, into traditional Javanese hierarchies, the Dutch's performance of colonial hegemony became highly—and deliberately—"Javanized."

As an example of this shift, under the Cultivation System Dutch colonial officials were encouraged to learn and speak vernacular languages, such as Javanese and Sundanese, in order to convincingly communicate their elevated social position. Since the days of the VOC, most Dutch officials conversed with their colonized subjects in Malay, the mercantile lingua franca of the Indonesian archipelago. This frequently resulted in tensions between Dutch officials and the Javanese elite (most egregiously with Prince Diponegoro in the years before the Java War), as Malay was an egalitarian language that lacked the clear differentiation and expression of rank and status that was so prevalent in Javanese. To address the issue, in an 1841 public lecture in front of King Willem I, preeminent Dutch linguistic scholar Taco Roorda advocated for an educational institution where prospective colonial civil servants could be taught vernacular languages.[66] Roorda argued that colonial civil servants should learn to employ the Javanese language hierarchy as a means of asserting their authority: they could then address their Javanese partners in low Javanese (*ngoko*), which required a response in high Javanese (*krama*). Such diglossia of the Javanese language reinforced both the prestige and superiority of individual Dutch civil servants and that of colonial authorities in general.[67]

Following up on Roorda's public call for an educational institution, Dutch minister of colonial affairs Jean Chrétien Baud soon composed his own detailed proposal to persuade the king to train prospective officials in Europe. Baud suggested that the Royal Academy in Delft add colonial studies to its program, stressing the importance of linguistic and cultural instruction for the success of future civil servants. He argued that it was a "tangible truth that a dominated people cannot be held in subjection for long, without violence, if the ruler does not make every effort to govern that people with fairness and justice, and above all, with respect for the local institutions, customs and prejudices." The principal means of acquiring this kind of knowledge, according to Baud, was "to become thoroughly familiar with the language of the country."[68] Clearly influenced by the recent experience of the Java War, this treatise effectively summarized the guiding principle of Dutch colonial policy for the remainder of the nineteenth century: by appropriating—or "respecting," in Baud's words—local institutions and customs, colonial dominance could be legitimized by consent rather than coercion. Baud's arguments swayed the king and in 1843, the Royal Academy in Delft accepted its first prospective colonial officials, supervised by Roorda, the institution's first professor of Javanese.[69]

The use of vernacular languages was an important component of a larger system of deference rituals and etiquette. In Javanese society, it was customary for those of lower rank or social standing to sit crossed-legged on the floor in a posture called *sila* in the presence of social superiors. When addressed, the social inferior would avoid eye contact and accompany each sentence with a gesture of respect called the sembah, bringing their palms together with their thumbs touching their mouth while their index fingers touched their nose. When encountering a person of higher social standing, one was expected to squat and only approach the superior on one's heels in an uncomfortable crouching-walk known as jongkok. Taken together, these deference rituals were known as *hormat*, which in Malay means "respect" or "homage." Under the aegis of men like Baud and Roorda, prospective colonial civil servants were instructed on how to employ both the vernacular language hierarchy and hormat rituals to legitimize colonial authority.[70]

The Javanization of colonial authority manifested in numerous other ways, as well, as Dutch officials sought to rule and perform like the Javanese elite. Regional administrators like residents and assistant residents were always accompanied by their gilded or semi-gilded payung, carried by a servant when touring on foot, mounted on their carriages when traveling by coach, or displayed on the veranda of their residences. In imitation of the Javanese priyayi, colonial officials also surrounded themselves with countless servants and traveled with a great entourage of local officials when touring their districts. They even insisted on being addressed with honorary titles like *kangdjeng tuan*—akin to "your highness"—and of course demanded observance of the proper language hierarchy and hormat customs, which were privileges previously beholden to Javanese royalty and nobility.[71]

Surprisingly, the process of Javanization also permeated less obvious arenas, such as food dishes and the manner of their consumption, which were employed as additional markers of social, racial, and cultural identities. What mattered was not only what was eaten but also how the consumption of a meal was performed. From the 1830s onward, the Dutch distinguished themselves as Java's new ruling class through a gastronomical spectacle known as the rice table (*rijsttafel*), rooted in Asian and European traditions. From a purely culinary perspective, the rice table consisted of a rice centerpiece in combination with a broad assortment of side dishes—vegetables, soups, sauces, meat, and fish, among others—which were to be served over the warm rice. These side dishes originated in the indigenous cultures of the Indonesian archipelago, including that of the Chinese diaspora, albeit modified to Dutch tastes. Symbolically, they represented the reach of the Dutch empire. The preparation of such a culinary feast was both labor and capital intensive, which meant that only the wealthy and powerful could offer it to their guests. In the course of the nineteenth century, the rice table evolved into a grand spectacle, with servants in procession presenting the diners with the side dishes. The larger the procession of servants, the greater the host's prestige. Tellingly, the rice table did not include tempeh—fried soybean patties widely consumed by all Javanese—as the Dutch considered them too lowly to eat. They did add beer and fried bananas to the rice table, which in turn were scarcely found on Javanese tables. In fact, the ordinary Javanese made do with rice and only a single side dish, if any. As this history of the rice table demonstrates, the production of colonial authority was extremely detailed and pervasive throughout colonial society.[72]

The Javanization of colonial authority also permeated colonial spaces. On arrival to the Indonesian archipelago in the seventeenth century, the Dutch initially transplanted European architecture to the tropics. They soon discovered that brick walls, small eaves, and few openings for ventilation were at odds with the hot and humid climate of Java. Over time, they made accommodations to create healthier and more comfortable living conditions, such as overhanging eaves to protect against the tropical sun and rain, spacious living quarters, and improved ventilation. However, it was not until the nineteenth century that vernacular architectural traditions were more fully incorporated into colonial spaces. In part, this transition can be attributed to the recognition that Javanese construction methods and design carried great climatic, and thus health, benefits. But this cultural adaptation also resulted from Dutch fascination with the lifestyle and authority of Java's elite. By trying to emulate and even outdo the priyayi, the Dutch sought to enhance their prestige and distinguish themselves as Java's latest rulers. Colonial architecture thus played a vital part in signaling and maintaining colonial hegemony.[73]

Moreover, implementing the Cultivation System required widespread infrastructural investment, from the construction of sugar factories, storehouses, port facilities, irrigation and drainage systems, roads, and bridges to new offices, residences, and outstations for colonial administrators. This building frenzy was

fundamental to exerting and preserving political and economic control over
the island, and the new structures' appearance was as crucial as their function-
ality. Their syncretic architectural design, combining Javanese and European
construction and décor, made these buildings appear familiar yet distinctive in
the colonial environment. Consequently, they became clear symbols of colonial
authority to rulers and subjects alike.[74]

This syncretism was most conspicuous in buildings representing state power,
such as residences, outstations (*passanggrahan*), and offices of colonial officials.
The nineteenth century colonial mansion in particular was modeled after the
houses of Javanese aristocrats, with local architectural traits such as a rectangular floor plan and a hipped roof (in which all sides slope downward) transferred
to colonial villas.[75] As with the Javanese language diglossia, the particular style
and pitch of the roof reflected the social status and rank of its inhabitants.[76] The
colonial mansion also mimicked the layout of Javanese houses, with a private
large interior section for family (*dalem*), a back porch (*gadri*), and a public front
porch (*pringgitan*). Arguably, the pringgitan was the most important part of
the colonial mansion, as it was where most public performances occurred. Its
function was derived from the Javanese *pendopo*—a square, open pavilion with
centralized wooden pillars supporting a hipped roof—that served as a location
for public meetings and celebrations. In contrast with Javanese traditions that
positioned the pendopo in front of the house, the Dutch expanded their front
porches in order for them to function *as* pendopos. Thus, the Dutch did not
simply duplicate Javanese traditions, but appropriated what they believed was
necessary while still maintaining a sense of difference.[77]

Such differentiation was evident in further design decisions made under the
colonial regime. The Javanization of colonial architecture coincided with the
widespread adoption of the "Empire style," a neoclassical style modeled after
Greco-Roman designs, resulting in a unique syncretism in colonial architecture.
It was Daendels who first utilized this style for colonial government buildings,
and the trend continued during the British interregnum. But it was not until the
construction frenzy brought on by the Cultivation System that Empire style became prevalent all over the island. For instance, neoclassical colonnades adorned
the porches of colonial villas, distinguishing them from their inspiration: the
Javanese pendopo. Moreover, in contrast to Javanese houses, those of the Dutch
were whitewashed, which was in part to reflect the tropical sun but also to clearly
identify colonial buildings. The colonial government even issued construction
manuals detailing how the residences of colonial officials (1854), bupati (1870),
and residents (1879) should be built. These standards not only ensured that the

appearance of colonial authority in Java remained ubiquitous but also visibly differentiated the homes of the ruling class.[78]

Another essential component of the Javanization of colonial authority was regulating dress. Due to a large Eurasian population, skin color alone did not distinguish colonizers from colonized. Thus, outward appearance was a marker of social and racial status, crucial in communicating one's position and ethnicity in such a stratified culture. As a consequence of the VOC's conjugal policies, colonial households had practiced local sartorial customs since the seventeenth century. In the private sphere, Eurasian women adopted the dress of their mothers, wearing a *kain*—a floor-length, uncut, dyed or plaid cloth wound around the waist—and a *kebaya*—a long-sleeved blouse extending to the hips. European and Eurasian men wore similar leisure and sleeping attire at home, but in public appeared in European dress. While Daendels and especially Raffles sought to Europeanize colonial officials' appearance, the Javanization of colonial authority institutionalized traditional clothing distinctions between an indigenized private sphere and a Europeanized public sphere.[79]

In the wake of the Java War, the Dutch symbolically displayed their reaffirmed control over the island by ending the Javanese elite's longstanding connection with batik fabrics. Since the Hindu-Buddhist period in Javanese history, the bupati were adorned in batik clothing to distinguish themselves from commoners. Batik was a perfect status symbol, as it was expensive (due to its time-consuming, wax-resistant dyeing technique) and allowed for the display of intricate designs reserved for royalty.[80] The Dutch appropriation of both batik production and usage was an unmistakable sign of a new balance of power. Women with European status adorned themselves in popular batik sarongs—rectangular cloths sewn into tubes—which were produced in batik shops owned and operated by Eurasian women. These shops created fabrics with unique designs and colors that became known as *batik Belanda* (Dutch batik), easily discernable from traditional Javanese batik. The growing importance of batik sarongs as status symbols resulted in shortening the white kebaya to allow onlookers to admire their designs.[81] European men likewise added batik clothing to their wardrobes, significantly replacing the traditional kain with a pair of batik trousers. By breaking with Javanese unisex attire, Dutch men contrasted their perceived masculinity with the appearance of Javanese men, which they deemed feminine. Such choices represent additional means by which the colonial regime justified its authority.[82]

Under the Cultivation System, the Dutch also regulated dress in the public sphere to reinforce a new racialized legal form of stratification that became the cornerstone of the colonial administration. Government regulations adopted

in 1854 and 1855 legally categorized inhabitants of colonial Indonesia as either
"European," "Native," or "Foreign Oriental" (primarily referring to people of
Chinese or Arab descent).[83] This legal differentiation mirrored the Dutch institution of indirect rule, leaving the Javanese administrative elite to manage the
colonized according to Javanese laws. However, as skin color was not sufficient to
discern these "legalized ethnic" groups, dress regulations became an indispensable means of communicating racial and social difference. Surabaya's police regulations of 1829 were the first to stipulate that it was prohibited for inhabitants
"to appear on the roads and streets in clothing that deviates from one's ethnicity
and social standing."[84] In the next decades, other towns and districts followed
Surabaya's example until provisions on ethnic dress were incorporated into police regulations that applied to the entire island in 1872.[85] As a consequence of
these regulations, "legal" categories became associated with ethnic stereotypes.
For instance, in public Javanese men were expected to don a kain, Chinese to
have a queue, Arabs to wear a turban, and Europeans to model a white suit. Europeans' sartorial transgressions in the private sphere, where they wore Eurasian
batik attire, similarly confirmed their privileged position in colonial society. But
in the public sphere, dress and appearance were vital, as they assigned a particular role and script that would determine other elements that were essential to
the performance of colonialism, such as the deference etiquette guiding an encounter. Through these and other deliberate manipulations of Javanese rituals
and status symbols, the Dutch asserted their power as colonial rulers.

From the perspective of the colonizer, the Cultivation System, the institution
of indirect rule, and the Javanization of colonial authority were a rousing success.
The forced cultivation of cash crops finally delivered the financial windfalls the
Dutch had so desperately desired. In the mid-nineteenth century, Java was the
envy of the colonial world, as profits enabled the Netherlands to pay off a significant part of its national debt, balance its budget, finance infrastructural projects
in the metropolis, compensate Surinam slaveowners for the abolition of slavery,
and delay the introduction of income taxes.[86] However, all of these spoils were
made possible by the excessive appropriation of labor and cash crops from the
ordinary Javanese, who, under the Cultivation System, suffered abuses not only
from Dutch colonial officials, but also from their own administrative elite—the
bupati. Both worked under a system of rewards that incentivized exploitation
of the peasantry, as percentages of their district profits augmented their regular
salaries. This arrangement effectively destroyed the traditional kawula-gusti relationship—which had imbued the elite and the peasantry with reciprocal responsibilities—and exacerbated the Cultivation System's impact on Javanese society.

The unbridled extraction of labor and resources resulted in the outbreak of typhoid fever (1846–50) and severe famines (1849–50). While most contemporary observers agreed that this distress indicated the Cultivation System's shortcomings, political and financial expediency dictated that the Netherlands could not forego it just yet. Instead, the Cultivation System was dismantled in stages until 1870, when it was finally abolished.[87]

Colonial Puppeteers and the Performance of Hegemony

The end of the forced cultivation of cash crops in 1870 marked the transition to a new system of colonial exploitation and administration known in the historiography of colonial Indonesia as the Liberal Period. During this time, the colonial economy opened to private commercial agents, welcoming Dutch planters and businessmen who replaced colonial officials as the drivers of economic exploitation. Rather than colonial administrators, entrepreneurs were now responsible for—and considered better suited for—advancing the colony's economy. It became colonial officials' primary responsibility to facilitate the capitalist development of Java while safeguarding the population against excesses like those under the Cultivation System. This form of quasi-capitalist exploitation, or so it was argued, would benefit the mother country, economically develop Java, and improve the welfare of the colonized.

These changes necessitated a new role for colonial civil servants. Whereas under the Cultivation System, Dutch officials had been chiefly responsible for overseeing agricultural production, the new system transformed them into powerful administrators. As such, they were tasked with maintaining colonial peace and order—an assignment that included protecting the ordinary Javanese from potential abuses instigated by both private interests and the Javanese aristocracy. Ironically, the bupati had acquired an unsavory reputation for exploiting the peasantry during the Cultivation System, even though it was the Dutch who had facilitated such mistreatment.[88] Now, colonial administrators were suddenly expected to protect the colonized. Moreover, managing the bupati was also under their official purview. As a result of these updated duties, Dutch bureaucrats interacted more directly and frequently with the Javanese, adopting a paternalistic attitude in the process. In a sense, the paternalistic turn in colonial administration can be interpreted as an attempt to restore a kind of kawula-gusti. To that end, the European civil service grew more powerful and influential at the expense of their Javanese counterparts and continued to rely on traditional forms of etiquette and deference to express their authority.

As the bupati once again lost political and administrative power, the Dutch compensated by increasing their symbolic power—a process that began in the 1860s, before the Cultivation System was completely abolished. In 1866, cultivation percentages—the incentives fostering the abusive exploitation of the Javanese peasantry—were eliminated, resulting in a significant loss in income for both European and Javanese officials. The bupati also saw their right to feudal services reduced, lost their right to private appanage entirely, and had to accept more overt and direct interference from European officials.[89] To compensate for their loss of income and decreased political and administrative power, the Dutch offered "payment" in the form of status symbols and deference. For instance, in 1867 the government bestowed on the bupati the right to decorate their yellow payung with a gilded circle, a significant status-enhancing gesture.[90] In addition, the government reassured them that they would maintain the principle of hereditary succession for their positions. The ironic consequence of these developments was that as the bupati became less powerful, they *appeared* more powerful than ever, receiving substantial ritualistic deference and surrounding themselves with a plethora of status symbols. The bupati clung to these traditional sources of authority in an attempt to maintain their standing and offset their loss of power to their European "colleagues."[91]

These seemingly diverging tendencies—a decrease in real power along with an increase in symbolic power—were also reflected in the broad expansion of the Javanese priyayi in general. The liberalization of the colonial economy and the government's new role in facilitating it resulted in a growing demand for cheap, specialized labor. In 1879, the colonial government sponsored the founding of Head Schools (*hoofdenscholen*) to prepare the children of the Javanese elite to work for the government in nontraditional (meaning non-administrative) professions, such as teachers, vaccinators, clerks, and irrigation officers.[92] These new and modern professionals were carefully incorporated into the traditional Javanese hierarchy and assigned specific titles, ranks, status symbols, and ceremonial rights. This in itself was nothing new. Forestry service leaders, senior heads of waterworks, and employees in the vaccination service, saltworks, and warehouses were already added to the ranks of the priyayi in 1824. But following the dismantling of the Cultivation System, this expansion accelerated considerably as the following professions were added: government tellers and prison guards (1874); teachers (1879); indigenous doctors (1892); veterinarians (1893); clerks for the post, telegraph, telephone, and railroad services (1896); conductors (1897); translators (1898); subdistrict chiefs (1900); forestry personnel (1901); and finally, pawnshop personnel (1906). As a sign of their priyayi status, all of

FIGURE 2. Meeting of the Native Court in Pati, Central Java, ca. 1865. The photograph captures the performance of colonial power in the nineteenth century. The Dutch resident is accompanied by his gilded payung (the top of his servant's head is just visible). The court officials are seated on chairs while lower officials sit on the floor, all donning ethnic garb. Source: Leiden University Library, Royal Netherlands Institute for Southeast Asian and Caribbean Studies (KITLV) 3516.

these "modern" professionals were assigned a payung. New color schemes were designed to reflect each branch of government: blue for indigenous administration and education, blue and green for a legal position, and brown for healthcare providers (see figure 2). The decision to implement traditional emblems and rituals for the bupati and priyayi was a clear indication that, despite liberalizing the economy and modernizing the administration, the Dutch still considered Javanese symbols of power to be indispensable within colonial rule.[93]

But perhaps even more surprising was that European officials, the purported modernizers of the colonial administration, similarly clung to a Javanized appearance of authority. They believed that adherence to local customs affirmed and naturalized their power in the eyes of their subjects and justified colonial authority more broadly.[94] This was not limited to the European civil service alone but permeated all layers of colonial society, including the growing number of European entrepreneurs in Java. Quick to follow the example set by colonial officials, they constructed villas in the hybrid colonial style, communicated with their workers according to the strict language hierarchy, expected traditional forms of deference, such as jongkok and sembah, and conformed to the sartorial order. Interactions within colonial households, where indigenous servants were the majority, were regulated by the same social etiquette. In short, the overall character of colonial society was profoundly local. This distinctive feature of Dutch rule in Java was not lost on outsiders. In the 1890s, a British traveler observed that rather than raising the Javanese to their "level" of civilization, the Dutch had sunk to the natives' level, and feared that they would "soon cease to be Europeans in anything but a traditional sense."[95]

"A Ridiculous Spectacle"

Dutch colonialism at the end of the nineteenth century invites an analogy to a traditional Javanese wayang performance. The beautiful *wayang kulit* (leather shadow puppets)—skillfully carved to the tiniest detail, patiently painted with several layers of bright colors, and finished with carved handles of buffalo bone—resemble the Javanese priyayi, clad in ceremonial attire and surrounded by various symbols of power and a large entourage. Both look exquisite, extravagant even, but most of all they appear powerful. However, the power is the hands of the *dalang* (puppeteer) who guides both puppets and priyayi. It is the dalang who makes the puppet move, who decides on its actions and direction. A Javanese bupati described this relationship with the Dutch succinctly: "They have degraded us from powerful chiefs to fancy civil servants with a high salary, beautiful titles, but in fact differing little from lower police officers. They (the population) consider us wayang puppets, who are moved by ever changing dalang, the European civil servants, without any free will or insight."[96] The bupati and other Javanese officials may have appeared as decorated and powerful as wayang puppets, but in fact they were nothing more than a shadow of their former selves. As the Dutch recognized, in the shadow theatre it is the source of light—power—and the dalang that makes or breaks the performance.[97] In the theatre of the colonial state, the Dutch relied on their coercive power to manipulate the appearance and performance of Javanese traditions to legitimize their authority. This suggests that the colonial theatre state, and the concept of the theatre state more generally, can only be understood by considering coercive and symbolic power as complementary.[98]

The Dutch were not simply puppeteers, stagehands, or prop-masters, but leading actors in their own colonial production. Their role in these performances visually reflected the colonial relationship as they imagined it and was meant to illustrate and imbue their dominance over their colonized subjects. Throughout the nineteenth century, the Dutch authored a hegemonic script that, while never static, increasingly centered on the Javanization of colonial authority. This was not simply the outcome of centuries of cultural and racial mixing due to the VOC's immigration and conjugal policies. Such an interpretation misses the deliberate nature of the Javanization of authority. At the opening of the nineteenth century, Java's colonial rulers used their familiarity with local culture to communicate their sovereignty to the Javanese courts. When this backfired—in the form of the Java War—they adjusted and intentionally embraced Javanese etiquette to appease the priyayi and ensure their collaboration. These policies were informed by Orientalist assumptions that Javanese culture was static and consensual, presuming that its appropriation would ensure passive acquiesce to colonial rule. Ironically, it was the Dutch attempt at ordering culture—through regulations on etiquette, entourage, dress, language, and more—that made it appear fixed. This façade created the illusion of colonial peace and order and obscured—even to many historians—the considerable coercion needed to stage the performance of power.[99] The Javanese did not merely comply docilely, but without a broad contestation of the hegemonic script, the performance remained intact at the end of the nineteenth century.

However, Raden Adjeng Kartini's observations around 1900, with which this chapter opened, demonstrate the existence of subversive interpretations of the Dutch hegemonic script. Kartini described the Dutch appropriation of Javanese deference rituals as a "ridiculous spectacle" that inspired jest and mockery at colonial officials' expense.[100] Her comments were not made in isolation, as a new educated elite began to challenge the colonial discourse the Dutch had so carefully crafted in the nineteenth century. It is to these challenges that the following chapters turn.

CHAPTER 2

"Sweet Was the Dream, Bitter the Awakening"

The Contested Implementation of the Ethical Policy, 1901–1913

I N JUNE 1905, A young medical student named Goenawan Mangoenkoesoemo published a pointed opinion piece in a progressive colonial newspaper, *Java Bode*. He argued that the prevalence of traditional Javanese
deference customs in colonial society was the primary obstacle to intellectual
and socioeconomic emancipation among the colonized. He invited his predominantly Dutch readership to see the world through Javanese eyes to help them
understand that apparent acquiescence to *hormat*—expressed through deference, honorifics, language, and dress—should not be mistaken for consent, nor
for an intrinsic respect for allegedly enduring cultural traditions. On the contrary, the younger generation of educated Javanese privately considered these
deferential performances to be prohibitive, time-consuming, and out of place in
the twentieth century. Goenawan contended that the social customs regulating
public contact between colonizer and colonized instilled a sense of inferiority in
the Javanese people, especially since other groups, like Chinese and Arabs, were
not burdened with similar constraints. He proposed leveling the playing field
by replacing Javanese deference traditions with, in his opinion, more egalitarian
and modern Western customs, and called on high-ranking colonial and Javanese officials to lead by example to accomplish progressive change. According
to Goenawan, most young Javanese feared insults, public humiliation, or arbi-
trary retribution in the form of a ruined career if they spoke out. But through
a friendly and benevolent attitude, influential European and Javanese administrators could convey that they no longer required excessive deference from their
subjects. In return, Goenawan assured his readers, the officials would soon enjoy
great popularity among the people.[1]

Goenawan's eloquent piece—written at age seventeen, no less—was a spirited
response to the unsuccessful implementation of a colonial government circular
issued in 1904. Popularly known as the hormat circular (deference circular), the

edict prohibited European civil servants from insisting on or accepting traditional Javanese deference in their interactions with their indigenous counterparts and subjects. Young Javanese like Goenawan received the decree with great
enthusiasm, as they no longer wanted to approach Europeans in a crouching
walk, sit on the floor in their presence, make gestures of respect after speaking,
and conform to the Javanese language hierarchy. However, conservative European civil servants simply ignored these instructions from the more progressive
central authorities, as they believed that the Javanization of colonial authority
was essential for maintaining peace and order. Even when these instructions
were repeated in additional hormat circulars in 1906 and 1909, conservative resistance persisted. Disillusioned with this protracted change, Goenawan later
wrote, "Sweet was the dream, bitter the awakening."[2]

The hormat circulars were a vital part of the Ethical Policy, the Dutch equivalent of the civilizing mission ideology that from 1901 onward sought to modernize colonial rule. Like the British "white man's burden" and French *"mission civilisatrice,"* the Ethical Policy was based on the presumption that with
Western superiority, rooted in scientific and technological prowess, came the
moral obligation to civilize and improve the welfare of the allegedly stagnant,
backward, and indolent colonized peoples. This idea was reflected in educational policies, agricultural reforms, and a modernized rationalization of colonial governance. In this context, the hormat circulars were meant to adapt the
nineteenth-century Javanized performance of colonial authority to this more
modern civilizing script. However, this civilizing mission ideology contained an
inherent contradiction: while the Dutch believed they had an ethical responsibility to civilize the colonized, they simultaneously accepted Social Darwinist
beliefs about race, which precluded the possibility that the colonized could ever
reach the colonizer's level of civilization, let alone become truly equal. These paradoxical perspectives divided colonial policy makers, officials, and civil servants,
resulting in a discrepancy between more emancipatory theory and conservative
practice regarding colonial rule.[3]

Although the hormat circular of 1904 did not lead to an immediate overhaul
of the outward appearance of colonial authority, it did encourage and facilitate
a more assertive mentality among Goenawan and his peers. This generation of
young, educated Javanese came of age attending government schools for indigenous doctors, teachers, and administrators.[4] In addition to their educational
training, here they learned that colonial subjecthood was a shared experience.
For instance, for Goenawan, the reading table at his medical school was the
cradle of the national awakening. It was there, in their free evening hours, that

he and other students read and discussed newspapers providing them a window to the world. They were inspired by the rise of Japan as an imperial power, social change in China, and anticolonial movements in British India. During their discussions they also realized that regardless of their own backgrounds, they all faced humiliating deference expectations and racial prejudice in their everyday lives. "In the streetcar, the train, or on the football field," Goenawan recalled, they were reminded that "the native had no real value other than as an object to wipe one's shoes with."[5] The rapid emancipation of the Chinese in colonial Indonesia further exacerbated their distress. As they founded associations and schools to advocate for their interests and demanded that Europeans treat them with more respect, the Chinese explicitly distanced themselves from the indigenous population, some even demanding traditional deference. Through these experiences, Goenawan and his peers became increasingly aware that if the colonized did not stand up for themselves, nobody would.[6]

By issuing and supporting the hormat circular, the colonial government created a space in which hegemonic public conduct and the colonial relationship in general were permissible topics for public discussion. Goenawan's opinion piece illustrates this perfectly, as the hormat circular provided him and his cohort with the opportunity to be critical, express their discontent, and demand emancipatory change. His writing exuded self-confidence, challenging the premise of the Javanization of colonial authority and disputing that Javanese compliance with traditional deference rituals was tantamount to consent. By revealing the veiled mentality of the colonized, Goenawan showed that the Javanese did not regard colonial authority with respect, but with fear. In doing so, he exposed what James Scott has described as the hidden transcript or the offstage critique of hegemonic power, in effect undermining the public transcript or the hegemonic display of power and consent.[7] The youthful medical student personified the new generation of educated colonial subjects who believed in progress, demanded respect, sought to break with repressive traditions, and wanted to organize themselves to achieve these goals. While not yet ready in 1905, within a decade this new generation would drastically disrupt the colonial performance of power.[8]

The turn of the twentieth century was a transformative period of social and cultural change in the history of colonial Indonesia, as these educated young Javanese joined progressive European authorities in contesting the enduring system of Dutch dominance and attempting to implement the Ethical Policy. Opposing their efforts were conservative European civil servants and the Javanese *priyayi*, who argued for the necessity of maintaining the status quo. This conflict was not merely an ideological struggle for hegemony, but one reflected and expressed in material culture and outward appearance. As the official ideology justifying colonial domination changed, there emerged an opportunity to redefine assumptions about social and racial relations as expressed through rituals regarding etiquette, dress, and language that regulated public conduct. It was under these unique circumstances that the colonized could demand a more active role in the colonial performance.

Turn-of-the-Century Transformations

During the nineteenth century, the Dutch firmly embedded themselves in Javanese society through a process of cultural appropriation that legitimized their authority. However, at the turn of the twentieth century, rapid technological innovation, evolutionary thinking, shifting demographics, the emergence and intensification of a Dutch civilizing mission, and the nascent national awakening began to challenge and finally transform this complex system of dominance. These developments resulted in greater European control over the colony, increased belief in Western superiority, and a growing emphasis on racial segregation in colonial society. The implementation of the Ethical Policy in 1901 was of particular importance to these outcomes. On the one hand, it provided the Dutch with a new discourse to legitimize colonial authority by emphasizing their relative modernity and civilization vis-à-vis the indigenous population. Consequently, those with this perspective rejected the profound cultural hybridity of the nineteenth century as a form of degeneration. On the other hand, the Ethical Policy created the conditions for the development of an indigenous nationalist movement, which became highly critical of the feudal aspects of the colonial relationship.

During the last three decades of the nineteenth century, technological innovations in transportation and communication greatly reduced the relative distance between the Netherlands and Java, enhancing colonial control and exploitation. For instance, the invention of steamships together with the opening of the Suez Canal in 1869 decreased the duration of the voyage from Amsterdam to Batavia from four months to a mere six weeks. By the mid-1880s, two large shipping companies—the Stoomvaart Maatschappij Nederland and the Rotterdamsche Lloyd—succeeded in establishing a weekly connection between the metropole and the new deep-sea harbor in Tanjung Priok, near Batavia.[9] Almost simultaneously, steam engines revolutionized overland travel with the construction of a railroad track between Semarang and Yogyakarta in 1873. Within decades, an extensive railroad network connected Java's large cities and towns and opened up the island's mountainous interior. Steam power did not remain the sole alternative to animal power for long, however; by 1899, the streetcars of Batavia operated on electricity, while the introduction of the automobile in 1900 further enabled European travel throughout its prized colonial possession.[10]

Technological advances also facilitated a more distinctively Western lifestyle in the tropics. Innovations in communications technology, most notably the telegraph (1870) and telephone (1929) but also the radio (1919), enabled Europeans to stay connected with friends and family and remain informed about developments at home. Technological progress also allowed for the proliferation of the latest European fashions, either imported in their finished state or created locally from designs and products from the continent. Department stores sprang up offering the latest European merchandise, including canned goods and less perishable foods such as cheeses, alcoholic beverages, cigars, and cigarettes. The rapid acquisition of electrical equipment, such as stoves, fans, lights, and radios, created a more hygienic and European household in a tropical environment. For many, these technological developments did not just enable the Europeanization of colonial society but were presented as evidence of European superiority.[11]

Developments in the biological and medical sciences were also employed to confirm and explain alleged Western superiority. The most obvious example was the application of Charles Darwin's revolutionary concept of evolution to human societies, known as Social Darwinism. When discoveries in the field of medical science excluded the possibility that non-Western people belonged to a different species than Europeans, a variety of evolutionary explanations were formulated to explain the West's supposed cultural, intellectual, and even physical dominance over those they had colonized. A popular concept in the Netherlands, and among colonial powers in general, was that there were various evolutionary stages of societal development and that Europeans had simply progressed to a more advanced stage. Indigenous societies were thus perceived as distant mirrors of an early, medieval self, passing through an evolutionary phase that Europeans had left behind centuries ago. A prominent member of Dutch parliament summarized this perspective as follows: "What the natives are now, we once were; what we are now, they will once become."[12] A strong sense of paternalism permeated this evolutionary discourse, characterizing indigenous peoples as immature children that required European parental support for their own benefit.[13]

Climate was considered the determining factor behind these distinct stages of evolutionary development. While the moderate European climate allegedly stimulated intellectual and technological advancement, a hot and humid tropical environment was thought to delay civilization's progress. Although this belief was largely discredited by the end of the nineteenth century, in part by Dutch Nobel Prize winner Christiaan Eijkman, climatologic factors were still thought to produce lazy, uncreative, and superstitious people. Such climatic determinism implied that Europeans who tried to acclimatize to the tropics would inevitably adopt some of these character traits and regress on the evolutionary scale. To prevent degeneration, Europeans not only sought protection against the heat but also reevaluated their use of cultural accommodation as a means of acclimating to the local environment. Since they considered indigenous people and their cultures to be backward, such influence on Europeans' lives should be minimized. Thus, evolutionary and climatological determinism fostered the Europeanization as well as the segregation of colonial society.[14]

The opening of the colony for private enterprise in 1870 following the abolition of the Cultivation System attracted a large number of Europeans who used recent technological advances to maintain a European lifestyle, resist cultural accommodation, and avoid degeneration as much as possible. In part, this was in response to civil servants' dominance in colonial society. Initially comprising more than half of the professional population (in both government and military service), European civil servants regarded their right to indigenous displays of deference as a particular source of pride.[15] By 1900, however, the majority of the European population worked in nongovernmental jobs, such as planters, lawyers, physicians, and journalists, and managerial personnel at mining companies, trade houses, and banks. In addition, the nature of government employ had changed with the addition of civil engineers, architects, and medical personnel to its ranks.[16]

Overall, the size and composition of the European population changed drastically at the turn of the century. Spread out over the archipelago, the total number of people with European status was 43,876 in 1860. In Java alone, this number had increased to 54,511 (38 percent women) by 1890 and 192,571 (47 percent women) by 1930. In the same period, the indigenous population of Java, which had only totaled 4.5 million in 1815, expanded from 12.5 million in 1860 to 23.6 million in 1890 to 40.9 million in 1930.[17] Between 1890 and 1920, the increase in European women (300 percent) was greater than that of men (200 percent).[18] Alongside the mixed marriage law of 1898, which stipulated that women assume the legal status of their spouse, the immigration of European women resulted in greater gender balance in Java's colonial society. Some historians have argued, almost nostalgically, that the increased presence of European women led to the destruction of a harmonious nineteenth-century colonial society.

However, as Frances Gouda has convincingly argued, the decision to allow
women to enter the colony was purposefully designed by the colonial authorities
to create a stronger European community. Even so, indigenous influences were
never far off, especially considering that by 1930 only 21 percent of all women
with European status were born in Europe. Until the end of colonial rule, the
combined locally born European and Eurasian population would remain far
greater than that of European immigrants.[19]

Taken together, these technological, economic, and demographic changes as
well as the evolutionary racism that supported the belief in Western superiority
led to the Dutch equivalent of a civilizing mission. Throughout the nineteenth
century, there had been occasional moral objections to exploiting the indigenous
people of Java for the sole benefit of the Netherlands, but it was not until the
end of the century that this criticism was more generally acknowledged among
the Dutch. This new perspective on the colonial relationship was famously articulated by lawyer C. Th. van Deventer, who argued that the Netherlands had
a "debt of honor" to fulfill in the Indies. Likewise, journalist P. Brooshooft proposed an "ethical direction in colonial policy" aimed at developing and civilizing
the indigenous people of the Netherlands Indies and creating a form of limited
self-government under Dutch patronage.[20] Finally, in 1901, this change of heart
regarding the colonial relationship was officially announced in the queen's annual speech, in which she stated that the Netherlands had a "moral duty" toward
the people of the Indies.

The Ethical Policy, however, was not a clearly defined set of policies, but rather
a new general outlook on the colonial relationship. A broad array of initiatives
fell under its umbrella, such as enhancing the socioeconomic condition of indigenous people, making Western education more widely available and accessible,
empowering the role of the colonized in the colonial administration, providing
a limited extension of democratic institutions, and improving infrastructure,
public sanitation and health, and irrigation systems. Many of these developments were both beneficial to indigenous people and highly profitable to Dutch
entrepreneurs and the colonial government. From the outset, this aspect raised
questions about the intentions behind the Ethical Policy among both European
and Javanese progressives.[21]

As the historiography of colonialism has demonstrated, the moral burden
of civilizing allegedly less developed peoples provided Westerners with a justi-
fication for their continued colonial enterprises.[22] On Java, the Ethical Policy
offered a new hegemonic ideology to legitimize Dutch rule that was strikingly
different from its nineteenth-century predecessor rooted in Javanese aristocratic

traditions. In fact, the contrasts between the two discourses could not have been greater: Javanization, feudalism, and autocratic rule were to be replaced with Europeanization, modernity, and democratic principles. However, although the Dutch and colonial governments supported the new hegemonic discourse, the Ethical Policy faced serious criticism from European civil servants and Javanese aristocrats on the ground in Java. Consequently, replacing one hegemonic discourse with another was far more complicated than anticipated. Moreover, the nascent Indonesian nationalist movement—in part a result of the Ethical Policy—produced its own hegemonic ideology, starting a fierce ideological competition that only made the social and political climate in Java more complex.

The Ethical Policy and indigenous national awakening in the Netherlands Indies did not develop in isolation from global events. The Spanish-American War of 1898 that resulted in the United States' annexation of the Philippines served as either a cautionary tale or hopeful example of how a colonial power could be ousted by a modern and progressive rival, depending on one's perspective. In a sense, the American presence in Southeast Asia forced the Netherlands to follow its civilizing example.[23] Around the same time, the Chinese community in the Indies joined the growing opposition to the Qing dynasty, and the successful revolution of 1911 fueled a renewed sense of Chinese identity and nationalism, offering another example for the nascent Indonesian nationalist movement.[24] Nationalists also looked toward British India for inspiration, pondering the increased participation in the civil service and the establishment of the Indian National Congress. Japan attracted the most attention, however, as rapid industrialization and development following the Meji Restoration of 1868 reached a symbolic conclusion with the defeat of Russia in the Russo-Japanese War of 1904–1905. Taken together, these Asian nations provided poignant examples that shaped both young nationalists' and Dutch colonizers' attitudes toward the future.[25]

In addition to inspiring the younger generation of Javanese ideologically, the promulgation of the Ethical Policy also accelerated the transformation of a segment of the *priyayi* from an elite class rooted in tradition and hereditary to one based on modernity and education. Since the middle of the nineteenth century, the colonial state had established schools to provide their growing administration with cheap, Western-educated, indigenous labor.[26] However, while the priyayi class expanded in conjunction with the general population as Java moved toward the twentieth century, the number of administrative posts remained by and large the same. As a consequence, an increasing number of educated lower priyayi was forced to seek work outside the administrative civil service, either in different government employ or in the private sector. Beginning in 1870 and especially with the Ethical Policy, the colonial state grew exponentially and began to rely on educated labor for, among other things, its pawnshop service, people's credit system, *opiumregie* (sale and production of opium), state railways, and postal, telephone, and telegraph services. Similarly, the liberalization of the colonial economy offered work opportunities for Western-educated priyayi in areas like agriculture, factories, and finance. This new group, who also worked as clerks, teachers, doctors, engineers, and overseers, comprised the majority of people who would become active in the nascent nationalist movement.[27]

During the first two decades of the twentieth century, this Western-educated indigenous elite emerged as the new middle class in colonial society. Theirs was a hybrid world between East and West. As students and professionals, they participated in a Western sphere in which they dressed like Europeans, spoke Dutch, read European literature, listened and danced to Western music, watched the latest Hollywood movies in theaters, and played European sports.[28] At the same time, considering the priyayi background of most of these intellectuals, they were also rooted in indigenous society with their own languages, social customs, and cultural performances. It was their challenge to combine these experiences—East and West—in their endeavor for *kemajuan* (progress), for which the notion of modernity was key. According to historian Takashi Shiraishi, this new elite strove for modernity as exemplified by the Dutch in particular and by Western civilization in general.[29] However, they disagreed on how to achieve it as well as if or how it would incorporate indigenous culture and religion and what the Dutch role would be in a modern state.

The proliferation of opinions on how to move through an age of progress to achieve modernity was reflected in the diversity of associations established within the nationalist movement. Some of these associations emphasized ethnic identities and interests; others focused more on religious values, ideologies, or secular principles. To complicate matters further, certain associations were politically oriented while others were mainly cultural, and some included elements of both.[30] As a consequence, it is difficult to speak of one distinct and teleological nationalist movement. Instead, it is better characterized as a broad national awakening reflected in an abundance of indigenous associations.[31] Depending on their outlook—ethnic, religious, ideological, secular—these associations formulated their own hegemonic ideologies as alternatives to, and in competition with, that of the European colonizer.

Ethical Shifts and the Hormat Debate

By the end of the nineteenth century, Dutch officials and civil servants stood at the apex of the colonial social hierarchy and enjoyed a privileged lifestyle on Java. Through the Javanization of colonial authority, these officials constantly reminded both the Javanese and European inhabitants of their inferior social ranks and positions. Deference rituals were arguably the most visible and sensitive Dutch adaptations of Javanese aristocratic culture, encompassing social behavior, dress codes, a stratified language system, honorific titles, regulations regarding an official's entourage, and other symbols of power. The Javanese were required to treat Dutch officials as they would their own aristocracy—to approach them in a crouching walk (*jongkok*), sit cross-legged on the ground (*sila*) in their presence, and place their hands together while bringing their thumbs to the upper lip (*sembah*) after speaking. The colonized also had to address colonial officials as *kanjeng tuan*, meaning "great lord," and observe strict language protocols, speaking to their superiors in high Javanese (*krama*) while he or she responded in low Javanese (*ngoko*). In addition, European residents were accompanied by a plethora of servants, one of whom carried a golden *payung* as a symbol of his power—historically the sole privilege of Javanese royalty. The official residency houses on Java also radiated a sense of prestige, with Roman columns on their verandas that gave them a Western appearance but featured architectural adaptations of the Javanese *pendopo* (open pavilion).[32]

Some Javanese traditions were not so much copied as they were reinvented by Dutch civil servants. For example, the Javanese aristocracy organized ceremonial festivities around family members' births, circumcisions, marriages, and deaths—ceremonies that were crucial for communicating power. The Garebeg Puasa celebration at the end of Ramadan is a prime example. To commemorate the conclusion of the fasting period, a *bupati* would proceed to a mosque in procession with his payung, after which he would hold court. Here, lower bureaucrats asked the bupati's forgiveness for their shortcomings throughout the year by approaching him with a low crouching walk, making the sembah, and performing a knee kiss (*sungkem*).[33] Inspired by the Garebeg Puasa, the Dutch hosted a similar court session on New Year's Day during which Javanese civil servants and village headmen paid their respects to their Dutch superiors. In the words of one Dutch official, this was a yearly "Day of Reconciliation" between European civil servants and their Javanese subjects.[34] However, with the absence of the traditional *kawula-gusti* relationship conveying mutual respect and responsibility, the Dutch ceremony was merely an elaborate performance of subservience.

Javanese language stratification was an essential component of the deference rituals upholding the colonial hierarchy. It was customary for a person of high rank to address his or her social inferiors in *ngoko* (low Javanese) and to receive a reply in *krama* (high Javanese).[35] According to colonial advisor for native affairs G. A. J. Hazeu, who was also a scholar and linguist, the subdivision of both language types was so highly refined that "all nuances of rank of a feudal society could be expressed therein."[36] The Dutch therefore consciously adopted the Javanese language stratification to legitimize their position as rulers. With the exception of high-ranking indigenous officials, such as bupati (regent) and *patih* (viceregent), all Javanese were to address Dutch officials in krama and expect a reply in ngoko. However, by the turn of the century, as an increasing number of Javanese aristocrats received a Western education which included learning the Dutch language, a significant addition was made to the colonial language hierarchy. European officials now addressed Western-educated Javanese in Dutch, although they still required that their reply be in krama. Remarkably, Dutch replaced low Javanese in these conversations, despite ngoko's status as an "inferior" language. However, it simply would not do for the Dutch to speak ngoko to the Javanese and have them answer in Dutch.[37]

Europeans' refusal to converse in Dutch with their indigenous colleagues in the civil service (in contrast, for example, to practices in French Indochina) was the topic of many spirited debates in the decades surrounding 1900. Knowledge of the Dutch language brought with it a certain level of social prestige. In a sense, it allowed indigenous speakers to distance themselves from traditional society and achieve more equal footing with Europeans. As early as 1890, the government encouraged European civil servants to communicate in Dutch with their Western-educated indigenous counterparts, but the fear of losing respect and weakening colonial rule prevented many from adhering to this circular. Instead, they demanded compliance with the traditional Javanese language stratification, albeit with modifications for including the Dutch language. The fear of offending Dutch civil servants was still too great, even for high-status Javanese aristocrats, to challenge the social order and request observance of the circular.[38]

Despite this fear, increased rumblings of discontent with hormat etiquette began to permeate indigenous society. Some Javanese regarded the Dutch emphasis on their own prestige as a "ridiculous spectacle" worthy of mockery but at the same time resented their adoption of Javanese deference customs to which traditionally only Javanese rulers were entitled.[39] In 1899, an anonymous author pointed out that the Dutch reliance on Javanese symbols of authority actually came at the Javanese aristocracy's expense, as they had been steadily losing their own power. The author was particularly bothered by the propensity of lower Dutch civil servants—whom he regarded as petty kings—for demanding deference from lower Javanese aristocrats, maintaining that it was they, not the Dutch, who had the traditional right to hormat.[40] Signaling this author's concern, an 1893 report submitted by the bupati of Demak, named Hadiningrat, reflected the changing balance of power between the indigenous and Dutch branches of the colonial civil service. Hadiningrat argued that during the last decades of the nineteenth century, the Javanese branch had lost considerable prestige in the eyes of the Javanese people and Europeans alike. This was due to the general population's increased direct contact with European civil servants, who, unlike their Javanese counterparts, maintained high educational standards. Alongside the highly educated Dutch in their midst, indigenous civil servants appeared far less formidable and authoritative. To compensate for their reduced power, Hadiningrat believed, many indigenous civil servants demanded more deference from Javanese people while showing more to their European superiors. Hadiningrat argued that only instituting more Western-style education could remedy this imbalance and bring real prestige back to the indigenous civil service.[41]

There were also Dutch colonial civil servants who opposed the use of Javanese deference rituals. One of the earliest challengers was H. E. Steinmetz, a young controller who was well aware of the pervasive deference practices on Java. In a book he wrote under a pseudonym in 1888, he severely criticized European civil servants' behavior toward their Javanese subordinates, specifically their abuse of hormat etiquette. Steinmetz sarcastically described the first years of a civil servant's career as the "hormat period," a time when he was most susceptible to acquiring a taste for Javanese deference rituals. It was not surprising then, he argued, that young civil servants quickly learned to be "angered when an indigenous person passes him or his house without uncovering his head nor dismounts his horse; when a lower ranking civil servant dares to address him in Malay; a *wedana* or tax collector enters his home with footwear, etc."[42] Early in his career, Steinmetz noticed that many Javanese considered it humiliating to engage in such deference, especially toward Europeans. He believed that this was because, as cultural outsiders, Europeans did not fully understand *their* role in hormat etiquette—that the reception of deference required a certain approachable attitude in return. According to Javanese tradition, deference was an expression of the principle of kawula-gusti. In the absence of reciprocity, the etiquette representing this relationship lost its value.

In essence, Steinmetz argued that the nineteenth-century policy of cultural adaptation to legitimize colonial authority had either failed, or worse, had never worked in the first place. He asserted that continued use of hormat etiquette was degrading, time-consuming, and did little to further European prestige. To those who believed that Dutch colonial rule depended on Javanese deference and status symbols, he retorted that they should worry more about the Dutch propensity to live with indigenous concubines, alcoholism, and godlessness. In his opinion, those habits were far more detrimental to colonial authority than a lack of hormat etiquette would be. Moreover, he cautioned that failure to modernize the colonial relationship made the Dutch more vulnerable to Javanese civil servants' manipulation, who, by showing exaggerated hormat, could try to improve their career opportunities. Steinmetz therefore proposed that the colonial government prohibit European civil servants from demanding traditional deference and using Javanese status symbols. However, in 1888 few were receptive to the young official's radical plea.[43]

This changed in the following decade, when the first appointed Advisor for Native Affairs Christiaan Snouck Hurgronje joined Steinmetz's cause. Originally trained in the Netherlands as an Arabic and Islamic scholar, Snouck Hurgronje found his way to the colonies after a research visit to Mecca. He believed that understanding Islam in general and local cultures specifically could improve the effectiveness of Dutch colonial policy. His inaugural post as advisor for native affairs, which he held from 1898 until 1907, reflected his ideas and the changing times. Crucially, the Office of Native Affairs enjoyed a direct and personal connection with the governor general, independent from the Department of the Interior, which was responsible for the conservative civil service. The advisor's role was twofold; namely, to serve as a barometer of the indigenous population's distress and to advise the governor general in that regard. Moreover, the advisor acted as a government liaison for the growing number of "educated natives." Snouck Hurgronje personally tutored several young Javanese of high birth and provided them with a Western education. Most of his students went on to hold prominent positions in colonial society in the following decades.[44]

As advisor, Snouck Hurgronje drew attention to a contradiction within colonial policy: the government's continued reliance on Javanese forms of deference while seeking to modernize the colonial relationship. After almost a century of indirect rule, many Javanese traditions regarding rank, titles, entourages, social deference rituals, and the like had become outdated as well as difficult to maintain due to shifting historical circumstances. Technological, political, social, and economic changes resulted in a society that was rapidly losing its harmony with time-honored aristocratic customs. Yet to Snouck Hurgronje's dismay, Dutch civil servants clung to the notion that deference etiquette not only remained relevant but was indispensable for upholding colonial authority. These divergent perceptions led to growing tensions between various social groups, old and new, in colonial society. It was not until the promulgation of the Ethical Policy in 1901, however, that there was finally enough political support to attempt to resolve these dualistic policies and modernize the outward appearance of colonial rule.[45]

Throughout the period of the Ethical Policy, it was the Office of Native Affairs that took the initiative in dismantling the Javanese aristocratic façade of Dutch colonial rule. For instance, in 1903, Snouck Hurgronje advised the governor general to prohibit European civil servants' use of large retinues while touring their districts. These honorary retinues, he argued, were a waste of time and money, and had no purpose other than fulfilling the European desire for display. He offered the example of a resident who required that his retinue of Javanese dignitaries run after his carriage. Several elderly Javanese had to beg his forgiveness, as they could not keep up.[46] Snouck Hurgronje proposed that the use of retinues for high-ranking civil servants when touring in a carriage be prohibited, and that an escort of Javanese civil servants only be required when their presence had an actual purpose. Four months later, his proposal became an official government circular that banned escorts and honorary retinues for European civil servants. It was the first sign of changes yet to come.[47]

The onset of the Ethical Policy as well as Snouck Hurgronje's presence inspired Steinmetz to argue for abolishing Javanese deference rituals and status symbols once again. Despite the 1888 publication of his censorious book, Steinmetz had successfully risen through the hierarchy of the colonial civil service and was eventually appointed president of the Diminished Welfare Committee. Founded in 1904, the committee was an institutional icon of the Ethical Policy, tasked with examining the causes of poverty and recommending solutions in Java. It was in this context that Steinmetz officially proposed barring European officials from demanding traditional Javanese deference, titles, honors, and servitude; in other words, that hormat abuses be eliminated.[48] Snouck Hurgronje concurred and, in a letter to the governor general, argued that the broadening horizons of the modern age, due to improved modes of transport and communication, had laid bare the backwardness of Javanese hormat etiquette. Citing Japan and Siam (Thailand) as models of more modernized Asian societies, he insisted that hormat culture be replaced with less outdated forms of deference.[49]

Just a few days after taking office, Governor General Van Heutsz received Steinmetz and Snouck Hurgronje's recommendations.[50] Van Heutsz immediately addressed his advisors' concerns, convinced that colonial authority should no longer depend on Javanese symbols of power and traditional deference. With military decisiveness, he signed and promulgated two circulars in November 1904 with the intention of modernizing the relationship between the European civil service and Javanese society, and colonial rule more broadly. The first, the so-called payung circular, prohibited European civil servants' use of payung, which was followed by the more expansive hormat circular prohibiting most other forms and rituals of deference.[51] In his private correspondence with Minister of Colonial Affairs Idenberg, Van Heutsz boasted that with the stroke of his pen, he had banned European civil servants from demanding traditional Javanese deference, surrounding themselves with large retinues of Javanese subjects, being received and honored with triumphal arches and fireworks, and, crucially, from carrying a golden payung as a symbol of their power.[52] In short, Van Heutsz had launched an almost all-encompassing attack against what he described as the "foolishness" of the nineteenth-century colonial order.

The language of the hormat circular of 1904 revealed both Van Heutsz and Snouck Hurgronje's underlying concerns and beliefs regarding the future development of the colony. The circular explicitly stated that more contemporary international forms of respect should replace traditional Javanese deference in order to stimulate increased participation in the modern world. According to the circular, traditional hormat etiquette was outdated, time-consuming, and humiliating for those whose sense of dignity had just been awakened, foremost the Western-educated Javanese. Moreover, it was counterproductive to the necessary development of trust between colonizer and colonized. In a sense, the circular intended to align the exterior appearance of colonial rule with the more modern administrative institutions and developments encapsulated by the Ethical Policy. Consequently, the hormat circular articulately challenged the nineteenth-century belief that Javanese traditions were necessary to legitimize colonial authority: "It is a false notion indeed to think that the authority, through simplification of indigenous social formalities, would be endangered and that maintenance of customs such as appearing before superiors without footwear, sitting on the floor, accompanying discussions with sembah etc. would involve an interest of state."[53] This was a judiciously worded warning to those who maintained that the circular would diminish European prestige and colonial authority.

Nonetheless, the hormat circular of 1904 left conservative detractors some wiggle room, since it stated that the process of change should be most strongly encouraged in areas of modern development (e.g., urban settings), thus excusing most of colonial Java from urgent and strict implementation.[54] In addition, in the Netherlands Indies, circulars were instructions that fell somewhere t strong advice and binding laws. This meant that compliance was expe most of the time not monitored or enforced by the colonial government. Instead, officials depended on local civil service representatives to execute their directives. Consequently, with respect to circulars, the theory and practice of colonial rule could be miles apart. Snouck Hurgronje acknowledged as much in 1904, stating, "The lips of a civil servant fold into a smile when pronouncing the word 'circular.'"[55] Thus, the promulgation of multiple government circulars challenged the aristocratic character of colonial society, but by no means signified its end.

Progressive Theory, Conservative Reality

The payung and hormat circulars of 1904 triggered a fierce debate in colonial society that lasted until the end of Dutch rule. Although the new and progressive Ethical Policy had its advocates, its opponents were far more prominent in both the civil service and the colonial press—a point clearly illustrated by contrasting editorials in colonial newspapers. Among the few who applauded the governor general's decision to prohibit hormat and the payung was the editor of the largest European newspaper in Surabaya. He argued that as long as hormat kept the Javanese stuck in past traditions, it would be impossible to uplift them into strong, self-consciously economical individuals. More importantly, he stated, colonial rule should not be based on traditional Javanese deference, but on the virtue and moral superiority of the colonizer. In other words, he interpreted the circulars as measures to redefine the grounds of cultural hegemony in the colony.[56]

In stark contrast, the editor of Semarang's largest newspaper completely rejected his colleague's reasoning, perceiving the circulars, and the Ethical Policy in general, as severe threats to the existence of the Netherlands Indies. In his opinion, the Javanized appearance of Dutch colonial rule was absolutely essential to maintain peace and order. It ensured that the colonizer did "not provoke complaints and resistance," which enabled control over "the numerically far larger indigenous population."[57] Abrupt changes to their style of rule, he cautioned, could force authorities to become more reliant on coercion. Representing the conservative argument, he insisted that hormat etiquette and the payung were essential parts of the Javanese social fabric that could not be so easily discarded. The editor of Batavia's newspaper agreed, concisely summarizing, "Payungs are cheaper than bayonets and less cruel."[58]

It was the prohibition of the payung, the nineteenth-century symbol of Dutch colonialism on Java, that conservatives in the colonial press especially lamented.

Colonial officials felt robbed and humiliated by the governor general's instructions. For them, the payung was not just a symbolic object but a physical extension of their authority, independently filled with power. To take away such a significant entity was to seriously weaken the prestige and ability of the civil service.
According to reports in the colonial press, the Javanese probably wondered if
Van Heutsz had punished his civil servants. Others claimed that the Dutch had
lost considerable respect and standing in the eyes of the colonized. What worried conservatives most was that Javanese civil servants were still entitled to their
payung. In part, Dutch officials were envious of their indigenous colleagues, but
there were also serious concerns that without the golden payung of the resident,
all ceremonial parasols would lose their importance. In other words, the Javanized system of colonial authority would collapse like a house of cards.[59] While
this was surely an exaggeration, several Javanese officials, such as Bupati Achmad
Djajadiningrat, decided to part with their own payung out of solidarity. However, Djajadiningrat was a pupil of Snouck Hurgronje, Western-educated, and
therefore the exception rather than the rule. The indigenous civil service's use
of the payung would continue until it was fiercely critiqued by the nationalist
movement in the following decades.[60]

   The anxiety surrounding the abolition of the payung was best captured in
a nostalgic poem published in Batavia's conservative newspaper. The opening
stanza of the poem, titled "A Resident's Farewell to His Payung," described how
the once-stately parasol suddenly degraded to the umbrella of a roasted peanut
salesman.[61] The poem portrayed the payung as the embodiment of colonial prestige and order: a majestic and noble symbol of power. The Dutch author remi-
nisced about a time when a servant was proud to carry his payung, how people
cheerfully honored it, and how official and payung were inseparable. The gilded
emblem decorated his gallery, stood gracefully on his coach, and followed him
as he paraded through Batavia. But no longer could the resident slumber in the
payung's protection nor count on its support. Without it, the author decried,
"I could do nothing," implying that deprived of the payung, European officials
lost their armor vis-à-vis the indigenous population of Java. This was the essence
of the debate about the payung as well as hormat circulars: conservative Europeans believed that without Javanese deference and symbols of power, they
could no longer command authority in the colony as they had before. Instead,
they assumed that colonial rule would revert to a reliance on the threat of coercion. Governor General Van Heutsz was squarely blamed for putting colonial authority in this perilous position as, according to the poem, the payung
floated away, wreckage "on the currents of anti-hormat." However, the circulars'

advocates—propelling the "currents of anti-hormat" forward—dismissed their concerns as foolish, and argued that sincere morality and modernity were a much stronger basis for colonial rule.[62]

When news of the circulars reached the Netherlands, it was evident that they hit a nerve within the Dutch colonial community there, as well. In The Hague, Minister of Colonial Affairs Idenburg found himself confronted by many disgruntled colonial veterans as well as civil service and military personnel, most of whom he characterized as conservatives. In a letter to Governor General Van Heutsz, Idenburg assured him that he fully supported the intent and content of the circulars, but conveyed that they had created many influential enemies in the metropole. The Dutch press argued that the hormat circular in particular undermined an "important principle of Government." Even Queen Wilhelmina reached out to Idenburg for an update on the sensitive issue. In their conversation, the minister of colonial affairs successfully convinced the Dutch queen that Van Heutsz's measures were morally just, which was an essential component of the Ethical Policy she herself had announced in 1901. In order to answer questions regarding the issue in Parliament, Idenburg requested that Van Heutsz keep him as informed as possible.[63] In his response, Van Heutsz thanked Idenburg for his support and posed a rhetorical question: who has more authority and prestige—those who rely on the payung or those who abolish it?[64]

In February 1906, Governor General Van Heutsz requested Snouck Hurgronje's opinion on the effectiveness of the payung and hormat circulars. In his response, Snouck Hurgronje explained that the payung circular had been quite successful, as it concerned such a strong visual symbol that was hard to ignore. However, he considered the hormat circular an utter failure. Apparently, European civil servants still demanded that their Javanese counterparts sit on the ground in the sila posture, present a sembah each time they spoke, and converse according to the Javanese language hierarchy. Snouck Hurgronje therefore pressed Van Heutsz "that a renewed, strong inculcation of the intentions of the Government in this regard seems anything but redundant."[65] Van Heutsz concurred with his advisor and rather quickly issued a new hormat circular in April 1906.[66]

Through the hormat circular of 1906, Governor General Van Heutsz expressed his sincere discontent with the European civil service's continued use of Javanese hormat etiquette. Civil servants who acted in accordance with the spirit of the circular were the exception instead of the rule, which resulted not only in the perseverance of the traditional character of colonial society, but also undermined the governor general's authority. The new circular emphasized that the days of the seigniorial civil servant were over and demanded that colonial officials follow the orders of the central bureaucracy in Batavia. The circular also provided explicit examples of undesirable behavior, such as adhering to the Javanese language hierarchy. Furthermore, European civil servants were reminded that Javanese civil servants remained entitled to ceremonial payung, suggesting that their response to the payung circular had been to inappropriately force their indigenous counterparts to relinquish theirs, as well.[67]

But rather than establishing a reluctant consensus, the hormat circular of 1906 exacerbated disagreements over the most effective approach to colonial rule. Within this debate, European civil servants represented those in favor of maintaining Javanese traditions, whereas central bureaucrats, such as the advisor for native affairs, advocated the Ethical Policy and modernization of the colonial relationship. According to a conservative Batavian newspaper, this debate existed between "men of reality" (civil servants) and "men of theory" (Batavian bureaucrats like Van Heutsz and Snouck Hurgronje).[68] The majority of the colonial press as well as the European public in the colony concurred with the more "realistic" conservative position. Betraying their anxiety about the social changes that would accompany Javanese emancipation, they also argued that the disadvantages produced by a smaller Dutch population in Java was offset by Javanese mental weakness (that made them prone to submission).[69] On the other hand, progressive European voices were not entirely absent from public discourse. Several authors argued that civil servants should stop obsessing over their prestige and alleged superiority and focus instead on actually serving the colonial community. Some mocked the officials who clung to their payungs and wondered if they also wanted to convert to Islam, wear Javanese ethnic dress, and don a headscarf.[70]

It therefore came as no surprise that in the last year of Van Heutsz's tenure, he was again forced to confront the persistent reality of European civil servants demanding deference from the Javanese. After reading in the newspapers about his own officials' continued defiance of his orders, Van Heutsz reached out to the advisor for native affairs once more.[71] G. A. J. Hazeu, who had replaced Snouck Hurgronje in 1907, confirmed that colonial officials remained unwilling to converse with civil servants and other educated Javanese in Dutch, fearing that they would consequently receive less traditional deference. To illustrate this point, Hazeu shared his experience during a visit to Cianjur (in western Java) in May 1907 during which he witnessed the local public prosecutor addressing the assistant resident in Sundanese while offering the sembah.[72] When Hazeu later talked to the public prosecutor himself, he was surprised to learn that he spoke fluent Dutch.[73] But by insisting on conversing in Sundanese, the assistant resident secured a more deferential attitude from the indigenous official. With hopes of finally eradicating these practices, Van Heutsz issued yet another hormat circular in 1909, its language permeated with anger and disappointment. It stated bluntly that the governor general "can and will not allow that his clear orders be considered unwritten."[74] Civil servants who refused to comply with previous hormat circulars were threatened with dire consequences (although they remained undefined).

Within six years, the third circular prompted another strong conservative rebuke toward the governor general. Civil servants felt cornered and mischaracterized by the accusations in the circulars, and two prominent officials wrote confidential letters to Van Heutsz to make their outrage known. In his letter, Resident Gonggrijp argued that the governor general was misinformed on the culture within the colonial civil service, either due to inexperience or malevolence—a not-so-indirect slight against past and present advisors for native affairs, whose ethical tendencies and influence on colonial governance were a thorn in civil servants' sides. Gonggrijp impressed on the governor general that in his twenty-five years of service, he never disobeyed orders from the government. European civil servants were not at fault; it was the Javanese themselves who prevented compliance with the circulars. According to Gonggrijp, Javanese civil servants simply refused to converse in Dutch with their European counterparts, as they did not want to come across as impolite. He insisted that even after years of encouragement, his own public prosecutor still did not wish to speak with him in Dutch.[75] In another private correspondence with Van Heutsz, Resident Boissevain echoed his colleague's interpretation of affairs. He argued that a bupati in his residency put it best when he stated, "Javanese traditions and speaking Dutch do not go together."[76]

The 1909 circular reflected more clearly than its predecessors the progressive colonial elite's frustration with the predominant conservatism among Europeans in the colony. However, Residents Gonggrijp and Boissevain's letters show that even in 1909, colonial civil servants rejected the assumptions within the Ethical Policy and blamed progressive officials and the Javanese themselves for the unnecessary tension in society. They urged the governor general to heed their advice before it was too late. Interestingly, there was no consensus among the Javanese elite about the proper role of deference in colonial society. While almost all wanted to end the custom of showing traditional respect to the colonizer, many conservative priyayi regarded these traditions as intrinsic to Javanese culture and identity. They rightly feared that the more progressive young generation wanted to also abolish these traditions from interactions among the Javanese. More conservatively inclined priyayi therefore emphasized hormat's significance for civilized conduct. To prevent social degeneration, the younger generation should be more, not less, respectful toward indigenous social superiors. They reasoned that it was not humiliating for the Javanese to crouch or offer the sembah to their own officials—those who truly understood the cultural significance of these gestures.[77] Some priyayi also accused progressive young Javanese of being hypocrites who argued in favor of abolishing hormat traditions from interactions with their superiors but continued to exact deference from their inferiors.[78] Thus, recognizing that the conservative pushback remained considerable, it became clear that Dutch advocates for a modern colonial relationship needed help from like-minded Javanese.

The Hormat Circulars and the Indonesian National Awakening

The hormat debate between 1904 and 1909 coincided with the birth of an indigenous nationalist movement in the Indies. This was not accidental, since both can be considered consequences of the Ethical Policy. The emergence of the "young Javanese," Western-educated and often employed in nontraditional professions, reignited the debate on Javanese deference traditions and changed its dynamic drastically. Whereas previously the question was to what extent Europeans could demand Javanese deference, the young Javanese questioned the pervasiveness of traditional deference as a whole. In other words, they did not just want to modernize interactions between Europeans and Javanese but among all members of society, just as older and more conservative priyayi warned. Interestingly, most of the young Javanese themselves originated from the privileged priyayi class, but as a result of their education and work outside the traditional civil service, many came to identify as a new class of intellectuals. Abdul Rivai, editor of the popular vernacular periodical *Bintang Hindia* (The Star of the Indies), dubbed this new generation the "*kaum muda*" (the young ones), whose desire to modernize Javanese society challenged that of the "*kaum tua*" (the old ones), who sought to preserve the status quo.[79]

Although the hormat circular of 1904 did not yield the anticipated overhaul of the appearance and performance of colonial authority, it had the unforeseen consequence of invigorating public discussion not only in colonial media, but also in the emerging vernacular press. Since the circular reflected the government's "ethical" intentions, it allowed for a public critique of everything believed to hinder its implementation. The new generation of Javanese seized on this opportunity to express their opinions forcefully and publicly. Goenawan's article, at the start of the chapter, perfectly exemplifies this newfound mentality, his critique is representative of a broader change in attitude that stimulated many of his contemporaries to publish their opinions as well. Discussions of the hormat circular thus contributed significantly to the emergence of what might tentatively be called public opinion. It was an empowering and inspirational moment, as the colonized openly dared to criticize the colonizer and demand progress.[80]

The central tenet of Goenawan's opinion piece in *Java Bode*, a progressive colonial newspaper, was that hormat traditions had a demoralizing and obstructive influence on Javanese intellectual and socioeconomic emancipation. He constructed his argument around the notion that deference customs should not be understood as enduring and essential elements of Javanese culture but instead as flexible traditions that developed over time. Goenawan pointed out that contemporary deference rituals originated in the court culture of Java's great kingdoms, during the Hindu-Buddhist era of the island's history. But it was only under Dutch colonial rule that these customs were increasingly appropriated by both the European and indigenous civil services. Thus, contemporary bupati were addressed as royalty with the honorific *Sampeyan-Dalem* (Your Majesty) and received deference that was formerly the sole privilege of monarchs and sultans. During the last decades of the nineteenth century, he continued, these customs became pervasive throughout civil service culture. His point was that just as easily these customs could be relaxed again. Adding yet another layer to his argument, Goenawan reasoned that deference etiquette was not merely a mental burden that communicated and instilled a sense of inferiority but also a physical one, as it gave the Javanese crooked legs from constantly sitting cross-legged on the floor. His hope that all Javanese would soon sit in chairs was thus as much about social emancipation as it was about public health.[81]

Unsurprisingly, Goenawan's article was not well received by Batavia's conservative colonial newspaper, where it provoked a condescending rebuke by an author using the pseudonym Wongso, meaning "people" in Malay. Wongso wrote a regular column titled "Sketches of Javanese Life," in which he explored the mysterious, primitive, and Eastern character of indigenous society for his European readership. In response to Goenawan, he boldly claimed to have a more profound understanding of Javanese culture than the young student. He refuted Goenawan's claims by arguing that Javanese deference traditions were not more time-consuming than shaking hands or taking off one's hat. He claimed that deference did not explain the Javanese's relative backwardness to Europeans and Chinese on Java; the Javanese were simply less entrepreneurial. Addressing

Goenawan's point about crooked legs, Wongso posited that this was the result of being carried in a *selendang* (cloth baby carrier) too long. Finally, Wongso ridiculed Goenawan's youthful iconoclasm, asserting that his arguments appeared to be about the right to sit in a chair. He warned Goenawan not to project his desires onto all Javanese. A mat was a beautiful piece of Javanese art in its own right. Who would exchange their culture for a piece of furniture? According to Wongso, such a proposition could only spring from "the mentality of someone who is on his way to denying their Javanese identity, on his way to renouncing his nationality—to being and to becoming neither indigenous, nor European, nor something else, but merely a hybrid."[82]

In a striking display of confidence, Goenawan wrote a scathing response in the colonial press. It was remarkable for a colonial subject to unabashedly repudiate a colonizer in a public forum. Even more significant was that Goenawan did so using his real identity, whereas the European Wongso hid behind a pseudonym. Goenawan was especially offended by Wongso's childish claim that he had a more profound understanding of Javanese culture than a native-born Javanese. If Wongso truly wanted to know what it was like being Javanese, Goenawan suggested that he dress in Javanese attire and try to purchase a train ticket while addressing the attendant in Dutch. Goenawan promised to let himself be skinned alive "if you are not rudely snubbed and are assisted in time."[83] None of this was just about the right to sit in a chair, to converse in Dutch, or to dress freely; it was about being treated with respect and equality. Goenawan blamed Wongso's misconceptions on the ethnographic stereotypes created by European academics that portrayed the Javanese as docile and submissive—descriptions he rejected as reminiscent of "babies and toys." Like Wongso, these scholars appreciated the Javanese as long as they remained "slaves to their traditions," but once people like Goenawan expressed deviating desires, they were labeled inauthentic.[84]

From Wongso's writing it is clear that he had not expected a public rebuke from a Javanese seventeen-year-old, but within a few weeks he retorted in kind. The author behind the pseudonym Wongso became more forceful in his writing, threatening even, as he tried to reestablish control over this defiant colonial subject. Ignoring Goenawan's invitation to dress as a Javanese, Wongso addressed the importance of the language hierarchy in colonial society. He asserted that it was only logical to converse in Javanese while in Java. European officials, planters, and train station attendants all spoke Javanese or Malay with the indigenous population out of respect for local culture and traditions, not to emphasize their social superiority. Moreover, the Javanese should speak their own language in their own country; doing so instilled in them a sense of self-worth and respect that no other language could provide. Wongso applied the same reasoning to deference and other cultural traditions, which were now being threatened by Goenawan's iconoclasm and desire to become European. In times of economic hardship, Wongso concluded, such ideas were not only demoralizing, but also encouraged anarchy by taking away people's self-respect and politeness.[85]

If conservative Europeans believed that they could silence Goenawan and other members of his generation, they were sorely mistaken. On the contrary, the release of the hormat circulars emboldened young Javanese to openly assert that they experienced their role in the colonial performance as humiliating, and they increasingly relied on the emerging vernacular press to voice their concerns. Rivai, editor of the richly illustrated biweekly *Bintang Hindia*, fully grasped the significance of a vernacular platform to share and discuss ideas. While Rivai praised Goenawan for publishing his opinion in a premier colonial newspaper, he believed that the student should have addressed his important message directly to his own people to convince them of traditional deference customs' harmful influence. Rivai therefore decided to reprint Goenawan's articles in the *Bintang Hindia* and provide them with additional commentary. Consequently, Goenawan's public standoff with a European journalist became widely known among the colonized.[86] The *Bintang Hindia* was the first vernacular publication to reach the whole of the indigenous elite (although it included Dutch articles, as well); it was read by government employees, students, and educated Javanese in private employ.[87] But Rivai's primary audience was what he called the *kaum muda*: the new generation of Javanese that rejected outdated traditions and embraced modernity and Western knowledge without losing their own identity.[88]

The articles in *Bintang Hindia* clearly illustrate that the hormat circular of 1904 significantly transformed the nature of public debate in the vernacular press. As a government-subsidized, vernacular periodical, the *Bintang Hindia* was in a unique position. Since it relied on government support, colonial authorities expected articles to promote "ethical" ideals. As editor, Rivai needed to strike a balance between being informative, educational, and emancipatory, but not too radical or provocative. This balancing act is reflected in articles on deference etiquette published before 1904, most of which offered uncritical accounts of its function in society. For example, one article emphasized the importance of showing traditional deference to one's parents, ancestors, siblings, and the elderly in general. Interestingly, the author made no mention of the requirement to honor someone based on rank. In another, a teacher from Batavia explored the diverse ways in which different ethnic groups in colonial society pay respect. He explained that Europeans salute, Arabs take each other's hands, Chinese bow to one another, and indigenous people crouch, sit on the floor, and offer the sembah after speaking. The author did remark that in Java's large cities many indigenous people had begun to follow the European example, but neither article includes an explicit discussion of what this all meant, why Europeans received Javanese deference, or if these traditions hampered the emancipation of the colonized.[89] However, the publication changed its standards for permissible content following the dissemination of the payung and hormat circulars.

With the proclamation of the Ethical Policy as well as the hormat circular of 1904, the government needed a more modern hegemonic script to legitimize colonial authority. As a consequence, the outward appearance and performance of power became legitimate topics for discussion in the vernacular press. This was especially visible in the *Bintang Hindia*, wherein articles on deference etiquette turned much more opinionated and critical. In a 1905 article titled "Jongkok and Sembah," a contributor explored what constituted proper deference in the context of colonial society. The primary cause of misunderstandings and anxiety, according to the author, was that the Javanese were required to show traditional deference to outsiders who did not fully comprehend local culture. In practice, this meant that colonizer and colonized interpreted deference etiquette differently. The Javanese understood a person crouching and offering a sembah after speaking as being respectful. To a Dutch observer, however, the same person appeared servile, afraid, and clearly inferior. Thus, the Dutch demanded deference to see their superiority confirmed, while the Javanese preferred to only honor those they respected. In the eyes of the Javanese, the author argued, the Dutch were not worthy of their respect, as they lived in sin with concubines (*nyai*), enjoyed vulgar talk about women, and held hands and kissed in public. He therefore welcomed the hormat circular as an opportunity to end misunderstandings around deference etiquette. To avoid any confusion in the future, he proposed distinguishing between a modern public sphere and a traditional private sphere. However, if the circular was not effective, he suggested that the Dutch who came to Java for financial gain have the decency to crouch for their hosts in accordance with local customs.[90] Such a defiant tone would have been impermissible before and exemplified the emboldened attitude of the new generation.

A recurring theme in the articles in the *Bintang Hindia* was the demand to be treated with more respect and dignity by the Dutch. One article in particular argued that after centuries of exploitation, the Dutch owed the Javanese some respect. The author noted that the hormat circular clearly exposed the ideological divisions between Dutch progressives and conservatives. The former

considered the Javanese as human beings, as equals even, and welcomed new regulations to reflect that. The latter differentiated themselves, in their eyes, from
the racially inferior Javanese and rejected the circular and the Ethical Policy. For
conservatives, the colonies were not so much a territory to be developed but one
to be exploited. The author called on young Javanese to work with progressive
Dutch in a joint effort to thwart conservative ideology. He reminded his readers
that the Dutch had subjugated Java for close to three centuries, during which
the Javanese had demonstrated themselves to be loyal subjects who enabled the
glory of the Dutch nation. They even fought in Dutch colonial wars to expand
their island empire. As a reward for this service, the Javanese did not seek mone-
tary compensation but merely dignity and respect. They wanted to be treated as
human beings who did not humiliate themselves by "crouching for the Dutch
or kissing the ground under their feet." The author concluded that by comply-
ing with the hormat circular, the Dutch could show that "the Javanese deserve
respect."[91]

In the wake of the hormat circular of 1906, criticism in the *Bintang Hindia*
became even more pronounced and militant. In an essay-length article, an anonymous author welcomed Van Heutsz's second hormat circular but questioned
if it could succeed where his first attempt did not, pointing out, "The Dutch
who are fond of receiving deference do not comply with these instructions." He
believed that the majority of the Dutch did not like change, making it "difficult
for the [colonial] government to develop the Indies and its children."[92] In other
words, the Ethical Policy could not be implemented as long as colonial officials
did not follow formal instructions. The author was skeptical that the latest hormat circular would yield a different outcome unless Dutch officials faced serious
repercussions for their noncompliance. He did qualify his comments somewhat
by granting that the situation was less severe in large cities, like Batavia, Semarang, and Surabaya, where the indigenous population was more educated and
the Europeans more progressive than in the countryside. However, the author
warned that a failure to modernize the colonial relationship was increasingly
estranging colonizer from colonized and slowing social change.

The author suggested that part of the problem was that the Javanese did not
publicly protest the current hormat situation or express their thoughts, fearing
the consequences of confronting their colonial superiors. But this was precisely
what they should do, the author insisted, beginning by holding officials accountable for their actions. As examples, he shared three comprehensive stories
of European officials who, against the spirit of the hormat circulars, continued
to demand traditional deference. The first case study he presented was that of a

newly appointed Dutch minor district administrator (*controleur*). While his predecessor addressed his Javanese colleagues in Malay, the newcomer insisted on
conversing in Javanese, including all its hierarchical levels. His subjects quickly
noticed an improvement in the administrator's temperament whenever they
showed him more deference than they were used to giving his precursor. They
addressed him as *gusti* (master) rather than *kanjeng tuan* (great lord), crouched
for him, and presented the sembah after speaking, and he became friendlier,
kinder, and more forgiving. The author of the article provided similar examples
from officials in the forestry service as well as plantation administrators and
European entrepreneurs. But he stipulated, "To honor these officials is not a
matter of respect, but merely serves to buy their affection."[93] By giving in to the
colonizer's desire for deference, the author suggested, the Javanese manipulated
them into receiving better treatment. Instead, they should openly demand not
just better but more dignified conduct.

During the continued growth of the vernacular press in the following years,
the discussion about the outward appearance and performance of colonial authority remained at the center of attention. In January 1912, a contributor to
the Batavia newspaper *Pemberita Betawi* repeated the argument that Goenawan
made in 1905, urging his fellow countrymen to stop showing old-fashioned
forms of deference to their superiors. He stated that these practices had their
purpose in the past but have no place in the modern present.[94] Reporting on
the topic increasingly focused on the issue of European compliance with the
circulars. A newspaper from Semarang, for instance, was highly suspicious of
the Netherlands Indies Railway Company (Nederlandsch Indische Spoorweg-
Maatschappij), which had recently instructed all European employees to become
fluent in high and low Javanese. The author believed that this dubious attempt
at customer friendliness was in effect a way to force indigenous personnel to
converse in Javanese rather than Dutch with their European colleagues, and
show them the accompanying traditional deference.[95] But just as the vernacular
press critiqued those who ignored the hormat circulars, it praised officials who
complied with them. For instance, the *Pemberita Betawi* commended the resident of Madiun for instructing his indigenous officials to refrain from showing
traditional deference to their European colleagues.[96] In this way, the payung
and hormat circulars had lasting effects, providing the young Javanese ongoing
opportunities to discuss and assess the performance of colonial power.

A Bittersweet Awakening

The turn of the twentieth century was a dynamic period in the history of colonial Indonesia marked by technological, economic, and demographic transformations. This coincided with the announcement of the Ethical Policy, the Dutch equivalent of the civilizing mission. Buoyed by the latest insights from evolutionary racism, the Ethical Policy held that based on their superior level of development the colonizer had the moral obligation to uplift the colonized. This new hegemonic script was strikingly different from its nineteenth-century predecessor, as the Javanization of colonial authority was to be replaced by an emphasis on Dutch and colonial modernity. But replacing one hegemonic discourse with another proved far more complicated than expected. It was out of frustration with the slow implementation of colonial authorities' "sweet" ethical promises that Goenawan Mangoenkoesoemo wrote his opinion piece on Javanese traditional deference in June 1905. But Goenawan's appeal to colonial and Javanese officials to lead by example largely fell on deaf ears; the conservative resistance—of colonial officials and priyayi—against progressive change was pervasive. Likewise, the initial hormat circulars proved unable to align the performance of colonial power with a new ethical hegemonic script. In response, Goenawan later characterized these experiences as a "bitter awakening." However, by focusing on everything that remained unchanged, he initially missed the significant transformations that did occur.

Goenawan's articles as well as the discussion in the vernacular press that followed reveal that the payung and hormat circulars provided young Javanese with a unique opportunity to openly discuss and critique not only the outward appearance of authority but also the colonial relationship more broadly. Knowing that they could rely on the support of central authorities in Batavia invigorated their desire for greater equality and respect and proved to be a profoundly empowering experience. Increasingly, the colonized spoke up, made themselves heard, and expressed their desire for emancipation in the burgeoning vernacular press as well as by establishing the first Indonesian cultural and political associations. Goenawan himself played a leading role in the foundation of Boedi Oetomo (Noble Endeavor) in 1908, the pioneering association founded with objectives of renewing an appreciation for Javanese culture and history, stimulating the development of Javanese land and people and advocating for the spread of Western education and knowledge.[97] Other cultural, religious, and political associations followed suit as institutional expressions of this new mentality among the colonized. Thus, in hindsight, it was perhaps not so much a "bitter" but rather a bittersweet awakening.[98]

Over time, however, the tone of the discussion became more radical and frustrated, conveying a sense of exasperation that progressive Europeans shared. Governor General Idenburg alluded to the schism that had developed within the European community between advocates of the Ethical Policy—which he described as a relatively small group that included himself and Hazeu—and "the large heap of Europeans" supporting the conservative policies of the previous century. According to Idenburg, at stake was the question of whether the Dutch were "sincere in uplifting the natives both mentally and materially or whether everything remains the same."[99] In fact, what he described in the Indies was a great fragmentation of social and political order.

For his part, Hazeu was unsurprised by the development of a more openly assertive mentality among the colonized. Only to the untrained observer, he argued in 1908, did the Javanese appear unchangeable and static—a sneer to his conservative adversaries—but he reasoned that many Europeans failed to notice this evolution because it "did not yet manifest itself in outward signs or appearance."[100] As long as the Javanese did not visually express their new mentality with transformed hegemonic conduct, including updated deference rituals, dress, and language, conservative forces could maintain that the colonized remained indolent and servile. Hazeu's observation struck at the heart of the debate over the hormat circulars; it was the absence of a visual representation and performance of the new progressive attitude that prevented broader Javanese emancipation. In other words, for the national awakening to take root, a hegemonic struggle over material and visual culture was going to be essential. During the first decade of the twentieth century, conservative forces were able to withstand the surge in nationalism but in 1913, the young Javanese took matters in their own hands.

CHAPTER 3

Disrupting the Colonial Performance

The Hormat Circular of 1913 and the National Awakening

I N FEBRUARY OF 1913, Raden Soemarsono, a young Javanese public prosecutor, was on his way to report to his new European superior, Assistant
Resident J. C. Bedding of Purwakarta (western Java). Soemarsono had just
been transferred from Batavia, the Dutch East Indies cosmopolitan capital, to
the backward provincial town of Purwakarta. On his arrival to the local police
court, he was shocked to see his fellow countrymen crouching before Bedding,
sitting on the floor, and addressing the European civil servant in high Javanese. After each sentence, they also brought their hands together in a gesture of
respect and obedience (*sembah*). For the Western-educated Soemarsono, these
longstanding traditional forms of deference, known collectively as *hormat*, were
considered a thing of the past. On the contrary, when Assistant Resident Bedding noticed that Soemarsono was dressed in European fashion (trousers and
a jacket), a clash between tradition and progress (*kemajuan*) ensued. Bedding
demanded that Soemarsono exchange his European trousers for a Javanese
sarong and sit on the floor. Soemarsono refused. He had attended a European
secondary school, spoke fluent Dutch, sat in chairs in the presence of Europeans,
and was used to being treated as an equal. Grudgingly, Bedding allowed Soemarsono to attend the meeting but provided him no chair. The prosecutor could
not sit on the floor because he was dressed in Western trousers—to do so was an
unequivocal sign of submission within Javanese deference tradition—and thus
would have been forced to stand throughout the meeting. Rather than submit
to that humiliation, Soemarsono excused himself to attend to the pile of paperwork that came with his new office.[1]

Soemarsono's disturbance of the colonial performance was representative of
the coming of age of a more assertive generation of Indonesians that demanded
greater equality and respect in colonial society. This new generation was highly
educated, multilingual, globally conscious, professionally employed, and aware

77

of the Ethical Policy's civilizing discourse. They began to organize in cultural, economic, and political associations, and like Soemarsono, many *performed* truth to power by refusing to submit to humiliating deference traditions. Their decisions about which language to speak, what to wear, how to approach someone, where to sit, and which gestures of respect to offer all became acts of hegemonic contestation. However, Soemarsono's confrontation with Bedding stands out because of a significant, albeit unintentional, consequence: the issuance of a new hormat circular in 1913. This final hormat circular was instrumental in energizing an Indonesian national awakening and irreparably damaging nineteenth-century colonial hegemony.

The hormat circular of 1913 was a remarkable piece of colonial legislation, as the government publicly acknowledged that its own officials had failed to comply with its previous circulars (1890, 1904, 1906, and 1909) and recognized that traditional deference rituals were incredibly humiliating for the colonized.[2] In addition, the circular was a promise that the government would insist that its civil servants adopt a more progressive attitude. Finally, it plainly encouraged the colonized to be more assertive in demanding respect from Europeans, suggesting that like Soemarsono (whose experiences were included in an anonymized addendum), one could adopt Western dress and thus make compliance with outdated deference traditions nearly impossible.

The hormat circular received vast public attention. Its implications were widely reviewed in the burgeoning vernacular press and, tellingly, the government actively collaborated with the Sarekat Islam, Indonesia's first mass political association (founded in 1911), to announce and interpret the significance of the circular's message. These discussions instilled in the colonized a great sense of confidence and justice that was instrumental in bringing about the transformative era in Indonesian history that Takashi Shiraishi so aptly described as "an age in motion"—a period of rallies, protests, demands, strikes, debates, and an emerging national consciousness.[3] Thus, by fanning the growing flames of advocacy for equality and respect, the hormat circular of 1913 played a crucial but often overlooked role in the development of the Indonesian nationalist movement. Once this impact became apparent, conservative colonial officials and Javanese aristocrats formulated a strong reactionary response, accusing the progressive coalition of young Indonesian intellectuals and Dutch proponents of "ethical" ideals of destabilizing colonial order and destroying traditional indigenous culture. These lamentations increased as the national awakening grew stronger and more assertive, resulting in fierce public debates over what constituted proper deference. This reactionary movement reestablished control over the government in the 1920s, but by then it was impossible to reimpose nineteenth-century colonial hegemony. Instead, the broad nationalist movement persisted in its assault on these traditions as markers of colonial and social authority. Still following Soemarsono's example, by the early 1930s it had accomplished this goal.

Performing Truth to Power: From Conflict to Circular

The small and dusty provincial town of Purwakarta seems an unlikely place for the confrontation between Bedding and Soemarsono. Although Purwakarta was part of the residency of Batavia, life in the town hardly resembled the hustle and bustle of the cosmopolitan colonial capital. Its relative isolation in the island's interior gave the town an aura of backwardness that seemed to shield it from modern developments such as the Ethical Policy and the national awakening. Purwakarta was a quintessential nineteenth-century colonial town with a layout reflecting the duality of colonial governance. The small European community and the residence of the assistant resident, constructed in the Empire style with a hipped roof (all sides slope downward) and rectangular floorplan based on Javanese designs, were located to the south of the pond in the town's center. The office of the bupati and the local mosque bordered the town square (*alun-alun*) with two holy banyan trees to the west of the pond. However, it was precisely because time seemed to move more slowly in Purwakarta that it was a prime location for a clash between a proponent of progress (*kemajuan*) and a defender of the old order.

Being of *priyayi* descent and Western-educated, Raden Soemarsono personified the tension between tradition and progress in turn-of-the-century colonial Indonesia. As his title *Raden* indicated, he was of noble birth, descended from the upper levels of Java's priyayi elite.[4] His grandfather had been the district head (bupati) of Grobogan (central Java), while his father was the public prosecutor (*jaksa*) at the native court in Magelang (central Java). Soemarsono was therefore well versed in priyayi culture and familiar with proper Javanese etiquette, language, dress, literature, gamelan music, and *wayang kulit* (shadow puppet theater).[5] His priyayi background also enabled him to attend one of the most prestigious secondary schools in the colony: the Gymnasium Willem III in Batavia. In 1901, he was one of only four non-European students—three Javanese and one Chinese—of the 148 who took and passed the admissions exam.[6] During his time at school, from 1901 to 1906, Soemarsono was immersed in a European cultural environment in which he wore European dress, conversed in Dutch, and socialized freely with his European classmates. On completing his education, he began his civil service career in 1906 as a clerk and rose through the ranks to become a public prosecutor in 1912. At age twenty-six he was appointed as jaksa of Purwakarta, for the first time in his young life substituting the progressive colonial capital for an "old-fashioned provincial town" where both European and indigenous officials "maintained a tradition of stiff conservatism."[7]

Considering Soemarsono's experiences in cosmopolitan Batavia at both school and work, the conflict with Bedding over appropriate deference was hardly surprising. In a correspondence with the resident of Batavia, H. Rijf-snijder, under whose authority the regency of Purwakarta fell, Soemarsono described his disbelief on learning that at meetings of the Purwakarta police court it was still customary for the public prosecutor to approach the assistant resident in a crouching walk and sit on the floor for the duration of the session. When he had appeared wearing trousers, he immediately sensed that Assistant Resident Bedding was ill disposed toward him. All of this surprised Soemarsono, who wrote that he could not possibly have known "that high ranking civil servants [in Purwakarta] still valued old-fashioned hormat traditions and customary law (adat)."[8] Very aware of the various government circulars regarding the issue, Soemarsono refused to submit to Bedding's demands. In the months following the confrontation, an adjunct public prosecutor took Soemarsono's place in the police court while he relocated to the native court, where the European judge worked outside of the civil service hierarchy and did not demand traditional deference. Soemarsono only returned to sessions of the police court in May when Bedding allowed him the "personal privilege" of sitting in a chair and wearing European dress. Soemarsono's perseverance in *performing* truth to power seemed to have paid off, but it was the events of the following months that explain how knowledge of his experience became widely shared.

While Bedding's concession cleared the air, Soemarsono's increasing involvement in the nationalist movement ensured that their mutual understanding was short-lived. During his time in Batavia, Soemarsono had joined Boedi Oetomo, colonial Indonesia's first modern association (founded in 1908) and established friendships with its founder, Wahidin Soedirohoesodo, and other prominent young intellectuals such as Soewardi Soerjaningrat and Tjipto Mangoenkoesoemo. Immediately after his arrival in Purwakarta, Soemarsono took the initiative to encourage what he called "association life," which, in his estimation, quickly "revolved around him." He acted as the local representative of Boedi Oetomo and was the driving force behind establishing a local branch of the Sarekat Islam in March 1913. Hosted by a local *hajji* (Muslim who made the pilgrimage to Mecca), the founding meeting was attended by approximately fifteen hundred people, including the district head, civil servants, teachers, merchants, *hajjis*, local village heads, and even peasants. Since Soemarsono's work as public prosecutor made it difficult to assume a daily role in the governing board, he acted as a special advisor to the association. He derived a great sense of purpose and happiness from his work with these associations, which he considered to be joyful signs of "the awakening of the people's consciousness and initiative."[9]

Assistant Resident Bedding was deeply troubled by these developments. He feared that the Sarekat Islam would escalate tensions among various ethnic groups in the district, especially between indigenous people and the Chinese. Riots between these two groups had already erupted in early March. Bedding credited the Sarekat Islam's success, and with it the risk of intergroup violence, to Soemarsono's use of his position as a civil servant to lend the association the "aureole of authority." He therefore scolded Soemarsono for his involvement in the organization and prohibited the group from meeting outside the town of Purwakarta.[10] Once again, the young public prosecutor opted not to yield to Bedding's demands, stating that nothing could "keep me from my duty to my people, that we aristocrats have neglected for so long."[11] In large part due to Soemarsono's support, the Purwakarta branch of the Sarekat Islam grew to fifteen thousand members by the end of the calendar year.[12]

Soemarsono's involvement in association life culminated in a public lecture commemorating the five-year anniversariy of Boedi Oetomo on May 25, 1913.[13] In front of a large audience, he argued that if indigenous people wanted to achieve real progress, increase their prosperity, and reclaim their dignity, they had to shed their servitude and contest colonial inequalities. He metaphorically described the colonial hierarchy as a seating arrangement, with indigenous people perched on the floor below the table looking up at the Chinese, who sat on chairs closer to the table, and further up to the Dutch, seated at the table itself. To challenge this colonial order, Soemarsono proposed that the colonized work together in associations, forge a distinct national identity (based on Islam and their Hindu-Buddhist past), and demand modern education for their youth. Most importantly, Soemarsono proposed a change in mentality. The Javanese should no longer be docile and submissive but rather self-confident and asssertive in advocating for equality. As if recalling his first encounter with Bedding, he suggested that they adopt modern clothes, at which time he presented his own outfit consisting of a blazer, pantaloons, and shoes. Encouraging his compatriots to emulate his example, Soemarsono conveyed his conviction that a change in appearance signaled a newfound self-respect and refusal to be humiliated.

Clad in modern trousers, they signaled a refusal to submit to traditional deference etiquette.[14]

In the days following his lecture, a rumor spread that Soemarsono had called
for the violent expulsion of the Dutch from Java if the colonial authorities would
not legally recognize the Sarekat Islam.[15] Bedding, who had not attended the lecture, immediately solicited witness accounts from indigenous civil servants who
had been present. According to these witnesses, Soemarsono had done nothing
of the sort, although they did suggest that he could have chosen his words more
carefully considering the largely uneducated audience. Despite these reports,
Bedding concluded that the incident confirmed his opinion of Soemarsono as
a troublemaker, especially because he believed that the lecture "had a fatal influence on the less educated priyayi, instigating them against the government."[16]
To prevent further disruption of colonial peace and order, Bedding suspended
all of the Purwakarta Sarekat Islam's activities until the government reached a
decision about the association's request for legal recognition. On Bedding's recommendation, even the governor general was informed of Soemarsono's speech.
The highest authority in the colony instructed the resident of Batavia to scold
Soemarsono and impress on him that if he wished to remain a civil servant, he
must refrain from expressing opinions that could be interpreted as inciting en-
mity against the government.[17]

At this crucial juncture, Soemarsono appealed for support from his former
high school mentor: the influential and progressive Dutch advisor for native
affairs G. A. J. Hazeu. When colonial authorities denied the Sarekat Islam's request for legal recognition in June 1913, the government directed further peti-
tions to officially approve the continuation of local branches to Hazeu's office.[18]
As the Purwakarta spokesperson of the Sarekat Islam, Soemarsono seized this
opportunity to share some of his frustrations with Hazeu and his assistant, D.
A. Rinkes. In late July, Soemarsono confided that he was severely distressed by
the official reprimand sanctioned by the governor general himself. He simply
could not fathom how standing up for the common people's interests led to accusations of "inciting" against the government or having "revolutionary tendencies." Disillusioned with his career, Soemarsono inquired about the possibility of
leaving the civil service and continuing his education in the Netherlands, which
would allow him to engage with "truly civilized and well-mannered Europeans
in their own environment."[19] Hazeu advised his former pupil to let bygones be
bygones, to be more cautious, and bide his time until he was promoted to a more
progressive district. Interestingly, Hazeu also reached out to the governor general about the situation in Purwakarta. He presented Soemarsono as a youthful

intellectual with a tendency to exaggerate but argued that it had been Bedding's treatment that left him feeling misjudged and confirmed his mistaken views. Hazeu's insinuation was clear: maybe Soemarsono's behavior was not the real problem.[20]

Despite Hazeu's counsel, Soemarsono found himself at the center of yet another dispute with his European superiors in early August 1913. After distributing a controversial pamphlet as a personal favor to the author, Soemarsono was interrogated under suspicion of transgressing the colonial press law. The pamphlet, Soewardi Soerjaningrat's *Als ik eens Nederlander was* (If I Were a Dutchman), was thought to incite ethnic hatred, as the author critiqued the upcoming centennial celebration of Dutch independence from Napoleonic France. Soerjaningrat argued that if he were a Dutchman, he would not hold "independence celebrations in a country where we deny the people their independence," effectively exposing colonial hypocrisy.[21] In a letter to Hazeu, Soemarsono maintained that he had acted in good faith in distributing the pamphlet, but that he also understood the gravity of his predicament. As Soerjaningrat himself had been arrested and exiled for this publication, Soemarsono expected to at least be suspended and at worst, discharged. However, he underestimated just how much Bedding detested him. The situation provided the Dutch official with the opportunity to rid himself of his troublesome adversary, and he advised the governor general to discharge and incarcerate Soemarsono.[22]

Aware of the danger facing his protégé, Hazeu requested that Soemarsono send him all relevant correspondence that could be used as evidence against him.[23] As he examined Soemarsono's materials, Hazeu became convinced that the real threat to colonial peace and order was not the young Javanese but rather the civil service itself. He believed that the arrogance of European officials and their persistence in demanding humiliating forms of deference, despite previous hormat circulars' explicit instructions, "literally drive *our* young Javanese to imprudence, anger, vexation, and eventually a pressing desire to rid themselves from such officials."[24] Such damaging responses emerged from the strikingly different social environments that Western-educated Javanese encountered during their studies and in their civil service careers. As students, they were treated as equals, sat on chairs, conversed in Dutch, and befriended Europeans. But, as Soemarsono's confrontations with Bedding demonstrated, as civil servants they were looked down on, considered racially and intellectually inferior, and expected to conform to outdated forms of deference. Hazeu was particularly incensed by a curt note that Bedding sent to the adjunct public prosecutor who, following Soemarsono's example, dared to sit on a chair during a session of the police court: "Considering you are expected at the session of the police court tomorrow, I notify you, that I do not allow you to sit on a chair, since that is a privilege I have only granted to Jaksa R. Soemarsono. You always used to sit on a mat and without my permission, you allowed yourself to sit on a chair. There is no reason for that."[25] To Soemarsono, this short notice illustrated the relationship between the modern and educated Javanese on the one hand, and those "European and indigenous civil servants, who still place value in the old worn-out hormat customs within the civil service" on the other.[26] Reading through Soemarsono's experiences in Purwakarta, Hazeu increasingly feared "serious consequences" if the culture within the civil service was not modernized, as the Javanese "no longer tolerate these humiliations as they used to."[27]

Within a day of receiving Soemarsono's evidence, Hazeu sent a lengthy and passionate defense of his protégé to the governor general's office in which he refuted the accusations against his former student and called for a comprehensive overhaul of the culture within the civil service. He argued that it should be impossible for someone like "Assistant Resident Bedding to have the power to decide individually if a native of modern development and civilization is allowed to sit on a chair in the company of European officials."[28] Hazeu proposed to resolve the situation in Purwakarta by transferring Soemarsono to a more progressive district, while officially reprimanding Bedding for his behavior. Moreover, as Bedding had many "spiritual doppelgangers," Hazeu urged that civil servants be forced to comply with the demands of the new ethical discourse by issuing a new hormat circular. The governor general was swayed by Hazeu's assessment and on August 22, 1913, only five days after Soemarsono sent his materials to his mentor, decided to transfer Soemarsono and scold Bedding. In addition, he issued the sternest circular to date, signaling an overhaul of colonial cultural hegemony rooted in Javanese deference rituals.[29]

The hormat circular of 1913 was a curious piece of legislation that sought to align the social etiquette and deference shaping colonial encounters with the civilizing discourse of the Ethical Policy. It was indicative of the great value that Dutch colonial authorities still placed on orchestrating the outward appearance and rituals of power to legitimize and maintain their dominance. In the decree, the government expressed concern over officials' demonstrated disregard for the previous hormat circulars (1890, 1904, 1906, and 1909), as tensions between the civil service and the growing number of educated Javanese had increased as a result. The circular stressed that the Javanese national awakening was not to be feared, but "instead, it should be interpreted as the first result of long-term efforts to civilize the natives."[30] In a confidential letter to civil servants accompanying the circular, Hazeu emphasized that the relationship between European and indigenous civil servants in particular needed to change. The document was clearly inspired by Soemarsono's experience in Purwakarta, discussed anonymously as an example of European officials' abuse of power. Hazeu used Soemarsono's incident to argue that Europeans should treat their indigenous counterparts more humanely and fairly, as "the old condition was destined to be replaced by a different one, more along European lines."[31] Both the circular and the confidential attachment thus forewarned European civil servants that those who continued to defy the government's instructions on the subject of hormat would be punished, although the penalties remained undefined.

European civil servants were taken aback by the latest hormat circular, which they considered a humiliating public affront by the colonial government. Resident W. Boissevain, for instance, wrote that it was tolerable when the vernacular press critiqued the civil service but not when the government did so. Their pride was further tarnished as the confidential letter to civil servants—which contained the most damning language—was leaked to the press and widely disseminated. The civil servants felt undervalued for their crucial work in the colonial administration and believed that the accusations against them were exaggerated. They blamed the Office for Native Affairs in particular, arguing that Hazeu had only theoretical and no practical knowledge of indigenous society. According to many civil servants and the conservative colonial press, the circular was a historic mistake, undermining European prestige by contradicting the supposedly innate Javanese sense of servility. Many Europeans even argued that the Javanese were themselves to blame for the perseverance of deference traditions, as they considered conversing in Dutch or wearing Western clothing to be impolite. How could European officials disagree?[32]

However, although it was Hazeu's letters that got the governor general's attention, it was Soemarsono's actions during his tenure in Purwakarta that truly ignited the overhaul of the hegemonic colonial cultural system beginning in August 1913. On the same day that the hormat circular was published, Hazeu informed Soemarsono that he did not have to fear for his position, as the governor general had sided with him and issued the hormat circular to ensure that behavior like Bedding's would not be tolerated. He further pointed out that this outcome was only possible because of the well-documented grievances and convincing evidence that his former pupil had provided.[33] It was thus Soemarsono's resolve during his confrontations with Bedding and his shrewdness in communicating with Hazeu that led to this significant—and ultimately effective—hormat circular. Soemarsono's response was full of gratitude but also indicated a sense of disappointment. He wondered why incidents always had to escalate before changes were made. In addition, he made it clear that the hormat circular was only the beginning, as he believed the Javanese also deserved suffrage and a national parliament. Although Hazeu urged him to practice self-control and strive for gradual change, Soemarsono's experiences in Purwakarta had pushed him in a more radical direction.[34] Moreover, in the following years, the hormat circular that resulted from his struggle became a rallying point for the Javanese national awakening as well as for a reactionary conservative movement that sought to put an end to attempts to modernize the colonial relationship.

Contesting Hegemony: Mass Rallies and the Vernacular Press

The impact of the hormat circular of 1913, especially compared to the circulars of the previous decade, was in part magnified by the colonial government's deliberate decision to collaborate with the Sarekat Islam to announce its publication. This partnership was surprising, given the government's ambivalent attitude toward the association. On the one hand, colonial authorities feared the Sarekat Islam's impressive mass following; on the other, they considered the movement to be the culmination—and therefore validation—of the Ethical Policy. The Dutch consequently opted to refuse legal recognition of a centrally led Sarekat Islam but offered their support in establishing local branches of the association, including the Purwakarta branch that Soemarsono had launched.[35] To signal the government's support of the movement, adjunct Advisor for Native Affairs D. A. Rinkes joined the charismatic chairman of Sarekat Islam, Oemar Said Tjokroaminoto, on a tour of Java in December 1913. Rinkes took on the role of mediator between conservative officials and representatives of the association.[36] For instance, in Purwakarta, Rinkes brushed aside Bedding's criticism of the Sarekat Islam, which he attributed to a personal grudge against Soemarsono. But Rinkes's task encompassed more than dealing with conservative officials. More importantly, he was expected to gain the trust of the Sarekat Islam's followers. The hormat circular was essential to achieving this goal.

In late 1913 and early 1914, Rinkes traversed Java to speak at large public gatherings sponsored by the Sarekat Islam. One can only imagine the murmurs in the crowd as the high-ranking Dutch colonial official took the stage to address the often thousands of people in attendance. Rinkes's speeches followed a singular script. He first explained that he was there to assist in establishing local branches of the Sarekat Islam. His presence, he continued, was a sign of the government's goodwill toward the association and support for the Sarekat Islam's program for economic, religious, and social emancipation, as long as it occurred within the boundaries of the law. He then introduced the hormat circular as evidence of the government's noble intentions. Occasionally, he read the circular aloud, but most often he summarized its contents. The message he delivered to the captive audience was clear: the governor general had prohibited humiliating deference rituals as a means of removing obstacles to equality and progress. This meant, according to Rinkes, that the colonized were no longer second-rate subjects in their own country. He stressed that civil servants were there for the people, not the other way around. Rinkes also explained that circulars were firm orders from the governor general that mandated all European officials' compliance. This declaration set up the apotheosis of Rinkes's performance: he publicly encouraged all in attendance to report transgressions of the hormat circular to the authorities. In a way, he urged tens of thousands of people to act like Soemarsono.[37]

Rinkes's words reverberated throughout colonial Indonesia, as they implied that colonial officials were fallible, would be held accountable, and that the colonized had a right, perhaps even a duty, to monitor their behavior. While Rinkes's presence was meant to defuse the Sarekat Islam, it effectively became a call for further political and social engagement. Moreover, he demonstrated that the hormat circular of 1913 could be weaponized as a powerful instrument to demand equality and bring about social change. Within Sarekat Islam circles, familiarity with the circular became widespread. At a meeting in Semarang in 1914, attendees carried a banner proclaiming: "2014: Do not forget this circular!" For those who missed the reference to the circular's administrative designation—it was listed as decision number 2014—another banner was more direct: "The Javanese do not want to squat like a frog."[38] In Sukabumi, Sarekat Islam followers distributed symbolic degrees to local district heads (*wedana*) for their compliance with the hormat circular, confirming Rinkes's prediction that once European civil servants were forced to change their habits, indigenous civil servants were bound to follow.[39] Perhaps most importantly, Sarekat Islam meetings turned into safe spaces in which people could openly discuss European civil servants' transgressions. In addition to abuses perpetrated by administrative officials like residents, such discussions incorporated other civil servants, such as those in the government run pawnshop service, forestry service, and the state service overseeing the production and sale of opium and salt.[40]

In the following years, the Sarekat Islam's leadership ingeniously adapted Rinkes's words to their Islamic nationalist discourse.[41] This was perfectly reflected in a speech at the Sarekat Islam's first national congress in Bandung in 1916. The speech, given by subdistrict head Prawiroatmodjo from Banten

FIGURE 3. Founding meeting of the Sarekat Islam in Blitar, 1914. This picture of the founding meeting of the Sarekat Islam in Blitar (eastern Java) illustrates how, like Soemarsono in Purwakarta, a change in dress was an important way to demand respect and equality. Source: Leiden University Library, Royal Netherlands Institute for Southeast Asian and Caribbean Studies (KITLV) 3719.

(western Java), heavily criticized the detrimental influence of Javanese deference traditions, especially the requirement to crouch and sit on the floor and
present the sembah. Prawiroatmodjo proclaimed, "As long as the people willingly submit to servile treatment, there can be no progress."[42] Echoing Rinkes,
he reminded his audience that civil servants were there to *serve* the people—a
sentiment that to him applied to European and indigenous officials alike. Crucially, Prawiroatmodjo argued that a servile attitude and the intricate system of
deference etiquette guiding social interactions and expressing social hierarchies,
which he referred to as *sembah-jongkok*, never were intrinsically Javanese but
rather cultural residues of Hindu dominance in Java's past. According to this
view, Hindu rulers had imposed humiliating deference rituals on the Javanese in
order to exploit them. Shedding these traditions in the present would therefore
not only lead to progress but also purify Java from damaging Hindu influences.
Prawiroatmodjo asserted that Islam actually prohibited the knee kiss (*sungkem*)
and sembah, stressing that this was not an argument against politeness and respect, of which he was in favor but against oppressive foreign traditions.

In addition to the Sarekat Islam's large public meetings, the burgeoning vernacular press provided a crucial platform through which Indonesians learned
about the 1913 hormat circular. As cultural and political associations developed
in the years preceding the circular, the vernacular press increasingly became an
extension of the nascent nationalist movement. Associations like Boedi Oetomo
and the Sarekat Islam founded their own publishing houses, newspapers, and
periodicals—publications that quickly turned quite opinionated and political.
Although financial stability was always an issue, as reflected in the high turn-
over rate of these publications, from 1914 onward the vernacular press expanded
rapidly and became a force to be reckoned with in colonial society.[43] The discussion of the hormat circular was arguably the first issue that clearly showcased
the vernacular press's new role in this regard. This role is particularly evident in
the periodical *Doenia Bergerak* (The World Is in Motion), founded in 1914 by
Marco Kartodikromo as the weekly publication of the Inlandse Journalisten
Bond (Union of Native Journalists) in Surakarta. Unlike Soemarsono, Marco
Kartodikromo belonged to the lower priyayi, received limited Western education, and was not fluent in Dutch. However, he was infatuated with moder-
nity and a highly critical observer of colonial society. Before founding *Doenia
Bergerak*, Kartodikromo gained journalistic experience as an apprentice to Tirto
Adhisoerjo, the "founding father" of Indonesian journalism, and as editor of the
Sarekat Islam's newspaper in Surakarta. Through his writing, Kartodikromo
sought to challenge colonial inequalities and achieve greater solidarity among

Indonesians. These goals were reflected in his decision to publish in Malay rather than in Dutch, the language of the oppressor, or in Javanese, a language with strict hierarchies. In *Doenia Bergerak*, Kartodikromo published critical and often sarcastic articles, letters, and complaints written by him and his friends. And throughout 1914, the latest hormat circular dominated its pages.[44]

In *Doenia Bergerak*, Kartodikromo praised the colonial government for issuing the hormat circular, echoing the consensus in the vernacular press.[45] He was cautiously optimistic that the circular was a significant step toward greater equality and mutual respect in colonial society. The circular, Kartodikromo believed, had the potential to accelerate the national awakening, as it encouraged the common people (*wong cilik*) to display greater self-confidence in their interactions with their alleged superiors. However, he pointed out that change would not come easily, as those in positions of power never willingly give up their privileges.[46] In an article titled "Deference Must Be Appropriate," readers were therefore advised to stand up for change by no longer "[showing] their masters respect like monkeys, while in their minds cursing them to die," but by being polite without humiliating oneself. This meant not treating superiors like gods by performing outdated deference rituals and addressing them with grandiose titles. That, the author argued, is "the way to progress [*kemajuan*] and freedom [*merdeka*]."[47] Another contributor conveyed the same message by pretending to be someone with high status—a popular expressive form since Soewardi Soerjaningrat's famous pamphlet. In the article, the author wondered why the Javanese would want to abolish sembah-jongkok, the time-honored traditions of their ancestors. He implored the reader to stop pursuing change, as it would no longer allow him to "oppress and suck your blood" by obtaining "your rice paddies for cheap," and turn the Javanese into a "clever, brave, and righteous people." In addition, the author beseeched his readers to avoid Western dress, offer sembah-jongkok, and to not cut their hair, as a cold head leads to a clear and clever mind.[48] These articles in *Doenia Bergerak* presented the hormat circular as a great opportunity, and emphasized that its implementation depended on the colonized themselves.

The pages of *Doenia Bergerak* make it clear that Marco Kartodikromo used the hormat circular to critique the behavior of both colonial and Javanese officials. While the hormat circular applied specifically to relations between colonizer and colonized, Kartodikromo forcefully argued that it should be extended to the priyayi in general and the bupati in particular. This signified a new direction in the hormat discussion that became increasingly important in the following decades. According to an article titled "Who Takes Care of

Whom?" the traditional patron-client relationship (*kawula-gusti*) between the common people and the priyayi was broken. The Javanese elite demanded excessive deference from the people without the customary reciprocation of beneficial leadership and protection. The author argued that compliance with the hormat circular could restore balance to this distorted relationship.[49] Inspired by Soewardi's pamphlet, another article titled "If I Were a Bupati" discussed the proper behavior and responsibilities of these traditional officials. Drawing on this fantasy, the author successfully exposed the hypocrisy of the age. He argued that as a bupati he would not demand sembah-jongkok but rather would permit his subordinates to sit in chairs and don European dress. In a veiled example of everyday resistance, he also reasoned that he would no longer demand the title *Gusti* (Lord or Master), as someone could "accidentally" address him as *Gusi*, referring to oral gums. He asserted that as a bupati, he did not wish to inspire fear and would only hire people based on merit, work toward emancipation, and establish a women's association and girls' school, as women were crucial to achieving real progress.[50] The latter was a reference to the emergence of various women's associations around the same time, which began to draw elite women out of the seclusion of the household and into the public sphere.[51]

In addition to these opinionated pieces, *Doenia Bergerak* and other vernacular publications assumed a more activist stance as they vigorously monitored European and indigenous officials' compliance with the hormat circular. This marked a significant turning point for the vernacular press, as readers were invited to share their experiences and observations. The editors of the *Oetoesan Hindia* (Messenger of the Indies), the Sarekat Islam's newspaper in Surabaya, justified this vigilantism by pointing out that the current hormat circular would have been redundant if European officials had complied with the circular of 1904.[52] Within months of the 1913 circular's release, the pages of the vernacular press were dotted with long and short exposés documenting transgressions. In June 1914, *Doenia Bergerak* published a letter from a pawnshop employee accusing his European boss of continuing to demand that he crouch and don traditional dress. According to the writer, his boss considered the Javanese to be animals rather than human beings.[53] *Doenia Bergerak* published many similar complaints, as did other vernacular newspapers.[54] In the Sarekat Islam's newspaper in Semarang, *Sinar Djawa* (Java's Radiance), a contributor threatened to expose the identity of an assistant wedana in Kudus who still ordered traditional deference from the people in his district.[55] Dutch colonial officials were equally branded, as with an assistant resident in Kendal who refused to let his Javanese colleagues sit in chairs.[56] The *Oetoesan Hindia* in turn reported on abuses within the state facilitated opium services, describing the department as outdated in the age of progress (*kemajuan*).[57] Together these complaints in the vernacular press helped bring about the realization that hormat abuses were a shared experience under colonialism—one that could only be undone by collective action. As such, the discussion of the hormat circular played an important role in the development of a nascent national consciousness.

One of the most significant and democratizing outcomes of these public discussions of the hormat circular was its publication in Malay, the nonhierarchical language of the people. Kartodikromo, who was involved in both the vernacular press and the Sarekat Islam, was among the first to dare publish the controversial circular in Malay, with the clear objective of familiarizing people with its message and providing them with the necessary information to stand up to hormat abuse. As Kartodikromo and other editors were quick to point out, knowledge was a powerful weapon that empowered the colonized to demand real change.[58] On the first anniversary of the hormat circular (August 22, 1914), *Doenia Bergerak* published an article expressing concern that many of the colonized had only limited knowledge of its contents. In a typical expressive form, the "circular" itself addressed the reader, lamenting its danger of being forgotten and requesting that it remain strictly enforced. The article went on to ask that all Javanese wear trousers and shoes to avoid traditional hormat demands (if they could afford to do so) and sit in chairs during meetings. It also insisted that all government circulars be translated into vernacular languages to ensure compliance.[59] It was in response to this article that Kartodikromo published a Malay translation of the official hormat circular in *Doenia Bergerak* on October 31, 1914.[60] Other vernacular newspapers followed suit. For instance, the Sarekat Islam newspaper in Bandung, *Kaoem Moeda* (The Young Ones), published the circular on its front page in November 1915 to celebrate the tenure of Governor General Van Idenburg, asserting that the hormat circular was the defining feature of his governance.[61] These Malay translations of the circular democratized access to information and inspired a new generation. Unintentionally, the hormat circular had played a crucial role in the formation of a more informed, critical, and politically engaged generation of Indonesians, willing to fight for change.

As widespread discussion in the vernacular press and at Sarekat Islam rallies illustrates, many Javanese interpreted the 1913 hormat circular as a public confession—the government admitting that the existing deference rituals were humiliating and no longer appropriate. They viewed it also as a pledge that they would be entitled to more respectful treatment in the immediate future, and as encouragement to proactively demand change by refusing to pay traditional homage to European officials. By instilling a sense of self-confidence and activism in the colonized, the 1913 hormat circular was a significant factor in bringing about a transformative period in Indonesian history that scholar Takashi Shiraishi has aptly described as an "age in motion." As Shiraishi demonstrated, the fifteen years following the foundation of the Sarekat Islam saw the proliferation of newspapers and journals, cultural and political associations, mass meetings and rallies, and trade unions and strikes, as the colonized increasingly expressed themselves politically. Gradually, their call for equal rights, political representation, and even a promise of independence became more widespread. It was through these experiences that the ethnically diverse inhabitants of the Netherlands Indies came to think of themselves for the first time as Indonesians.[62]

For his part, Soemarsono, the little-known spark behind these developments, was transferred to the district of Purworedjo in central Java in September 1913. The restlessness that had characterized his tenure in Purwakarta followed him there as he continued to balance his activities in associations, especially Boedi Oetomo, and his career as a public prosecutor. Within Boedi Oetomo, he became one of the most vocal proponents of a more overtly political course, primarily by demanding democratic reforms. It was therefore apt that he made the association's candidacy list for the first People's Council, an advisory body to the colonial government inaugurated in 1917. Although he was not voted into the People's Council, Soemarsono was elected to Batavia's city council the following year. By this time, the government had discharged him from employment, officially for missing police court proceedings but more likely for being unable to combine his professional and political activities.[63] After serving as a regular contributor to the Javanese nationalist periodical *De Wederopbouw* (Restoration) throughout 1920 and 1921, Soemarsono disappeared from the forefront of "association life," as well as from historians' radar.[64]

Continued Debate: The Hormat Circular and Its Implications

While the 1913 hormat circular was widely praised among the Javanese and instrumental in initiating a national awakening, European colonial officials reacted less positively. They too interpreted the document as a confession—one in which they were publicly scolded and humiliated by the colonial government. The circular's distribution and subsequent Javanese resistance to hormat rituals generated a reactionary movement among conservative colonial officials who sought to reinstate the feudalism that had previously characterized their rule.

D. A. Rinkes's partnership and lecture tour with the Sarekat Islam after the hormat circular's release in 1913 particularly irked European civil servants and the European colonial press. Moreover, to their dismay, Governor General Van Idenburg fully supported Rinkes's speeches and the growth of the nationalist association. Not only was a confidential and humiliating letter leaked to the press, now the colonial government added insult to injury by debating the recent circular publicly with Javanese nationalists. A periodical for European civil servants insisted that Rinkes's ideas could only result in complete disobedience from the Javanese, who were instructed to no longer show deference to their superiors. This was a grave mistake, according to the press, since obedience and servitude were important Javanese character traits. The press argued, "Whoever disconnects the Javanese of these traits, changes their character, takes away their most precious possession, and turns them into anarchists during this current phase of their evolution."[65] In the years that followed, both European civil servants and the traditional Javanese elite would use this argument about the preservation of Javanese culture and identity to justify their intention to re-feudalize Javanese society.

In late 1916, Hazeu, the advisor for native affairs, reached out to the governor general to express his concern over the growing disquiet permeating colonial society. He argued that the agitation primarily stemmed from conservative Europeans' unreasonable rejection of the indigenous population's national awakening, which he emphasized was the desired result of the Ethical Policy. According to Hazeu, the reactionary movement among Europeans was the real threat to colonial peace and order. To reinforce his argument, he brought up Assistant Resident M. B. van der Jagt's recent publications, in which he mused nostalgically about the aristocratic spirit at the root of colonial authority and lamented the loss of the payung as a powerful symbol of colonial power. Van der Jagt's writings reflected the reactionary conviction that the Ethical Policy encouraged the Europeanization of indigenous society, transforming a naturally deferential and servile people into insolent and assertive nationalists. Such arguments implied that halting or even reversing the Ethical Policy and the 1913 hormat circular could restore the subservient Javanese.[66]

Waxing wistfully about the good old days, Hazeu warned, would not reverse the direction of societal development—quite the contrary. To clarify his perspective, he shared his impressions of the Sarekat Islam's first national meeting in 1916, where the association's representatives and members formulated clear aspirations, such as participation in government administration, political representation, legal certainty, an end to arbitrariness, and to be treated as equal citizens rather than as inferior or lesser people. Hazeu reported that, while the association greatly appreciated the colonial government's recent support, specifically the hormat circular, he observed a growing awareness among the attendees that they were not given what they were due. Recognizing this as an enduring change in mentality, he therefore argued that it was imperative to not turn back the clock, as the reactionaries proposed, but to continue working with indigenous leadership to guide the nationalist movement, as "time is running out."[67]

Heeding Hazeu's counsel, the government continued to view the national awakening as a positive development. However, at the same time, the tone of the debate in both the colonial and vernacular press hardened considerably. As the presses catered to different readerships, there was initially little direct discourse between the opposing sides. Their dissociation suddenly changed with the inauguration of the People's Council (Volksraad) in May 1918. Originally intended to be a European advisory committee to the colonial government, the People's Council was reconfigured to include indigenous Javanese, Chinese, and Arab representatives. While it was not a truly representative body—half of the members were not elected but appointed, and the majority were still European—the People's Council did provide a relatively safe place for open discussion, as members were protected from censorship law on the council floor. As a result, the inaugural meeting featured feisty debates between conservative Europeans and progressive nationalists.

Van der Jagt was sworn into the People's Council to represent the interests of the European colonial civil service. By this time, he had firmly established himself as one of the strongest proponents of the reactionary movement, advocating for strict observance of hormat, reinvigorating the Javanese aristocracy to counter the nationalist movement, and protecting indigenous people from negative European influences. Above all, Van der Jagt was convinced that colonial rule depended on the maintenance of Javanese traditions, such as aristocratic culture, etiquette, and deference. During his first address in the People's Council, he underscored this belief by again recalling the payung from distant memory, describing it as an inexpensive emblem of power, similar to a crown in the West. He argued that discarding the payung destroyed "the symbolic bridge between an Oriental people and the Western bearer of authority."[68] Like many other colonial officials, Van der Jagt believed that this loss of symbolism resulted in subversive behavior among the colonized. For instance, Van der Jagt himself was offended when the president of the Sarekat Islam in his district dared to address him in Dutch, and without waiting for permission, seated himself in a chair during a meeting. Irritably, Van der Jagt described the local leader's attitude as a "hybrid mixture of Western and Javanese allures and manners and a childish naivety with refined impertinence."[69] Moreover, just as he had reprimanded the Sarekat Islam leader for his behavior, he fiercely criticized the Ethical Policy in the People's Council meeting. While there was some pushback from Europeans—for instance, the liberal editor Stokvis argued that hormat was "one of the causes of a not very symbolical distancing between colonizer and colonized"—this time around, the strongest rebuttal of Van der Jagt's reactionary ideas came from indigenous representatives in the People's Council itself.[70]

Governor General Van Limburg-Stirum personally appointed several prominent nationalist movement figures to the People's Council—a gesture symbolizing the coalition between progressive Dutch and indigenous nationalists. These representatives voiced the strongest condemnation of Van der Jagt's reactionary position. First to speak was Tjipto Mangoenkoesoemo, one of the cofounders of the Indische Party (Indies Party) and an intellectual driving force in the national awakening. Tjipto immediately tested the limits of his mandate, publicly calling into question the legitimacy of the council and insulting European civil servants outright. In unmistakable terms, Tjipto argued that Van der Jagt's comments illustrated that European officials were trapped in the past and unable to accept that they were mere servants of the government rather than the dictators of yesteryear—petty kings within their administrative districts. Instead of adapting to the times, he accused Van der Jagt and his colleagues of trying to bring back the "older sister of Miss Ethics, the hag Mrs. *Ancien Régime*." This old but familiar character, he continued, "needed to chase us back to sleep, tamper our desire for human rights, and delay our march to a brighter future."[71]

Tjokroaminoto, president of the Sarekat Islam, concurred with Tjipto's assessment, and was quick to point out the centrality of the hormat circular to the entire discussion. He proclaimed that the hormat circular was perhaps the most remarkable government regulation in Indies history, as it essentially constituted an acknowledgement of indigenous people's national awakening and grievances, and a public self-reflection on colonial officials' behavior. He also recalled how, with Rinkes's help, Sarekat Islam members learned that indigenous people had the same right to humane and just treatment as Europeans. But to officials like Van der Jagt, Tjokroaminoto continued, the circular made indigenous people arrogant and bold: "Where they used to crouch and show respect to every European, to everyone wearing a coat and trousers and hat, they now dare to assault Europeans." The latter was a reference to increasing social tensions that found their expression in strikes, attacks on estates, and racial riots in Kudus in October 1918, all attributed to Sarekat Islam agitation. Tjokroaminoto concluded that Van der Jagt's words could only be interpreted as a call to forcibly re-instill a sense of respect for European officials among indigenous people before it was too late. This was an anathema to Tjokroaminoto, as it went against everything that the government and the national awakening had worked so hard to achieve.[72]

In his retort the following day, Van der Jagt demonstrated that he was much better at doling out criticism than receiving it. Tjipto and Tjokroaminoto's words clearly hit a nerve. Van der Jagt was affronted by the public nature of the criticism of the European civil service in the vernacular press and, now, on the floor of the People's Council. How dare the colonized challenge and insult the colonizer so directly? Dropping all pretenses, Van der Jagt accused Tjipto and Tjokroaminoto of "breaking and dismantling" Javanese traditions by pushing for Europeanization. Van der Jagt was particularly bothered by the cultural modes of resistance encouraged by the hormat circular, such as the adoption of Western dress, insistence on conversing in Dutch, and refusal to crouch. He no longer considered these acts to be innocent growing pains of a "forward looking primitive people," but rather, "malicious, even criminal, action masked by sweet words and phrases and slogans that lead the Javanese astray" from their traditions, culture, and identity.[73] In short, the innocence of the nationalist movement was long gone. For Van der Jagt and his conservative cohort, it had become a danger to colonial authority *and* Javanese tradition that needed to be stopped.

The confrontation among the three men did not end there but continued during a preparatory meeting of the People's Council exploring the possibility of a native militia. As a government representative, Hazeu also attended the gathering, which made a lasting impression. For instance, the advisor was stunned that Van der Jagt purposely addressed a Javanese committee member in low Javanese (*ngoko*) because he was unsure if the person was "worthy" of a conversation in either Dutch or high Javanese. With such behavior, Van der Jagt publicly defied the hormat circular—in the presence of its author, no less. The atmosphere in the meeting worsened when someone proposed to only enroll intellectuals—meaning educated—Javanese into the potential native militia, which then prompted Van der Jagt to proclaim that there were no Javanese intellectuals. According to Hazeu, the assistant resident even declared that there was more culture in his own chair than in the Javanese people, since all of the culture in Java was imported from abroad. This was too much for Tjipto to tolerate. He stood up and politely told Van der Jagt, "The difference in opinion between the two of us is too considerable for me to be able to cooperate with you," and angrily left the room.[74] Van der Jagt stood by his remarks, and continued to proudly represent the conservative bloc within colonial politics in the People's Council.

Hazeu found Van der Jagt's behavior profoundly unsettling and once more took up his pen to write the governor general. He made his position very clear: behaviors and comments such as those made by Assistant Resident Van der Jagt should be impossible under the latest hormat circular. More importantly, according to Hazeu, Van der Jagt was not alone in his beliefs; his mentality was widely shared among European officials as well as Javanese aristocrats. Therefore, he urged the governor general to take a powerful stand against those civil servants who still ignored, opposed, or ridiculed these government regulations. From a disciplinary perspective, Hazeu wrote, such persistent contempt for the highest authority could not be tolerated, as indigenous leaders could interpret government inaction as a lack of commitment to the national awakening.

In contrast to August 1913, this time Hazeu's warning fell on deaf ears.[75] Governor General Van Limburg-Stirum was not convinced that another hormat circular, public reprimand, or other form of chastisement directed toward the European civil service was politically expedient. Tensions in the Indies had reached a boiling point, as the end of World War I brought the specter of socialist revolution to the colonial world. The outbreak of revolution in Russia in 1917, in Germany in 1918, and ever so briefly in the Netherlands in November 1918 filled colonial authorities with dread, fearing they would inspire the nationalist movement. The governor general sought to stymie the development of these tensions by promising reforms in meetings of the People's Council in November 1918. These so-called November promises (*November beloften*) comprised colonial authorities' vague intent to grant indigenous people greater participation in governance, specifically by expanding the People's Council's responsibilities. While indigenous leaders received these promises with cautious optimism, conservative European civil servants, planters, and citizens fiercely rejected them. Thus, the November promises ultimately enhanced the reactionary movement enormously, strengthening conservative Europeans' conviction that the Ethical Policy had reached its limits. Van Limburg-Stirum had no intention of stoking these anxieties further by following Hazeu's advice.[76]

In 1919, the polarization of colonial society continued, eventually resulting in Hazeu's professional downfall as well as the breakdown of the coalition between progressive Dutch and progressive Indonesians. On top of the strikes, mass meetings, and protests of the previous years, the outbreak of violent incidents linked to the Sarekat Islam in 1919 further reinforced the reactionary bloc's position. In June a Dutch civil servant was murdered in Toli-Toli (Sulawesi) following a Sarekat Islam leader's propaganda tour in the region. The following month alleged Sarekat Islam followers in Garut (western Java) were believed to have plotted an armed resistance and were killed by the authorities. While Hazeu continued to defend the Sarekat Islam as the desired outcome of the Ethical Policy, most Europeans came to see it as an association of radicals and agitators that threatened colonial peace and order. The advisor for native affairs was mocked in the colonial press as a contemporary Don Quixote, searching for an imaginary "Ethical Dulcinea." Reactionary journalists blamed Hazeu for indoctrinating successive governor generals with dangerous ethical ideals. His name became a synonym for weakness in dealing with the colonized, and in one of the more personal attacks, a conservative newspaper called him a moron, "a being stripped of all strength; a weak, hesitant, old-hag; a sentimental boy, too dull to exercise any authority."[77] These assaults had their desired effect. Hazeu lost the governor general's trust and subsequently announced his repatriation to the Netherlands to be a professor. With his departure in March 1920, the reactionaries crowed victory while indigenous leaders mourned the loss of a powerful ally. His retreat also signified a devaluation of the Office of Native Affairs, as reactionary forces' influence on colonial policy increased at Hazeu's successors' expense. The vernacular press no longer depicted the Office of Native Affairs as an ally, but rather as an instrument of the authorities to spy on and control indigenous society.[78]

With Hazeu out of the way, the reactionary call to return to a more traditional form of colonial power grew louder. Illustrative of this change was Van der Jagt's promotion to resident in 1922, as opposed to being reproached for his attitude and comments in the People's Council, as Hazeu had suggested. That same year, J. W. Meijer Ranneft—Van der Jagt's successor in the People's Council—argued in an essay intended for civil servants that, simply put, the Ethical Policy had failed. Using the recent institution of mobile police units to make his point, Meijer Ranneft wrote, "A democratic instrument of power, such as a modern police force, costs several millions more than the old Asian instrument of power: hormat."[79] To ensure colonial stability and end the reliance on coercion, he therefore suggested restoring the prestige of the European and indigenous civil services to their nineteenth-century glory. Their aristocratic aura would serve as a counterweight to the nationalist movement.[80]

This reactionary turn in colonial politics instilled in Indonesian intellectuals a great sense of distrust and disappointment. From the outset, the vernacular press criticized Van der Jagt's public speeches, and journalists wondered how many European officials agreed with him.[81] One author noted that even the Europeans who conversed with educated Indonesians in Dutch always addressed them with the informal pronoun *jij* and expected the formal pronoun *U* in return.[82] A deep suspicion toward the reactionary movement was clearly reflected

FIGURE 4. Advertisement for a Sundanese language course suggests that by learning
to speak Sundanese—a hierarchical language, like Javanese—European planters can
transform insolent subjects into obedient ones who show them customary deference.
Source: *Algemeen Landbouwweekblad voor Nederlandsch-Indië*, April 22, 1921.

in numerous newspaper articles suggesting that the government had revoked the
1913 hormat circular and required that the colonized crouch again. A contributor to the *Sinar Hindia* even went so far as to compare revoking the circular
to being forced to lick old and stinking saliva from the ground. While other
reactions were less unsavory, they all agreed that the general populace could not,
and would not, return to old-fashioned feudal customs.[83]

For all its nostalgic musings, the reactionary turn did not result in a return to
the nineteenth-century hegemonic script. The hormat circular was far too influential, instilling a growing number of Indonesians with the self-worth, language,
and actions to irreparably disturb the colonial performance. This is an important
but often overlooked aspect of the "age in motion," brought on by Soemarsono
and others like him who demanded equality. As the vernacular press rightly

observed, reestablishing such traditions was an impossibility that would require physical coercion and destabilize colonial society completely. Rather than take that route, the reactionaries sought to halt the modernization of indigenous society—to slow down changes that could result in challenges to their supremacy. Even so, the Javanese nationalist movement continued to push for modernization and emancipation in the final years of the colonial era.

Broad Emancipation and Assertive Advocacy

In November 1926, members of the Communist Party (Partai Kommunis Indonesia, PKI) revolted in the streets of Batavia and in the Banten residency. However, due to internal discord, poor planning, and government intelligence, the intended overthrow of the colonial government rapidly descended into failure. A separate revolt in January 1927 in Minangkabau (western Sumatra) similarly turned into a fiasco. Nonetheless, the intent behind the revolts shocked colonial authorities, which resulted in a far more repressive colonial regime. Rebels were arrested, imprisoned, executed, or placed in internment camps in New Guinea. Press censorship increased, as did political oppression. As historians have pointed out, this marked the definitive end of the Ethical Policy era in colonial Indonesia. The outbreak of open violence and the government's reliance on its coercive apparatus raised the question of whether there could have been a way to restore colonial peace and order before the eruption of such conflict.[84] The authorities found it hard to reconcile their own notion of the colonized as docile and submissive with these events and eagerly blamed outside interference by foreigners, especially China, for the outbreak.[85] But it also brought back to the fore the question of the outward appearance of colonial authority. In response to the communist revolts, both European conservatives and Indonesian moderates lobbied to fortify the civil services by either restoring traditional forms of deference or completely disavowing them.

In the minds of many Europeans, the communist uprisings confirmed what the conservative colonial press had propagated for years: that the abolition of traditional forms of deference and status symbols would inevitably result in a cycle of anticolonial insurrections and repressive countermeasures.[86] Karel Wybrands, one of the colony's most conservative newspaper editors, rhetorically questioned if "the communist revolts and radical agitation could have reached such heights if deference etiquette had not been relaxed."[87] The obvious answer, according to Wybrands, was no. The colonial press identified the hormat circular of 1913 as one of the primary causes of the revolts with a curious mix of apprehension and vindication. There was great concern about the largest insurgence since the Java War a century earlier, but to conservatives, these events exposed the Ethical Policy's shortcomings more than anything else. According to Samuel Kalff, a retired newspaper editor, it was now evident that "an Eastern people, which still has great respect for outward appearance, needs to be governed according to Eastern traditions."[88] Promoting this perspective, the conservative press argued that reintroducing traditional deference etiquette and other symbols of power would strengthen the colonial civil services, restore colonial peace and order, and pacify the communist and nationalist movements. They further justified this reactionary proposal with the culturally relativist claim that the government should not intervene in local customs but rather leave it to Indonesians themselves to change over time. But unsurprisingly, the colonized had no desire to turn back the clock.[89]

Moderate Indonesians' response to the communist uprisings was precisely the opposite of the reactionary proposal. Their perspective was most pointedly articulated by Achmad Djajadiningrat, the progressive bupati of Batavia. In meetings of the People's Council in June and July 1927, Djajadiningrat suggested that communism might be contained by increasing the indigenous civil service's influence on the population. This, he reasoned, could not be achieved by reintroducing outdated deference rituals, as the "glory of the payung belongs to the past," but by strongly emphasizing merit and character.[90] According to Djajadiningrat, this was the only way to entice educated Indonesians into a civil service career without the fear of having to submit to humiliating displays of deference. Subsequently, the overall quality of the civil service would improve, as would its social standing.[91] Other Indonesian representatives on the People's Council echoed Djajadiningrat's analyses but added that the idea would require substantial changes to the civil service. Traditional deference forms were still prevalent in both branches, but especially among indigenous administrators. Representative Soeroso shared his amazement that officials, "in a time of elegant footwear and Zeiss-glasses... still dare to require such deference."[92] His colleague Soejono, a progressive bupati from Pasuruan, concurred and publicly called for a new hormat circular that applied to the indigenous civil service explicitly, rather than to European officials alone.[93]

In his 1929 opening address to the People's Council, Governor General De Graeff finally addressed the intensifying debate on the outward appearance of colonial authority. In front of his assembled advisory council, he praised the European and indigenous branches of the colonial civil service as pillars of colonial rule. However, he impressed on his audience that the pillars' stability did not depend on their rigidity but on their flexibility to adapt to changing circumstances. He implied that the prestige of colonial officials—and by extension the authority of the government—could not depend on "artificially preserved traditions and etiquette" but on the intrinsic quality of their work and character. Referencing Djajadiningrat's observation that educated young Indonesians preferred careers outside the civil service, De Graeff warned that clinging to outdated deference etiquette alienated the colonized from the colonial authorities. With a sense of urgency, he asserted, "Obsolete hormat traditions can no longer be retained," and expected colonial officials to display proper manners and civilized behavior in accordance with the times.[94] To ensure that his message came across, De Graeff deliberately opted for a public announcement in the People's Council rather than another circular. And although the governor general specifically directed his words toward those European civil servants who still ignored the hormat circulars of the previous decades, he strongly implied that their meaning extended to indigenous civil service culture and interactions between officials and colonial subjects more broadly.[95]

Unsurprisingly, the European colonial press and officialdom were highly critical of the so-called hormat passage in De Graeff's annual address. Just as in 1913, they particularly resented the public nature of the governor general's stern comments, which they feared further undermined European standing in colonial society.[96] B. J. Suermondt, the representative for the Association for European Civil Servants, articulated these sentiments in the People's Council. Recalling the prohibition of the ceremonial payung in 1904, Suermondt claimed that the "hormat passage" resulted in a loss of prestige that could only be compensated with higher police expenditures.[97] Regarding the demand that officials display "civilized behavior," he wondered aloud what civilization the governor general had in mind. In a twist of cultural relativism, Suermondt reminded the council that colonial Indonesia was home to various civilizations—Western, Chinese, Javanese, and more—and argued that none should be elevated over another. Suermondt also repeated a frequent claim made in the colonial press: that the majority of Indonesians, especially those in rural areas, did not find it humiliating to show deference to their superiors by squatting, crouching, or presenting a sembah. It was this silent majority that needed the government's protection from the damaging whims of culturally estranged, Western-educated intellectuals.[98] In other words, a change in deference traditions should stem from within indigenous society, not be imposed by the colonial government.

Among Indonesian representatives on the People's Council, as well as in the vernacular press, there was widespread appreciation for De Graeff's "hormat passage."[99] Representative Wiranatakoesoema expressed "profound gratitude" for the governor general's words, while Soejono described them as "coming straight from his own heart." In addition, Dwidjosewojo praised the passage for its "broad social significance."[100] Interestingly, it was this topic that guided the ensuing debate, as discussants considered the speech's impact on the culture within the indigenous civil service and on interactions between people in positions of power and commoners in general. European civil servants' alleged (mis)behavior was conspicuously absent—an omission that reflected a transformative moment in the ongoing discussion about the outward appearance of authority. The conversation was no longer merely about demanding equality within colonial society, but about establishing a clearly defined, modern national cultural identity. For instance, Soejono rhetorically wondered if the Menadonese, Ambonese, or Sumatrans were impolite for not conforming to Javanese deference etiquette and dress. Clearly they were not, as each community had its own deference and sartorial traditions. However, according to Soejono and his peers, the challenge would be to rewrite the script guiding social interactions in such a way that worked for *all* Indonesians. They would need to apply this sort of agreeable modification to the indigenous civil service, as well.[101]

During the deliberations in the People's Council, several speakers brought up Bupati Nitinegoro of Probolinggo (east Java). Nitinegoro had recently attempted to modernize the indigenous civil service in his regency by issuing a local hormat circular. This initiative was applauded as an example of self-improvement that could be emulated elsewhere. Bupati Nitinegoro's actions were informed by concern about the civil service's dwindling popularity among young Indonesians, whom he believed were essential to proper governance in his regency. He believed that civil servants too often masked their own ineptitude by demanding servile deference—a mandate that deterred talented youth—and implied that a competent civil servant was one who did not rely on excessive deference. Nitinegoro looked to Turkey and Egypt for inspiration, arguing that while Java remained backward, these two countries had successfully shed the outdated cultural traditions that had previously held them back. His own hormat circular, issued in December 1928, stipulated that civil servants were not allowed to squat or crouch. In addition, he no longer expected them to present the sembah but permitted anyone who was uncomfortable with the change to offer it once on arriving and once on departing a meeting. With regards to clothing, the bupati allowed his civil servants to wear European dress (defined as a suit and shoes) but always in combination with a Javanese headscarf (*ikat kepala*). As these terms demonstrate, Nitinegoro sought to adapt Javanese traditions to the modern era.[102]

Bupati Nitinegoro's hormat circular provided an inspiring blueprint for those interested in reforming the indigenous civil service. In nearby Surabaya (only sixty miles from Probolinggo), the local branch of the Persatoean Prijaji Bestuur Boemipoetera (PPBB; Association of Indigenous Civil Servants) formed a special committee tasked with formulating hormat policy. In June 1929, the committee presented its recommendations, which reflected those in Nitinegoro's circular. The committee proposed that civil servants converse in Dutch if possible, or alternatively, in Malay; always wear European clothes and footwear (and, if needed, glasses) in combination with a Javanese headscarf during meetings; and no longer sembah-jongkok.[103] The Surabaya branch presented their proposal at the national PPBB meeting in Surakarta in August 1930, where it was embraced.[104] The PPBB also recommended government punishment for civil servants who did not conform to these regulations, but as De Graeff had made clear in his speech, the indigenous civil service was free to decide how to shape interactions within its own ranks.[105] The PPBB campaign's success was reflected in the organization's growing membership: about half of the bupati in Java had joined by 1932 and accepted the hormat conditions as decided by the association.[106]

However, not all Indonesians were impressed by the massive changes in indigenous civil service culture and by extension, indigenous society. For progressive social and political activists, these transformations were too little and too late. For instance, Soetomo, a doctor and cofounder of both Boedi Oetomo and the Indonesische Studieclub (a study club for Western-educated Indonesian intellectuals) was highly critical of Bupati Nitinegoro's circular. In the Indonesische Studieclub's periodical, he described Nitinegoro as out of touch with both reality and the times. He was offended by the language used in the document, such as the stipulation that it applied to visitors to the bupati's palace. As Soetomo was quick to point out, this terminology insinuated that the bupati considered himself to be a great lord or king, rather than a regional administrative servant. Moreover, he reminded his readers that the bupati did not write anything original; Kartini, the early voice of women's emancipation, had proposed similar changes decades earlier, as did the Sarekat Islam, while Prince Mangkunegoro IV, ruler of one of Java's principalities, prohibited sembah-jongkok in his palace in 1904. Soetomo also argued that Nitinegoro's proposal was actually less progressive than it appeared, as it still expected civil servants to wear a traditional headscarf. If the governor general did not require his indigenous servants to wear a headscarf, he reasoned, why should a bupati? In Soetomo's opinion, Nitinegoro deserved ridicule rather than praise and insisted that the priyayi's self-congratulatory attitude would only create more resentment and anger among the people.[107]

As Soetomo's fierce criticism demonstrates, opinions about what constituted proper deference were not limited to civil service circles; it was a topic with broad social, cultural, and political appeal. For the many young educated professionals in Indonesia's urban centers, this was a debate about self-respect and cultural identity. They considered themselves to be participants in the modern world—a status increasingly reflected in their preferred manners, language, dress, and consumption patterns. The continued practice of sembah-jongkok was at odds with this self-image, as it made them appear backward and inferior to outsiders, like the Dutch and Chinese. To them, these customs were tools of oppression that kept the colonized weak and hindered the development of a truly national identity. Rather than clinging to outdated traditions, many young Indonesians proposed disregarding them entirely in order to forge a new, more egalitarian national identity. Their Islamic faith provided a useful rationale to achieve this. In discussions, sembah-jongkok was increasingly depicted as a legacy from the Hindu Javanese period that was simply incompatible with Islamic principles of equality—the foundation behind the community of all-believers (*ummah*). Muslims were only allowed to crouch and worship during their prayers to Allah.[108]

The public discussion of appropriate social deference reached its peak in 1931 when the bupati of Lamongan (eastern Java) reprimanded teachers in his district for refusing to perform and instruct sembah-jongkok at local schools. Following the example of the civil servants united in the PPBB, many other young professionals working in the public sector demanded to be treated with respect, as equals. Teachers were one of the largest professional groups to do so. At school, they were still expected to crouch and pay homage to social superiors, such as principals, school inspectors, and civil servants. Increasingly, teachers considered these traditions to be demeaning obstacles to progress. In the periodical published by the Perserikatan Goeroe Hindia Belanda (Association of Teachers in the Netherlands Indies), numerous articles called for an end to sembah-jongkok to bolster teachers' self-confidence.[109] Perhaps these publications inspired the young teachers in Lamongan when they spoke truth to power and announced that they would no longer humiliate themselves at work. The local bupati was incensed and immediately issued a circular ordering the teachers not only to show traditional deference themselves but also to instruct their students in these traditions, as these were essential skills for pursuing a career.

When the vernacular press got wind of these events, this local incident suddenly became a national topic of discussion.[110] Once again, journalists played a vital role in drawing readers' attention—primarily educated Indonesians— to the misconduct of people in positions of power, with the ultimate goal of bringing about societal change. For instance, under the headline, "Disrespect-ful?" (*Koerang Adjar*), the Batavian newspaper *Bintang Timoer* published and discussed the bupati's circular. Just as in 1913 with the infamous hormat circular, publishing an internal government document allowed readers to judge for themselves whether the teachers in Lamongan were insolent or if the bupati was arrogantly craving deference. Of course, the editors offered their own interpretation, commenting that the circular could not be dated August 7, 1931, as its contents suggested that it was composed in the early 1800s.[111]

Interestingly, the fiercest criticism and most original attempt to mobilize public opinion originated in Java's cultural heartland: Yogyakarta. Living up to its name, the Malay-language newspaper *Aksi* (Action), partnered with Javanese-language newspaper *Sedio-Tomo* to organize a public referendum on Javanese deference forms. Both newspapers published a ballot with which readers could vote on whether they agreed or disagreed with the abolition of sembah-jongkok. The editors of *Aksi* urged readers to let their voices be heard, as silence implied agreement with the current situation. Referencing the poll, the editors of *Aksi* echoed *Bintang Timoer*, writing that their readers clearly indicated the time had come to break with the "frog system" (*kodok-systeem*)—a popular idiom for the crouching that characterized Javanese deference traditions—once and for all.[112]

In central Java, this position was still controversial and invited a rebuke from Javanese nationalists. *Darmo Kondo*, a Javanese-language newspaper in Surakarta, engaged in a polemic exchange with *Aksi* over the place of Javanese deference in the modern era.[113] The editors of *Darmo Kondo* argued that social change could not be forced or imposed from above; rather, change would come gradually once society was ready to embrace the new and let go of the old. For instance, while the editors acknowledged that jongkok had fallen out of favor, they believed that the sembah was still a powerful and essentially Javanese gesture. Using the sembah in social interactions was not a sign of submission or cowardice but a culturally relevant Javanese convention. The editors' main argument was that becoming modern did not require mimicking Europeans in every way. They asserted that all people use hand gestures as signs of deference: Europeans salute each other, while the Chinese use the fist-and-palm salute. How, they asked rhetorically, are these different from the sembah? To drive this argument home, the editors wondered if the Javanese should then also adopt the Dutch custom of kissing in public. The answer was obvious to readers—of course not; such acts of public affection were taboo. Other publications also defended Javanese traditions. Similar arguments could be found in *Djawa*, the periodical for

FIGURE 5. Opinion ballot on "sembah djongkok." The editors of the newspaper *Aksi* ask their readers to indicate on this polling ballot whether they agree (*moefakat*) or disagree (*tidak moefakat*) with the statement that traditional deference (sembah and jongkok) is outdated. Source: *Aksi*, October 13, 1931.

the Djawa Institute in Yogyakarta. For a contest about how to reform Javanese etiquette, the winning articles likewise preached an evolutionary perspective. Interestingly, these articles suggested that deference traditions only be performed for or in the presence of Javanese, but no longer for Europeans or anyone else. This, the authors claimed, would make these customs less humiliating while maintaining a strong Javanese identity. But by this time, such ideas had become untenable among modern Indonesians.[114]

In a series of articles, *Aksi*'s editors refuted *Darmo Kondo*'s reasoning and advocated for revolutionary rather than evolutionary change.[115] They recalled that two years earlier, several Indonesian journalists, including the editor of *Darmo Kondo*, were forced to crouch, sit on the floor, and present the sembah during celebrations at the Surakarta *kraton* (palace) while their European and Chinese colleagues sat comfortably in chairs.[116] They effectively employed this example to show that Javanese etiquette made Indonesians look like submissive and weak "frogs" to outsiders. As the example demonstrated, the *sembah* differed from the European salute and the Chinese fist-and-palm salute in that it emphasized social difference. According to *Aksi*, presenting the sembah to someone of higher rank immediately made the presenter feel inferior and small. To honor God or one's parents, the editors reasoned, the sembah was a proper Javanese gesture, but it was no longer appropriate in a multicultural colonial society of Europeans, Chinese, and a plethora of Indonesian officials all demanding it as a right. In this moment, the sembah and other Javanese deference traditions had become obstacles to progress and self-respect, without which the Indonesian nationalist cause was doomed to fail. The editors understood that many Javanese considered their culture to be an essential part of their identity. However, they explained that just as wars were now fought with revolvers instead of daggers, outdated deference traditions needed to join ceremonial daggers (*kris*) in museums.[117]

"No Time to Waste, Change Your *Kain* for Trousers!"

By drawing attention to the myriad ways through which colonial authority was communicated and contested, the remarkable history of the hormat circular of 1913 captures the significance of the colonial performance of power. The circular sought to align the enactment colonial power with the new Ethical Policy's hegemonic script. Conservative forces in colonial society—primarily colonial officials but also entrepreneurs, journalists, and others—resisted the transition away from the nineteenth-century Javanization of authority, which they argued would necessitate greater reliance on the coercive apparatus of the state. In contrast, supporters of the Ethical Policy, like Hazeu, believed that failure to implement the circular would further alienate and agitate a new generation among the colonized and inevitably result in escalating social tensions. However, the hormat circular's timing and success can only be explained by the disturbance of the colonial performance by Soemarsono and others like him. Their refusal to sit on the ground, offer humiliating customary deference, observe the Javanese language hierarchy, and conform to ethnic dress codes exemplified how the colonized could contest and negotiate the hegemonic script. This new generation of educated, professional, multilingual, and globally conscious colonial subjects changed their attitude to demand respect and to be treated as equals in the colonial encounter. The circular's message—acknowledging that government officials were fallible, recognizing that deference traditions were humiliating, and a pledge to rectify that—emboldened the national awakening, as reflected at Sarekat Islam rallies and its extensive discussion in the vernacular press. In fact, the prompt proliferation of everyday discursive acts around 1913—so easy to overlook in favor of later, more direct political resistance—constituted a broad social transformation and change in mentality from which open politicization would ultimately emerge.

The intensity of the debate over social etiquette and deference only subsided during the last years of Dutch colonial rule. The vernacular press remained a critical social observer, as it continued to expose abuses committed by European and indigenous civil servants, but the frequency at which these reports were published decreased significantly.[118] On the one hand, this decline was due to the more explicitly political nature of public discourse; on the other, it indicated that many traditional social etiquette and deference forms had retreated from public life. To observers, it was clear that modern Indonesians no longer crouched for anybody—European or indigenous—but showed and demanded respect in more modern ways. This was an instrumental development in the construction of an Indonesian national identity. Discussions in the People's Council followed a similar pattern. After the fierce debates in the late 1920s and early 1930s, representatives increasingly used the past tense when bringing up the issue of hormat in their deliberations. In 1936, Representative Soetardjo even claimed that the "jongkok system" was all but eradicated among civil servants, and to a large extent was no longer the norm in interactions with commoners. One of the most important reasons for this rapid change, according to Soetardjo, was the introduction of a new modern costume for civil servants, a European suit, which made the practice of sembah-jongkok much more difficult.[119] Tellingly, a few years earlier the editors of *Aksi* advised their readers a tactic that Soemarsono had already used in 1913: "No time to waste, change your *kain* for trousers!"[120] As the next chapter demonstrates, a change of clothes was indeed a powerful way to challenge colonial hierarchies.

CHAPTER 4

Contesting Sartorial Hierarchies

From Ethnic Stereotypes to National Dress

I N NOVEMBER 1913, Raden Moehamad Enoch, a junior engineer at the Department of Public Works, patiently waited in line to purchase a second-class train ticket at the Bandung railway station. Dressed in a European suit, Enoch exemplified his generation of young Javanese who enjoyed a Western education, were fluent in Dutch, and had roots in the lower aristocracy but worked in nontraditional professions. When it was his turn, Enoch approached the window and, in Dutch, kindly requested a train ticket to Madiun, his hometown. The European ticket officer, clearly annoyed, replied to Enoch in Malay and told him to wait. When he then immediately accepted a European patron at his window, Enoch stepped up to another officer at the counter for third-class tickets, only to be denied service once more. On Enoch's inquiry as to why he was not served at either window, the ticket officer yelled at him—this time in Dutch—and told him unmistakably to either shut up or suffer the consequences. Enoch refused to back down, which provoked the ticket officer into bellowing: "You are a native, and thus need to buy your ticket at the window for natives." Instead, the proud Enoch demanded to speak to the station chief. When the chief arrived, he was forced to acknowledge Enoch's right to purchase his ticket at any window he pleased—a right that was previously limited to Europeans.[1]

On the train to Madiun, Enoch described the episode in a letter to Advisor for Native Affairs G. A. J. Hazeu. From their correspondence, it is evident that Enoch was particularly bothered by the fact that although he wore European attire and spoke Dutch, the ticket officers still refused to treat him as an equal. He emphasized this point when recalling the moment the ticket officer scolded him for his impudence, writing with palpable astonishment and disbelief, "[But] I was dressed in European style."[2] While Enoch believed that he could breach the divide between colonizer and colonized by dressing "up," the European ticket

officers interpreted his actions as a transgression of the colonial order. However, their attempt to humiliate and re-educate Enoch backfired; he was well
aware of his rights and unwilling to relinquish them. As a result of the Ethical
Policy's attempt to modernize the colonial relationship, recent government circulars explicitly allowed him to wear European attire, converse in Dutch, and
be treated with respect. Not only was Enoch ultimately permitted to purchase a
second-class train ticket, his correspondence with the advisor for native affairs
also resulted in a reprimand for the European personnel of the Bandung railway
station and an official apology from the head inspector of the Netherlands Indies
State Railways.

The incident at the Bandung railway station constituted a considerable challenge to the predominant ethnic sartorial hierarchy of the nineteenth century.
Before 1900, strict sartorial regulations were a significant component of Dutch
attempts to legitimize their colonial authority by appropriating local etiquette.
Through the Javanization of colonial power, the Dutch essentialized indigenous
culture, in effect codifying ethnic stereotypes in laws and decrees. Police regulations stipulated that everyone in the colony dress according to their ethnicity
or position. As overseers of these regulations, the colonizers thus demanded the
right to determine what constituted proper Javanese, Sundanese, Madurese,
Malay, Arab, and Chinese costume. These ethnic sartorial regulations were relaxed and eventually abolished as part of the Ethical Policy; a modern colonial
state could not limit the clothing choices of its population. But although this led
many Javanese to cautiously experiment with composite dress by adding European elements, it did not effectively end the ethnic sartorial hierarchy.

Moehamad Enoch's experience in November 1913 was not an isolated incident. In late 1913 and early 1914, the colonial and vernacular press published
numerous accounts of young Javanese men discarding their sarong and *kebaya*
for trousers, shirts, jackets, and ties. The timing of what effectively constituted
a sartorial revolution was certainly no coincidence. It followed in the wake of
the hormat circular of August 1913, which prohibited European officials from
demanding traditional forms of deference from the colonized. The vernacular
press and Sarekat Islam rallies not only informed the public about the circular but also encouraged them to force European compliance, emphasizing that
dressing "up" in European style was an important way to signal a refusal to participate in humiliating deference rituals. Clothing thus became an important
site of the contestation of colonial hegemony. By changing their appearance,
Javanese demanded to be treated with respect and to be considered civilized
and modern.

The widespread sartorial transformation in colonial society was an expression of larger social and intellectual changes that characterize a significant turning point in Indonesian history, yet this crucial connection has not been established in the elaborate scholarship on dress in colonial Indonesia.[3] This sartorial shift was a profoundly visible political statement that took many by surprise, making dress and the social body increasingly contested sites in the colonial relationship. As anthropologist Emma Tarlo has argued, the key to unpacking these controversial moments is to focus on the question of "what to wear rather than a description of what is worn."[4] In this formulation, the human body is a social rather than a physical entity around which clothing serves as a marker of various identities.[5] When the Javanese embraced European attire, Dutch colonizers were forced to change their appearance accordingly, as they could not continue to don seemingly indigenous dress that was widely discarded by the Javanese themselves, even in the semiprivate sphere. To reassert their dominance in colonial society, the Dutch increased their own sense of sartorial correctness by dressing "up" in the latest European fashions, while at the same time ridiculing identical Javanese attempts to appear modern. Even so, for the colonized, these experiences were empowering and inspired contemplation of what it meant to be modern and how clothes reflected one's ethnic or national identity. Similarly, Europeans were challenged to rethink their own identity in the colonial world. Crucially, these experiments with dress were highly gendered, raising questions about how clothing reflected and, in some cases, challenged gender roles in society. This sartorial hegemonic struggle was thus a significant factor in the emergence of new ethnic, national, and gender identities in colonial Indonesia.

Colonial Hegemony and the Creation of Ethnic Stereotypes

In nineteenth-century Dutch colonial Java, dress was a crucial social and racial marker that distinguished between colonizers and colonized. Due to a long history of racial mixing among Europeans and Javanese, as well as other groups in Java such as Chinese and Arabs, skin color alone did not set people apart. Many Eurasians appeared racially Javanese but held European status, and vice versa. This posed significant challenges, as nineteenth-century colonial society was structured around a plural administrative and legal system. Dutch colonial law sorted the population into "Europeans," "Natives," and "Foreign Orientals" (mostly Chinese), and the conflation of race and legal status had far-reaching consequences. Europeans, Natives, and Foreign Orientals were governed by different civil service branches, prosecuted in different courts, and subject to different legal statutes that regulated work, travel, and more. It was therefore essential that the authorities be able to easily discern to which legal or racial group an individual belonged. Consequently, strict regulations required everyone in the colony to dress according to his or her ethnicity.[6]

The institution of dress regulations coincided with the formation of the Dutch colonial state in the nineteenth century. At first, these regulations were issued locally, by city or district, but in 1872 they were all superseded by police regulations that applied to the entire colony. These included stipulations regarding dress for Europeans and natives, specifying that "whoever appears in public, disguised in a different dress than the one corresponding with one's ethnicity or position, with the exception of masked or costumed-parades" would be punished "with a fine between sixteen and twenty-five guilders."[7] For the colonized, this was an especially exorbitant penalty. Moreover, these regulations empowered the colonizer to categorize colonial subjects, assign them fixed ethnic costumes, and effectively define their cultural identities.[8] This included specifying dress, language, traditions, and customs for Javanese, Sundanese, Malay, Madurese, Chinese, and Arabs, as well as Europeans. Considering the deep histories of cultural and racial exchange in the region, this was an overtly ambitious if not outright impossible task. The assumption that only the Dutch could make colonial society comprehensible testified to the arrogance of the colonial mindset and indicated a profound belief in the necessity of ethnic categorization for colonial rule.

The institution of this ethnic sartorial hierarchy was an indispensable part of the nineteenth-century Javanization of colonial authority. In the multiracial and culturally hybrid colonial world, dress was a visual reflection of a person's rank, position, gender, ethnicity, and legal status—all of which determined social and interpersonal etiquette. In the everyday experience of colonialism, external appearance at a glance made social interactions and relations legible. Who was required to show deference to whom? What honorifics were appropriate? And in what language(s) would the conversation be conducted? Without dress as a visual marker, the proper etiquette for social interactions would have been impossible to ascertain. It is therefore no coincidence that dress regulations coincided with the Javanization of colonial authority—the Dutch appropriation and codification of Javanese cultural traditions. Prior to the 1872 police regulations, the colonial authorities clearly circumscribed the attire of the bupati and priyayi in specific guidelines issued in 1820 and 1824, respectively.[9] Together these regulations ensured that colonial hierarchies could be read instantly and reinforced through the Javanized performance of colonial power.

The history of the sarong, a traditional wraparound skirt, and kebaya, a short or long-sleeved blouse closed in the front with pins or brooches, illustrates the complexity of assigning fixed sartorial identities. Traditionally, men and women in Java wore a variety of long cloths around their lower body, precursors of the sarong. Whereas men went bare-chested, women who could afford it wore a breast wrap (*kemban*). Most likely under the influence of Hindu-Javanese court culture (eight to fifteenth centuries), aristocratic women wore a sheer fabric blouse over their kemban. Due to the spread of Islam from the thirteenth century onward, this sheer garment was slowly transformed into a more concealing blouse, the kebaya, which eventually became common among the Javanese. Around the same time, Javanese men began to wear long-sleeved shirts to cover their torsos as well as a form of headdress, varying from a headscarf to a cap. The sarong likewise evolved with changing circumstances. In the seventeenth century, Eurasian and European women adopted both sarong and kebaya and elaborated on their design. In the nineteenth century, Eurasians and Chinese disrupted the monopoly on batik production in Java and developed batik stamps (*batik cap*) as opposed to hand-drawn patterns (*batik tulis*). Production soared and made the batik sarong available to those outside the traditional elite, such as Europeans, Chinese, and lower-class Javanese. The importation of imitation batik from the Dutch textile industry further accelerated the process. Thus, although the sarong and kebaya became increasingly associated with local ethnic identities, their history reveals diverse origins and a development that was never static.[10]

The Dutch colonizer's position in this sartorial hierarchy was ambiguous in the nineteenth century. European men and women wore European dress in the public sphere as an indication of their prestige and privilege but changed into clothing akin to Javanese dress in the private sphere.[11] Women wore a batik sarong and white kebaya. Men wore trousers made from batik, which they found less feminine than the sarong, in combination with a white collarless shirt. Although this seems counterintuitive to the sartorial hierarchy's objective, European dress in the private sphere was still clearly recognizable as that of the colonizer. The Dutch appropriated the batik, a familiar indigenous marker of status, in the wake of the Java War, thus breaking its exclusive connection with the Javanese aristocracy. However, they did not simply adopt Javanese batik styles, but under the entrepreneurial initiative of Eurasian women, designed their own patterns known as *batik Belanda* (Dutch batik). Like their embrace of the *payung* and traditional Javanese forms of deference, the Dutch used batik as a status symbol to legitimize their colonial authority.[12]

In addition to batik cloth, European colonial attire included another visual marker of colonial power. Both in the public and private spheres, Europeans wore white. Their white shirts and kebaya in the private sphere as well as the high-collared white colonial suit (*jas tutup*) that men wore in public (also known as a tropical suit) were of course practical in the hot and humid climate of Java. But the Dutch display of spotless white garments was also an effective sign of status, as it communicated that the wearer did not perform manual labor and could afford the expensive acquisition and maintenance of white clothes. More-over, that white had strong connotations of Christian purity and sacrifice—as opposed to in Java, where it was traditionally associated with death and mourn-ing—only aided in the colonizer's appropriation of the color. Toward the end of the nineteenth century, an increased number of *hajjis* (Muslims who had undertaken the Hajj pilgrimage to Mecca) also donned white garb but by this time white clothing had already become, in the words of the editor of Batavia's conservative colonial newspaper, the protective armor of colonial authority and prestige.[13] In this way, the Dutch used clothing to maintain and visually express their distinction from and superiority to their indigenous subjects.[14]

The Ethical Policy and the Overhaul of the Sartorial Hierarchy

In the last decades of the nineteenth century, several groups in colonial soci-ety gradually began to push back against the ethnic sartorial hierarchy. In large part this was due to Java's economic opening in the 1870s and the island's en-suing interconnectedness with the wider world. As people, products, and ideas moved more freely, maintaining fixed cultural traditions and stereotypes proved increasingly difficult. For instance, the opening of the Suez Canal in 1869 and the introduction of steamships enabled the exponential growth of Hajj travel to Mecca from the Indonesian archipelago.[15] On their return to colonial Java, pilgrims wanted a visual indicator of their newly acquired status as *hajji*. For some, this consisted of a white *jubah* (an Arab robe), while others opted for a white European jacket over their sarong, and almost all adopted the Arab tur-ban.[16] Around the same time, members of the small Arab Hadrami community living in colonial Indonesia used the same transportation networks to study in Ottoman Turkey. On completion of their studies, they returned to Java wear-ing modern Turkish attire consisting of a European suit and fez, instead of a turban.[17] The proliferation of *hajjis* and Arab students created a conundrum for colonial authorities: should and could colonial subjects be permitted to change their ethnic attire and identities?

This question was further complicated by Japan's rise as an imperial power and the simultaneous decline of the Qing dynasty in China, which impacted sartorial developments throughout Asia. Japan embraced Western appearance to symbolize the country's rapid modernization and industrialization following the Meiji Restoration in 1868, projecting Japanese power by replacing traditional Samurai clothing and hairstyles, like the topknot (*chonmage*), with Western suits, uniforms, and haircuts.[18] This led many to speculate about whether Japanese modernization was related to their change of dress. This question became particularly pressing following China's humiliating defeat in the Sino-Japanese War of 1894–1895. Chinese reformers contrasted the modern appearance of the Japanese with their own traditional look, dominated by the queue (pigtail), which was increasingly associated with the oppressive Qing dynasty and Chinese backwardness. Beginning in the 1890s, Chinese revolutionists cut their queue as a form of protest.[19] These tensions affected colonial Indonesia, especially following the Dutch decision in 1899 to grant European legal status to Japanese in the colony, an acknowledgement of Japan's new international prestige. This ruling energized the large Chinese diaspora in Java who, feeling slighted, demanded the same privileges as the much smaller Japanese community. They expressed their push for equality by forming associations, schools, newspapers, and economic cooperatives but perhaps most strikingly by embracing Western dress and cutting their queues.[20]

These sartorial developments among the Japanese and Chinese provided the indigenous people of colonial Indonesia with a model to emulate. Associating European dress with modernity, progress, and respect, many Javanese began to adopt composite fashion, consisting of both local and European clothing.[21] For instance, one observer remarked that women were replacing earrings made of rolled coconut leaves and pineapple fiber pins with silver, nickel, and tin alternatives to secure their kebaya. Paradoxically, these sartorial experiments were enabled by Western imports. Following the economic opening of the colony, European imitation batik, colorful linen, cotton, and silk as well as leather belts, chainwatches, jewelry, and other consumer products found their way into Java.[22] The introduction of innovative technology, like sewing machines in the 1880s, allowed local tailors to create modern Western attire from imported cloth.[23] By the turn of the century, the streets of Batavia offered a diverse array of fashion choices among indigenous people, from those donning any combination of jackets, trousers, tropical helmets, shoes, and boots to those who went barefoot in a simple sarong and open shirt.[24] Yet very few Javanese dressed entirely in European attire to the extent that they became indistinguishable from Eurasians.

This was the authorities' foremost concern, as skin color was not a reliable indicator of ethnic and legal status. Even so, the proliferation of composite dress—even minimal changes like natives wearing shoes—created much anxiety in the colonial press and among Dutch officials, which was reflected in the upsurge of fines issued for sartorial transgressions.[25]

In formulating a more formal and extensive response to these turn-of-the-century sartorial challenges, the colonial government relied on the insights of Christiaan Snouck Hurgronje. As a specialist in Islamic and Oriental studies and the colony's first advisor for native affairs, he played an important role in the practical implementation of the Ethical Policy. A central tenet in Snouck Hurgronje's numerous reflections on the issue of dress from 1890 and 1905 was his belief that appearance, like European fashion, was always in flux. He therefore argued that it was "unfathomable, that a civilized government would force Arabs to wear a turban, Chinese a pigtail, and natives a sarong over their trousers, when these subjects have rejected these elements of their appearance themselves."[26] Snouck Hurgronje considered the universal adoption of Western attire to reflect the growing interconnectedness of the age. Only those who loved the picturesque, were obsessed with their own prestige, and did not believe that the colonized could ever be equal to Europeans, could support maintaining these artificial ethnic stereotypes through "tyrannical measures." He therefore suggested a less narrow interpretation of the existing police regulations to allow colonial subjects the individual freedom to dress as they pleased, as long as they did not intend to evade the law or cause harm by disguising themselves.

In his capacity as advisor for native affairs, Snouck Hurgronje considered a request to wear European attire, submitted by Javanese physician Raden Moekadi in 1903, demonstrating the social complexity of sartorial questions at that time. Although he had attended the School tot Opleiding van Inlandsche Artsen (STOVIA) medical school, spoke fluent Dutch, and was used to socializing with Europeans, Moekadi petitioned to be allowed to wear a European suit in combination with a Javanese headdress because he was still expected to don traditional Javanese dress. According to Snouck Hurgronje, Moekadi was not the only one with the desire to change his attire; many other educated Javanese longed for the same privilege. This was part vanity, he reasoned, as lower officials sought to mimic their superiors. But it was also because European clothes were simply better suited for the modern era; trousers were more practical than the traditional sarong, which restricted the wearer's movements. Likewise, modern life required shoes rather than bare feet. Moreover, Snouck Hurgronje recognized that Western-educated Javanese were ashamed of their ethnic attire, well aware that Europeans associated it with lower social status and an inferior civilization. He agreed that wearing European clothes was an effective way to appear more civilized and modern.[27]

But perhaps most importantly, Snouck Hurgronje believed that Moekadi's request was motivated by his wish to evade, in the physician's own words, the "onerous formalities" of Javanese society. According to the advisor, the more European the appearance, the less appropriate it was to engage in deference rituals and conform to the Javanese language hierarchy. Snouck Hurgronje felt that abandoning such customs was an emancipatory development that should not be allowed to run its "natural course" and saw no reason to deny Moekadi's request to dress "in a more or less European fashion" or to withhold the same rights from others. As the physician intended to continue to wear a Javanese headdress, there could be no confusion about his ethnic status, so he was not violating the police regulations. However, he did caution against too rapid—or unnatural—a pace of change. As a Western-educated Javanese, it was Moekadi's responsibility to adjust his appearance and behavior depending on the social context. This meant that he could wear European attire in urban centers but might have to change into a sarong and offer traditional deference in Java's more conservative interior. Moreover, he cautioned Moekadi that wearing European clothes did not give him the right to treat others in a way he tried to avoid for himself; namely, by insisting on deference. Snouck Hurgronje's elaborate deliberations on the request were published as a circular in June 1903, intended to remind European civil servants to be more open to sartorial changes. It was the first step toward relaxing the nineteenth-century sartorial hierarchy.[28]

Within two years, the official ethnic sartorial hierarchy was dissolved entirely. This was not a result of the 1903 circular but primarily due to the rapid emancipation of the Chinese community in colonial Indonesia. As the Chinese community's demand for respect and equality grew more assertive following the colonial government's decision to grant European status to the Japanese, the colonial press reported with increasing frequency about Chinese men cutting their queue. The European press was worried that the Chinese would become indistinguishable from the Eurasians and Japanese in their midst. European civil servants were unsure about what to do in these situations; some arrested and fined Chinese men without their queue, while others condoned the new hairstyle.[29] In an attempt to formulate a cohesive and unambiguous response to these sartorial challenges, the government once again relied on Snouck Hurgronje for advice. This time, the advisor for native affairs suggested completely abandoning the superficial connection between ethnicity and appearance.[30] The colonial administration issued a dress circular in March 1905, which stated that the government wished "to leave her subjects free from interference with regards to their hairstyle and dress as long as it is evident there is no intent to evade or break the law."[31] In theory, colonial subjects were now free to dress and style their hair as they pleased, but in practice, it took several years before the policy was implemented.

Although the dress circular of 1905 did not immediately impact everyday life for the majority of the colonized, it did spark a debate among young Javanese. Two students initiated the discussion in the periodical *Bintang Hindia*. A young medical student named Moesa took issue with his peers' desire to don European clothes, inspired by Moekadi's successful appeal.[32] He described a recent incident in which, on his way home from a gamelan performance in Batavia, Europeans and natives (ethnic Malay) jeered at him and shouted, "Telur asin" (literally "salted egg") in mocking reference to the knot in his traditional central Javanese headdress (*blangkon*). On returning to his dorm room at the STOVIA, Moesa cast off his Javanese clothes in anger and humiliation, but almost instantly regretted his actions as he considered the love, time, and effort his mother had put into making his batik sarong. This experience prompted him to argue that there was a logic to the colonial sartorial hierarchy, as each ethnic or national group looked most elegant, natural, and appropriate in their own costume. European clothes also obscured Javanese nationality and made them indistinguishable from Eurasians in Western dress, who were not only held in low regard by Europeans and Javanese alike but also, due to their legal status, paid higher fares on trains and at theaters. As a final caution, Moesa warned that employers frowned on Javanese who emulated Europeans in every way.

In response to Moesa's article, a student attending the European secondary school in Semarang (Hogere Burgerschool) argued that the Javanese should not be so preoccupied with futilities, like appearance or deference traditions, but instead be concerned with transforming their mentality. If they wanted to compete with Europeans and Chinese in what he tellingly described as the "struggle for life," the colonized needed to become more innovative, courageous, entrepreneurial, and diligent. He reasoned that appearance did not hinder the Javanese in their glorious past nor did it prevent many of his contemporaries from graduating from European universities. He also pointed out that the Dutch were not bothered by similar concerns, rhetorically wondering if anyone believed that Europeans who were honored as Javanese with traditional deference ceased to be Europeans in their hearts and minds. Of course not, he argued, and therefore he and his peers could similarly acquire Western knowledge as long as they remained Javanese in spirit. Regardless of "the clothes we wear and traditions we follow, we are and will remain Javanese."[33]

Many subsequent contributors disagreed with both students and argued that a change in appearance and a change in mentality were inextricably connected. For them, dress was not simply an expression of a more assertive mentality; it was a material extension of it that was essential to suppress outdated traditions like deference etiquette, demand equality, and instill a sense of self-respect. Attire and other cultural traditions were not at all futile, but vital to the Javanese emancipation movement. One author recalled that only a decade earlier he was scorned and fined by Europeans for adopting European clothes and considered an infidel (*kafir*) by his own family. He felt vindicated by the dress circulars and argued that the twentieth century had proven that European clothes were more comfortable, practical, and egalitarian than his ethnic costume.[34] In addition to altering their clothing, many young Javanese also cut their traditionally long hair, which according to another author, could be traced back centuries to the Hindu-Javanese era. But just as the Javanese had later embraced Islam, they were now free to adopt a neater and more hygienic hairstyle, taking inspiration from the Chinese in Java who had recently cut their queue and the Japanese who had cut their topknot.[35]

These discussions in *Bintang Hindia* were conducted within a small circle of educated Javanese, an elite group that was enthralled with modernity and the desire to be considered equal to Europeans. But such conversations about dress did not reach nor involve most of the colonized, especially the majority living in the countryside. Even in Java's cities, where there was plenty of experimentation with composite dress, most of these attempts did not blur ethnic distinctions. Nonetheless, they were the cause of great anxiety within the colonial press. For instance, a European author ridiculed a Sundanese dandy he observed wearing shoes, linen trousers under a shortened sarong, a high-collared dress shirt, cufflinks, a colorful necktie and pocket square, a fitted jacket, a watch chain and pocket watch, and a Javanese headscarf.[36] But underneath such scorn was fear of the possibility that the colonized would soon be indistinguishable from Europeans. Without a larger source of motivation to encourage an indigenous sartorial makeover, however, their worries remained gratuitous.

Dressing "Up": The Sartorial Revolution of 1913

Moehamad Enoch, the confident young engineer with whom this chapter began, purposefully adopted European clothing to signal that he was a cosmopolitan man of the modern age. This message would have been clear to observers on both sides of the colonial divide, his clothes and posture communicating that he was educated, probably fluent in Dutch, and professionally successful. But Enoch's appearance would also have been immediately recognized as a contestation of the racial and cultural hierarchies of colonial society. His European suit was very much intended as a provocative means of demanding equal treatment by Europeans in colonial spaces, and it was perceived as such when he strode into the Bandung railway station on a Sunday afternoon in November 1913. By insisting on his right to communicate in their language and travel in their class, and then complaining to colonial authorities when these rights were withheld, Enoch proved to be anything but the submissive subject that the Dutch believed the Javanese to be. His new European appearance was clearly accompanied by a recalcitrant attitude. And although Enoch's story is one of exceptional nerve, his was by no means an isolated incident.

In late 1913 and early 1914, tens of thousands of young, educated, indigenous professionals—teachers, physicians, railroad employees, pawnshop personnel, clerks, and lower civil servants—cut their hair and adopted European clothing, especially trousers, shoes, and jackets. These sartorial transformations proved extremely contagious; a quick succession of newspaper reports describing this vibrant makeover emerged within several months. The atmosphere and landscape of colonial society noticeably changed as colonial subjects donned their new outfits in public squares, parks, streetcars, trains, railroad stations, theaters, markets, fairs, and offices. Both the colonial and vernacular press discussed the sudden popularity of European dress at great length. One of these dress-related press reports concluded, "There is a sociological relevance to this surprisingly rapid development that began in September 1913; with every age a new costume comes into vogue and anyone who still doubts the dawn of the liberation of the people in the Indies should, with a little sociological insight into these symptoms, come to the conclusion to change the décor."[37] The author recognized the revolutionary nature of these sartorial changes. This was not an expression of mere dandyism or a desire to appear modern, nor was it a straightforward challenge of nineteenth-century dress regulations. By defying the etiquette, policies, and rituals regulating public conduct—elements that communicated colonial power—the new generation of Javanese did not just seek to change their appearance, but the underlying assumptions of the colonial relationship more broadly. For some, the goal was to force the implementation of the Ethical Policy; for others it was merely the first step toward independence from the yoke of colonialism.

This sartorial revolution was part of the larger challenge to colonial authority that arose following the hormat circular of 1913—a pivotal moment that forged a progressive coalition between Dutch proponents of the Ethical Policy and Javanese nationalists. While previous studies of dress in colonial Indonesia have focused primarily on the dress circulars of 1903 and 1905, sartorial change was slow and far from widespread until 1913.[38] With the hormat circular, the government sought to finally align the colonial performance of power with its new "ethical" discourse, publicly working with the nationalist association Sarekat Islam to announce that civil servants were there for the people and not the other way around. Emboldened by the hormat circular and ensuing encouragement from the Sarekat Islam and the vernacular press, many Javanese demanded the right to sit in chairs during meetings, shake hands, and converse in egalitarian languages like Dutch or Malay as well as choose their manner of dress. They made an explicit connection between attire and emancipation, arguing that when one dressed in European clothes, especially trousers, one could not perform traditional deference. Donning European attire thus became a provocative weapon to exact equal treatment from conservative Dutch and indigenous forces in colonial society, and many Javanese rapidly adopted European dress in the months following the hormat circular of 1913.

The Sarekat Islam, the first Indonesian association to have a mass following, played a major role in promoting this view about freedom of dress to the public, presenting a change in costume as an effective method of resistance. Adjunct Advisor for Native Affairs D. A. Rinkes, who attended these gatherings to show government support for the association, was struck by the numerous followers donning European attire, particularly trousers, at meetings and rallies. He witnessed progressive members encouraging each other to adopt European dress as a means of evading traditional deference demands and commanding more respect from Europeans and Chinese alike. Several local branches of the Sarekat Islam even issued their own dress regulations stipulating that members wear trousers and shoes.[39] However, Rinkes also reported that indigenous support for the sartorial makeover was not unanimous. Some Javanese nationalists feared the loss of traditional culture and identity and were also concerned about the potential destruction of the batik industry. In addition, according to Rinkes, orthodox Muslims argued that wearing European attire constituted emulating *kafir* (infidels) in thought or appearance, which was strictly prohibited. In response, progressive Sarekat Islam followers circulated a *fatwa* (religious ruling) from Egypt, the center of the Islamic modernist movement, stating that wearing trousers was not in conflict with the Islamic faith.[40] In this and other ways, progressive nationalists embraced sartorial transitions as an important step toward emancipation.

The vernacular press reported extensively on the sartorial makeover as it transpired in colonial society. Press coverage made it clear that the protagonists of this movement were primarily young, educated professionals who hailed from the lower priyayi and the nascent middle classes. It was precisely these groups that felt most frustrated with and humiliated by the continued prevalence of hormat etiquette, and they embraced dress as way to end these degrading customs. These reports played an important role in adding momentum to the transformation that was taking place, instilling confidence in and providing inspiration for their readership. For instance, when articles about school teachers in Batavia who voted to wear European attire to work were published in November 1913, reports of teachers doing the same in Malang, Bandung, and Surabaya soon followed.[41] Similar reports appeared about other professional groups, such as civil servants, pawnshop personnel, and railroad employees.[42] From his exile in the Netherlands, Soewardi Soerjaningrat saluted these developments, exclaiming, "Bravo! This proves the unwillingness to be treated as inferior in the future. This is what happened when one was dressed in indigenous clothing. If one appears European in the Indies, one looks more prominent. That is the right that the indigenous peoples demand for themselves, to be prominent and engaged."[43]

Emphasizing that shifting circumstances shaped fashion, a contributor to the *Oetoesan Hindia* (Messenger of the Indies) reminded readers that it was only natural for clothing to adjust to the times. Even what many considered traditional Javanese dress, he argued, in part originated elsewhere. For instance, the white cloth necessary for batik production traditionally came from the Indian subcontinent, while under Dutch colonial rule they were imported from Europe. The batik stamps that enabled the mass production and consumption of batik cloth were only invented after the Java War (1825–1830), and their use pioneered by European and Chinese entrepreneurs. As for the traditional shirt (*baju*) worn by Javanese men, the author argued that it was inspired by Spanish and Portuguese influences in the archipelago. Most Javanese men would have originally gone bare-chested like the indigenous peoples of Papua (western New Guinea). Finally, he claimed that Arab, Chinese, and European norms inspired Javanese footwear. By explaining the diverse roots of Javanese clothes, the author argued that ethnic groups did not have fixed costumes nor did their identity depend on them. After all, the modern Japanese and Chinese did not lose their identities when they discarded their kimonos and queues.[44] For those who feared a loss of identity or prestige by wearing trousers, the author suggested that if they insisted on a traditional look, they would have to wear a costume made from banana tree fibers.[45] In other words, the Javanese should feel free to don European clothes, as they were most suited to the modern era.

However, many understood that these changes in appearance were about much more than simply adjusting to the times; they were part of a broad movement for social emancipation that was closely linked with the issuance of the hormat circular of 1913. For instance, in the typical satirical style of editor Marco Kartodikromo, several contributions to his periodical *Doenia Bergerak* (The World in Motion) sketched out what was at stake by taking the perspective of power holders like Dutch civil servants and bupati.[46] In an article about the hormat circular, an imaginary official asked the reader directly: "Why are you discarding your sarong and headscarf and replacing them with shoes and a suit?" Does the reader not realize, the author continued, that without their traditional outfit, "you do not want to worship or crouch for me anymore?" The author went on to wonder why the reader had cut their hair: "Because if you cut your hair your head will feel cold, if your head is cold, you gain a clear mind, which makes you smarter, and when you are smarter you no longer want to honor me."[47] The author declared that not receiving such deference would surely kill him! This was a recurring theme in *Doenia Bergerak*; another article claimed that a bupati fainted on seeing a Javanese in European attire, while a different bupati allegedly had a heart attack when he spotted a Javanese wearing shoes. The author suggested walking past his house often in order to make him sick.[48]

Unsurprisingly, the majority of the traditional Javanese ruling class fiercely contested the sudden acceleration in the westernization of indigenous appearance, in defense of their own aristocratic privileges and rank in colonial society.[49] As an author in the *Oetoesan Hindia* explained, the adoption of Western dress undermined the entire system of deference that informed all social interactions. As an example, he presented an awkward situation that unfolded when a European controller met with a subdistrict administrator (*wedana*) wearing traditional dress and an indigenous teacher donning European clothes. The wedana sat on the floor during the meeting, as was customary, but the teacher, wearing trousers, could not. Since offering him a chair would further insult the higher-ranking wedana, the teacher had to stand throughout the meeting.[50] Another article recounted that to avoid such a situation, a bupati simply refused to receive an indigenous engineer from the Department of Public Works because he wore European dress.[51] For similar reasons, local officials in Bojonegoro tried to prohibit young people from wearing European footwear in order to maintain clear class distinctions.[52]

However, such attempts became increasingly difficult to enforce, as assertive young Javanese had the support of the colonial government, the Sarekat Islam, and the vernacular press.

Kartodikromo took a direct, activist stance toward the many letters and reports he received from indigenous people who wanted to wear European clothes but were either intimidated or thwarted by their superiors or did not even dare try for fear of the imagined repercussions. In order to familiarize colonial subjects with government regulations and better understand their rights, he decided to publish a Malay translation of the dress circular of 1905, in which the governor general had confirmed years earlier that people had the right to dress according to their own desires. Kartodikromo's goal was to create an informed and critical readership that could stand up for itself and hold its superiors accountable. To offer further reassurance, so "that the readers of *Doenia Bergerak* do not worry too much about wearing European clothes," he insisted that he never encountered any problems while donning European attire himself.[53] He even argued for an egalitarian, standard dress style for the people of the Indies, which he believed should reflect European norms.

The vernacular press provided a crucial platform for readers to not only share their experiences but also put pressure on those unwilling to comply with the existing dress regulations. When a government employee sought Kartodikromo's advice about his Dutch boss who did not allow him to wear European attire to work, *Doenia Bergerak* printed a response. In his editorial commentary, Kartodikromo encouraged the reader to persist in dressing as he pleased, as was his right, even if his supervisor was "crazy for deference."[54] In several other articles, Kartodikromo encouraged his readers to not give up the fight and stand up for their rights.[55] *Doenia Bergerak* as well as other publications were filled with complaints and recommendations like this.[56] Disclosing negative incidents was cathartic; it demonstrated that being denied one's rights was a shared experience and created an awareness among the colonized that they were not alone. They enacted their awakening by shedding their native dress along with their indolence, and became more assertive in colonial society. This sartorial revolution heralded, according to one journalist, the arrival of the "age of progress" in colonial Indonesia.[57]

Dress and Identity: Ethnicity, Nationality, and Gender

The sartorial revolution of 1913–1914 was a pivotal moment in the hegemonic struggle to remove cultural traditions as obstacles to progress. The pace and character of these changes took many by surprise and raised questions about what it meant for Javanese ethnic, national, and gender identities. Had the Javanese gone too far in their emulation of Europeans? Could one truly become equal to them by donning their dress? Had they lost their identity in the process? And what were the distinct implications for men versus women? Differing opinions on these issues reflected a division within the national awakening, as Javanese grappled with the implications of breaking with nineteenth-century norms. At the heart of these disagreements between those known as Javanese nationalists and those known as Indies nationalists were the questions of who belonged to the newly imagined nation and what represented the nation. Javanese nationalists valued the nation's aristocracy, characterized by its elite culture, including hierarchical deference and etiquette traditions. They sought to restore the greatness of Majapahit's fourteenth-century Hindu-Javanese kingdom. In contrast, Indies nationalists believed that the colonized formed a single nation that through modernization and democratization could become an independent nation-state. For both sides, clothing signaled these distinct hopes for the future; the ostensibly egalitarian power of the European suit appealed to proponents of Indies nationalism but threatened Javanese nationalists' vision.[58]

Two contributors to *De Indiër* (The Indian), a weekly publication established by exiled leaders of the nationalist Indies Party in the Netherlands, promoted these divergent opinions. Soetatmo Soeriokoesoemo was one of the most vocal advocates of Javanese nationalism and a staunch defender of Javanese dress. In his contributions, he expressed shock and amazement at the "fast and unexpected change of clothes" in colonial society. Soetatmo quickly linked this development to the hormat circular of 1913, questioning if this transformation in appearance transpired for the right reasons. He warned his countrymen, "A slave is and will remain a slave even if he wears the costume of a king," and urged them not to adopt trousers and European hats as a means to avoid traditional deference.[59] In Soetatmo's eyes, anyone who tried to hide his servile character with trousers was a hypocrite. Arguing that Europeans only respected the clothes, not the person, he encouraged his compatriots to act like *satryas* (Hindu caste of warriors) and don indigenous dress with pride. Doing so would inspire their people to join the nationalist cause, not estrange them by wearing European attire.[60]

Soetatmo's Javanese nationalist opinion drew a strong rebuke from Soewardi Soerjaningrat, at the time a clear advocate for the more inclusive Indies nationalism. According to Soewardi, national identity did not reside in a sarong or headscarf but in the hearts of the people. He agreed that Javanese dress should not be discarded too easily but at the same time argued that European attire had its benefits, characterizing it as more affordable and practical for daily use. Most importantly, Soewardi argued, European dress emancipated indigenous people by exempting them from servile obedience: "Time and again it is surprising to witness the change in the servile attitude and manners, yes even of the opinions, into unforced, frank, but always Eastern-polite manners, because of a change of clothes."[61] Soewardi considered European clothing a "weapon with which we force the colonizers to give our people their legitimate rights."[62] For Soewardi, the ends—emancipation, equality, and eventually independence—justified the means of adopting European attire.

In the following decade, the debate about dress continued along these lines, both sides echoing Soetatmo's and Soewardi's respective sentiments.[63] The outbreak of World War I intensified the discussion, as it laid bare the West's moral shortcomings and suggested that scientific and industrial development alone did not inevitably signify civilization and progress.[64] This raised the question of whether it was necessary or even desirable to emulate the West in order to become modern and civilized. Perhaps the Javanese could simply revitalize and adapt indigenous heritage to the modern age.[65] On the streets of colonial Java, people continued to experiment with their appearance and find ways to reflect their desired identity. A new consensus gradually emerged in the 1920s, as men adopted the European suit while women continued to wear traditional attire. This gendered divide on the issue of dress seemingly resolved concerns over cultural loss, as even proponents of ethnic dress supported this surprising turn of events.

For instance, in 1923, the Java Institute, founded several years earlier to promote and preserve Javanese culture, organized an essay competition through its periodical *Djawa* on the advantages and disadvantages of European dress.[66] The second-place essay, a passionate defense of Javanese dress, was never published and remained hidden in the *Djawa* archives. The piece was clearly written by an ardent Javanese nationalist who sought to reconcile Javanese cultural traditions with the modern age. The author considered his countrymen's rejection of the sarong and traditional headdress as "a negation of Javanese culture" that imperiled the batik industry and Javanese culture and identity along with it.[67] The author acknowledged the appeal and benefits of European dress, recognizing that even when a Javanese in traditional attire was "more educated and intelligent than a white person," Europeans still treated him with contempt. In addition, he understood that "modern natives find the indigenous traditions too subservient, servile, and deferential and therefore consider European clothing to be more in accordance with their free spirit." Yet he was convinced that sporting European clothing was not the solution. Like Soetatmo a decade earlier, the author reasoned that it took "moral and ethical courage to present oneself as an indigenous person in a circle of European mediocrity." As a compromise, he suggested that Javanese dress be worn outside of work hours, such as at home, while going out with women, and during parties, holidays, and other social gatherings. Finally, he urged nationalist and community leaders to don traditional attire with pride to not only set an example but also to ensure the preservation of the batik industry and Javanese identity.

In stark contrast, the winning essay, written by Javanese teacher Roesalam Dwidjadisastra, emphasized the benefits of European attire over traditional Javanese dress. His essay was optimistic rather than nostalgic in tone. As a man of the modern era, the educator from Madiun constructed his argument around the latest notions of hygiene. He referred to studies that claimed that wearing a headscarf in hot tropical climates was an impediment to one's intellectual abilities. He also asserted that the traditionally open Javanese wooden sandal (*terompah*) did not protect its wearer from injuries, worm larvae, or snakebites. In his experience, European clothes were more affordable, especially for the common man, and did not wear out as quickly. Moreover, he emphasized the greater practicality of European dress by reasoning that it allowed for more freedom of movement when partaking in sports, such as cycling, running, horseback riding, tennis, and gymnastics. Crucially, he also repeated Soewardi's argument that European clothes communicated that one had too much self-respect to crouch or crawl for another person, and thus allowed the wearer much more freedom in social interactions. But Roesalam Dwidjadisastra's most original argument in favor of European dress was that because Javanese clothes were only worn by the ethnically Javanese, and not by other inhabitants, they could not define a *national* dress. The European suit was thus not only more hygienic, practical, affordable, and aspirational but most importantly, a potential symbol of Indonesian national unification and identity.[68] This idea about Indonesian identity reflects significant changes to Javanese society that began in the 1920s.

While the voices of Javanese women were underrepresented in discussions about dress, their appearance featured prominently in debates about clothing and identity. The nationalist discourse that emerged in the 1920s was centered on the "new Indonesian man," for whom European suits represented political power. Women, on the other hand, were directed toward subordinate positions and retained traditional Javanese dress to reflect their status as guardians of national culture.[69] However, this outcome was not foregone in the immediate aftermath of the sartorial revolution in 1913. The vernacular press offers numerous indications that many Western-educated Javanese girls and women experimented with European clothing just like their male counterparts.[70] Yet conversations about their attempts to adopt Western fashion were not framed as part of the struggle against Dutch colonial rule or oppressive deference traditions but instead in terms of morality, sexuality, decency, and social freedom. Javanese women's experiments with Western and composite dress posed a dual challenge: to the colonial hierarchy and the Javanese gender hierarchy.[71]

Most Javanese women who experimented with adding European clothes to their appearance came from a privileged background and had attended government-run elementary schools. The dress codes at these institutions prescribed European attire for girls, such as dresses or skirts, as opposed to nongovernmental institutions like the famous Kartini schools, where indigenous attire was mandatory.[72] Javanese boys outnumbered Javanese girls by a wide margin at government schools. In 1915, only 5,494 students in attendance were female, a little less than 19 percent. By 1940, attendance had increased to 33,925 (38 percent). Compared to Java's population of approximately 35 million, this number was a pittance, but these students became influential women in society as activists in women's associations, teachers, secretaries, nurses, telephone operators, and more.[73] Unlike boys, however, they could not continue their education at the secondary level—expected to retreat into the patriarchal private sphere, clad in traditional attire—which, according to the vernacular press, not all women did. By the late 1910s, frequent reports indicated that educated Javanese women embraced European dress. Although there were some positive progressive responses to this development, the Europeanization of Javanese women's appearance was most often associated with an assault on traditional gender roles.

The rapid Europeanization of the appearance of Javanese men immediately raised the question of the implications for Javanese women. In 1913, the author who analyzed the "sociological relevance" of the sartorial transformation encouraged women as well as men to cast aside their traditional attire. He considered clothing a means of spiritual revolution and strongly opposed the "poor fools who go up against the spirit of the age."[74] Several years later, another progressive observer expressed support for women in European clothing, which he linked to their entry into the public domain as working professionals in previously all-male environments.[75] But these responses were the exception rather than the rule. Soetatmo, for instance, strongly argued against women dressing in European clothes, as such Western tendencies were in stark opposition to the Eastern dignity of Javanese women. In addition to jeopardizing the development of a steadfast female character, the ever-changing whims and fancies of Parisian fashion threatened a man's finances. According to Soetatmo, nothing was more dreadful than for a Javanese woman "to put on the airs of a fashion doll or a suffragette." She would be much better off as a loyal housewife.[76] Others agreed that women should be educated to run a modern household, not to compete with men in the job market.[77] Even the victor of *Djawa*'s essay contest, who strongly advocated for Javanese men to adopt European dress, argued that women should not follow their example, claiming that such attire was impractical and unflattering.[78] Clearly, although men disagreed about their own appearance, they found common ground on the appearance of Javanese women. Dress provided them with an opportunity to challenge colonial hegemony, while simultaneously maintaining traditional gender roles that worked to their benefit.[79]

Many observers in the vernacular press warned that Western culture negatively influenced Javanese girls and women both socially and sexually. The sensual character of European dress, by virtue of the amount of skin left exposed, was considered an affront to Javanese and Islamic traditions alike. Girls were deemed especially susceptible to such immorality, adopting short skirts and thin European clothes that left little to the imagination. Authors cautioned that scantily clad young women incited lust and passion in men when participating in gymnastics at school, attending dances, or merely cycling around town.[80] In addition, there was great concern that girls in Western dress demanded the right to socialize freely with their friends—of both genders—going out unsupervised to movie theaters or strolling arm-in-arm through fairgrounds.[81] Many in the vernacular press argued that young Javanese women were simply too different from their European counterparts to safely imitate them. Whereas European girls enjoyed a socially free upbringing, Javanese girls did not and were thus ill-prepared to navigate male advances in public. This was further complicated by the assumption that Javanese girls allegedly blossomed earlier than Europeans, which enhanced the danger of social interactions with the opposite sex.[82] During the 1920s, authors increasingly advised that female adolescents only adopt from Western culture what was practical, like knowledge about running a household, and ignore dangerous components like improper dress and carefree social contact.[83] These reports demonstrate that Javanese women did experiment with European attire and its social and political implications alongside their male counterparts. However, despite a lasting sartorial revolution for Javanese men, widespread gendered anxiety prevented westernized appearance—and behaviors—from taking hold among Javanese women.

European Responses: Putting Down and Dressing Up

The abolition of nineteenth-century ethnic dress regulations and the rapid sartorial transformation in 1913 challenged Europeans' understanding of their alleged superiority. A peculiar situation arose, as the colonized embraced European dress while the colonizers continued to wear attire akin to indigenous garb in the semiprivate sphere. Troubling questions emerged with this new distinction: which of the two appeared more modern, and how would these changes affect both Dutch and indigenous status in colonial society?[84] The possible blurring—or worse, reversal—of the boundaries between colonizers and colonized was cause for great anxiety among the Dutch, for whom dress was employed as a significant social marker demonstrating European superiority and legitimizing colonial rule.[85] In response, the Dutch tried to differentiate themselves from the dressed "up" Javanese by out-dressing them in European fashion. A similar phenomenon occurred in British India, where scholar Emma Tarlo found that the increasing European appearance of Indian men encouraged "the British to make their own sense of sartorial correctness more rigid."[86] In Java, this process heralded the marginalization of the sarong, kebaya, and batik trousers in Europeans' wardrobes.

Dutch anxieties about clothing and appearance found expression in the conservative colonial press. Dramatically declaring that the sartorial transformation signaled an imminent end to colonial rule, editor Karel Wybrands argued that the abolition of traditional deference rituals and the sartorial hierarchy had irreparably damaged colonial authority. He mourned the loss of the privileged "white jacket," which after serving as the white man's armor in the colonies for generations, had lost its symbolic power when widely adopted by the colonized. According to Wybrands, there was a direct correlation between the Javanese embrace of trousers and white jackets and their increased rebelliousness. Referencing the emergence of the nationalist movement and reports that indigenous workers were increasingly standing up to plantation owners, he wrote, "The blunderer [Governor General] Van Heutsz has allowed natives and Chinese to dress like us. . . and now the attacks on Europeans are frequent."[87] Given this context, it is no wonder that the Sarekat Islam's mass meetings attended by thousands of indigenous people in white suit jackets were particularly intimidating. Europeans, like the Javanese, understood that these forms of cultural resistance had shifted the dynamic of the colonial relationship.

The initial European response to Javanese experiments with composite dress was to ridicule their appearance. As Patricia Spyer demonstrates, in the colonial

FIGURE 6. "The past and the present!" Illustrative of the Dutch
ambivalence toward sartorial changes in society, the cartoon suggests
that without the nineteenth-century sartorial hierarchy, colonial subjects
become more impertinent. Source: *De Reflector*, July 14, 1917.

context mockery was an effective means of emphasizing difference and otherness
and was also meant to affirm the Dutch's continuing superiority.[88] But in the
wake of the sartorial revolution of 1913, conservative Europeans could no longer
consider Javanese dressed in "a slit coat, borrowed blue glasses, brown shoes, and
two pens in the upper pocket" as an innocent expression to be tolerated with a
smile.[89] Instead, conservative civil servants like M. B. van der Jagt believed it

evil, even criminal, that the Javanese politicized European attire to become more vocal, demanding, and assertive. According to Van der Jagt, although wearing European dress instilled in the colonized a naïve belief that "within limited time their place on the world's stage will be equal to that of her European educator," this was merely a façade.[90] The dissolution of ethnic dress regulations created the *illusion* of equality, while in reality dressing similarly only obscured intrinsic differences between colonizer and colonized. With similar rationale, the conservative editor Wybrands encouraged the Javanese to remain Eastern: "If against all laws he tries to molest his being by adopting Western ways to look like a Westerner, he becomes just as much of a misnomer as the Westerner who tries to be an Easterner."[91] The implicit cultural relativism in this remark implied that the Dutch themselves should be more distinctly Western—a suggestion that many Europeans began to take seriously.

Thus, in addition to putting down Javanese in Western garb, the Dutch dressed "up." By making their own appearance more distinctively European in both the public and private spheres, they sought to reassert control over the colonial sartorial hierarchy. Their Europeanization marked the colonizer as modern and civilized and reaffirmed their superiority and right to rule. Historiography on dress primarily ascribes this process of Europeanization to external forces, such as the increased immigration of men and especially women from Europe. Technological and scientific advancements in transportation, communication, medicine, and hygiene allowed these newcomers to maintain a European lifestyle in the tropics. Informed by Social Darwinist notions, they regarded everything that derived from indigenous society as suspect and with potentially degenerative powers.[92] However, this is only half the story, as it does not adequately explain the particular timing of the Dutch sartorial transformation. When we consider dress as an interactive site of contestation, a hegemonic struggle between colonizer and colonized, a more dynamic narrative emerges. The same technological developments that enabled a more European lifestyle in the tropics—faster shipping, the telegraph and printing press, frequent imports of clothes and textiles, and sewing machines—also facilitated Javanese experimentation with composite dress at the turn of the century. From that moment onward, the colonizer and colonized made sartorial choices that increasingly shaped one another—a process that suddenly accelerated with the Javanese sartorial transformation in 1913 and Europeans' response.

As mentioned previously, by the late nineteenth century, European women wore a sarong and kebaya and men wore batik trousers in the semiprivate sphere, which included the house, its porches and gardens, hotels, and even social visits and strolls in the neighborhood. The public visibility of their attire made it a defining feature of the Dutch experience in Java. The first criticism of these clothes as too similar to indigenous dress emerged around the turn of the century. In 1900, author Bas Veth published a scathing analysis of colonial society in which he described the sarong and kebaya as indecent, unceremonious, and immodest. Employing racist language, he sarcastically encouraged "pure" European women to at least wear a peignoir instead because "the sarong and kebaya originate from the kampong, the peignoir from Europe."[93] At the time, Veth's criticism was not yet widely shared. Out of many rebuttals to his piece, one described the sarong and kebaya as the most hygienic, comfortable, and beautiful clothing for European women living in Java's paradise.[94] But public opinion gradually started to shift. By 1908, a popular household guide meant to prepare European women for life in the colony argued that a European "cannot be dressed like a coolie, drape himself like a native, even if he wore clothes from the most exquisite materials."[95] A guide from 1910 echoed this sentiment, stating that no self-respecting young European woman would allow herself to be seen on the streets in a sarong and kebaya.[96] Both books suggested that sarong and kebaya only be worn in a much more restricted private sphere, and that the public sphere be a site of exhibiting and performing European identity.

However, sarong, kebaya, and batik trousers began to be discarded entirely in response to the widespread Javanese embrace of European dress in 1913. After returning to Java for the first time since his retirement seven years earlier, former advisor for Chinese affairs and novelist Henri Borel was struck by the Europeanization of colonial society. He noted that all icons of nineteenth-century colonial culture seemed to have disappeared; the colonial house, rice table, and quasi-indigenous attire were all replaced with European equivalents. In a report to a Dutch newspaper, he claimed that after several months in Java he "had [yet] to see the first [European] lady in sarong and kebaya."[97] To his surprise, European women did not wear a sarong and kebaya anymore; they all donned peignoirs, skirts and blouses, or kimonos. The popularity of the latter was both a form of Japonisme, a Western obsession with Japanese culture, as well as a cultural recognition of Japan as a civilized imperial power. Similarly, in the semiprivate sphere European men had exchanged their apparently vulgar batik trousers with English pajamas. Respectable men no longer wore the traditional white jacket but rather a "shantung silk jacket with a nice cardigan, a stiff collared shirt, tie, and cuffs."[98] According to Borel, the Dutch had seemingly decided to follow the English custom and dress themselves in European style despite the smothering tropical heat. Another observer agreed that the age of the sarong, kebaya, and batik trousers was now clearly in the past, while household and travel guides also discussed the former mainstays of Indies dress solely in the past tense: they had become "unfashionable" and "obsolete."[99] The marginalization of the sarong, kebaya, and batik trousers among Europeans resulted in the decline of the Eurasian batik industry in the 1920s.[100]

A 1917 political cartoon perfectly captured this transformation in European appearance. In adjacent frames portraying the past and the present (*lain doeloe! lain sekarang!*), the cartoon depicts a European couple promenading past a colonial subject. The contrast between the two images is striking. A fashionable dress displaying her lower legs had replaced the European woman's sarong and kebaya, while a modern suit complete with necktie and hat had replaced the man's batik trousers and kebaya. The couple appears to have been directly transported from a Parisian boulevard. The transformation of the Javanese native in the image is just as revealing. Whereas he used to cower, squat, remove his hat, and avoid eye contact, he now stands tall, his conical hat firmly in place, and looks straight at the passersby as well as the viewer. The cartoon clearly conveys the understanding that in colonial society, changes in dress were not so much about fashion as they were about power.[101] This nostalgic undertone, reminiscing about a past in which the native was submissive, was pervasive in the colonial press. In 1918, one author even dedicated a rather sexist poem to the sarong and kebaya, asserting that they were much more sensual (i.e., revealing the female form) and becoming than European attire. It therefore saddened him that young European women boasted about never having worn them.[102] While this was most likely an attempt at contemporary humor, in hindsight it illustrates Europeans' changing appearance.

To reinforce their own sense of sartorial correctness, Europeans in colonial Indonesia were infatuated with the latest fashion in Europe and the United States. Modern technology and the networks of trade, transport, and information it sustained enabled Europeans to keep up with developments on the other side of the globe. Regular fashion columns in periodicals and newspapers in the colony reported on the styles worn in Paris, London, Berlin, New York, and San Francisco. Special mail-order catalogs enabled European inhabitants of Java to order the latest fashions with only the slightest delay. For those who could not wait or could not afford the luxury of ordering clothes from Europe, hiring an indigenous seamstress (*jait*) to re-create European fashions from patterns or images was a great solution. In addition, in the 1910s and 1920s, large department stores opened their doors in Java's principal cities, facilitating a modern shopping experience. With names like Aux Palais de Modes, these "fashion palaces" left little to the imagination, providing a modern space where Europeans could finesse their appearance and further the occidentalization of colonial society.[103]

Advertisements and illustrations accompanied fashion columns in the colonial press and provide yet another example of how Europeans sought to reassert their authority through dress. A fascinating case is a 1926 advert for Petodjo lemonade with the slogan, "Nine types, one taste."[104] This catchphrase appears beside an illustration of nine people with different ethnic backgrounds. A European family of four is depicted as entirely modern but the others are shown in their respective ethnic dress, seemingly immobilized in the past. Anny Oldenziel, a fashion columnist for the popular illustrated weekly *D'Oriënt*, used a similar strategy of exclusion in the drawings alongside her articles. Her column not only kept Europeans informed about the latest fashions, but also through her drawings enabled them to imagine them in the colonial context. In one such image, Oldenziel depicted European women with angular and elongated bodies wearing short sleeveless summer dresses. Their hair is cut short in a bob reflecting the 1920s modern global ideal.[105] The women use small Japanese parasols—another form of Japonisme—to protect their exposed skin from the tropical sun. Oldenziel often portrayed European men in modern white suits with dress shirts, open jackets, ties, and tropical helmets. But in sharp contrast to these modern images of Europeans, she continued to illustrate the Javanese in their traditional sarong and kebaya, emphasizing their difference and backwardness. There is no sign of a modernized Javanese or "Indonesian dandy." Through images like these, the Dutch tried to establish a new sartorial hierarchy, maximizing the distinction between ruler and ruled, colonizer and colonized, master and servant.[106]

As European men sought to bolster their prestige and status by changing their appearance, like Javanese men they found that doing so upended prevailing gender roles. The presence of European women in Java increased significantly in the early twentieth century due to immigration, thereby changing the ethnic and gender makeup of the European population. The Dutch believed that the arrival of white women, for whom the colonies were a temporary home, would bring civilization to the local European community and ward off threats of physical degeneration and moral decay.[107] Gradually, the proliferation of European women and their "civilizing" mission began to marginalize Eurasians and mestizo culture.[108] The change in women's clothing, especially the rejection of the sarong and kebaya, symbolized these anxieties, which were exacerbated by 1920s Western fashion trends featuring exposed arms, legs, necks, and shoulders. Further aggravating the tension was the question of women's emancipation. In addition to suffrage, which was granted in the Netherlands in 1919, Dutch women demanded access to education, the workplace, and the public sphere more broadly. They did not leave these demands behind in the metropole but transferred them to conservative colonial society. In Java, it quickly became apparent that women's sartorial transformation encompassed much more than the preservation of European prestige. As a male contributor to a popular weekly observed in 1927, "The revolution in women's outward appearance mirrors her inner evolution, specifically her growing independence in society."[109]

The colonial press addressed this "growing independence," depicting the modern girl or woman as assertive, determined, and self-sufficient. She wore the latest European fashions, such as skirts, dresses, blouses, and hats, which marked her as modern. She had a bob or shingle haircut, which according to observers signaled her demand to be treated as equal to men and deserving of the same opportunities.[110] She was also athletic and graceful; she swam, played tennis, and rode horses, all in appropriate modern sporting attire.[111] Perhaps most crucially, she worked in offices, stores, schools, and medical institutions, and increasingly behaved more freely in the public sphere. She socialized unsupervised with men and women, smoked, danced, drank, and went to the movies.[112] In effect, she represented a radical break with the past, especially in the conservative colonial setting. While it is uncertain to what extent this idealized modern girl or woman actually existed in colonial society, frequent discussions of her presence in it and perceived threat to it are indicative of the acute anxiety surrounding changing gender roles. But perhaps most importantly, the dressed-up European woman did not just jeopardize the traditional gender order; to conservatives, she also jeopardized the preservation of colonial authority.[113]

Whereas the attire worn by European men supposedly radiated colonial power and superiority, women's dress appeared to do just the opposite. The gradual shortening of skirts and increased exposure of arms, shoulders, backs, and necks—so emblematic of the 1920s in the West—were thought to undermine European prestige in the eyes of indigenous peoples. Many argued that European women's fashion was simply unsuited for colonial society, as it invited derision rather than respect from the predominantly Muslim population. According to one author, it was one thing for women to dress this way in Europe, where at least the climate forced them to cover up when outdoors, but in Java, "All Easterners, most of whom stand on a lower step of civilization, can ogle the modern-dressed woman."[114] However, even if Dutch women avoided Western attire, it was not difficult for the colonized to find imagery of scantily clad European women; they proliferated in movies, advertisements, public performances, and even magazines.[115] The colonial press was especially obsessed with the way women were depicted in Western films, convinced that it could negatively influence the colonized. For instance, in 1918 there was some consternation following a screening of *The Triumph of Venus*, a movie featuring lust, sensuality, jealously, and sex in which women wore skimpy attire and were often subject to the whims of men. One viewer worried that the film showed indigenous viewers "how to break a [European] woman's resistance."[116] Some argued that without respect for European women colonialism was doomed to fail. This provided European men with the opportunity to reassert their control by protecting their wives and daughters against the indigenous male gaze by advocating for film censorship and segregated spaces, such as swimming pools.[117]

From Ethnic to National Dress

By the late 1920s, the Indonesian nationalist movement was fragmented and severely weakened. Following the communist revolts in 1926 and 1927, the communist party was destroyed. The Sarekat Islam had long lost its political momentum, and a multitude of smaller associations that focused on ethnic, regional, or religious identities remained.[118] In response, there were several attempts to articulate a unified Indonesian national identity, the first of which was the establishment of the Indonesian National Association (Perserikatan Nasional Indonesia; PNI) in 1927.[119] Led by Soekarno, who would later become the first president of an independent Indonesia, the PNI advocated secular nationalism, noncompliance with the Dutch colonizer, and eventual independence as its main objectives. But perhaps even more significant than the PNI, at least symbolically, was the increased collaboration among diverse youth associations within colonial Indonesia. Meeting together in Batavia in October 1928, members took a Youth Pledge (*Sumpah Pemuda*), swearing their allegiance to one country, one people, and one language. Attendees imagined that the colonial state with its great diversity of people and languages would be transformed into a single cohesive nation with its own unifying, egalitarian language: Indonesian (*Bahasa Indonesia*).[120] And at this moment, of "triumph of the idea of Indonesia," the question of what constituted national dress for both men and women became particularly relevant.[121]

By the end of the 1920s and into the early 1930s, the conversation about appearance and its relationship to ethnic, religious, and national identities had intensified. At its core, this was a debate about how to appear modern and independent without alienating or rejecting local culture and traditions. Incidents regarding dress, such as the rejection of a bupati from a European club in

Surabaya because he was clad in Javanese attire, and a similar episode involving two students at a European cinema, elicited extensive discussions in the vernacular press. According to some newspapers, such incidents could easily be avoided if the Javanese would just wear "international"—meaning European—clothing that made them indistinguishable from Eurasians. Others maintained that donning international dress would not increase Dutch respect and only result in a loss of cultural identity.[122] Batavia's largest vernacular newspaper, the *Bintang Timoer* (Star of the East), offered another perspective. According to editor Parada Harahap, these incidents illustrated the need to develop distinctive national dress: "Discarding Javanese, Buginese, Batak, Acehnese, and Minangkabau attire, except during special occasions and festivities, so that in public one no longer appears Javanese or Malay, but . . . Indonesian."[123] For men, he proposed a European suit in combination with the Indonesian *peci*, a flat-topped conical cap.[124] By bridging ethnic differences, the suit had a universalizing and egalitarian effect on the new Indonesian man, while the peci simultaneously differentiated him from the colonizer.[125] In the private sphere, Harahap stipulated that men could continue to wear traditional ethnic attire.

The following year, the *Bintang Timoer* further explored the question of what to wear in an in-depth, six-part series titled "National Clothing" (Pakaian Nasional).[126] Here, the editor elaborated his argument for the necessity of national dress for both genders. As before, he identified a suit—trousers, a shirt, tie, and jacket—and a peci for men. This commanded respect and was considered the most practical attire for the modern era, as evidenced by newly established national dress in independent states like Turkey, Japan, and Siam.[127] The peci was the distinguishing feature of Indonesian national dress. While its name derived from the Dutch *petje* (small cap), the peci was most likely inspired by the Ottoman fez worn by some Muslim men in the Indonesian archipelago in the nineteenth century. According to the *Bintang Timoer*, it was only in the 1920s that the peci—under its secular name—was embraced as a national symbol. Soekarno experimented with the peci as a unifying emblem, wearing it to meetings of the youth association Young Java in 1921.[128] Although he certainly played a large role in turning the black cap into a national icon, Soewardi Soerjaningrat and Tjipto Mangoenkoesoemo wore similar headwear in 1913 when they founded the Indies Party.[129] According to the editor of the *Bintang Timoer*, by 1931, the peci had become popular with the Indonesian intelligentsia, including lawyers, physicians, engineers, and even members of the People's Council.[130] The peci was thus embraced as a vital component of Indonesian men's national costume, the only downside being that Eurasians might wear one to try to get into fairgrounds or movie theaters at the discounted rate for natives.[131]

Advertisements in the vernacular press clearly reflected the crystallization of men's national dress. The European suit was already widely advertised, as it had become popular during the sartorial makeover of 1913. Clothing stores and tailors with names like "Stylish" and "Fashionable" promoted the latest trousers, shirts, and shoes in European styles, all branded as products of the "modern age" (*zaman modern*). By the early 1930s, Java's stores offered the most modern Palm Beach gabardine suits from Europe.[132] In advertisements for other consumer products, such as cigarettes, soap, biscuits, watches, and tea, Indonesian men were more often than not depicted in a modern suit.[133] The peci also increasingly appeared in vernacular advertisements. For instance, a 1931 advert for a hatter in Medan included an image of three modern Indonesian men, each wearing a suit, tie, and peci. The accompanying text assured readers that there was a peci for every Indonesian: young and old, teachers and students, civil servants and private professionals alike. The store offered the latest models from Medan, Padang, and Batavia.[134] Another advertisement for a peci factory in Batavia clearly illustrated that the black cap was both a symbol for the nation and of the modern age, emphasizing that the factory used electric-powered machinery to produce its peci, which were the same quality as those worn by Indonesian leaders.[135] With the peci and European suit firmly cemented as their national costume, Indonesian men were prepared to enter the "modern age." Indonesian women, however, were tasked with a different mission: to safeguard tradition.

According to the lengthy exposé printed in 1931 in the *Bintang Timoer*, Indonesian women had settled on the traditional batik sarong and short kebaya as their national attire. Interestingly, as the article observed, in colonial society a batik sarong and white kebaya used to be associated with indigenous nannies to European families (*baboe*) and Dutch men's concubines (*nyai*). In recent years, however, many educated and prominent Indonesian women embraced this attire as their national dress, making it respectable in the process.[136] Whereas Indonesian men adopted the European suit as a symbol of their elevated status and prestige, European dresses, skirts, and blouses had the opposite effect on Indonesian women. As had been argued for years, European women's fashions were sinful and shameless; they showed too much bare skin and left little to the imagination, thus inviting the male gaze.[137] Some newspapers even described such attire as more befitting of prostitutes.[138] A contributor to the periodical *Pembela Islam* (Defender of Islam) argued that it was necessary for Indonesian women to strive for less disgrace in society. It was important to avoid showing exposed arms and calves, let alone thighs or cleavage. The author was not only bothered by Western clothing, but also by many (poorer) women's practice of bathing in rivers and streams, displaying their nudity in public like "American Beach Beauties."[139] He therefore called on women to dress more decently, meaning in a sarong and kebaya, and urged wealthy benefactors to establish public bathhouses for women.

Critics of Western clothing disapproved of the way they adorned a woman's body, but also of what such attire represented: freer interaction between the sexes, and women's presence and confidence in the public sphere. Many men were very concerned about women potentially entering professional spaces, as secretaries in offices, for instance.[140] In this moment of flux—the modernization of colonial society and Indonesians' increasing assertiveness—the future of Indonesian gender roles was uncertain. For men, establishing national dress was a visual expression of their attempt to undo the emasculation they experienced under colonial rule. In their new clothing, they would assert themselves against European colonizers and over Indonesian women.

Interestingly, conservative Indonesian women's associations supported this endeavor and shared in the censure of European women's fashion. Their considerable influence on the issue became clear during the first Indonesian women's congress in 1928. A majority of representatives from various associations voted against a proposal to adopt Western skirts (*rok*) as acceptable attire.[141] Instead, ethnic dress like the sarong and kebaya remained common, as was the practice for members of conservative associations like Muhammadiyah.[142] Subsequent conferences reinforced ethnic attire as women's national costume. Moreover, in a parallel move, they increasingly defined the Indonesian woman through her motherhood, infusing her identity with the responsibility of caring not just for her own family, but for the nation as a whole.[143]

In the last decade of colonial rule, economic crisis further cemented the presence of Indonesian national dress. The colonial economy, heavily dependent on exports, was hit hard by the Great Depression. During the recession, Indonesian intellectuals looked to Mahatma Gandhi's Swadeshi movement as a possible model for economic relief, arguing, like British Indian nationalists, that their national dress needed to be locally produced and affordable for all. They looked immediately to the batik industry, which was controlled by Eurasian and Chinese interests. By buying batik from Indonesian producers, they claimed, consumers could support national industry as well as the development of national dress and identity. Once again, the burden of this position fell disproportionately on women, who were now often the only ones wearing batik. Men were expected to purchase their peci from Indonesian hatters and their suits from local tailors, rather than importing them from Europe or the United States. But it was women's responsibility to avoid the temptation of Western dress and buy batik sarong from local producers, thereby supporting the national economy and maintaining indigenous tradition.[144]

"The Minute an Indonesian Dons Trousers He Walks Erect like Any White Man"

In the everyday lived experience under colonialism, clothing was absolutely essential in making social relationships and interactions legible. Dress visually reflected a person's legal status—European, Native, or Foreign Oriental—as well as ethnicity, social position, and gender. All of these markers of identity determined proper etiquette. By stipulating that all members of colonial society dress according to their ethnicity, the Dutch crafted an ethnic sartorial hierarchy in the nineteenth century. It was only as part of the Ethical Policy that these sartorial regulations were relaxed and the colonized allowed to freely decide what to wear. However, while some experimented with forms of composite dress, the dress hierarchy remained the norm until 1913, when the prevalence of new attire comprised nothing short of a sartorial revolution. These events are best understood in conjunction with the hormat circular, as the colonized publicly advocated a change in clothes as the best way to signal a refusal to perform traditional deference etiquette. In the process, they transgressed not just the sartorial hierarchy but also through their clothes challenged the colonial performance of power and the racial and gender inequalities that it sustained.

In his 1965 autobiography, Soekarno reflected on these sartorial transformations with language surprisingly similar to that of the Javanese who adopted European dress in great numbers in 1913. He condemned traditional dress for Indonesian men as demeaning, converting its wearer into a servile and subservient creature. In contrast, "The minute an Indonesian dons trousers he walks erect like any white man."[145] But although those like Soekarno strove for and celebrated Indonesian men's access to (Western) modernity, they denied Indonesian women the same entry into the modern world. Despite moments of ambiguity and experimentation, the selection of traditional attire as Indonesian women's national dress illustrates that clothes enabled men to challenge colonial hierarchies while maintaining traditional gender roles. As these comments show, the sartorial revolution of 1913 was not merely about self-respect, but as much about changing identities in a rapidly changing world. This was true for colonizer and colonized alike. The Javanese embrace of Western clothes forced the Dutch to increase their own sense of sartorial correctness and reconsider what it meant to be European men and women in the tropics. As both colonizer and colonized became more explicit about creating their new identities, anxieties increased about the need to protect them. These discussions were not limited to dress, as the next chapter shows, but pervasive throughout all aspects of colonial society.

CHAPTER 5

East Is East, and West Is West

Forging Modern Identities

I N 1918, READERS OF the newspaper *Sinar Hindia* were introduced to "Student Hidjo" (Student Green), a fictional character created by Marco Kartodikromo whose experiences encapsulated the social anxieties of the period. The serial publication follows Hidjo, a quiet, smart, Western-educated son of a Javanese merchant, on his journey to the Netherlands to pursue a degree in engineering, which his parents believe is a sure way for him to join the ranks of the *priyayi*. Before his departure, his mother reminds her son of his engagement to his cousin and warns him about the sexual promiscuity of Dutch women. Almost immediately after boarding the steamship to Europe, Hidjo experiences the wisdom of his mother's words, as two young Dutch women openly flirt with and eye him amorously. For readers, it was no surprise that after arriving in the Netherlands, Hidjo eventually succumbs to the advances of a Dutch woman, Betje, the daughter of his landlord. But after their first romantic escapade, Hidjo receives letters from his Javanese fiancée and friends that make him immediately regret his actions. He realizes that if he does not leave the Netherlands soon, he will turn into a Dutchman, marry a Dutch woman, and alienate himself from his own family, people, and country. He decides to return home to the bride his parents selected for him and remain Javanese. For her part, Betje ends up in the same Javanese town married to a Dutch colonial official with similar philandering behavior.[1]

One of the most important takeaways for readers of the Student Hidjo serial was to stay true to oneself, as the differences between Eastern and Western culture and morality were unbridgeable. Kartodikromo's work was not the only one that echoed the opening line of Rudyard Kipling's infamous "The Ballad of East and West" (1889): "Oh, East is East and West is West, and never the twain shall meet."[2] In September 1924, *D'Oriënt* published on its cover a photograph of a young Javanese woman clad in traditional dress holding up a handmade batik cloth against a background of tropical vegetation. The accompanying caption read, "East is East. . ." and invited the reader to turn the page to find the second half of the trope. This showed a photograph of a young European woman with bobbed hair, bangs, and lipstick, wearing a bathing suit and standing on the beach while refreshing ocean waves crashed on the rocks around her.[3] The contrast between the women was clear, and many vernacular publications made similar insinuations, using Kipling's words to convey the intrinsic differences between East and West, colonizer and colonized.[4] One author in the Sino-Malay newspaper *Sin Po* even used Kipling to argue that the greatest danger for the national awakening did not derive from the Dutch but from overly Westernized Indonesians.[5]

These examples illustrate the increasing hardening of beliefs about difference in colonial society among both the Dutch and Indonesians. Underlying these concerns were assumptions that identities were fixed, that mixing was degenerative, and that unwanted influences could and must be purged to prevent a loss of self. These anxieties intensified in the decades around the turn of the century, as advances in Western science—particularly in the fields of climatology, evolutionary biology, and medicine—stressed racial difference as a marker between colonizers and colonized. For the Dutch and Javanese, just as important was the introduction of the Ethical Policy, which no longer legitimized colonial authority through Dutch immersion in Javanese aristocratic culture but instead based it on the colonizers' modernity and alleged higher degree of civilization. These developments led increasingly to the rejection of cultural accommodation, acclimatization, and racial mixing in favor of the cultivation and firm delineation of racial and cultural boundaries. This was reflected in the Dutch fear of degenerating to the level of the "natives" and obsession with the maintenance of "white prestige" in the colony. Indonesians were not passive bystanders to these transformations in colonial discourse, as many cultural, religious, and political associations called for alternate approaches to modernity and resistance to "westernization." Such concerns led to debates over lifestyle and moral issues, such as interracial relationships and the consumption of alcohol and opium.

These negotiations on both sides of the colonial divide cannot be separated; they were part of a singular and cohesive discourse that profoundly shaped everyday life. Dutch anxieties about the physical and moral consequences of Java's tropical climate and social interactions with the "natives" were mirrored in Indonesian disquiet about the free interaction between the sexes, dancing, and consumerism of colonial modernity. The redefinition of identities through these ideas—what it meant to be European or Asian, Dutch or Indonesian, colonizer or colonized, modern or primitive—was not merely speculative but experientially performed, expressed, and communicated in everyday colonial encounters. The discourse of difference was thus reflected in appearance, etiquette, sexual morality, social customs, culinary traditions, and consumer patterns. These modes of individual and social comportment became sites of contesting and negotiating colonial hegemony for both the colonizer and colonized as they fashioned new identities in a modern world.

Shifting Paradigms: Acclimatization, Race, and Identity

During most of the nineteenth century, the prevailing belief in the Netherlands Indies was that Europeans could acclimatize to tropical environments by following indigenous customs concerning clothing, diet, and lifestyle. Thus, professional medical views supported Dutch colonial policies of cultural accommodation, racial mixing, and the Javanization of colonial authority. However, in the second half of the century, biological racism—the pseudoscientific belief in inherent racial differences—challenged theories of acclimatization and acculturation. An increased emphasis on the concept of race supported the belief that it was impossible for European bodies to adjust to the tropical environment. Instead, Europeans in the tropics could expect physical, cultural, and moral degeneration if they did not maintain European lifestyles and limit their stay in the colonies. By the turn of the twentieth century, this racialized perspective gained prominence in the Netherlands Indies—a shift reflected in the adoption of the Ethical Policy and the modernization of colonial authority. Where science had once supported Javanized colonial rule, biological racism now tipped the scales in the opposite direction. This raised immediate concerns regarding racial identity, culture, and lifestyle for Europeans living in colonial Indonesia.[6]

As Hans Pols has shown, early-nineteenth-century physicians approached the issue of acclimatization from the prevailing Hippocratic tradition, emphasizing the influence of the environment, morality, and lifestyle on the human physical constitution.[7] Within this framework, bodily characteristics were perceived as fluid and adaptive, which meant that the human constitution could adjust to new variables. Migration between different climate zones, physicians reasoned, triggered necessary changes in the body's metabolism, thermoregulation, muscle activity, and skin activity (i.e., perspiration), and a body required a transition period to become familiar with a new environment. Known as "seasoning," this period was characterized by physical discomfort and disease but would ultimately resolve and leave the migrant as good as new. For instance, on arrival to Java in 1842, the physician Cornelis Swaving described suffering bursts of sweating, anorexia, congestion of the liver, fevers, ulcers, lack of physical strength, listlessness, and sleeplessness alternating with insomnia, among other maladies. Luckily, Swaving soon developed a healthy physical constitution the likes of which he had not even experienced in European summers.[8]

German physician Carl Waitz similarly believed that humans were conditioned to particular climate zones but, like animals and plants, had the ability to physiologically adjust to different environments.[9] Waitz argued that embracing elements of the Javanese lifestyle would expedite the process for Dutch settlers. For instance, he claimed that European dress was the greatest obstacle to acclimatization in the tropics, and European food was too difficult to digest in the warm environment. In contrast, the Javanese dressed lightly, consumed small portions of easily digestible food, did not perform physical labor during the hottest hours of the day, and frequently bathed in cool water. Waitz estimated that by following the Javanese example, the process of acclimatization would take about a year. However, if one maintained a European lifestyle in the tropics, the duration of this process would extend considerably.[10]

Despite some dissenting opinions warning that European bodies simply could not survive the tropics, most physicians in the Netherlands Indies remained optimistic about the possibility of adapting.[11] In part, this can be explained by continued tolerance toward racial mixing and the large proportion of Eurasians within colonial society. More significantly, however, medical arguments about acculturation coincided with the conscious Javanization of colonial authority. Once implemented, Dutch rule *relied* on cultural accommodation in order to function. Under these circumstances, a pessimistic perspective on acclimatization would be detrimental to the system of colonial governance and to maintaining social control. The Javanization of colonial rule, reflected in deference etiquette, status symbols, and sartorial and language hierarchies, was thus extended to key aspects of everyday life, including hygienic practices, food preparation and consumption, physical activity, and daily routines.[12]

Until the late nineteenth century, Dutch physicians emphasized the importance of adapting one's lifestyle to the climate, especially by taking cues from the indigenous population.[13] Bacteriologist Christiaan Eijkman, who would go on to win the 1929 Nobel Prize in Physiology or Medicine, was the primary Dutch influence on the question of acclimatization. During his long career in the colonies, especially as Director of the Medical Laboratory in Weltevreden (1888–1896), Eijkman made several valuable discoveries that changed the debate on European adjustment to the tropics. First and foremost, through extensive comparative experiments, he was able to demonstrate that heat-induced tropical anemia—a point of consensus among nineteenth-century scientists—did not exist. He found that the blood count, specific gravity, and water content of Europeans in the tropics was no different from those of either the indigenous population or Europeans living in cooler climates. He reached similar conclusions by comparing metabolism, respiratory functions, perspiration, and temperature regulation in Europeans and indigenous peoples. In other words, Eijkman had scientifically proven that Europeans *did not* physically change their constitutions in the tropics *nor* did they differ physiologically from the indigenous population in the first place.[14]

Having disproved heat-induced tropical anemia, Eijkman wondered why so many Europeans felt listless and worn out in the tropics. He concluded that acclimatization depended on adopting habits more suited to the tropical climate (external processes), rather than changes to one's physical constitution (internal processes). From this perspective, Eijkman believed that "the sobriety of food consumption of the indigenous people, their airy clothing, their *festina lente* ['to make haste slowly'], their calm and resigned attitude, all merit, from a purely sanitary perspective, to serve as an example for the white tropical inhabitant."[15] Arguing that imitating the Javanese lifestyle was beneficial for Dutch settlers' health, Eijkman's research thus worked to support colonial strategies of Javanization.

By the turn of the twentieth century, however, physician and anthropologist Jacob Herman Friedrich Kohlbrugge had replaced Eijkman as the leading Dutch voice on European tropical acclimatization, and his perspective was much more pessimistic. During his career (1892–1906) in the Indies, Kohlbrugge became fascinated with the comparative anatomy of Europeans and indigenous peoples, and what he called the "Javanese psyche." His research on the brains of his deceased European and Javanese patients confirmed Eijkman's conclusion that there were no physiological differences between the two. He therefore determined that if Europeans and Javanese had the same brains, perceived differences in intellectual and cultural development must be due to external factors. The most likely candidate, in his opinion, was the tropical climate, which limited humans' physical and mental exertions. Based on climatological differences, Kohlbrugge thus argued that the West stood for progress, innovation, individualism, freedom of thought, reason, science, and physical strength, while the East was characterized by tranquility, collectivism, despotism, mental confusion, emotion, and physical weakness. Due to the climate, Kohlbrugge concluded, the Javanese were intellectually less-developed "children" compared to Europeans, who had evolved to "adulthood."[16]

Kohlbrugge was in good company among other European scientists and physicians. In the second half of the nineteenth century, developments in science and medicine had gradually infused the acclimatization debate with the issue of race. The "evolution revolution" in the biological sciences inspired social theorists to apply and distort Charles Darwin's notion of evolution to human societies and thereby proclaim the superiority of the white race.[17] But while race was increasingly used to mark difference in the British and French colonial world, scientific research in the Netherlands Indies continued to promote the significance of European acculturation on the island of Java.[18] It was not until Kohlbrugge came on the scene that these notions began to change.

Needless to say, Kohlbrugge's conclusions were not without political implications. In his climatic determinism, he proved to be a staunch opponent of the Ethical Policy, arguing that the civilizing mission could not overcome these climate-induced evolutionary differences. The Javanese would always remain intellectually inferior and childlike compared to Europeans who, as the inhabitants of more moderate climates, were the most productive people on earth. Claiming that it was impossible for Europeans to acclimatize to the tropics, Kohlbrugge warned that those who permanently migrated to Java would undergo a process of familial degeneration, as their offspring would "transform gradually, but surely, into Indo-Europeans and finally into Javanese."[19] The pace of this process depended on whether a man brought a European wife with him, married a Eurasian woman, or conceived children with an indigenous woman, but due to the climate, any descendants would be infertile and the family line would terminate by the third generation. The only manner by which Europeans could survive Java's tropical conditions was to physically strengthen themselves through racial mixing, which, according to Kohlbrugge, defeated the purpose of European settlement. Even though Eurasians were more fertile and viable, their character was so radically different that they ceased to be Europeans at all (despite their official legal status as European).[20] Echoing Kipling's infamous line, Kohlbrugge warned: "We cannot turn the West into the East and the hot East into the cool West."[21]

Increasingly, the vast majority of Europeans in colonial society shared Kohlbrugge's view. A columnist for a popular weekly, for instance, argued that the difference between Javanese and European's level of civilization could be explained by ten degrees Celsius: "Take them away and man invents railways, wireless telegraphs, canned flower cabbage, and crystal palaces."[22] Insisting that any attempt to uplift the Javanese was doomed from the outset, he therefore advised the government to put the Ethical Policy on hold until the temperature around the equator equaled that of the Netherlands. The widespread embrace of Kohlbrugge's climatic determinism was even reflected in government documents, such as a 1914 report investigating the causes behind the Javanese's perceived civilizational weakness. Permeated with evolutionary discourse, the report explained that a combination of the climate and character flaws was responsible for the low level of intellectual, cultural, and economic development among the Javanese. The tropical heat created a situation that negated both the "struggle for survival" and a process of "selection." The fertile volcanic soil facilitated year-round harvests, and the absence of cold winters enabled the Javanese to live free of clothing and housing concerns. Moreover, the lack of seasonal cold prevented Javanese society from developing strong physical constitutions and eliminating the weak. Consequently, the report stated, there was no incentive to work hard, be innovative, or strive toward progress, leaving the Javanese lingering in a developmental stage that the Dutch had—allegedly—passed through ages ago.[23]

For most of the nineteenth century, Dutch physicians and scientists had argued that acclimatization to the tropical climate was possible by adjusting one's lifestyle and habits to the new environment. But by the early twentieth century, Kohlbrugge's climatic determinism and belief in evolutionary differences became predominant, changing Dutch colonizers' understanding of their circumstances, role, and identity on Java. The result was an increased emphasis on the cultivation of difference—in other words, on ideas of racial superiority and inferiority—as European identities were continually besieged by the dual threat of the climate and the Javanese's alleged primitive development. As Kohlbrugge himself put it, "If Europeans go to the Indies and stay too long, [they] are doomed to degenerate."[24]

"No One Walks Underneath the Palm Trees Unpunished": Combating Dutch Degeneration[25]

As colonial discourse shifted away from racial mixing, cultural hybridity, and the Javanization of colonial authority, the Dutch began to emphasize the significance of European modernity as a means of racially and culturally purifying colonial society from degenerative influences. Just as Javanese social and political etiquette was no longer needed to legitimize colonial authority, Dutch efforts to adapt to the tropical environment were now considered obsolete, even dangerous. Moreover, these new ideas transformed the Javanese people from reliable guides to life in the tropics to primitive, unhygienic, degenerative disease vectors that must be kept at a safe distance. In contrast, the Dutch now considered themselves (and Europeans in general) to be superior, modern beings that were far more civilized, hygienic, and intellectual than the natives. This newfound modern identity not only pervaded the Ethical Policy and shaped twentieth-century approaches to legitimizing colonial rule but also became an essential strategy for combating the risk of degeneration. The acclimatization argument lingered, but most agreed that Java's tropical climate had a negative impact on Europeans. While the extent of this impact was up for debate, many Dutch believed that establishing a modern European colonial lifestyle would offer protection against the degenerative influences of both the climate and indigenous people and culture.

During the first decades of the twentieth century, there was a sudden rise in cases of tropical neurasthenia among Europeans living on Java. Introduced by American neurologist George Beard in the 1860s, neurasthenia was a catchall diagnosis used to describe varied physical and mental symptoms caused by anxieties about modern life.[26] In the tropics, it became a prevalent diagnosis for an assumed disorder of the central nervous system that could not be attributed to a single causative factor. Consequently, a broad agglomeration of symptoms was associated with the illness, such as listlessness, depression, headache, irritability, nausea, constipation, diarrhea, respiratory problems, insomnia, excessive sleep, heart palpations, and impotence. The alleged causes of tropical neurasthenia were almost as varied as its symptoms, including the continuous tropical heat and humidity, consumption of spicy food, concerns over hygiene and tropical diseases, the materialism and individualism of colonial society, and loneliness.[27]

Of the European civil servants who received furlough in the years 1915 to 1924, almost half were diagnosed with tropical neurasthenia.[28] The popularity of this diagnosis reflected lingering ambiguity about climatic determinism as well as anxieties about physical degeneration among the European population. Attempts to prevent or cure the condition centered around circumventing its causes and recreating a European environment in the tropics. Dutch colonials retreated to the dry, moderate climate of Java's mountains, consumed European food, followed Western hygienic conventions, and sought out cultural and intellectual interactions with other Europeans. In other words, they tried to institute a Western lifestyle that resembled that of Europe.

Western pharmaceutical companies also joined the effort to treat tropical neurasthenia and, accordingly, fears of degeneration, by introducing an array of medications to counter the disorder, employing savvy advertisement campaigns that anticipated European anxieties. Nerve medicines like Sanatogen, produced by Bayer, were presented as the scientific solution to Europeans' need to adapt to living in the tropics. By purportedly strengthening the bones, muscles, and nerves, Sanatogen was said to cure diverse symptoms of tropical neurasthenia, such as anemia, listlessness, depression, sleeplessness, and eating and intestinal disorders.[29] Presented as "The Nerve Strengthening Food," advertisements printed in newspapers and periodicals often featured a depressed European man or woman, sometimes with another illustration of the person in better health after taking Sanatogen.[30] One of the campaign's more interesting advertisements depicts a European mother with two children playing in an outdoor springtime scene, described as "fresh, young, and happy" without any "dust, heat, and weakness." Lest the colonial observer despair over the contrast between a healthy European environment and their unhealthy Javanese reality, the accompanying text provides some reassurance: "A Dutch spring is probably an impossible ideal at present, but you can certainly achieve that 'spring-feeling' of happy, cheerful health with Sanatogen."[31] Along with other nerve medications, such as Biocitin and Virol, Sanatogen came to be considered an effective cure for European degeneration in the tropics.

In addition to medical supplements, Europeans became convinced of the need to physically strengthen their bodies to heighten their resistance to the tropical climate. Strengthening one's muscles, central nervous system, and immune system through exercise was deemed a crucial way to maintain physical and mental health. Travel guides and household manuals advised Dutch colonials residing in the tropics to be physically active during the cooler mornings and evenings, preferably by engaging in sports that also strengthened social bonds within the European community.[32] This was not difficult to do, as the early twentieth century witnessed an international explosion of sports associations and leagues for swimming, tennis, football, field hockey, cycling, rowing, sailing, golf, croquet, skittles, hiking, mountaineering, horse riding, and gymnastics. In the colonies, most of these associations were for Europeans only; swimming in particular was strictly segregated by race. Although the Javanese began to play some of these sports themselves—soccer, for instance—they had to establish their own leagues.[33]

Finally, to address concerns about neurasthenia and degeneration, Dutch colonials sought a reprieve from both the tropical climate and indigenous culture. Reflecting this desire, mountain resorts proliferated in late-colonial Indonesia, creating spaces in which pseudoscientific concerns about race, civilization, and the climate coalesced. In contrast to British and French hill stations in Asia, mountain resorts in Dutch Indonesia were not semiannual retreats but weekend getaways near Java's major urban areas. In the mild mountain climate, colonials relaxed in European-style hotels and lodges, cozied up next to fireplaces, consumed hearty European meals prepared by European chefs, and enjoyed flora and fauna that reminded them of home. By protecting the European physical body, mentality, and cultural identity, mountain resorts were crucial in facilitating the colonial project. Here, the sick could recuperate, the healthy strengthen their bodies, and all find shelter from the indigenous conventions permeating the island. As an antidote to degeneration, it was believed that these resorts provided the colony with physically strong and mentally healthy Europeans to advance the colonial project and uphold European prestige.[34]

"The Cancer of Indies Society": Purging Eastern Influences

Medication, physical exercise, and mountain resorts could only go so far to protect European bodies on Java. Drawing heavily on evolutionary understandings of racial difference, Dutch colonials also sought to purge their households and everyday lives from the degenerative influences of indigenous people, culture, and society. Unsurprisingly, Kohlbrugge identified the overwhelming presence of indigenous servants in the colonial household as a primary threat to European lives. Most Europeans depended on a variety of indigenous servants such as a houseboy (*djongos*), cook (*kokkie*), gardener (*kebon*), nanny (*baboe*), and seamstress (*djait*) to manage their households. While the number of servants had long signified status in colonial society, their place in the colonial household became contentious as Europeans came to regard their servants as uncivilized, unhygienic, and, due to scientific advances in germ theory, carriers of disease that posed a danger to the health of colonial families.[35]

The conviction that Europeans were inherently more sanitary than indigenous people strikingly contrasted with the reality in which Javanese servants prepared their food, washed and fitted their clothing, cleaned their homes, and most importantly, took care of their children. This ambivalence was reflected in European household manuals and the colonial press, which simultaneously described servants as lazy, dirty, and unreliable as well as gentle, skilled, and compliant. As Elsbeth Locher-Scholten argues, this incongruity mirrored the prevailing political discourse that on the one hand cultivated racial difference but on the other aimed to civilize indigenous society. Under this rubric, servants were considered both useful children in need of European guidance and a serious threat to colonial families.[36]

The baboe became the embodiment of the danger that servants in particular, and indigenous society in general, posed to European culture and identity on

Java. According to Kohlbrugge, the baboe submitted to children's every whim. She allowed them to hit her and give orders, did not enforce eating only at meal-times, and refused to let infants cry themselves to sleep. In contrast to a decent European upbringing, this allegedly resulted in children with no sense of obedience, restraint, duty, or work ethic. The baboe's unhygienic native habits further set a bad example and even endangered the children when she dressed, fed, and bathed them. In addition, many argued that children in a baboe's care spoke Malay better than Dutch, believed in indigenous superstitions, and were susceptible to the low sexual morality of the natives.[37] In colonial public opinion, indigenous women's "lack of civilization and development" made them "absolutely unsuitable as nanny for [European] children."[38] The baboe was a "curse," causing them to quickly degenerate to the level of the natives, which endangered the survival of European culture and identity in the tropics. Consequently, "baboe-ism" escalated to a "vice" of sensational proportions in the colonial press, referred to as the "cancer of Indies society."[39]

Such views presented the European mother as both the reason for and antidote to the baboe's corrupting effect on children and, indirectly, the future of the European community in the tropics.[40] European mothers' tendency—especially Eurasians, who held European status—to delegate their children's upbringing to indigenous women was now an indication of their own degeneration. It was their laziness, indolence, egocentrism, and vanity—character traits often ascribed to Indo-Europeans—that resulted in the decision to employ a baboe. The vicious cycle of degeneration therefore did not start with the baboe but with the children's mother, or if one wanted to uncover the root of the problem, their indigenous ancestors. The only way to break or even reverse this cycle was for the mother to reclaim charge over her children's upbringing following bourgeois European standards. It was not accidental that this idealization of European motherhood coincided with the rapid increase of European women in the colony. But although they came to be considered the guardians of European identity and cultural values, their presumed role in baboe-ism simultaneously reinforced continued oppression from male counterparts. For instance, when European women lobbied for suffrage in the colonies, one commentator flatly stated: "First do your duty, then demand your rights."[41]

In addition to this anxiety about baboes and motherhood, food and the kokkie who prepared it became crucial issues for Europeans on Java. The kokkie's place in the household gradually came under much scrutiny that emphasized the assumed unsanitary conditions of her kitchen and her inability to prepare a decent European meal. Again, it was European women who had caused this problem and also had the power to solve it. They were encouraged to take control over their kitchens, either by closely supervising the kokkie or by preparing meals themselves. Household guides and periodicals offered an abundance of advice on hygiene and cooking, while modern novelties like refrigerators and gas and electric stoves also made the kitchen a more sanitary space for food preparation. By reclaiming their role in the colonial kitchen, European women would protect the physical wellbeing of their families and halt cultural degeneration in its tracks. [42]

However, there was more at stake than the issue of who prepared the food; the Dutch also began to scrutinize the food itself. With rice as their staple and the rice table as a significant social practice, some worried that the latter in particular was both a cause and indication of degeneration. For instance, a popular commentator described the rice table as a "ravenous, gluttonous, animalistic agglomeration of extremely stinking food"—a hodgepodge that allegedly undermined one's taste and propriety.[43] Such assertions implicitly suggested that European bodies and minds required European food to thrive. Western companies like Quaker Oats played to these sentiments, claiming that oats were ideal for the tropics, "much better than rice." Advertisements promoted oats as a nutritious substitute that allegedly strengthened the blood, muscles, and bones, improved athletic abilities, and produced superior breast milk. Arguing that oats were the best food for growing babies, toddlers, teenagers and adolescents, the Quaker Oats campaign incorporated colonial anxieties about children's protracted physical development to sell the product.[44]

The invention of light, airtight canisters and freezers aboard ships enabled the importation of goods like Quaker Oats to colonial Java, making a wide array of European food products available in the colony.[45] This emphasis on European food was also reflected in agricultural initiatives on Java itself. Private entrepreneurs expanded the cultivation of numerous European vegetables as well as dairy products in Java's mountains, while the colonial government experimented with the largescale cultivation of wheat.[46] Although rice and the rice table did not disappear, changes in food consumption played an important role in combating fears of degeneration and developing a European identity in the tropics.

Thus, during the final decades of colonial rule in Indonesia, the Dutch became increasingly concerned with Java's influence on their physical and cultural wellbeing. Embracing theories of climatic determinism and evolutionary racism, they now considered themselves outsiders in a hostile climate living among backward people with an alien culture. To assert their modernity and alleged superiority, they emphasized their Europeanness and sought ways to replicate a Western lifestyle in the tropics. In the process, they forged new racial and cultural identities in opposition to the Javanese, which gradually shaped a new approach to legitimizing their authority on the archipelago. By the 1920s, the once-fashionable idea of a colonial collaboration between East and West had become an illusion, and Dutch colonial rule firmly relied on the cultivation of difference.

The "Seven M's": Negotiating Western Modernity

The rapid changes within colonial society triggered by the Ethical Policy, the national awakening, scientific and technological innovations, and developments in the wider world forced a reconsideration of the colonial relationship as well as a reinvention of colonial identities. As the Dutch redefined themselves by re-interpreting the impact of the tropical climate and their Javanized approach to power, the Javanese were redefining their own identity against this new colonial discourse. Central to this process was an ongoing debate about how westerniza-tion would influence conceptions of Indonesianness, which were simultaneously being forged through the national awakening. Questioning to what extent they could embrace Western modernity without a loss of self, Indonesians sought to purge alleged vices and bad habits, and promote attitudes and behaviors that would increase their power and standing in the colonial arena. In this way, their goals aligned with those of the colonizer (albeit from a different angle), as both attempted to develop modern identities within a shared discursive space.[47]

The early decades of the twentieth century saw the emergence of a largely urban Indonesian middle class. Because they were essential in staffing the co-lonial state's expanding bureaucracy as well as private enterprises, middle-class men (along with the traditional elite) were the almost exclusive beneficiaries of extensive Western education. This education, work opportunities, and accom-panying financial advantages meant that they were the group most exposed to Western modernity on Java. According to historical anthropologist Henk Schulte Nordholt, the nascent urban middle classes were characterized not by their political ambitions, such as independence, but rather by their aspiration to modern lifestyles. This concept of modern life was loosely associated with West-ern social values, including the nuclear family; Western fashions in clothing and furnishings; habits such as smoking, dancing, drinking, and reading newspapers; Western technology, especially watches, bicycles, and gramophones; and West-ern perceptions of beauty and hygiene. Interestingly, westernized individuals and social groups often bought into the Ethical Policy's civilizing discourse that

had replaced the Javanization of authority in 1901. But while the middle classes
provided essential support for the revised colonial project, they did not uncritically embrace Western norms and behaviors. In their encounter with Western
modernity, the Indonesian middle classes formulated their own alternate understandings of modernity and progress. Though approaches varied, they shared a
common determination to create a distinct, though Western-influenced, modern Indonesian identity. Thus, Kipling's trope was not just popular with the
colonizer.[48]

From the outset, it was clear that the West was not the only, or even most
desirable, model to emulate in articulating varied ethnic, religious, and national
identities. Members of Boedi Oetomo, for instance, were profoundly inspired
by the Japanese, who during the Meiji Restoration (1868) selectively broke with
what were perceived to be outdated traditions and embraced Western science,
technology, and education without losing their own cultural identity. The
Chinese revolution of 1911 and the emancipation of the Chinese diaspora in
Indonesia suggested a similar path. Others, such as the Sarekat Islam and Muhammadiyah, were drawn to the transnational Islamic modernist movement
that originated in Mecca and Cairo and swept through the Muslim world at
the turn of the twentieth century. In an attempt to reconcile Western colonial
dominance with the superior teachings of Islam, the Islamic reform movement,
as it was also known, accepted certain elements of Western modernity, above all
scientific and technological knowledge, while amending cultural and societal
practices to bring them into accordance with Islamic teachings. These associations propagated the pursuit of self-betterment, behavioral moderation, and
the strict observance of the five pillars of Islam.[49] Similarly, Indonesian associations with a more overtly political outlook—like the Indische Party or later, the
Partai Nasional Indonesia—emphasized the importance of the right to vote,
equality under the law, and self-determination, while also formulating a distinct national identity. All of these viewpoints aspired to be modern, defined by
political rights, self-improvement, and embracing science and technology, but
their ultimate acceptance was always contingent on being distinctively Eastern.

The question of to what extent Western cultural accommodation became
problematic was one of the most discussed subjects in the vernacular press during
the final decades of colonial rule. Countless articles considered whether it would
be best to only adopt from the West what was deemed useful or, alternatively,
to reject Western materialism and individualism altogether in favor of Eastern spirituality and collectivism—perspectives widely considered throughout
the colonial world.[50] The underlying fear was that imitating the Dutch would

eventually lead to a societal and individual loss of identity.[51] These anxieties became more concrete with numerous specific examples of westernization ranging from the modernization of deference rituals and the question of what to wear, to trepidation regarding language, education, science, technology, architecture, interior design, consumption, the arts, and music. Advocates of the various currents within the nationalist movement offered diverging perspectives on these and other issues. As a result, an array of competing Indonesian identities began to emerge.[52]

Generally speaking, the colonized sought to identify the vices of colonial modernity and replace them with virtues more befitting indigenous traditions. At the turn of the twentieth century, the most common among them became popularly known as the "seven M's" (*mim pitu*), referring to seven vices beginning with the letter M: *main* (gambling), *madon* (chasing after women; prostitution; adultery), *minum* (alcoholism), *madat* (opium use), *maling* (thievery), *mada* (lying), and *mangani* (gluttony). There were many reasons for opposing these vices, including the fact that they did not conform to Islamic morality, and the belief that engaging in them subdued the colonized while financially benefiting the colonizers. Although the idiom preceded the emergence of the nationalist movement, it was through Indonesia's first political and cultural associations that it took on special meaning as a way of challenging colonial modernity. In 1909, it became an oft-used expression at Boedi Oetomo meetings, where it was used as a call to action to claim dignity and self-respect.[53] A few years later, Tjokroaminoto, as chairman of the Sarekat Islam, frequently brought up the seven M's at the association's meetings and rallies, impressing on his audiences that they must strive for self-improvement. This included moderation in behavior, self-education, working hard, and eschewing criminal activities and lying. The Sarekat Islam's reformist agenda specifically identified alcoholism, opium use, gambling, and prostitution as social evils that must be reduced, if not exterminated.[54] In the program for the 1917 Sarekat Islam Congress, tackling these vices formed the core of the movement's social objectives.[55]

In addition to these larger organizations, a number of self-help associations established throughout Java during the 1910s also embraced the principles behind the seven M's. For instance, members of the aptly named Mim Pitu, founded in Batavia in 1914, promised to adhere to agreed-on moral guidelines—namely, rejecting the seven M's.[56] Another self-help association organized in Salatiga (Central Java) committed to a similar moral code. Named Insulinde's Dageraad (Indies' Dawn), the association was started by Dutch schoolteachers in 1913, but its indigenous members quickly took over leadership, dedicating themselves to living a clean life, honoring women and the elderly, and refusing the consumption of alcohol, opium, and cigarettes.[57] Interestingly, many of these associations, as well as Boedi Oetomo and the Sarekat Islam, defined the seven M's slightly differently. They often used vices that began with the letter M interchangeably, at times adding new ones—such as *misuh* (cursing) and *matenni/modol* (murder)—to the list and subtracting others. The fluidity of the concept only enhanced its popularity.

Alcoholism—one of the original seven—was perhaps the most disconcerting vice associated with colonial modernity. Although Java had a long history of producing fermented beverages from rice or sugar palm juices, their widespread consumption had been inhibited since the fourteenth century by the arrival of Islam.[58] However, as members of the Javanese aristocracy sought to create an aura of authority by dressing, wining, and dining like the Dutch, the consumption of alcoholic beverages gradually increased in the nineteenth century.[59] This attempt to appear powerful through mimicry motivated many aspiring Javanese to consume alcohol, as well, which was also facilitated by the import of Dutch gin (*jenever*). As a consequence, by 1900, the consumption of alcohol had grown significantly among the Javanese.[60] For those questioning the morality of Western modernity, this increase was not a welcome development. Sarekat Islam rallies promoted the idea that alcoholism was the result of the westernization of society and the cause of moral decay, physical deterioration, a loss of prestige, and financial ruin among Indonesians.[61] In addition, observers always pointed out the colonial government's dubious role regarding the presence of alcohol on Java; officially, the authorities discouraged its consumption, but at the same time profited handsomely from excise and import duties on gin. As one commenter noted cynically, the Dutch first "introduced alcohol to the Indies, profited from its sale, and subsequently promulgated circulars and organized conferences to fight its consumption." The government claimed to want to protect the indigenous population, but the author wondered, "How much profit does the government make with its monopolies again?"[62] Thus, resistance to alcohol was about more than Islamic reforms; it was also part of a larger struggle against colonial exploitation.

Like alcohol, the Dutch imported opium to Java but in contrast, the Dutch themselves did not consume opium. The clientele of Java's opium dens consisted primarily of indigenous and Chinese people, while the profits of these enterprises flowed back into the coffers of the colonial state. Until 1918, at least 10 percent of the state's total annual revenue came directly from the government's sale of opium. As part of the Ethical Policy, in 1910 a more "humanitarian" government-controlled system of opium production and sale called the *opium-regie* replaced the financially lucrative opium farms. This would purportedly enable the government to proactively discourage the use of opium, but to the impartial observer it was clear that in terms of consumption, little changed. A journalist for *Bintang Soerabaja* scathingly wrote that the overhaul of the farm system "was intended to reduce opium consumption, just as the government intended to reduce the number of debtors, travelers, phone customers, and slaughtered animals through its pawnshops, railroads, telephone-company, and slaughter houses."[63] More explicitly than with alcohol, the anti-opium movement was characterized as a struggle against colonial exploitation. Tellingly, it was not government propaganda and actions that ultimately curbed opium consumption in colonial Indonesia, but cultural and political associations' campaigns against it, including Boedi Oetomo, the Sarekat Islam, Muhammadiyah, and Taman Siswa. And as consumption dwindled, so did the share of opium profits in colonial revenue.[64]

Conspicuous consumption—or gluttony—was another vice that was strongly associated with westernization, moral decay, and colonial exploitation. At Sarekat Islam rallies, Tjokroaminoto reasoned that Europeans were merely humans who, like the Javanese, had strengths and weaknesses. Perhaps foremost among their weaknesses, he argued, was their obsession with material wealth and conspicuous consumption, which he contrasted with Eastern spirituality and asceticism.[65] Like many others, Tjokroaminoto encouraged the colonized not to naively emulate Europeans, but to adopt only those aspects of Western modernity that supported their struggle for respect and equality.[66] This meant resisting the many temptations of Western materialism, including modern consumer products such as watches, radios, gramophones, bicycles, electric lights, refrigerators, soaps, perfumes, and canned food, as well as entertainment and events from movies, restaurants, and concerts to international expositions. Tjokroaminoto asserted that conspicuous consumption did not only run counter to Javanese morality but also benefited the colonizer. Western products and services were provided by European companies. Tempting the Javanese to live above their means, ensuing indebtedness forced them to turn to government-run pawnshops to return their consumer products. In popular culture, the pawnshop became a corrective site where people without self-discipline were forcefully stripped of material symbols of Western modernity. Evoking the humiliation of a visit to the pawnshop, advertisements, political cartoons, and speeches given by Tjokroaminoto and others effectively discouraged people from such gluttonous consumption.

DJANGANLAH SAMPAI LOEPA DARATAN!

Sarwan: Wah, lihat si Toing belaga memanggil taxi!

Diman: Addoeh, pakaiannja serem, kerén! Ajoh, kita gontjeng, lihat maoe kemana!

Sarwan: Ai, ai, dibioskop masoeknja djoega dikelas satoe!

Diman: Ei, ei, lihat si Toing gadaikan barang!

Sarwan: Tjoba, kemarén ia belaga, sekarang pergi gadai!

FIGURE 7. "Don't forget where you come from!" A cartoon cautioning against the temptations of modern life. Wearing a suit, riding a taxi, and buying first class cinema tickets can easily result in a visit to the pawnshop. Source: *Pandji Poestaka*, January 31, 1940.

Finally, one of the most controversial topics in these discussions of Indonesian westernization was social mixing between men and women. Traditionally, Javanese boys and girls, especially the children of elites, were separated from the age of twelve onward. Girls were secluded within the privacy of the household and family life, where they remained until they were married, usually to a partner selected by their parents. However, Western modernity brought with it many new social habits and temptations, such as movie theatres, public concerts, restaurants, night markets, and, of course, dances. Interactions between the sexes were increasingly less inhibited in these venues, as adolescents mingled, held hands, hugged, and even kissed in public. This behavior contrasted sharply with the beliefs of Islamic modernists seeking to purge society from modern vices, of which the public social engagement between adolescent boys and girls and unmarried men and women was one of the most troubling.

In the vernacular press, Western dances became the focus of anxieties about free social interaction. In contrast to traditional Javanese dances where participants were all of the same sex, men and women danced together in close physical contact at Western-style dances. In the women's journal *Isteri*, several authors expressed concern about what they regarded as highly sensual activities, which they argued were likely to lead to improper public behavior, premarital sexual relations, and children born out of wedlock. In addition, they asserted that allowing youths to participate in these dances suggested parental approval of immoral behavior.[67] One author called on all Indonesian mothers to protect their daughters from the menace of Western dances.[68] As this appeal indicates, indigenous mothers—and indigenous women in general—were often cast in a significant and often paradoxical role in these discussions about the negative effects of Western modernity. In the vernacular press, "authentic" Javanese women (which depended on participation in the nationalist movement) were deemed guardians of the nation—a role that carried honor but also the weighty responsibility of purging all the immoral Western influences threatening themselves, their progeny, and the emerging Indonesian state. At the same time, the press often insisted that women—and, by extension, children and the nation—needed protection from westernization's harmful impact.[69] The topic of social mixing, and dances in particular, was a common avenue toward such discussions of modern Indonesian womanhood.

Contesting Western vices was an important step in redefining what it meant to be a colonial subject, a Javanese man or woman, a Muslim, and, increasingly, an Indonesian. But as the examples of alcoholism, opium, and conspicuous consumption, and freer social interaction illustrate, the Javanese confrontation with colonial modernity was far from a uniform, let alone a nationalist, one. A variety of perspectives emerged through which Indonesians sought to modify Western modernity to fit their desired lifestyle. Their burgeoning identities and corresponding choices and debates reflected these negotiations, and as such played an important role in the struggle against colonial oppression.[70] For many, these issues came to a head with changing norms and ideas around interracial relationships between Indonesians and Europeans.

Concubinage and Mixed Marriages: Race, Gender, and Colonial Identities

As Indonesians and the Dutch constructed new identities in response and opposition to one another, both had to negotiate—and in many ways disentangle—the blend of East and West that characterized colonial society. The adoption and rejection of new moral codes was central to this process of self-definition, and many focused on an area of entanglement that had shaped life on Java since the VOC's arrival: intimate encounters between colonizer and colonized. Attitudes toward such relationships—concubinage and mixed marriages, in particular—changed significantly during the final half-century of colonial rule, on both sides. For the Dutch, shifting views toward marriage and sex were often rooted in theories of acclimatization and biological racism. Whereas explorations of this shift have been at the center of scholarly inquiry, Indonesian perspectives have received far less attention. Interestingly, however, Indonesians also came to consider these unions to be dangerous and degenerative, often invoking the same racist rhetoric espoused by the colonizer.[71] Indigenous intellectuals who had studied in the Netherlands (as well as some educated in the Indies) inevitably came into contact with European notions of race. As with the adoption of democratic and enlightenment discourses—which the Javanese effectively used to expose the hypocrisy of the colonial project—some educated and informed Indonesians also employed Western racial discourses. This is not to say that they fully bought into these ideas but utilizing them allowed Indonesians to turn racial discourses against the institution of colonialism and cultivate nationalist sentiment.

The new Dutch position on interracial relationships marked a substantial departure from colonial authorities' tacit approval, even encouragement, of racial mixing that had reigned since the seventeenth century. The VOC preferred to recruit bachelors for service in the Indies but limited the immigration of European women and at the same time placed limitations on marriage to indigenous women.[72] The reasoning behind these policies was that indigenous women were less expensive to maintain and less likely to encourage their partners to partake in illegal trade. With the exception of high-ranking employees, who were either accompanied by a European spouse or married a converted indigenous or Eurasian woman, most European men sought the company of enslaved or free indigenous women as concubines (nyai). Although temporary marriages or concubinage was a common feature of trade diasporas in Southeast Asia, in colonial Batavia they uniquely formed a more permanent Eurasian society. These relationships served to anchor European men in the colonies, encourage the growth of a stable colonial settler community, and provide guidance regarding local lifestyles, culture, and climate. The institution of concubinage changed nominally with the abolition of slavery in 1860, but widespread poverty facilitated indigenous women's willingness to continue serving as concubines—now referred to as housekeepers—to European men. By the end of the nineteenth century, an estimated 50 percent of European men cohabitated with a housekeeper.[73]

However, the institution of concubinage was gradually discredited from the 1880s onward due to growing concerns about acclimatization, European prestige, and the dangers of physical and moral degeneration. To live outside of marriage with an indigenous woman with no legal rights—she could be discarded with or without her children at any moment—came to be regarded as immoral and indicative of a lack of piety. Critics of these unions argued that it was impossible for officials, civil servants, and soldiers, as representatives of Dutch authority and European civilization, to command respect when living in concubinage. The advantages once associated with the lifestyle were either dismissed or transferred to the care of European women.[74] Moreover, while the nyai had long been regarded as an invaluable guide to indigenous society and the tropical environment, she was now considered a degenerative influence on her partner. By encouraging indigenous approaches to dress, food, customs, and superstitions, she would inevitably turn him into a lazy, egocentric, and indifferent person. In addition, the relaxation of conjugal restrictions with indigenous women and the growing presence of European women on Java made it no longer necessary for the nyai to serve as a perceived remedy for loneliness, boredom, alcoholism, sodomy, prostitution, and the spread of venereal diseases among European men.[75] These changes and growing concerns led the government to prohibit concubinage for all civil servants in 1904, and to gradually reduce its presence in army barracks between 1913 and 1928. Following the authorities' example, concubinage in the private sector also diminished after 1920.[76]

The decrease in concubinage in colonial society led to an increase in mixed marriages between European men and indigenous or Eurasian women.

Marriages between Europeans also increased as immigration restrictions for European women lessened, but the reality remained that Dutch men outnumbered Dutch women on Java until the end of colonial rule. And while most Europeans believed that mixed-race procreation was to be avoided regardless of the nature of the sexual relationship, there were also many who justified mixed marriages with religious or moral arguments, claiming that they were preferable to living in sin.[77] The numbers reflect this attitude, as mixed marriages rose from 13 percent of all European marriages in 1900 to 20 percent in 1920 and 27.5 percent in 1925, before dropping back down to 20 percent in 1940.[78]

Even so, the growth of mixed marriages created a new racialized and gendered class hierarchy in colonial society. The legal foundations for this hierarchy, as well as for authorizing mixed marriages in the first place, can be traced to government regulations from the mid-nineteenth century. Until then, marriages between Christians and non-Christians were prohibited, and indigenous partners had to convert before wedding a Dutch Christian. In 1848, legal status replaced religion as the primary criteria for permitting mixed marriages. This meant that indigenous individuals had to submit to European civil and commercial law before they could marry a European. And since the legal division between populations largely corresponded with ethnicity—Europeans, "Foreign Orientals," and indigenous people—the term "mixed marriage" had highly racialized connotations.[79]

By the turn of the century, colonial authorities' perspective on mixed marriage changed again when they realized that the 1848 regulation was enabling unions between women with European status—mostly poor Eurasians—and indigenous men. On average, only three of these marriages occurred per year between 1886 and 1897, but officials still considered them a blow to European prestige. To discourage these relationships, revised marriage regulations were issued in 1898, stipulating that women now inherited the legal status of their husbands, as did any children born from these unions. This statute aligned with European, Islamic, and Chinese law, and its official reasoning was that the family's viability benefited from legal equality. Unofficially, though, the regulations were purposefully designed to discourage white European women from marrying indigenous men. As the law's explanatory text made clear, colonial authorities could tolerate poor Eurasian women—who were already considered partly degenerate in their minds—marrying indigenous men, but it was "most contemptible" if European women who did not "straddle the border between the races" did so.[80] This racialized and gendered class hierarchy affected men's choices, as well, as immigrant and locally born European men and affluent Eurasian men were expected to marry "white" or "pure" European women. Conversely, poor European and especially Eurasian men could now marry indigenous women without much social consequence since according to colonial ideology, they too were already lacking in prestige.

However, it was not only European attitudes toward concubinage and mixed marriages that changed in the late-colonial period. Interracial relationships were increasingly scrutinized by the colonized, as well. The Sarekat Islam was instrumental in voicing criticism of the institution of concubinage at rallies and meetings and in its vernacular publications. As a union not only out of wedlock but also crossing a religious divide, Islamic reformists considered concubinage a reprehensible sin. Moreover, in 1913, the association identified opposition to concubinage as one of its main objectives, framing it as a quintessential symbol of colonial exploitation. Followers were reminded that European men primarily came to Java in search of riches and sought poor young women as temporary housekeepers and concubines. Women only accepted such positions due to poverty and, crucially, had no legal rights, as there were no official records of these relationships. When the European man made his fortune and repatriated or chose to marry a European woman, he could discard his concubine at will and either take his children or leave them behind as he desired. Used and abused, the nyai returned to poverty. The nyai thus became emblematic of colonialism itself, which benefited the Dutch and left the Javanese bereft.[81]

Just as with the opposition to deference rituals, public criticism of concubinage as a colonial injustice forced the Dutch to reconsider the custom. Yet there was no consensus among the Javanese as to what should replace the institution. Some promoted mixed marriages as a possible solution, as that would put an end to the moral ambiguity of cohabitation outside of marriage as well as give indigenous women legal rights regarding their children, divorce, and inheritance. From this perspective, these unions could ultimately symbolize a true partnership between East and West. This was unacceptable, however, for Islamic reformists, including Sarekat Islam's leadership, who insisted that mixed marriages could only be legitimate if the European converted to Islam.[82]

However, many indigenous commentators also echoed European concerns about race, most often conceptualized through ideas regarding purity of blood (*darah*). For instance, in an article about a nyai accused of poisoning her former master, a contributor to the newspaper *Kemadjoean Hindia* (Indies Progress) categorically rejected interracial unions. Writing under a pseudonym, he argued that interracial relationships—"mixed blood" (*berdarah campuran*), in his words—hampered Javanese national progress. Since children inherited their father's status, the offspring of mixed unions were foreigners, destined to also

inherit harmful European interests and customs. The author suggested that the
system of concubinage and all mixed unions be forbidden altogether.[83] Many
agreed, as phrases like "the betrayal of one's race," "the degradation of our race,"
and "loyalty to one's race" became commonplace in the vernacular press, and the
"contamination of Javanese blood" framed discussions of Eurasian children who
resulted from interracial unions.[84]

Such discussions in the vernacular press were heightened by the 1915 announcement of the engagement of Raden Adjeng Soehito, a bupati's daughter,
to Hubert Dorren, a lieutenant in the colonial army. Up until then, the focus
had been on relationships between European men and poor Javanese women,
but the bride's social status made this a highly sensitive topic. Being of priyayi,
or aristocratic, descent made Soehito an unlikely spouse for a European man.
Traditionally, aristocratic adolescent women lived in seclusion after their twelfth
birthday until the moment of their arranged marriage. The fact that Soehito
and Dorren were able to meet each other at all implied that the bride enjoyed a
relatively progressive social upbringing that allowed her to socialize more freely
with men. Conservative commentators in the vernacular press presented the engagement as an example of the dangers of freer social interaction between the
sexes and of westernization in general. In addition, they considered Soehito's
choice of a European lieutenant instead of a fellow member of the priyayi to be a
slight against Javanese tradition and rejection of Javanese men. There were also
concerns that Soehito would be seen as a concubine in the eyes of the common
Javanese.[85] Apparently, the consequences of interracial relationships were much
more acute when they involved the elite.[86]

Responses to Soehito and Dorren's announcement were not uniform, however, and alongside concern and alarm were some positive reactions. A contributor to the newspaper *Sinar Djawa* (Java's Radiance) described the engagement as
the "fruits of progress" and a sign of Javanese women's successful emancipation.
The marriage proved that European men no longer felt too superior to marry a
Javanese woman and dared to display their affection publicly and legally. Moreover, since women had more rights in European marriages and European men
allegedly treated their spouses better than Javanese men did, the author reasoned
that mixed marriages could be a great opportunity for Javanese women. And
if Javanese men did not like it, they needed to treat women better.[87] In stark
contrast, Islamic reformists vehemently opposed any marital union between a
European man and Javanese woman, as it went against religious prescripts. In
the newspaper *Kaoem Moeda* (Youth), a contributor therefore described the Soehito's engagement as the "sour fruit of progress" and wrongly argued that she

was now obliged to convert to Christianity. Interestingly, the author had fewer qualms about mixed marriages when European women converted to Islam in order to wed Javanese men.[88]

In the following decades, the marriage between an aristocratic or Western-educated Javanese woman (the two often were interchangeable) and a European man almost guaranteed a resurgence of the debate over mixed marriages.[89] The preference for a European over a Javanese husband was perceived as a significant challenge to Javanese masculinity, and the potential motivations behind Javanese women's choice was a hotly debated topic in the vernacular press. In the newspaper *Perempoean Bergerak* (Women's Movement), one author argued that before criticizing women's decision to engage in interracial relationships, the underlying causes must be understood and addressed. She suggested that perhaps upper-class women were disillusioned with Javanese marriage customs in which women had no rights and were always at risk of child marriage, repudiation and divorce, and polygamy. By marrying a European spouse, women gained legal rights and protections against these threats. The author also found it unfair to criticize poor women seeking stability and security as either a nyai or wife to a European man.[90] Another female contributor presented a similar argument in the newspaper *Padjadjaran*, writing that since Javanese men all too often took their wives for granted and could renounce her at any time, educated Javanese women in particular preferred the company of Europeans.[91] Such arguments posed by female authors were mostly rejected by their more numerous male counterparts, who increasingly blamed Western education and cultural depictions of chivalrous and gentlemanlike European men. Countering the idea that women could better relate to men who were their intellectual and modern equals, they argued that adulation for everything European would only result in veiled concubinage.[92]

Frustrated with the prevalence of interracial relationships between European men and Javanese women, commentators in the vernacular press openly wondered how the Dutch would respond if the tables were turned. Would they allow a European woman—especially of high social standing—to marry an indigenous man, her alleged racial inferior and a Muslim on top of that, and lose her legal status in the process?[93] To taunt the Dutch and bolster public opposition to mixed marriages, several newspapers devised a unique manner of protest. Alluding to advertisements in which Europeans solicited the companionship of an indigenous woman, the newspaper *Sinar Pasoendan* published its own advertisement featuring a Western-educated indigenous man seeking a European woman under the age of twenty as his spouse. Interested parties were asked to submit photographs for consideration. Below the ad, the editors explained that they did not mean to offend but merely to point out how insulting the European practice was to the Javanese. In bold letters they added that the objective of their symbolic protest was to quicken emancipation and achieve full equality with Europeans.[94]

Despite this alleged intention, marriages between Western-educated Javanese men and European women were in fact on the rise. Although Dutch investments in education were minimal overall, they did enable the sons of the Javanese elite to receive a Western education. A select few continued their studies in the Netherlands, where they freely socialized with European women. These interactions resulted in a steady increase in mixed marriages between Indonesian men and Dutch women, who were not discouraged by the 1898 law dictating that wives inherit their husband's legal status. Seeking to suppress interracial unions, colonial authorities instead focused their efforts on dissuading Indonesian students from pursuing them. In September 1914, the study committee of the Association of East and West, which supported Indonesian education in the metropole, addressed a letter to students as well as their parents in the colony. The Dutch committee explicitly stated that after completing their studies, it was best for every young man to take a wife of his own people and thus share his educational experiences, instead of alienating himself by marrying a European woman.

Sam Ratu Langie, president the Indonesian students association in the Netherlands (Indische Vereeniging), felt that his Dutch mentors were forcing him and others to avoid relationships with European women. He countered by arguing that Indonesian students came to the Netherlands to gain knowledge and advance the development of their homeland. Consequently, if they fell for a European woman, she must have demonstrated great compassion for their cause. In addition, Ratu Langie presented the educational gap between indigenous boys and girls as an important reason why students like him could more easily relate to European women.[95]

In response to the study committee's letter, the student association decided to organize a discussion for its members and the committee's Dutch representatives on June 30, 1915. The evening brought together an array of viewpoints on the issue of mixed marriages. The Dutch ethical advocate J. H. Abendanon, representing the study committee, explained that the letter's intention was to elucidate that marrying an indigenous woman resulted in sharing the students' knowledge, which would benefit the whole of indigenous society. Moreover, he warned the students that returning with a European wife could be interpreted as a belief that indigenous women were too inferior to be their spouses. During the subsequent discussion, some students agreed with Abendanon, arguing that having a European wife would be counterproductive, as common Javanese did not trust Europeans and the immediate family would consider her an outsider. Soewardi Soerjaningrat added that the contrast between Indies spirituality and European nationalism was too great for mixed marriages to work, unless they involved Indies-born Europeans and Eurasians who better understood indigenous peoples.

Some students employed strong racial and evolutionary language in their rejection or defense of mixed marriages. For instance, one student argued that Indonesian blood should remain "pure and unadulterated," while another contended that Eurasian degeneration stemmed from the combination of mostly poor European men and Javanese women, whom he implicitly equated with prostitutes. This line of thinking led him to encourage interracial marriages only between European and indigenous intellectuals. Remarkably, and in stark contrast to the debate in the vernacular press, religion was only peripherally mentioned as a possible obstacle for mixed marriages.[96]

The study committee's recommendation failed to discourage Indonesian students from marrying Dutch women. On the contrary, many returned to the archipelago with a European fiancée or spouse. Ratu Langie himself married Suzanne Houtman who, as a scientist and physician, was not a typical European woman in the Indies. Their marriage was far from an isolated incident, as numerous Indonesian students and European women found each other in love.[97] Clearly, highly-educated European women were not deterred by the 1898 marriage regulations, nor did indigenous men refrain from these marriages in favor of sharing their education with a less-educated indigenous spouse. The vernacular press did not reject these interracial unions outright; in fact, there was a certain delight about the role reversal in these marriages. Finally, Dutch men were experiencing the emasculating pain and humiliation that Indonesian men had felt for centuries. This response was highly gendered, of course, as those who harbored this opinion continued to disavow marriages between European men and Indonesian women.[98]

Despite this reaction among some commentators, many Javanese increasingly deemed all interracial relationships undesirable.[99] Vernacular novels reflected these changing attitudes and emphasized an essential incompatibility between Europeans and Indonesians. The Western-educated youth who alienated himself from his own people and turned arrogant was a popular theme. Through these novels, readers learned that there were innate differences in culture, mentality, and spirituality between colonizer and colonized. Marko Kartodikromo's

Student Hidjo (1919), with which this chapter opened, presents the perils of Western free love to which the protagonist almost succumbs during his studies in the Netherlands. Fortunately, he finds happiness in an arranged marriage to a Javanese woman by the story's end.[100] In contrast, Abdoel Moeis's *Salah Asoehan* (Wrong Upbringing, 1928) explores the struggles of Hanafi, a young man from the Minangkabau region on Sumatra enthralled with the West and in search of love, status, and the meaning of life. He falls in love with Corrie, a Eurasian woman, and asks for her hand in marriage. Both sets of parents advise against it; Corrie's father invokes Kipling's trope about East and West to underscore how misguided their plans are. But the lovers persist, get married, and painfully learn the truth of their parents' advice, as they are ostracized by Europeans and Indonesians alike and become fully dependent on each other until the marriage becomes unbearable.[101]

Habib St. Maharadja tells a similar tale in *Nasib* (Fate, 1932), which features the relationship between Nasib, an Indonesian man who finds his way to Holland, and Elly, a Dutch woman whom he meets there and marries. Their relationship begins to unravel the moment they move to Java. Their identities change in the colonial world; Elly is snubbed and looked down on by Europeans, while Indonesians distrust Nasib. Their insurmountable cultural differences are exposed when Nasib invites his parents to live with them without consulting Elly, allowing them to try to convert his wife to Islam and play a large role in raising their daughter. Elly ultimately flees to Europe, and Nasib finds real love with a Javanese woman. In the story, a friend of Nasib's sums up the changing attitude toward mixed marriages very well: "Oil and water do no mix, oil is attracted to oil, water is attracted to water."[102]

Such beliefs sometimes worked to undercut the moral authority and prestige of Indonesian men with European wives, resulting in serious consequences. This was the case with Raden Soetomo, one of the most prominent figures within the Indonesian national awakening. Soetomo was the driving force behind the founding of Boedi Oetomo in 1908; he was an active member of the Indonesian Students' Association (Perhimpoenan Indonesia) while studying in the Netherlands from 1919 to 1923, and on his return to Java founded the secular nationalist Indonesian Study Club in Surabaya, which became a center for political discussion among educated Indonesians.[103] Surprisingly, Soetomo did not meet his future spouse, Everdina Johanna de Graaff-Brüring, in the Netherlands but on Java during his time as a physician in the missionary hospital in Blora before embarking on his European studies. Recently widowed, De Graaff-Brüring came to Java as a nurse in search of a new purpose. The two eventually fell in love and got married in 1917. Interestingly, although Soetomo suggested that he request Dutch legal assimilation to protect his wife's European status, De Graaff-Brüring rejected the offer, fearing that it would inhibit her husband's ability to work for his land and his people. In Soetomo's words, "My wife's marrying me truly required a sacrifice on her part."[104]

Soetomo and De Graaff-Brüring's marriage shocked the colonial world. Although Soetomo always considered his relationship to be a source of personal strength, many saw it as a liability. Indeed, this belief came to fruition in the late 1920s and early 1930s, when colonial repression of social and political leaders caused a rift within the nationalist movement. Soetomo's continued insistence on a cooperative relationship with colonial authorities as well as his conviction that Islam and communism were not viable pillars of Indonesian identity made him an increasingly divisive figure. Rather than engaging Soetomo intellectually, his opponents questioned his loyalty by attacking his marriage. The vernacular press accused him of being an alienated nationalist, arguing that European women, as members of the ruling "race," would never support their cause nor could they truly understand the Indonesian mentality and worldview. Thus, they could never become genuine members of Indonesian families and their children, raised by a European mother, could never be considered Indonesians, let alone nationalists.[105] Islamic modernists also maintained that Soetomo, and all Muslims in mixed marriages, willingly ignored their religious duties.[106] Others called Soetomo's marriage an insult to Indonesian women, as it implied that they were not good enough for him.[107] There were some exceptions to this barrage; several authors defended Soetomo, claiming that his actions, not his marriage, demonstrated his commitment to the cause.[108] But the critics' voices remained the loudest. Even so, Soetomo stayed the course. At De Graaff-Brüring's funeral in 1934, he made his wife a promise: "I will continue my struggle for righteousness and justice in honor of you."[109]

"And Never the Twain Shall Meet"?

In the final decades of colonial rule, both the Dutch and Indonesians negotiated Western modernity to forge new identities. Kipling's oft-referenced trope about East and West captured this process of redefinition, as each highlighted the perceived intrinsic differences between them. Dutch understanding of themselves as Europeans, Dutch nationals, and colonizers shifted, just as perceptions among the colonized changed about what it meant to be Javanese, Sundanese, Madurese, Malay, Indonesian, and a colonial subject. The articulation of these new identities did not occur in a vacuum but within a shared discursive space best described as colonial modernity. Eastern and Western stereotypes were constructed in conversation with and against one another; the new self was defined as much by what it was as by what it was not. Yet the reality was messier; identities were porous, fluid, malleable, everchanging, and never uniform. Through appearance, language, etiquette, consumerism, displays of virtuous behavior, and the rejection of vices, both colonizer and colonized actively experimented with, communicated, and performed their new modern identities.

The everyday *meeting* of East and West—colonizer and colonized—was thus the site of a pervasive hegemonic struggle in colonial society. As the Dutch understanding of their circumstances, role, and identity changed due to the alleged impact of the climate, they increasingly cultivated difference by performing a modern European colonial lifestyle devoid from supposedly degenerative local influences. However, the colonized did not acquiesce to the roles assigned to them but redefined their own identity by classifying vices associated with Western modernity—such as conspicuous consumption, alcoholism, and the use of opium—and rejecting concubinage and mixed marriages. New identities were thus forged in contradistinction to the Dutch and helped create a substitute script authored by the colonized. These encounters were more widespread in late-colonial Indonesia than ever before due to the emergence of the nascent middle classes and a larger educated elite. They were especially visible and tangible in spaces associated with modernity, such as offices, railroad stations, stores, restaurants, movie theatres, and public parks. But the fairground was perhaps the most illustrative space of the modern colonial encounter. As the next chapter will show, fairgrounds facilitated a uniquely modern meeting of East and West and constituted an important stage for the performance of the hegemonic struggle.

CHAPTER 6

Staging Colonial Modernity

Hegemony, Fairs, and the Indonesian Middle Classes

I N A POPULAR WEEKLY, a Dutch journalist described that at Surabaya's 1907 *jaarmarkt*, the city's third annual fair, Arabs, Chinese, Sundanese, Javanese, Madurese, Malay, Eurasians, and Europeans all promenaded the fairgrounds adorned in their best ethnic dress, seemingly in accordance with the sartorial colonial hierarchy. He was therefore startled to encounter several of what he called "modernized" or "fake Javanese" partly clad in European clothes. The columnist disdainfully described them as "Pithecanthropus Erectus" (Eugene Dubois's "Java Man") with a brown slouch hat on their heads, wearing a dress shirt, striped tie, green waistband, black jacket, and gold chain watch and carrying a cheap *payung*. Only their sarong and smelly *terompah* (sandals) he deemed authentic.[1] For the author, "modernized Javanese" were out of place at the fairgrounds, as they subverted and blurred colonial hierarchies by not donning ethnic costume. Moreover, their presence ostensibly undermined the primary objective of the fair, which was to stimulate the indigenous artisan industry and conserve traditional Javanese culture.

Unbeknownst to the European journalist in 1907, by the 1930s his "modernized Javanese" would be omnipresent at the fairgrounds, which proliferated in twentieth-century colonial Indonesia to the point at which every major city and town hosted its own fair, exhibition, or *pasar malam* (night fair). Notably, the Dutch colonial regime used the organization of fairs to stage modernity and legitimize its authority.[2] However, negotiating the fairs enabled the primarily indigenous visitors to shape a distinct middle-class lifestyle and identity—quite an unintentional consequence of this demonstration of Dutch power. Fairs were large physical sites of interaction that attracted hundreds of thousands, if not millions, of people annually from different ethnic backgrounds and walks of life. And while they were far from egalitarian, they constituted a unique shared experience in the colonial world. As public spaces, fairs provided a forum

II. De Gemoderniseerde Javaan.

FIGURE 8. "The Modernized Javanese." A Dutch journalist mockingly depicts the composite appearance of what he describes as the "modernized Javanese," consisting of a sarong, Western shirt, tie, and jacket. Source: *Weekblad voor Indië*, 1907.

for the negotiation of political, economic, and social anxieties that could not be openly communicated due to the realities of colonial inequality. They also offered visitors the opportunity to experience modernity through architecture, educational exhibits, performances, entertainment, advertisements, and commercial displays. Moreover, they were spaces in which indigenous visitors actively shaped their identities in relation to one another, to colonial discourse, and to modernity. In this context, the appearance of the "modernized Java-nese" at Surabaya's jaarmarkt signified the emergence of the Indonesian mid-dle classes and reveals the importance of fairs as discursive spaces in the late colonial-world.

Given their scope and prominence in late-colonial society, it is remarkable that annual fairs have received scant attention from scholars of colonial Indo-nesia and colonialism more broadly. Developments in Indonesia were not iso-lated events; thus, similar fairs emerged simultaneously throughout the colonial world, such as the Foire de Hanoi and the Manila Carnival. Although such fairs have figured in several histories—for instance, those on the performing arts—they have not been the main object of study.[3] This has changed only recently with publications by Yulia Nurliani Lukito on the hybrid architecture of the Pasar Gambir (Gambir Fair) in Batavia and the various ways in which it shaped interactions between colonizer and colonized.[4] The only other work that signifi-cantly addresses the proliferation of fairs, albeit indirectly, is that of Joost Coté on the 1914 colonial exhibition in Semarang, which was actually not an annual fair at all, but was modeled after world's fairs and exhibitions.[5]

At first glance, the proliferation of annual fairs in the colonial world appears reminiscent of similar exhibitions in the West. However, the very different na-ture of their locations, intended audience, and objectives set them apart as unique colonial phenomena. These annual fairs were organized in Batavia, Hanoi, and Manila, rather than Amsterdam, Paris, or Washington, DC; the colonized were the main audience rather than components of an ethnographic display; and mo-dernity rather than indigenous traditions was the celebrated feature.[6] As such, they were important instruments in the modernizing and civilizing projects of the twentieth-century Dutch colonial state.[7] However, annual fairs were signif-icant parts of their hegemonic project, as well. With the advent of the Ethical Policy and its civilizing discourse in 1901, the legitimacy of the colonial state increasingly came to rely less on coopting the Javanese aristocracy and more on the ability to modernize the Netherlands Indies. Generating support among the nascent Indonesian middle classes was central to this mission.

Within this context, fairs can be interpreted as stages on which hegemony was performed and communicated. The architecture of the buildings, the design of the fairgrounds, the presence of a plethora of both indigenous and Western merchandise, and the appearance of indigenous visitors themselves were all cru-cial parts of the décor. The juxtaposition between Western merchandise, ranging from gas stoves, bicycles, the latest fashions, and cigarettes on the one hand, and traditional Javanese batik, *wayang* puppets, and gamelan instruments on the other, was intentional. Here, Dutch colonizers presented themselves as guides—the harbingers of modernity and developers of technological and scientific advantages. This position demonstrated their supposed superiority and legitimized their continued colonial domination. It was thus a performance in contrasts: the modern Dutch versus the backward Javanese.

Such performances of colonial modernity at the fairs were intended for a specific audience: the nascent Indonesian middle classes that had gradually become more central to maintaining colonial rule. The rise of the middle classes coincided with the emergence of a new urban mass culture that was primarily visual, guided by advertisements and illuminated by films.[8] The fairgrounds incorporated all of these experiences into a single space, which enabled the state to connect these urban middle classes with their hegemonic project.[9] Crucially, though, while the fairs were extremely popular, the nascent middle classes were not simply buying what the Dutch were selling. Like modernity itself, fairs were, as Vincent Houben points out, "a discursive space. . . that was both empowering and unsettling."[10] At the fairgrounds, the nascent Indonesian middle classes both embraced and contested colonial modernity, welcoming certain elements while rejecting others. It was especially through consumer practices at colonial fairs—leisure, exhibits, food, and commodities—that they shaped and performed a new middle-class identity and culture characterized by distinctive appearance, language, morality, and social practices, including attention to gendered roles and responsibilities.[11]

Fairs as Civilizing Instruments

The emergence of annual fairs coincided with the implementation of the Ethical Policy (1901) that claimed to promote the development of the land and people of colonial Indonesia. In part, this was to be achieved through stimulating the indigenous artisan industry, which had suffered from the economic recession of the 1890s and the competition of Western imports. Of the various studies the colonial government commissioned on the condition of the artisan industry, the first and most ambitious was conducted by J. H. Abendanon, director of the Department of Education, Religion, and Industry and a vocal advocate of the Ethical Policy. During a research tour of Java for his study in the spring of 1904, Abendanon proposed that the colonial authorities could improve the artisan industry, and by extension the welfare of the colonized, through the organization of annual fairs. In his final report, he explained that fairs would allow artisans access to larger markets to sell their products, gain a wider clientele, compare their work with that of others, and as a result improve their overall business opportunities. The report further suggested that combining entertainment with the exhibition of native arts and crafts could attract a greater number of visitors.[12] While the bulk of Abendanon's plans were deemed too radical and costly, his proposal on the organization of annual fairs was immediately adopted and became a staple in subsequent reports on how to counter the indigenous population's declining welfare.[13]

The towns selected to premiere these fairs combining trade and leisure were Batavia and Surabaya, where local authorities had committed to Abendanon's proposal during his tour of Java.[14] In the summer of 1904, Batavia organized its first fair—Pasar Gambir—with the stated objective of "promoting indigenous trade and industry."[15] Surabaya followed suit with its jaarmarkt in 1905, officially intended to promote indigenous craftsmanship and products, create a larger market for indigenous artisans, and encourage them to work more regularly.[16] The authorities in both cities drew on existing traditions in organizing these first annual fairs. In the colonial capital, the initiative was undertaken by Oost en West (East and West), a private association known for its ethical propensities, of which Abendanon himself was a founding member. Oost en West combined organizing exhibits of indigenous arts and crafts with annual festivities celebrating the Dutch queen's birthday and the Javanese tradition of night fairs (*pasar malam*), which were often held around special occasions.[17] Similarly, in Surabaya, local controller J. E. Jasper used his experience with area arts and crafts exhibitions to organize the city's first fair for Hari Mulud, the holiday commemorating Mohammed's birthday.[18]

In accordance with Abendanon's proposal, Batavia's Pasar Gambir and Surabaya's jaarmarkt focused primarily on encouraging the artisan industry. Local and regional artisans displayed their arts and crafts in stands at the fairgrounds. Both fairs also reserved large sections for live crafts exhibits where artisans showed off their workmanship. In Batavia's Kampong Kerajinan (Crafts Village) and Surabaya's Kampong Tukan (Artisan Village), visitors could admire batik painting, stamping, and waxing, woodworking, weaving, bamboo plaiting, rattan weaving, and ivory tuning, as well as gold and silversmiths, horn, bone, stone, and turtle cutters, tanners, and pottery bakers at work. The fairs further hosted a variety of traditional Javanese entertainments, including daily gamelan, wayang, and dance performances, to draw people to the exhibits. Interestingly, as these amusements alone did not attract enough people, the organizers added cinema, sports (cycling and equestrian competitions), carousels, and *stamboel* performances (modern music and theatre performances). According to newspaper reports, these supplements quickly turned into the fairs' main draws.[19] Even so, the fairs' organizers deliberately emphasized traditional Javanese culture, as defined by colonial experts' selection of entertainment and exhibits. This reflected the paternal aspect of the Ethical Policy, which sought to develop, respect, and conserve indigenous culture under Dutch tutelage.[20]

Western import companies and their modern products were conspicuously absent from these first fairs. This was not a coincidence, as the organizers intended to bolster the artisan industry by excluding foreign competitors. According to contemporary reports from indigenous civil servants, Western imports had significantly impacted the Javanese lifestyle by the turn of the century. For instance, the *bupati* of Serang, Achmad Djajadiningrat—one of the principal organizers of the first Pasar Gambir—argued that the availability of affordable and reliable Western products created new desires and increased the Javanese cost of living. Specifically, Western goods tempted common Javanese to consume conspicuously to enhance their social status by imitating Europeans and the priyayi. Among the products that were widely available at local markets were Swiss sarong and headscarves, silk *slendang* (baby sling) from Lyon, Swedish matches, perfumes, European clothing, jewelry, wristwatches, and canned food, such as Huntley and Palmer biscuits. By boycotting these products at annual fairs, the organizers sought to reduce conspicuous consumption and protect and stimulate the artisan industry, encouraging the sale of payung instead of European umbrellas, for instance. Taken together, they hoped to increase the prosperity of the indigenous population.[21]

The first annual fairs were thus complicated spaces in colonial Indonesia that exemplified the tension in ethical discourse between conserving traditional culture—stimulating artisan industry—and modern development—including modern amusements and access to Western products. Pulled in opposite directions, the fairs were a mixed success. While they drew large crowds, most people were more enticed by the amusements than by the exhibits and artisan stands. Tellingly, in 1908—the same year that the Pasar Gambir drew a record-breaking two hundred fifty thousand visitors in less than two weeks—the organizers canceled its forthcoming Kampong Kerajinan due to budgetary problems. Instead, they merely offered entertainment for the queen's birthday celebration. This is not to say that the goal of stimulating the artisan industry was unsuccessful. According to reports of Surabaya's jaarmarkt, the diversity, quality, and originality of the arts and crafts on display improved significantly between 1905 and 1908, which was reflected in the fourfold increase of their sales revenue.[22] The jaarmarkt and Surabaya's Kampong Tukan were more successful than Batavia's

Pasar Gambir, and continued until 1915. By then, however, World War I prevented any fairs from being organized for several years.[23]

Hegemony through Education and Entertainment

The disruption in annual fairs due to the war and its fallout in Europe allowed for a reassessment of their utility and purpose. The colony's precarious international position and the socioeconomic and political anxieties that permeated colonial society challenged officialdom to reconsider its policies. The social-cultural and mental transformation of indigenous society following the foundation of the Sarekat Islam in 1911, the issuance of the hormat circular in 1913, and the subsequent sartorial revolution added to these concerns. With regards to the fairs, these anxieties resulted in a shift in focus from primarily promoting the indigenous artisan industry to instigating broad modernization and industrialization of the colonial economy. Moving forward, less emphasis would be placed on the conservation of Javanese culture and tradition, and more on modern economic development.[24] The first fair to exemplify this new approach was in Bandung in 1919. In the capital of the Priangan residency, local officials pushed for a European-style industrial fair (*jaarbeurs*) where importers, producers, local manufacturers, and retailers could come together. On the side, the organization added amusements and local artisans to draw visitors. However, as Java was far from industrialized, for years Bandung's jaarbeurs was an industrial fair in name alone. Instead of company representatives and trade partners, Western import companies, indigenous artisans, entertainment, and consumers came to dominate its fairgrounds.[25]

Two more years passed before Batavia's Pasar Gambir resumed in 1921 and its organizing committee had no intention of hosting an industrial fair. But while stimulating the artisan industry remained its official objective, Western import companies and their consumer products dominated the fairgrounds. Surabaya's jaarbeurs in 1923 was highly contentious, as it coincided with the one held in Bandung.[26] Moreover, Surabaya's committee proclaimed that their city was much better situated to host an industrial fair, directly challenging the existence of the jaarbeurs in Bandung.[27] These differences were resolved through government intervention, ensuring that Bandung remained the only town with an industrial fair—at least in name—and that Surabaya followed Batavia's model. To prevent inter-city competition, the Association for the Promotion of Annual Fairs was founded in 1928 to coordinate a fair cycle: Bandung's jaarbeurs in June, Batavia's Pasar Gambir in August, and Surabaya's jaarmarkt in October.[28]

However, due to the sheer size and plethora of vendors, advertising, food, amusements, sporting competitions, and exhibits, the Pasar Gambir established itself as Java's ultimate annual fair. It was renowned for its temporary bamboo and palm leaf buildings, which drew architectural inspiration from Javanese, Asian, and Western styles. The resulting "Oriental fairy-tale" pavilions were adorned with thousands of electric lights, which reflected the Dutch under-standing of the colonial relationship: through the enlightened Dutch example, the Javanese could, in time, achieve modernity. The fairgrounds were quite lit-erally the stage of the Dutch hegemonic performance.[29]

The changing character of annual fairs in Java is best described in the writings of A. E. Simon Thomas, who, as secretary of a local trade association, served as a member on the Pasar Gambir organizational committee from 1922 to 1937.[30] According to Simon Thomas, the new annual fairs were intended to inform and civilize the indigenous population by presenting government programs, creating new consumer markets for Western-manufactured commodities, and strength-ening colonial order. The extent to which these objectives could be realized de-pended on the organizing committees' ability to attract visitors. Simon Thomas argued, similar to Abendanon before him, that entertainment was a crucial means to this end. People tended to flock to fairgrounds, not to exhibitions. Thus, the goal was to offer entertainment that would appeal to all members of colonial society.[31]

The pedagogical intentions of annual fairs notwithstanding, most people did visit them for their elaborate entertainment. Whereas indigenous amusements had characterized fairs before World War I, Western attractions predominated in the years after. No fair was complete without movie theatres showing Holly-wood's latest productions or stages for listening or dancing to Western music, varying from classical to jazz. Spectator sports like soccer, field hockey, baseball, and track and field, and competitive entertainment, such as dance contests (i.e., foxtrot or waltz) and automobile and motorcycle races, were among the most popular attractions. Fairs offered another form of visual entertainment, as well: the diorama and panorama. Popular subjects included Mecca during the Hajj, Jerusalem in the time of Christ, and the Battle of Waterloo. Visitors could also enjoy typical Dutch fare—a rarity only a decade earlier—at the more exclusive restaurants, including pickled herring, *rolmops* (pickled herring with savory filling), *spekbokking* (cold smoked herring), mackerel, mussels, Russian salad, Dutch cold cuts, *kroket* (croquettes), and sausage rolls.[32]

Many of the more popular attractions at Java's colonial fairs actually came from the Philippines. American entrepreneur Eddie Tait was the owner of the

Manila Shows, with which he annually toured colonial Southeast Asia. The Manila Shows were famous for their mechanical attractions, such as carousels, giant strides, caterpillar rides, bumper carts, and Ferris wheels. In addition, visitors to Tait's shows could marvel at clowns, Mexican dancers, and performers with such nicknames as the "human fountain," the "living skeleton," and "Jolly Nelly" (a woman weighing four hundred fifty pounds). Tait also brought "Hula-Hula" girls to Java, without whom, he once remarked, the Pasar Gambir would not be complete. The Hula-Hula girls, dressed in nothing more than thatch skirts, a wrap over their breasts, and some Hawaiian decorations, were amongst the most hotly debated draws at Java's fairs, and the topic of many visitors' dreams. The success of Tait's Manila Shows, as well as the organization of similar fairs in the Philippines and elsewhere in colonial Southeast Asia, suggests that such amusements were part of a larger regional trend. Throughout Southeast Asia annual fairs were organized to legitimize colonial power and create new consumers of western products in the process.[33]

Whereas mechanical rides and Western-style performances emphasized Western modernity, the fairs' indigenous entertainments and exhibitions were rooted in Java's past. Although these sections had become relatively small compared to their early-twentieth-century equivalents, all the major forms of indigenous craftsmanship could still be admired, such as batik and the creation of wayang puppets. In addition, several musical presentations (gamelan and *angklung*) and dance performances (*ronggeng* and *topeng*) occurred throughout the day.[34] However, it is significant that colonial fairs depicted indigenous people and cultures through the eyes of the colonizers. The contrast between Western ice cream, jazz music, and Hollywood films, and *nasi goring* (fried rice), gamelan music, and wayang performances was intentionally produced. The implied message behind this contrast was straightforward: it signified to the indigenous observer what they were—primitive—and what they could become—modern.[35]

By successfully drawing hundreds of thousands of visitors to Java's annual fairs with spectacular and diverse entertainment, organizational committees effectively created large-scale sites of interaction that facilitated, according to Simon Thomas, a "seemingly unnoticed and unintentional visual education" of indigenous visitors.[36] The fairgrounds themselves, the architecture of the buildings, the many visually engaging stands and exhibitions all served to convey the benevolence of Dutch colonial rule. The visual aspect was particularly important, since the majority of visitors were not expected to be fully literate. These so-called ethical goals remained embedded in the statutes of Java's dominant fairs, which all incorporated the promotion of indigenous agriculture, livestock, fisheries, trade, and industry among their main objectives.[37] To this end, various government agencies contributed exhibits detailing their involvement in the development of indigenous arts and crafts, agricultural improvements, and the promotion of hygienic practices among indigenous peoples.[38]

Although they only occupied a small portion of the fairgrounds, these *inheemse nijverheid* (indigenous arts and crafts) exhibitions were arguably the most important displays organized by the colonial government. At most fairs these exhibits were prepared by the Afdeeling Nijverheid (Subdivision of Arts and Crafts) of the Department of Agriculture, Industry, and Trade. This government agency was specifically tasked with promoting indigenous arts and crafts and creating larger markets for the sale of such products.[39] The Afdeeling Nijverheid also played a crucial role in trying to improve the quality of the products, in effect pushing for some traditional items to be considered works of art. Another way in which these commodities were made more appealing was by tailoring them to European tastes and desires. For instance, the agency stimulated the production of batik tablecloths and pillowcases, leather fans, and wooden toys.[40] At most fairs, the exhibition of indigenous arts and crafts was still accompanied by a kampong (village) for artisanal demonstrations. On the one hand, visiting the kampong served as pedagogical experience for all who attended, while on the other it had become a major tourist destination. For many Europeans, a visit to the artisanal kampong was a unique opportunity to familiarize themselves with indigenous culture and pick up a souvenir, such as wayang puppet, batik sarong, copper work, or woodcarving. This is indicative of just how "other" Javanese culture had become in the eyes of the Dutch, who as recently as the turn of the century embraced indigenous culture and traditions in their households, daily lives, and to legitimize their authority.

Recurring exhibitions on hygiene and sanitation were a new addition to annual fairs in the 1920s and 1930s. Similar to exhibits on indigenous arts and crafts, these were pedagogical expositions that both propagated the work of colonial agencies and demonstrated the Dutch commitment to the Ethical Policy. Hygienic exhibitions were organized by the Department of Public Health and often included contributions from other health organizations, such as the Institute for the Blind in Bandung, the Institute Pasteur in Batavia, and other local clinics and hospitals. At most fairs, the hygienic exhibits were organized around an annual theme. For instance, Batavia's Pasar Gambir hosted exhibits addressing malaria, tuberculosis, the plague, eye diseases, infant health and mortality, food preparation, drinking water, the danger of rats and flies, and first aid.[41] Bandung's jaarbeurs, which from 1924 onward organized specialized large exhibitions alongside the fair, hosted the Eerste Hygiënshce Tentoonstelling in Nederlandsch-Indië (EHTINI: First Hygienic Exhibition in the Netherlands Indies) in 1927. The main objective of the EHTINI—and all hygienic exhibitions, for that matter—was to promote and disseminate knowledge of hygiene and its practical applications among all strata of the populace.[42]

According to M. A. J. Kelling, secretary of the EHTINI's organizing committee, the importance of this pedagogical task went beyond the improvement of physical health; it would also reduce related mental weaknesses in indigenous character that resulted from unsanitary living conditions, such as "a lack of obstinacy, thrift, perseverance, and productivity."[43] Consequently, Kelling reasoned, since the majority of the indigenous audience was still illiterate and mentally adapted to primitive living conditions, these exhibitions included very few tables, graphs, and statistics, and instead featured paintings, drawings, dioramas, and models. For instance, the Pasar Gambir of 1930 visually demonstrated the health dangers of flies through a contrast between dioramas depicting unhygienic behavior—uncovered food at a *warung* (small food stall or restaurant), open wounds, and filthy latrines—and paintings showing the preferred hygienic alternatives—covered food, bound wounds, and clean latrines. The dioramas conveyed the superiority of western hygiene—and science in general—over local practices, reminding the viewers of the alleged benevolence of Dutch colonial rule.

In Kelling's opinion, the EHTINI disproved that annual fairs were primarily for financial gain. Quite the opposite, he argued, as the Dutch took on the moral responsibility of educating indigenous visitors about the benefits of Western science and hygienic practices. This had the added benefit, he believed, that "whoever makes the people healthy, strengthen their rule."[44] Other colonial agencies' exhibits also rested on the principle that promoting the government's civilizing work would stabilize colonial authority. For instance, the Bureau voor Volkslectuur (Balai Poestaka—the agency that published informative literature for the indigenous population) provided visitors with educational pamphlets on a wide range of topics, such as purifying water, personal hygiene, and the dangers of opium and alcohol addiction. Similarly, the exhibits of the Landbouwkundige Voorlichtingsdienst (Department of Agricultural Promotion) on agriculture, livestock, poultry, and horticulture informed visitors about the great strides that had been made through Dutch guidance and example, and possibilities for further improvement.[45]

Fairs and the Creation of Desire

While Simon Thomas claimed that he greatly valued the pedagogical aspect of annual fairs, he believed that their most important objective was "the creation of new needs and desires" by familiarizing the indigenous masses with the latest commodities and other expressions of Western culture.[46] The president of the annual fair in Surabaya, G. J. Dijkerman, voiced similar beliefs, stating that modern fairs were distinct from traditional pasar malams because of their focus on Western import companies and their commodities.[47] However, creating demand for new manufactured products among the largely illiterate indigenous population was not an easy feat. Simon Thomas argued that advertisements in periodicals and billboards were an expensive and ineffective means of reaching Java's analphabetic masses. Instead, the millions of potential consumers needed to be convinced by product demonstrations. The experience of seeing, touching, trying, and if applicable tasting, new commodities was crucial for the successful creation of desire among the Javanese. Annual fairs, Simon Thomas maintained, facilitated precisely these kinds of interactions between representatives of Western companies and the "indigenous millions."[48]

While there were alternative ways in which indigenous consumers could be reached, according to Simon Thomas none was more cost efficient than annual fairs. For instance, following World War I the British American Tobacco Company (BATC) embarked on a large-scale sales campaign in Java. To create a market for its white cigarettes, as opposed to locally produced *kretek* (clove cigarettes), the BATC sent salesmen and interpreters in Ford vans out into Java's countryside to hand out samples, sell cigarettes, and post advertising materials. It was a highly successful campaign for the BATC, which soon opened two factories in Java (Cirebon in 1925 and Semarang in 1929), but it was a costly promotional strategy that most businesses could simply not afford. The annual fairs provided a viable alternative by bringing Western producers, importers, and indigenous consumers together. Similar to the BATC campaign, the fairs allowed for sensory marketing in which touch played a crucial role: it allowed potential consumers to create a symbolic connection and sense of ownership over items that were simply absent in regular displays or advertisements.[49]

In their search for new global growth markets, Western companies found that Java's colonial fairs were effective intermediary institutions in reaching millions of potential consumers. When fairs resumed in the early 1920s, Western commercial interests quickly came to dominate the fairgrounds. For instance, between 1925 and 1927, Western companies accounted for approximately

65 percent of the commercial stands at the Pasar Gambir. Of the remaining stands, Foreign Orientals (a legal group consisting principally of Chinese) rented out around 20 percent and indigenous entrepreneurs 15 percent.[50] The products on display ranged from luxury items intended for colonial elites to mass-produced commodities for mass consumption. One could thus find advanced forms of transportation, such as cars (i.e., Fiat, Ford, General Motors), motorcycles (i.e., Harley Davidson), and bicycles, as well as electrical appliances for household convenience or leisure including refrigerators (i.e., Kelvinator, Frigidaire), cameras (i.e., Kodak, Agfa), and gramophones and radio players (i.e., Edison, Philips, Columbia Records). The majority of the products, however, were mass-produced merchandise for personal hygiene and appearance (i.e., Colgate and Pepsodent toothpaste, Lux and Lifebuoy soaps, Cutex lipstick, perfumes), medicines (i.e., Bayer, Lakeroll), food items (i.e., Blue Band, Droste's Cacao, Sun-Maid Raisins, Coca-Cola, Victoria Biscuits), alcoholic beverages (i.e., Bols, Amstel, Bavaria, and Heineken beer), tobacco products (i.e., British American Tobacco, Camel, Faroka, MacGillavry, Van Nelle), and shoes (i.e., Bata, Keds, Jack).[51]

The fairgrounds were a space of aggressive advertising and competition between producers and importers in search of new markets.[52] Stands at the fairs were designed by emerging advertising agencies that created elaborate displays and stunning decorations that often included electrical lighting. According to an Indonesian reporter for the *Pandji Poestaka*, this was *"zaman reclame!"*—the age of advertising.[53] At a time in which *kampongs*, villages, towns, islands, and countries were more interconnected than ever, he argued, a new space for commerce had emerged. Moreover, advertising at colonial fairs became a prerequisite for success, as it allowed producers to vie for the attention of potential customers through distinctive kiosks. In 1925, the Pasar Gambir even organized a special exhibit demonstrating how businesses could effectively advertise products or services in the colony and provided several successful examples. Thus, annual fairs became famous for their spectacular advertising, which for many was an important part of their appeal.[54]

The broad variety of commodities at colonial fairs, both in terms of price range and brands, presented nascent consumers with a new kind of experience: the ability to shape their identities through their consumption choices. While the majority of indigenous visitors would not have been able to purchase many products, let alone any of the luxury items on display, they could selectively purchase more affordable items depending on their discretionary income. In this way, consumption choices resulted in varying degrees of association with

modernity. At the lower end of the spectrum, one could purchase locally produced, Japanese, or Chinese knockoffs of modern products such as soap, shoes,
or bicycles, which could be replaced with Western premium brands when their
financial fortunes improved. Consequently, consumption was not merely reflec-
tive of a new lifestyle but also of social status.[55]

Anticipating criticism that the commercial aspect of colonial fairs solely advanced Western business interests, Simon Thomas insisted that fairs had much
to offer indigenous visitors, as well. He acknowledged that the fairs, with their
plethora of entertainment and enticing commercialism, were places in which visitors could easily spend excessively. However, as long as the pedagogical benefits
outweighed the costs, he believed this was acceptable. Alternatively, he reasoned,
people would spend their money on less useful things or experiences. Instead,
Simon Thomas assumed that conveying government agencies' important work
and creating new consumer needs would motivate the indigenous population
to work harder, earn more money to satisfy their new desires, and consequently
raise the prosperity of society as a whole. For Simon Thomas and most of his contemporaries, colonial fairs therefore did not merely fulfill an economic function,
but more importantly, a political one.[56]

The promotion of benevolent—*ethical*—policies and the creation of new consumer demands effectively encouraged indigenous visitors to buy into colonial
modernity. Fairs were an essential part of the Dutch attempt to create a new
form of cultural hegemony, anchored in the Ethical Policy. This was a significant
departure from colonial legitimization in the nineteenth century, which was
constructed around collaboration with the Javanese traditional elite and relied
on its aristocratic culture. In contrast, the Ethical Policy was aimed at the Western-educated elite and the growing number of Javanese participating directly
in the modern colonial economy. Colonial authorities believed that gaining
the "consent" of these emerging elites and middle classes could not be achieved
with reference to the traditional past, but instead by focusing on cosmopolitan modernity. Consequently, fairs contrasted Western modernity with Javanese backwardness in a highly visual manner to legitimize colonial authority.
Through these fairs, the Dutch staged their technological and scientific prowess
as indictors of their alleged superiority. However, high attendance and increased
consumption did not mean that the Javanese simply bought into modernity or
colonialism. Instead, the fairs were spaces in which the meaning of colonial modernity was very much contested.

Colonial fairs reflected the paradox of all civilizing discourses by inviting visitors to participate in colonial modernity seemingly as equals, while

simultaneously reinforcing difference and social hierarchy. This was most clearly reflected in distinct entry fees. For instance, in 1925, entry fees for Europeans, "Foreign Orientals," and indigenous visitors at the Pasar Gambir were fl. o.50, fl. o.25, and fl. o.15, respectively.[57] All other major fairs instituted similar price differentiations. Colonial hierarchies were further reinforced on entering the fairgrounds. There were segregated restrooms, dining facilities, movie theatres, parties (such as dances and masquerade balls), and seating arrangements at sporting events for Europeans and non-Europeans. Moreover, the sporting events themselves were segregated based on ethnicity, which meant, for instance, that there were separate soccer tournaments held each year. Although akin to an apartheid regime, the key difference was that segregation was not based on skin color alone. An educated and affluent Javanese clad in a European suit and fluent in Dutch could, if he wanted, attend most European entertainment. For instance, the report following the first annual fair in Semarang in 1908 bluntly stated that although indigenous people were not prohibited from dining at the fairgrounds' European restaurant, they were charged an additional fee of fl. o.10—an expenditure intended to deter indigenous guests.[58] The increased segregation of colonial society in general, and the fairs in particular, drew fierce criticism from the Indonesian nationalist movement and vernacular press, which argued that the Dutch were "whitening" the colonial elite. In 1925, news that a "municipal" swimming pool was only accessible to Europeans incited the vernacular newspaper *Hindia Baroe* to call for a boycott, which never transpired, of the Pasar Gambir.[59]

Colonial Modernity, the Middle Classes, and Conspicuous Consumption

In 1929, an article in the *Pandji Poestaka* claimed that Batavia's Pasar Gambir and Surabaya's jaarmarkt had become local traditions similar in stature to the Sekaten celebrations in Yogyakarta and Surakarta commemorating the birthday of the Prophet Muhammad. While this comparison underestimated the religious significance of the Sekaten, the massive crowds and positive attention in the press confirm that fairs had indeed become seemingly indispensable institutions in colonial society. In trying to explain the appeal of the postwar modernized fairs, the author described how visitors at the Pasar Gambir were struck by the "bright electric lights, colorful flags and paper decorations, advertising, shouts of artisans and vendors, food stands, entertainments, and the crowds."[60] They came, he argued, to enjoy themselves, attend performances and other entertainments, and to eat and drink but also for flyers and free commercial samples such as tea, biscuits, and cigarettes. The fairs, in other words, facilitated a sensory exploration of modern life through the spectacular design of pavilions and stands, the omnipresent sounds of performances and crowds, the smell and taste of diverse food offerings, and the ability to try unfamiliar commodities. Without naming it as such, the author's description suggests that people flocked to fairs to experience what might be called colonial modernity and the activities associated with it, especially consumerism.[61]

The fairgrounds themselves were arguably the greatest attraction of Java's colonial fairs. Their architecture, layout, and design often differed greatly from one city to another, ranging from Batavia's temporary bamboo-and-thatch hybrid-Oriental style, Surabaya's semipermanent entry pavilion inspired by a ship's bow, and Bandung's permanent modern exhibition halls, but all were clearly recognizable as contemporary and modern spaces.[62] This was due in part to the extensive use of electric lighting for decorative purposes. At the Pasar Gambir, testing the lights prior to the fair's opening alone drew thousands of visitors. More than anything else, electric lights and appliances were associated with the modernity on display at the fairs. Not surprisingly, lights were not only used for decoration but also for advertising purposes. A striking example is an electric billboard promoting the cigarette company Mac Gillavry. The billboard showed a well-dressed man smoking a cigarette, and each time he exhaled, consecutive lights created the illusion of smoke in the shape of the brand name: Mac Gillavry.[63] This billboard, like the elaborate designs adorning commercial stands, was a must-see for the fair's visitors.

Another defining feature of the modern fair experience was the large, ethnically diverse crowd. For instance, in a letter to a friend, a Dutch schoolteacher explained how at Batavia's fair visitors from "all races wriggled into a motley," while a Javanese journalist similarly described, "All categories of our society meet at the Pasar Gambir."[64] Where the first Pasar Gambir drew 334,985 visitors, at its peak in 1930 it welcomed a remarkable 516,980 guests. This impressive increase in visitor numbers of the Pasar Gambir was mirrored by the fairs in Bandung (from 58,221 visitors in 1920 to 226,227 in 1929) and Surabaya (from 192,216 visitors in 1923 to 413,902 in 1930).[65] The statistics are especially impressive given that fairs only lasted two weeks (i.e., thirteen days in Batavia, sixteen days in Bandung and Surabaya). As many other towns organized fairs as well, it can be assumed that on Java more than one million people visited them annually. In the case of the Pasar Gambir, between 1921 and 1939, 18 percent of these visitors on average were European, 23 percent Foreign Oriental, and an impressive 59

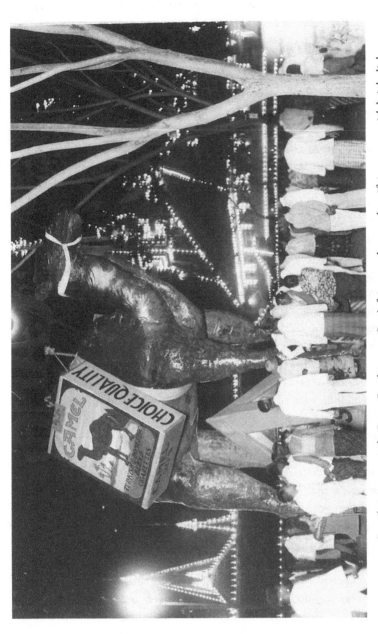

FIGURE 9. Camel cigarettes at the Pasar Gambir, 1930. Java's fairgrounds were electrifying spaces with bright lights, entertainment, and merchant displays that invited visitors to participate in modernity. Source: Leiden University Library, Royal Netherlands Institute for Southeast Asian and Caribbean Studies (KITLV) 16580.

percent indigenous.[66] Surprisingly, this meant that the indigenous population was underrepresented, as Europeans made up 7 percent of Batavia's total populace, Foreign Orientals 16 percent, and indigenous 77 percent.

However, ticket sales only partially reflect the multitudes attracted by the fairgrounds. According to the European and indigenous press, the roads leading toward the fairs were littered with street vendors selling food, drinks, toys, fabrics, and more. These temporary fairs thus created economic opportunities for salesmen and women, retailers, and peddlers who could either not afford or opted not to rent stands at the official fairgrounds.[67] According to a European journalist, for "people for whom a dime is a fortune" (the entry fare for indigenous peoples), these stands outside the fairgrounds were an opportunity to experience the excitement, marvel at the spectacular buildings draped in electric lights, listen to distant musical performances, and watch the fireworks at night.[68] Attempts by the less privileged to sneak or peak into the fairgrounds were popular cartoon themes in the *Pandji Poestaka*, which once again suggests that fairs were only for those who could afford them.[69]

The fairs' ticket sales mirrored the development of the national and global economy. The fairs expanded with an economic recovery beginning in 1924, shrank with the Great Depression that impacted the Netherlands Indies, especially from 1931 to 1934, and slowly grew again from 1935 until 1938, after which the specter of war in Europe brought an end to the fairs even before the Japanese occupation in 1942. The eerie similarity of this curve to the development of the gross domestic product (GDP) per capita in the Netherlands Indies during this period seems indicative of the consumer character of the fairs. When the GDP per capita increased or decreased, and with it, discretionary income, consumer practices and fair attendance similarly adjusted.[70]

These statistics suggest that visitors to Java's colonial fairs consisted primarily of those with discretionary income and an interest in consumer practices. In other words, these were people who were not simply interested in modern experiences but could actually afford them. This most certainly did not mean that the fairs were only for the wealthy, as they allowed for several levels of engagement, from watching from outside or paying the entrance fee to merely stroll the fairgrounds, to more extensive and expensive consumption options involving entertainment and luxurious dining. The fairs were thus an aspirational experience where one was always left wanting more. This feature was reflected in many exhibits, like one on home furnishings at the Pasar Gambir in 1938. Here visitors could observe different displays based on income level (fl. 25–125 and fl. 250–500 per month, respectively). According to one observer, the first exhibit was aimed at a broad middle-class audience and by far drew the most attention. But while lower-middle-class visitors dreamt about the furnishings in the first exhibit, the middle classes themselves marveled at the more luxurious display in the second.[71]

Taken together, it seems reasonable to assume that the majority of the fairs' indigenous visitors consisted of what can be described as the nascent lower and "middle" middle classes.[72] The income level associated with the less expensive home furnishings display corresponds with the annual income level of about 5 percent of the population of Java and Madura in the 1930s. As Henk Schulte Nordholt has argued, the nascent middle classes can be considered "children of the colonial state," as they emerged to fill the needs of the modern colonial economy with comparatively cheap labor. This resulted in a class of mainly white-collar professionals, such as teachers, railroad workers, pawnshop personnel, clerks, and civil servants, that had enjoyed some level of education and whose job security was often tied, directly or indirectly, to the colonial state. Conversely, the functioning of the colonial state depended on their work. It is therefore not surprising that this was the primary group that fairs' organizers had in mind as the intended audience. Fairs were one of the more prolific manners by which authorities tried to "sell" colonial modernity as a way to legitimize and strengthen the colonial system. However, this did not mean that the nascent middle classes "bought" what the Dutch were "selling." At the fairs, modernity was not simply imposed on indigenous visitors; instead, fairs were spaces where modernity—and colonial hegemony—was contested and negotiated until it became part of a new autonomous middle-class culture and lifestyle. This process of negotiation often occurred through commodified performances.[73]

In discussions of fairs in the colonial and vernacular press, the danger of overconsumption and conspicuous spending were recurring themes.[74] The fairgrounds were often described as too tempting for the average visitor, encouraging extravagance and reckless spending. This discussion was not limited to the press—it even reached the floor of the People's Council several times, especially during the Great Depression—but it never resulted in fairs being canceled.[75] One journalist remarked that the Pasar Gambir should not be considered a *volksfeest*, a celebration for all people, since the level of engagement depended on social position. The fairs' visitors, he argued, could be divided into three classes: the *hartawan* (wealthy), *budiman* (wise), and *nekat* (reckless). The minority of the visitors belonged to the rich category, those who "swam in money" and could enjoy the fairs to their hearts' content. They could attend all the performances and dine luxuriously. The wise were also a marginal group that consisted of people who consumed responsibly—never beyond their means. But the majority of the visitors belonged to the class of the reckless and irresponsible. At the fairs, they gave in to their desires and spent conspicuously to impress others, trying to appear wealthy and with great social status. Ironically, according to the author, their visit to the fairgrounds often ended at the government's pawnshops.[76]

The frequent association between conspicuous spending and colonial fairs suggests that the fairgrounds were spaces where the emerging middle classes actively shaped new identities through consumer culture. Take, for example, Hardjo Soë (a pseudonym), a columnist at the middle-class periodical the *Pandji Poestaka* who described several visits to the Pasar Gambir with his wife. According to Hardjo Soë, he originally belonged to the class of the wise, advocating for saving money to enjoy themselves at Batavia's annual fair. However, his wife did not agree, as she argued that it was more important to look elegant and important at the fair. Otherwise, people might think that he could not support her, or worse, that she could not run a proper household. To prevent such embarrassment, the couple purchased silk voile and brocade clothes for her, and gabardine and Palm Beach suits for him. For the cost of accumulated debt, they looked neat, elegant, and indistinguishable from people with a higher income at the Pasar Gambir's opening.[77]

Hardjo Soë's recollection illustrates the importance of seeing and being seen at the fairs. This was a space where people experimented with changes in appearance to create new social markers. Hardjo Soë even claimed that people's appearance at the fairs was one of its main and most popular exhibits, as appearance measured social status. According to him, "In the modern era clothing styles are manifold," and their meanings could be interpreted in various ways, from "down to earth, unpretentious, brave, slightly elegant, very elegant, modern, and hyper-modern."[78] The common Javanese still predominantly wore traditional dress, which consisted of a sarong, shirt, and *peci* (cap) or headscarf for men, and a sarong and kebaya for women. However, the majority of visitors' clothing might best be described as composite dress, as many people combined traditional and modern elements in their appearance. This could range from shoes, pants, colorful scarves, walking canes, and sunglasses, among others, as well as cosmetics, like lipstick and foundation, for women. Only those who could afford and wanted to be considered extremely modern adopted Western dress in its entirety. This meant a suit, shoes, and a hat for men, and a skirt with a modern blouse for women. By the late 1930s, most middle-class men had adopted the Western suit in combination with a peci, while Javanese women still wore a sarong and kebaya, as they were considered guardians of traditional culture.[79]

Without realizing it, Hardjo Soë had described the omnipresence of the "modernized Javanese" at Batavia's fair. While in 1907, the "modernized Javanese" was out of place at Surabaya's jaarmarkt, by 1937 the annual fairs had clearly become places where they belonged. Appearance was only one of the commodified performances that occurred at the fairs, albeit the most visual. But it was through consumer practices in general that the nascent middle classes created their identity. For instance, for Hardjo Soë, simply wearing a Palm Beach suit did not suffice. Instead of walking or taking a *sado* (two-wheeled horse-drawn carriage) to the Pasar Gambir, he and his spouse took a taxicab. While owning an automobile—a powerful symbol of modernity—was still an elite privilege, being able to afford a cab ride was a significant marker of middle-class status. At the fairgrounds, the couple engaged in further conspicuous consumption by visiting the European restaurant. Not to be outdone by members of the traditional elite, such as civil servants and aristocrats, they pretended to be familiar with the strange dishes and drinks they consumed, like *huzarensla* (Russian salad), compote, beer, and mineral water. To their shock, the food was not very tasteful or satisfying, but it was rather expensive. Hardjo Soë's anecdote is one of many that illustrate the importance of conspicuous spending at the fairs. But it also provides a clear indication that there was a gender bias to these consumer practices. Throughout his narrative, Hardjo Soë depicts his wife, and women in general, as someone who easily succumbs to consumer impulses. It was because of her concerns about social status that they purchased modern clothing and ate at a fancy restaurant. Moreover, according to Hardjo Soë, she purchased many products at the fair's exhibits and stands. As with clothing, his depiction of their experiences demonstrates that middle-class identity and lifestyle was gendered at colonial fairs.[80]

Fairs as Discursive Spaces: Contesting Colonial Hegemony

Contrary to what the visitor statistics might suggest, there was substantial criticism and skepticism toward the colonial fairs among the Javanese. In the vernacular press, and especially in critical publications as the *Persatoean Indonesia*—the periodical of Sukarno's Partai Nasional Indonesia—the fairs were considered as legible discursive spaces. According to observers, Java's annual fairs, very much like the colonial and world fairs in the Western world and ethnographic exhibitions in museums, conveyed that the colonized were worse off without the colonizers, whose guidance was essential in bringing civilization to the colonial world. The fairs were spaces that endorsed colonialism and the right of the colonizer to rule over the colonized.[81] It was argued this happened in two distinct manners. First, the obligatory artisanal sections of the fairgrounds presented the colonized as enduring ethnic stereotypes, clad in traditional dress and primarily capable of producing old-fashioned arts and crafts. These exhibits, observers noted, denied any societal progression and modernity among the Javanese. Secondly, by highlighting ethnic, linguistic, and religious differences among the colonized, for instance between the Javanese, Sundanese, and Madurese on Java, the Dutch repudiated the existence of an Indonesian national identity. The organizing principle behind these fairs, these publications argued, was anathema to the nationalist associations that fought for recognition of Indonesian modernity and nationality.[82]

The discussion of annual fairs focused primarily on questions as for whose benefit these fairs were organized, and to what extent they damaged Javanese traditions, culture, and identity. One of the strongest and most eloquent criticisms of annual fairs was printed in an editorial of the biweekly periodical *Timboel* in October 1928. Published in Surakarta, *Timboel* was a nationalist periodical that openly contested the ongoing westernization of Javanese society. According to the editorial, modern fairs had not emerged naturally out of the traditional Javanese pasar malam but were the result of European appropriation of this custom. While the original intent among ethical organizers had been to promote Java's culture and economy, European business interests had become predominant at modern fairs. The editors claimed, "The annual fairs in Surabaya, Bandung, Weltevreden [Batavia], not to mention their local equivalents, increasingly served to advertise and sell European mass-produced commodities."[83] They cynically added that indigenous artisans were merely tolerated because of Europeans' desire to purchase exotic souvenirs.[84]

Gradually, the editorial continued, the Javanese character of the fairs had receded into the background. Javanese artisans could only afford stands in the poorly lit fringes of the fairgrounds, from which they could gape at elaborate displays of imported commodities bathed in electric light. Here the editors both invoked and undermined the popular notion of the Dutch's enlightened example, arguing that the fairs only benefited the colonizer, not the colonized. Europeans' "desire for conquest" similarly affected the fairs' entertainment. Amoral dancing, nude dancers, and carousels had replaced traditional Javanese gamelan, *angklung* (musical instrument made from bamboo tubes), and wayang performances. To resist further economic exploitation and cultural degeneration, the editors called for a broad popular resistance to the Western penetration of Javanese culture and society. They believed that by reestablishing traditional pasar malam, they could purge Javanese national identity from foreign cultural influences. This sentiment was shared by others, especially in the Principalities where Javanese nationalists lamented the decline of the annual Sekaten celebrations, which were rooted in local cultural and religious traditions. By more purposefully organizing a fair accompanying the Sekaten, it was argued, the Javanese could take back control, organize a fair that was truly beneficial to indigenous society instead of Western interests, and one that was in line with local traditions and propriety.[85]

Although the great number of indigenous visitors at modern fairs can easily be interpreted as an indication of unconditional fascination, the concerns raised by *Timboel*'s editors were widespread. Even annual coverage of the fairs in *Pandji Poestaka*, a government periodical aimed at indigenous civil servants, revealed a certain level of ambivalence.[86] *Pandji Poestaka*, like *Timboel*, was produced by and for Indonesian Western-educated elites whose social position was tied to the colonial order. The articles in these periodicals can best be described as supportive of the colonial government's civilizing discourse. However, by reading against the grain, one can clearly discern anxieties about the fairs within their pages. For instance, throughout the 1920s and 1930s, articles in *Pandji Poestaka* repeatedly emphasized the various benefits of organizing and attending Java's annual fairs. The apparent necessity of insisting that fairs were not merely entertaining, exploitative, or a waste of money but instead enlightening experiences that broadened visitors' horizons, can be interpreted as an indication that the concerns raised by *Timboel*'s editors were more widespread. *Pandji Poestaka*'s counterargument stressed the fairs' significance for economic progress and development. Exhibits on native arts and crafts, for instance, were not intended for European tourists but meant to stimulate indigenous industry and instill a sense of cultural pride.[87] Similarly, *Pandji Poestaka* presented the colonial government's pedagogical exhibits as opportunities to learn how to improve one's living conditions.[88] And instead of interpreting the fairs as exploitative, they were hailed as driving forces behind the movement of people and goods, as well as the creation of new commercial markets that facilitated Java's economic integration.[89]

There were of course more explicit critiques of the modern fairs in the vernacular press, many of which focused on the financial consequences of a visit to the fairgrounds. Although most newspapers agreed with the stated objective of the fairs, namely to promote artisanal industries, stimulate the local economy, and by extension the welfare of the people, they openly questioned whether it could be achieved. One contributor wondered why the common people were encouraged to attend the fairs and spend money they did not have. He posed a simple question that could be found throughout the vernacular press: why make the poor poorer? In answering this question, some were more direct than others, stating that the Javanese were simply being exploited, their wallets pillaged by the Dutch. The message was simple, the Javanese could better spend their hard-earned money elsewhere. In Pekalongan, home of one of the largest annual fairs on Java outside its major cities, some people even founded a committee against the fairs (*anti-tontonan*) whose members committed to not visiting the fairgrounds.[90]

One of the more scathing critiques on fairs and their harmful influences on society was published as series of articles in the Malay language newspaper from Semarang with the Dutch name *De Samenwerking* (Cooperation)—a reference to its willingness to work with the authorities in furthering the emancipation of the indigenous people. In the articles the editors openly questioned who benefitted from the fairs. Did Batavia's Pasar Gambir or Surabaya's jaarmarkt actually stimulate the indigenous artisan industry or economy? Were these fairs beneficial for the indigenous people who were poor and destitute? The editors answered both questions in the negative. Instead, the real beneficiaries of the modern fairs, they argued, were Western companies.[91] And while the fairs did not pose a threat to educated people, for the "99% of indigenous people still living in ignorance, the fairs [were] extremely poisonous."[92] The plethora of entertainments attracted indigenous people to the fairgrounds, where clever and manipulative entrepreneurs took advantage of them. As a consequence, the "fair[s] promoted gambling, the fair[s] promoted prostitution, the fair[s] created thieves, and the fair[s] were the hubs for immoral behavior."[93] The authors suggested that only the registers of local pawnshops truly reflected the economic damage done to society. As part of their campaign, the editors published a letter addressed to all Dutch residents, Javanese bupati, and the government's Committee on Public Welfare on their front cover, publicly calling for an intervention from the authorities, beginning with a prohibition on gambling at Java's fairs, to protect the indigenous visitors against manipulation and their own worst instincts. While the authorities agreed in principle, the editors' advice went unheeded.[94]

The articles in *De Samenwerking* illustrate that public debate over the influence of fairs on indigenous people was not limited to economic concerns but very much included anxieties over cultural and moral degeneration. While fascination with modernity attracted many people to the fairs, it also challenged visitors to consider how this engagement might affect their identity. They wondered to what extent modernization—which, according to many, meant westernization—resulted in a loss of self. This question was part of a larger debate within the vernacular press and nascent nationalist movement.[95] The answer to this query depended on one's political outlook; for instance, Javanese nationalist, Islamic reformist, or modern secular. Interestingly, it was the discussion of the consequences of westernization on indigenous women specifically that determined the acceptable extent of cultural accommodation and the creation of new identities.[96] In the vernacular press, including the *Pandji Poestaka*, westernized indigenous women were often contrasted with an idealized woman—one considered more "authentic," who needed protection from the alienating Western influences that threatened her, her progeny, and the future of the nation.[97] It was this woman that, in 1931, the Federation of Indonesian Women's Associations (Perikatan Perhimpunan Isteri Indonesia) proclaimed to be the mother of the nation.[98] But while women, through their capacity for motherhood, came to be defined as guardians of national identity and culture, men were allowed greater liberties in balancing Western influences in their lives.[99]

Although negotiating colonial modernity through gendered concerns about morality was not specific to colonial fairs, they did provide a rather unique discursive space in which new middle-class identities were being shaped. The fairs combined many contentious modern experiences, such as watching movies, listening to music, dancing, sports, conspicuous consumption, and drinking, to name only those most discussed in the popular press. A striking example is the concern about women's clothing at the fairs. The adoption of Western dress was deemed inappropriate for Indonesian women, as it was too revealing and left little to the imagination.[100] Even the *Pandji Poestaka* critiqued the manner in which European women dressed at the Pasar Gambir, pointing out that parts of their bodies were visible for all to see and sorely needed to be covered.[101] The sensual character of European dress—the amount of skin left exposed and the way it accentuated the feminine form—was considered an affront to Javanese and Islamic traditions alike.[102] This did not mean that Indonesian women did not experiment with European or modern dress; however, by the late 1920s and 1930s, they did so by wearing colorful, nontraditional clothing items, like scarves or blouses, in combination with the more traditional sarong. While even this drew some ridicule in the vernacular press—the *Pandji Poestaka*, for instance, likened these composite styles to fireworks—they did not draw the fierce criticism that European dresses and skirts did.[103]

Unsurprisingly, experimentation with more cosmopolitan social norms at the fairs received copious amounts of attention in the vernacular press. Compared to traditional Javanese society, where interactions between men and women were circumscribed, the fairs were public spaces where the sexes mingled relatively freely. Adolescents demanded the right to socialize with their friends of both genders. At the fairs, they often went out unsupervised, walked arm-in-arm, shook hands, kissed, visited the movie theatre, attended musical performances, or simply enjoyed a carnival ride.[104] European dances, which meant dancing with a single partner of the opposite sex, were especially criticized for arousing participants' excitement.[105] This was considered particularly inappropriate for young women, who ran the risk of losing their "innocence." The aforementioned correspondent of the *Pandji Poestaka*, Hardjo Soë, described this modern activity as indecent, shameful, and embarrassing.[106] Others contrasted European dancing with traditional Javanese dances, which never "degenerated into the unbecoming embrace between men and women."[107] Traditional Javanese dances were imagined as performances to be observed, not to partake in.

Through the eyes of its criticasters, the annual fairs were spaces that portrayed the colonized as backward, denied them a national identity, and where they were economically exploited and morally corrupted. These deficiencies were not just articulated by observers, they also formulated possible solutions to negate them. The issue was straightforward: how to make the fairgrounds *fairer* spaces? Some, like the editors of *De Samenwerking*, demanded government intervention in the form of stricter oversight to prevent social ills as gambling, conspicuous consumption, indecent performances, licentious behavior, and thievery. Others called for a boycott of annual fairs until the Dutch treated the colonized as equals.[108] When the Great Depression made itself felt in colonial Indonesia it became popular to encourage Indonesians to buy locally produced products at the fairs, foremost batik, *lurik* (woven cloths), kretek, and tea. Inspired by Gandhi's swadeshi movement, buying products made in and by Indonesians was believed to strengthen the local economy as well as national self-esteem. Through consumer choices and commodified performances, one could effectively support national emancipation at the fairs.[109]

But perhaps the most ambitious—and most insightful—response to the massive success of Java's colonial fairs was for Indonesians to take the organization of fairs into their own hands. In April 1930, at a meeting of the Indonesian Study Club in Surabaya—founded by Soetomo in 1924 as an intellectual meeting space to promote a national consciousness—one of its members proposed to organize a *pasar malam derma* (a night's fair for a good cause) that was run by and for Indonesians and specifically *national* in character. The idea immediately got traction and resulted in the institution of a special committee chaired by Soetomo himself.[110] The new fair was symbolically dubbed Pasar Malam Nasional (The

National Night's Fair), a clear indication that it was conceived in opposition to the colonial fairs. The guiding principles behind the fair made this clear as well. Soetomo argued that the primary function of the fair was to educate and enlighten its visitors and stimulate the economic development of the nation. This meant that entertainments needed to be meaningful, as they easily allowed for slippage in moral behavior. Performances that violated common modesty, such as sensual dances, were prohibited. In the same vein, alcoholic beverages were not sold on the fairgrounds, nor was any form of gambling tolerated. The visitor experience consisted of walking past exhibits of Indonesian artisans and taking in traditional theatre, literature, music, and athletic performances. Crucially, all profits from the fair's organization and a percentage of the earnings of exhibitors was donated to several charities, including a local boarding school for girls, a women's home, an outpatient clinic of the association Muhammadijah, a public library, and the construction of a national building (*gedong nasional*) to house the Study Club and host discussions about the future of Indonesian people in general. The fair was thus a modern celebration of Indonesian artisanal and artistic accomplishments, benevolent, and safe.[111]

The first *Pasar Malam Nasional* was opened on May 31, 1930, by Nji Mas Hadji Mansoer, the chairwoman of the local branch of Aisjijah, the women's association of Muhammadijah that sought to empower women by striving for access to education, health care, and social opportunities.[112] That Mansoer performed the ribbon cutting was no accident of course. Most of the selected charities were run by Aisjijah. But her presence also signified that the fairgrounds were a safe and respectable space without all the moral ambiguities of the colonial fairs. In her appearance she represented the idealized Indonesian woman, donning a batik sarong and kebaya to indicate her care of the nation and its culture. In contrast, the men—who otherwise predominated the opening ceremony—were without exception dressed in a suit and tie to which most had added the peci. The men represented the modernity of the Indonesian nation.[113]

Like colonial fairs, visitors entered the *Pasar Malam Nasional* through a large ornamental gate that opened up onto a rectangular fairground lined by approximately sixty exhibition stands. There was also ample space for performances of a brass band, string orchestra, gamelan orchestra, *wayang orang* (human reenactment of Hindu epics), *ketoprak* (theatre performance based on Javanese history), *ludruk* (comedic theatre performances), *sandur* (performance art), *pencak silat* (Indonesian martial arts), cyclists, and weightlifters.[114] And of course, there was a restaurant offering affordable Indonesian, Chinese, and some European dishes and nonalcoholic beverages to "cool the esophagus and fill one's stomach."[115]

The fairgrounds were deliberately decorated as a *national* space. Red and white flags proudly waved in the wind around the terrain. These were the banner colors of Java's fourteenth-century Majapahit empire and embraced by Indonesian students in the previous decade as the colors of the emerging nation. Some of these flags were decorated with the head of a Javanese wild bull (*banteng*), which symbolized the power of the people of Indonesia.[116] Contrary to the colonial fairs, Indonesian national identity was front and center at the Pasar Malam Nasional.[117]

The first Pasar Malam Nasional was a resounding success. In ten days, the fair sold a remarkable 111,877 tickets and was able to make a significant financial contribution to its designated charities.[118] While there was some disappointment with the lack of European visitors—prompting some in the press to call for a retaliatory boycott of the Surabaya jaarmarkt—foremost a great sense of pride predominated.[119] The committee proved that by working together Indonesians could, within an extremely short time-span of two months, organize a fair that was educational, economically stimulating, and national in character, without running into any significant problems or delays. The secret behind this success, according to the special issue report in the Study Club's periodical *Soeloeh Ra'jat Indonesia*, was the willingness to cooperate and donate time, labor, materials, and money to the cause. The same report concluded that the experience proved the strength of the "Indonesian National Spirit." It proudly proclaimed: "Hurrah for Unity! Hurrah for Indonesia!" Although the Pasar Malam Nasional never became a real competitor for the colonial fairs—the Surabayan jaarmarkt drew almost four times as many visitors in 1930—its organization exemplifies the formulation of a counter-hegemonic performance and discourse.[120]

The colonial fairs on Java were quite literally "electrifying" spaces with a strong gravitational pull that drew approximately a million people in annually. From the exhibits to the entertainments, the fairs provided a quintessential modern experience. Yet, the colonized were aware that they were attending a hegemonic performance justifying the colonial relationship. Instead of uncritically engaging with or even buying into the discourse of colonial modernity, the indigenous visitors at Java's fairs contested those elements that did not conform to their cultural or moral beliefs and sense of self. This does not mean that visitors were not fascinated with the display of modernity at the fairgrounds, but it illustrates that there were some considerable limitations to the extent to which they would adopt it. Taken together, the commodified consumer performances and the moral negotiation of modernity resulted in the formation of a new, albeit fluid, modern middle-class identity and lifestyle that was particularly suited to the Indonesian context.[121] While fairs were merely one of the stages on which this modernity was fashioned and performed, due to their sheer size and reach, they were among the more prominent in the late-colonial world.

The Omnipresence of the Modern Indonesian

The organization of annual fairs and exhibitions in late-colonial Indonesia was an essential part of the larger hegemonic attempt to legitimize colonial authority. The fairgrounds were a physical representation of the Ethical Policy, showcasing the benevolence of government programs through special exhibits and stimulating indigenous artisan industries. The fairs constituted a staged modern experience that stressed Western cultural, technological, and scientific superiority and contrasted it with local culture and traditions. Crucially, the fairs' intended audience was the nascent Indonesian middle classes, who were enticed to consume Western products and the lifestyles and aspirations associated with them. The Dutch deemed this group's adoption of Western modernity and the colonial hegemonic worldview essential to the maintenance of colonial rule. But while the middle classes were indeed enthralled with the modernity on display at the fairgrounds, they did not simply buy into the hegemonic discourse but actively negotiated and contested it through their appearance, consumer behavior, and social attitudes. The fairgrounds were thus intriguing sites of interaction, discursive spaces that illustrated the tensions in society at large.

Whereas in 1907 a Dutch journalist at Surabaya's annual fair was appalled by a Javanese man's audacity in daring to appear in a sarong, dress shirt, tie, jacket, and hat, by the 1930s the modern *Indonesian* in a Western suit was no longer extraordinary. Rather than mocking the "modernized Javanese," Dutch visitors to colonial Indonesia's urban fairs in the 1920s and 1930s were confronted with the absurdity of their prejudices that characterized the colonized as rude, uncivilized, and inferior, and were struck instead by their neatness, civility, and sophistication. Like Mrs. Kuyck in 1929, Dutch visitors must have realized that many Indonesians "consider themselves completely equal to the Europeans."[122] By changing their appearance, speaking a more egalitarian language like Dutch or Malay, taking liberties where they previously had not, and displaying a different attitude in the colonial encounter, Indonesians subverted colonial hierarchies and signaled their equality. Moreover, Indonesians experimented with and crafted new identities at the fairs. As they enjoyed modern entertainments, such as movies, musical performances, and sports, ate and drank a variety of cuisines and beverages, spent conspicuously on consumer goods, and tested the limits of free social interaction, they articulated a modern identity that was not modeled on the West but distinctly their own. As part of this transformation, sartorial ethnic distinctions became less visible and relevant over time and a more uniform Indonesian appearance emerged. At the fairs, Indonesians subverted Dutch colonial hegemony by new identities and everyday forms of resistance. Their actions reveal the broad social transformation of society that comprise a successful national awakening.

Epilogue

Pawnshops as Stages of the Colonial Performance of Power

I N JANUARY 1922, the sudden outbreak of a strike among indigenous employees of the government's pawnshop service sent shockwaves throughout colonial society. Fearing that the strike would spread to other government services, the authorities brought in strikebreakers and fired all picketers. A political cartoon published in the sensationalist colonial weekly *De Zweep* (The Whip) showed two indigenous strikers clad in modern outfits—shoes, trousers, dress shirts, ties, jackets, pocket squares, hats, canes, and a cigarette in each of their mouths—while a strikebreaker passed by wearing a traditional sarong, *kebaya*, and Javanese headdress (*blangkon*). The cartoon further reinforced the juxtaposition between the characters in the accompanying text, as the two strikers expressed their amazement at the strikebreaker's appearance and behavior, noting with disdain that he was dressed as a common native, seemingly willing to carry teacups to the auction hall like a lowly servant. The protestors' ostensibly misplaced arrogance, smugness, indifference, and laziness are positioned in sharp contrast to the calm, honorable, and submissive strikebreaker. The cartoon perfectly captures the essence of the performance of power, showing both how Indonesians successfully subverted colonial hegemony by changing their appearance and the Dutch attempt to restore their formerly dominant worldview through ridicule and mockery. As such reactions make clear, incidents like strikes were not merely about improved working conditions but also about the changing character of the colonial relationship more broadly. Although the causes for the pawnshop strike of 1922 were not straightforward, being treated with more dignity and respect was among strikers' primary objectives.[1]

Like the numerous other sites of colonial encounters discussed in this book—from the civil service and private households to fairs, roadways, and railroad stations—pawnshops were important stages for the performance of power on which both colonized and colonizer actively communicated, expressed, and contested the discourse of colonial hegemony. In fact, the history of the pawnshop service in colonial Indonesia aptly encapsulates the various "acts" of this performance as outlined in this study. Pawnshops initially reinforced the Javanization of colonial authority, turned into spaces of its contestation around 1913, and ultimately played an important role in the forging and enactment of new modern

FIGURE 10. "The Pawnshop Strike." This cartoon effectively contrasts the noble and submissive attitude of the strikebreaker, donning traditional dress, with the misplaced arrogance of the striker clad in a suit. Source: *De Zweep*, January 15, 1922.

identities. Each of these acts demonstrates that through language, etiquette, appearance, material symbols, and attitudes, the Dutch tried to confirm and strengthen colonial hierarchies of race, class, and gender, while the colonized destabilized them through discursive everyday actions.

The first act of the colonial performance of power opens in the nineteenth century, when the Dutch sought to strengthen the legitimacy of the colonial state through collaborating with the *priyayi* and by adopting local deference etiquette, symbols of power, sartorial hierarchies, lifestyles, and architecture.

Through the Javanization of colonial authority, as I call this deliberate process of acculturation, the Dutch attempted to instill a sense of compliance throughout the colonial populace. The hegemonic script for the colonial encounter was never static, however, but was continuously adapted to changing circumstances. For instance, as the priyayi lost influence in actual governance vis-à-vis European officials, the Dutch compensated them with additional symbolic vestiges of power. As the character of colonialism itself began to change—in part due to new insights in evolutionary science, the privatization of the colonial economy, and the rise of Japan and the United States as new imperial powers in Southeast Asia—the Javanization of authority seemed increasingly inadequate. In response, the Ethical Policy (announced in 1901) proclaimed that the Dutch had a moral responsibility to "civilize" the colonized, producing a new hegemonic script that divided colonial officialdom. While some agreed with the necessity of Dutch tutelage and Western examples, others believed that "civilizing" the colonized was an impossible task and that maintaining Javanized colonial rule was the only way to keep the peace. Consequently, there emerged a discrepancy between emancipatory theory and conservative practice.

The ambiguity of this first act of the colonial performance is strikingly reflected in the establishment of the pawnshop service in 1904. The Dutch ostensibly sought to use the pawnshop service to protect the colonized against the supposed abuses of Chinese middlemen. On the one hand, ordinary Javanese used government pawnshops for easy access to cash; on the other, the pawnshop service provided several thousand Javanese with coveted government positions. Employment in this sector essentially represented admission into the priyayi class of aristo-bureaucrats, since those who joined as administrators, appraisers, tellers, and clerks were mostly recruited from the grey area between the lower priyayi and the common people. As a symbol of their newly acquired social status, pawnshop employees were granted the right to carry a *payung* in 1906.[2] Although the government had prohibited the payung for European officials in 1904 as part of the attempt to modernize the colonial relationship, it continued to rely on the Javanization of authority by incorporating indigenous pawnshop personnel into the payung hierarchy. Just as in colonial society more broadly, these contrasting signals caused considerable tension among indigenous and European pawnshop personnel.

Pawnshops remain a key site for explicating the second act of the colonial performance, in which the sudden proliferation of everyday discursive challenges to colonial power in 1913 signaled a broad social transformation—the Indonesian national awakening. Although most pawnshop workers were not necessarily highly educated, they did (or aspired to) belong to the new generation of Indonesians that articulated their desire for equality and respect in the vernacular press and in cultural and political associations. It is therefore no surprise that following the distribution of the hormat circular in August 1913 (which prohibited European officials from requiring traditional deference from the colonized), indigenous pawnshop personnel were among the first—along with teachers, physicians, railroad employees, and civil servants—to demand the circular's immediate and complete implementation. They expressed their activist mentality through a change in appearance, substituting their Javanese sarong and kebaya for a Western suit in an attempt to evade European administrators' calls for traditional deference. Their superiors, however, did not budge willingly, as acquiescing to the circular would have been analogous to granting their indigenous employees' equal social status.

Alongside their contemporaries, pawnshop employees turned to the vernacular press to air their grievances. For instance, one author in the periodical *Doenia Bergerak* wrote that his European boss treated his staff like animals rather than human beings, insisting that they continue to sit on the floor in his presence and speak in accordance with the Javanese language hierarchy.[3] But as reports like these demonstrate, the colonized resisted such treatment through publishing their transgressions in the vernacular press as well as everyday discursive acts, such as speaking Dutch, wearing trousers, or demanding a chair. In 1919, another pawnshop employee pledged in the newspaper *Oetoesan Hindia* that he refused to "speak Javanese, to crouch, or to make the sembah" any longer for his European bosses.[4] Frustrated with the protracted struggle for emancipation within the pawnshop service, a representative of the indigenous pawnshop workers union declared that there was only one choice left: "To strike or to crouch!"[5]

The pawnshop service strike of 1922 must be understood within the context of this prolonged cultural struggle between colonizer and colonized. According to former Advisor for Native Affairs G. A. J. Hazeu, the strike was the result of Europeans' failure to "acknowledge and take account of the change of mentality among Indonesians." He wrote that, on the contrary, all expressions of emerging self-awareness among the colonized, as well as their roots, were willfully ignored.[6] It is telling that the spark that ignited the strike was an incident at a pawnshop in Yogyakarta in which an employee refused to carry pawned items to the auction hall (as referenced in the political cartoon). As a member of the priyayi, he felt he should be exempt from performing menial labor, generally relegated to special servants, but recent spending cuts dictated that the task was now his responsibility. Angered by his refusal, his European superior fired him on the spot, setting in motion a chain of events that caused the strike to spread like wildfire over Java, ultimately encompassing a third of all pawnshop personnel. Despite this widespread fervor, the strike ended with an anticlimactic thud, as all the indigenous employees involved lost their jobs along with their priyayi status.[7] Even so, the history of the pawnshop service strike illustrates how a broader and more conscious challenge to the colonial order emerged out of everyday struggles. This is an important revision to the prevailing narrative of the Indonesian national awakening—it was not just a movement incited by a small political elite from the top-down but one that also grew out of large social transformations from below.

The third act of the colonial performance of power opens in response to these profound changes around 1913. As it became clear that the Javanization of authority was unsustainable, the Dutch began to contrast their sense of their own modernity with the alleged backwardness of the colonized. This resulted in the propagation of a more European lifestyle in the colony along with increased fear of the degenerative influences of both the tropical climate and the colonized themselves. Similarly, while the colonized sought new identities as modern Indonesians—attempts that the Dutch ridiculed and feared—they worried about the negative influences of Western culture. The colonial performance of power continued as both sides negotiated colonial modernity to articulate their new identities. They again did so in the everyday colonial encounter, expressing and communicating their approaches to modernity through changes in social customs, sexual norms, culinary preferences, and consumer behavior.

Pawnshops perfectly capture the anxieties surrounding the performance of new modern identities. As the strike of 1922 shows, the Dutch clearly equated Indonesians' changing appearance, comportment, and attitude with their increased demands for emancipation, equal opportunity, and respect. Ironically, with the pawnshop service European officials found an institution that could potentially offset these changes by taking away precisely those items through which Indonesians signaled their modernity and equality—clothing, sunglasses, shoes, canes, umbrellas, cigars, and more. For instance, in response to an earlier strike in 1920, a colonial newspaper mockingly declared, "Thousands and thousands of workers know no road as well as that from their home to the pawnshop and back."[8] The author's implication was clear: Indonesians trying to present themselves as something they were not—modern, civilized, and equal—would eventually be forced to sell their "luxury items" at the local pawnshop. Thus, the colonial mindset celebrated the pawnshop as an institution that corrected this co-optation and exposed people for who they really were: their native subjects.

The political cartoon discussed above draws on this same dichotomy, as the artist associates an Indonesian in European dress with arrogance and indolence and one in indigenous dress with modesty and obedience.[9]

Perhaps surprisingly, Indonesians also considered pawnshops to be crucial spaces where costumes and props for the performance of new identities could be bought and sold. For instance, a 1940 political cartoon in the periodical *Pandji Poestaka* depicted an Indonesian man clad in a suit and *peci* (cap) hailing a taxicab to go see a movie in the first-class section—all privileges associated with European or elite status (see figure 7). As to how he could afford these luxuries, the reader learned that, in fact, he could not; he had spent too conspicuously and was forced to pawn his suit and other belongings at the local pawnshop. But while seemingly similar to Dutch political cartoons, the message here is significantly different. Whereas the Dutch saw the pawnshop as an institution that exposed indigenous people's backwardness, Indonesians viewed these spaces as moral scales that weighed and judged modern vices within this changing cultural context. The cartoon's caption reminded the reader that it was important "not to forget where you come from," warning not against Indonesian modernity but rather against the dangers of excessive westernization and conspicuous consumption.[10] Pawnshops were thus spaces that facilitated the condemnation of uncontrolled Dutch mimicry, and cartoons like this encouraged readers to filter their modern identities through indigenous cultural and religious traditions and to retain only the beneficial elements of Western modernity. If one failed to do so, a visit to the pawnshop was inevitable.

Tracing the development and evolution of the performance of power in colonial Indonesia thus uncovers a dynamic and engaging history of Indonesian agency and resistance. It brings into sharp focus the myriad ways in which power was continuously communicated and contested through a complex array of social performances and material culture in the everyday colonial encounter. Rather than privileging outright forms of political resistance, this emphasis expands the Gramscian concept of cultural hegemony and suggests new ways to analyze the interplay between culture and power. The value of this approach is not limited to Indonesian history or colonial societies, but by emphasizing people's decisions and lived experiences in seemingly unexceptional interactions, extends to the study of social relationships more broadly.

Japan abruptly put an end to Dutch colonial rule in Indonesia in 1942, but the performance of power persisted into the postcolonial era.[11] While this larger history lies outside the scope of this book, dress remains an illustrative example of the perpetual nature of the hegemonic struggle. Changes in appearance continued to play a crucial role in the performance and contestation of power. Following the trauma of Japanese occupation (1942–1945) and the Indonesian revolutionary war (1945–1949), President Sukarno sought to strengthen national identity and unity through the creation of a pan-Indonesian batik design. The design reflected his attempt to appease various political and religious movements—foremost among them nationalists, Muslims, and communists—as well as to bridge the many regional and ethnic divisions in the newly independent country. While Sukarno succeeded in promoting Indonesian batik, the country was nonetheless torn apart in 1965 and 1966 by mass violence targeting communists. It was in the wake of mass murder that Indonesian leadership once more turned to dress to restore unity and national identity. In 1972, Governor Ali Sadikin of Jakarta was the first to encourage and popularize open-collar batik shirts for men, instead of Western dress shirts and jackets. President Suharto embraced this new style and commissioned a special batik shirt as formal wear for civil servants, thus reinstating batik as a symbol of state power. Through this initiative, batik was also reintroduced into Indonesian men's wardrobes without giving up their trousers—a design element that rendered batik representative of Indonesian modernity. Discussions of outward appearance did not end here; they continue today in debates over headscarves for women. The persistence of this and other topics of routine significance is a stark reminder that the performance of power—as well as its contestation—endures into the twenty-first century.

NOTES

Abbreviations

BKI	*Bijdragen tot de Taal-, Land-en Volkenkunde* (Journal of the Humanities and Social Sciences of Southeast Asia)
HDC	Historical Documentation Center for Dutch Protestantism
IG	*De Indische Gids*
IPO	*Overzicht van de Inlandsche en Maleisch-Chineesche Pers* (Survey of the Native and Malay-Chinese Press)
JSEAS	*Journal of Southeast Asian Studies*
JWH	*Journal of World History*
KITLV	Royal Netherlands Institute for Southeast Asian and Caribbean Studies
KT	*Koloniaal Tijdschrift*
NL-HaNA	Nationaal Archief, Den Haag (National Archives, The Hague)
NNI	*Het Nieuws van den Dag voor Nederlandsch-Indië*
PPBB	Persatoean Prijaji Bestuur Boemipoetera (Association of Indigenous Civil Servants)
SEAP	Southeast Asia Program Publications
TBB	*Tijdschrift voor het Binnenlandsch Bestuur*
TNI	*Tijdschrift voor Nederlandsch-Indië*
UBL	Leiden University Library, Special Collections
VOC	Vereenigde Oost-Indische Compagnie (Dutch East India Company)
WVI	*Weekblad voor Indië*

Introduction. The Performance of Power

1. T. Hellwig to G. A. J. Hazeu, February 25, 1913, in Collection Hazeu, H 1083, no. 29, UBL.

2. Indonesian independence was declared on August 17, 1945; however, it took four years of violent conflict before the Dutch's eventual recognition of it on December 27, 1949.

3. Heather Sutherland, *The Making of a Bureaucratic Elite: The Colonial Transformation of the Javanese Priyayi* (Singapore: Heinemann Educational Books, 1979); H. W. van den Doel, *De stille macht: het Europese binnenlands bestuur op Java en Madoera, 1808–1942* (Amsterdam: Bert Bakker, 1994); C. W. Newbury, "Patrons,

213

Clients, and Empire: The Subordination of Indigenous Hierarchies in Asia and Africa," *Journal of World History* 11, no. 2 (2000): 227–63. An exception is Sanne Ravensbergen, "Courtrooms of Conflict: Criminal Law, Local Elites and Legal Pluralities in Colonial Java" (PhD diss., Leiden University, 2018), http://hdl.handle.net/1887/61039.

4. Jean Gelman Taylor, *The Social World of Batavia: Europeans and Eurasians in Colonial Indonesia* (Madison: University of Wisconsin Press, 1983); Ulbe Bosma and Remco Raben, *Being "Dutch" in the Indies: A History of Creolisation and Empire, 1500–1920* (Singapore: NUS Press, 2008); Leonard Blussé, *Strange Company: Chinese Settlers, Mestizo Women and the Dutch in VOC Batavia* (Dordrecht: Foris, 1986).

5. Benedict Anderson, *Language and Power: Exploring Political Cultures in Indonesia* (Ithaca: Cornell University Press, 1990), 133–34.

6. O. W. Wolters, *History, Culture, and Region in Southeast Asian Perspectives* (Ithaca: SEAP, Cornell University, 1999), 11–57; Jan Wisseman Christie, "Rāja and Rāma: The Classical State in Early Java," in *Centers, Symbols, and Hierarchies: Essays of the Classical States of Southeast Asia*, ed. Lorraine Gesick and Michael Aung-Thwin (New Haven: Yale University Southeast Asia Studies Monographs, 1983), 21–35; Soemarsaid Moertono, *State and Statecraft in Old Java: A Study of the Later Mataram Period, 16th to 19th Century* (Ithaca: SEAP, Cornell University, 1981), 14–24; Michael Adas, "From Avoidance to Confrontation: Peasant Protest in Precolonial and Colonial Southeast Asia," *Comparative Studies in Society and History* 23, no. 2 (April 1981): 217–47.

7. Anderson, *Language and Power*, 28.

8. Clifford Geertz, *Negara: The Theatre State in Nineteenth-Century Bali* (Princeton: Princeton University Press, 1980), 13.

9. Henk Schulte Nordholt, *The Spell of Power: A History of Balinese Politics, 1650–1940* (Leiden: KITLV Press, 1996).

10. Jan Breman, *Mobilizing Labour for the Global Coffee Market: Profits from an Unfree Work Regime in Colonial Java* (Amsterdam: Amsterdam University Press, 2015), 262–71.

11. John Pemberton, *On the Subject of "Java"* (Ithaca: Cornell University Press, 1994), 10, 22–23, 64–66.

12. Antonio Gramsci, *Selections from the Prison Notebooks of Antonio Gramsci*, trans. Quentin Hoare and Geoffrey Nowell Smith (New York: International Publishers, 1972), 5–23, 52–58, 161–70; Steve Jones, *Antonio Gramsci* (London; New York: Routledge, 2006); Walter L. Adamson, *Hegemony and Revolution: A Study of Antonio Gramsci's Political and Cultural Theory* (Berkeley: University of California Press, 1980); Perry Anderson, "The Antinomies of Antonio Gramsci," *New Left Review* 1, no. 100 (1976): 5–78.

13. Douglas Haynes and Gyan Prakash, eds., *Contesting Power: Resistance and Everyday Social Relations in South Asia* (Berkeley: University of California Press, 1992); Dagmar Engels and Shula Marks, eds., *Contesting Colonial Hegemony: State and Society in Africa and India* (New York: British Academic Press, 1994); David Arnold, "Gramsci and Peasant Subalternity in India," *Journal of Peasant Studies* 11, no. 4 (1984): 155–77; Bernard S. Cohn, *Colonialism and its Forms of Knowledge: The British in India* (Princeton: Princeton University Press, 1996).

14. Breman, *Mobilizing Labour*, 347–67.

15. Jackson Lears, "The Concept of Cultural Hegemony: Problems and Possibilities," *American Historical Review* 90, no. 3 (1985): 567–93.

16. Ranajit Guha, *Dominance without Hegemony: History and Power in Colonial India* (Cambridge: Harvard University Press, 1997).

17. Gramsci, *Prison Notebooks,* 52–58, 161–70.

18. Sutherland, *Bureaucratic Elite*; Leslie H. Palmier, "The Javanese Nobility under the Dutch," *Comparative Studies in Society and History* 2, no. 2 (1960): 197–227.

19. James Rush, *Opium to Java: Revenue Farming and Chinese Enterprise in Colonial Indonesia, 1860–1910* (Ithaca: Cornell University Press, 1990), 83–135; Patricia Tjiook-Liem, *De rechtspositie der Chinezen in Nederlands-Indië 1848–1942: wetgevingsbeleid tussen beginsel en belang* (Amsterdam: Leiden University Press, 2009).

20. Jaap de Moor, "The Recruitment of Indonesian Soldiers for the Dutch Colonial Army, c. 1700–1950," in *Guardians of Empire: The Armed Forces of the Colonial Powers c. 1700–1964,* ed. David Killingray and David Omissi (Manchester: Manchester University Press, 1999), 53–69.

21. Raymond Williams, *Marxism and Literature* (Oxford: Oxford University Press, 1977), 108–14.

22. James C. Scott, *Domination and the Arts of Resistance: Hidden Transcripts* (New Haven: Yale University Press, 1990); James C. Scott, *Weapons of the Weak: Everyday Forms of Peasant Resistance* (New Haven: Yale University Press, 1987).

23. Robert Elson, *The Idea of Indonesia: A History* (New York: Cambridge University Press, 2008), 1–25.

24. Scott, *Domination and the Arts of Resistance,* 87; Ann Laura Stoler, *Along the Archival Grain: Epistemic Anxieties and Colonial Common Sense* (Princeton: Princeton University Press, 2009); Remco Raben, "Ethnic Disorder in VOC Asia: A Plea for Eccentric Reading", *BMGN – Low Countries Historical Review,* 134, no. 2 (2019): 1115–28.

25. Michael Adas, "From Footdragging to Flight: The Evasive History of Peasant Avoidance Protest in South and South-East Asia," *Journal of Peasant Studies* 13, no. 2 (1986): 64–86; Breman, *Mobilizing Labour,* 347–67.

26. F. A. Stoett, *Nederlandsche spreekwoorden, spreekwijzen, uitdrukkingen en gezegden* (Zutphen: W. J. Thieme & Cie, 1923–25), 181.

27. Raden Adjeng Kartini to Stella Zeehandelaar, January 12, 1900, in *Letters of a Javanese Princess,* trans. Agnes Louise Symmers (Kuala Lumpur: Oxford University Press, 1976), 40–42. Also see Raden Adjeng Kartini, *The Complete Kartini: The Collected Works of R. A. Kartini,* trans. Joost J. P. Coté (Clayton: Monash University Publishing, 2013).

28. Jürgen Osterhammel, *The Transformation of the World: A Global History of the Nineteenth Century* (Princeton: Princeton University Press, 2015); Tony Ballantyne and Antoinette Burton, *Empires and the Reach of the Global, 1870–1945* (Cambridge: Belknap Press of Harvard University Press, 2014).

29. Eric Tagliacozzo, "The Indies and the World: State Building, Promise, and Decay at a Transnational Moment, 1910," *BKI* 116, no. 2/3 (2010): 270–92; Kees van Dijk, *The Netherlands Indies and the Great War, 1914–1918* (Leiden: KITLV Press, 2007) 1–90.

30. Elsbeth Locher-Scholten, *Ethiek in fragmenten: vijf studies over koloniaal denken en doen van Nederlanders in de Indonesische Archipel, 1877–1942* (Utrecht: HES Publishers, 1981); Maarten Kuitenbrouwer, *The Netherlands and the Rise of Modern Imperialism: Colonies and Foreign Policy, 1870–1902* (New York: St. Martin's Press, 1991); Suzanne Moon, *Technology and Ethical Idealism: A History of Development in the Netherlands East Indies* (Leiden: CNWS Publications, 2007); Steven Wedema, *"Ethiek" und Macht: die niederländisch-indische Kolonialverwaltung und indonesische Emanzipationsbestrebungen, 1901–1927* (Stuttgart: F. Steiner, 1998); Marieke Bloembergen and Remco Raben, eds., *Het koloniale beschavingsoffensief: wegen naar het nieuwe Indië, 1890–1950* (Leiden: KITLV Press, 2009); R. B. Cribb, ed., *The Late Colonial State in Indonesia: Political and Economic Foundations of the Netherlands Indies, 1880–1942* (Leiden: KITLV Press, 1994); Wim Ravesteijn and Jan Kop, eds., *For Profit and Prosperity: The Contribution Made by Dutch Engineers to Public Works in Indonesia, 1800–2000* (Leiden: KITLV Press, 2008).

31. Fenneke Sysling, *Racial Science and Human Diversity in Colonial Indonesia* (Singapore: NUS Press, 2016); Frances Gouda, *Dutch Culture Overseas: Colonial Practice in the Netherlands Indies, 1900–1942* (Amsterdam: Amsterdam University Press, 1995); Jan Breman, Piet de Rooy, and Ann Laura Stoler, eds., *Imperial Monkey Business: Racial Supremacy in Social Darwinist Theory and Colonial Practice* (Amsterdam: VU University Press, 1990).

32. Kartosiswojo, "Kamerdika'an," *Sinar Djawa*, April 8, 1914.

33. Bart Luttikhuis and Arnout H. C. van der Meer, "1913 in Indonesian History: Demanding Equality, Changing Mentality," *TRaNS: Trans-Regional and-National Studies of Southeast Asia* 8, no. 2 (2020): 115–33.

34. Locher-Scholten, *Ethiek in fragmenten*; Kees Groeneboer, *Gateway to the West: The Dutch Language in Colonial Indonesia, 1600–1950* (Amsterdam: Amsterdam University Press, 1998); Robert van Niel, *The Emergence of the Modern Indonesian Elite* (The Hague: W. van Hoeve, 1960); Rudolf Mrázek, *Engineers of Happy Land: Technology and Nationalism in a Colony* (Princeton: Princeton University Press, 2002); Andrew Goss, *The Floracrats: State-Sponsored Science and the Failure of the Enlightenment in Indonesia* (Madison: The University of Wisconsin Press, 2011).

35. Michael Francis Laffan, *Islamic Nationhood and Colonial Indonesia: The Umma Below the Winds* (New York: Routledge, 2003); Michael Laffan, *The Making of Indonesian Islam: Orientalism and the Narration of a Sufi Past* (Princeton: Princeton University Press, 2011); Chiara Formichi, "Indonesian Readings of Turkish History, 1890s to 1940s," in *From Anatolia to Aceh: Ottomans, Turks and Southeast Asia*, ed. A. C. S. Peacock and Annabel Teh Gallop (Oxford: Oxford University Press, 2015), 241–60; Deliar Noer, *The Modernist Muslim Movement in Indonesia, 1900–1942* (Kuala Lumpur: Oxford University Press, 1973).

36. Takashi Shiraishi, *An Age in Motion: Popular Radicalism in Java, 1912–1926* (Ithaca: Cornell University Press, 1990); Akira Nagazumi, *The Dawn of Indonesian Nationalism: The Early Years of the Budi Utomo, 1908–1918* (Tokyo: Institute for Developing Studies, 1972); A. P. E. Korver, *Sarekat Islam, 1912–1916: opkomst, bloei en*

structuur van Indonesië's eerste massabeweging (Amsterdam, Historisch Seminarium van de Universiteit van Amsterdam, 1982); Chiara Formichi, *Islam and the Making of the Nation: Kartosuwiryo and Political Islam in Twentieth-Century Indonesia* (Leiden: KITLV Press, 2012); Safrizal Rambe, *Sarekat Islam: pelopor nasionalisme Indonesia, 1905–1942* (Jakarta: Yayasan Kebangkitan Insan Cendekia, 2008); Sartono Kartodirdjo, *Pengantar sejarah Indonesia baru: Sejarah pergerakan nasional dari kolonialisme sampai nasionalisme*, vol. 2 (Jakarta: Gramedia Pustaka Utama, 1992).

37. Ahmat Adam, *The Vernacular Press and the Emergence of Modern Indonesian Consciousness (1855–1913)* (Ithaca: Cornell University Press, 1995); Tom G. Hoogervorst, *Language Ungoverned: Indonesia's Chinese Print Entrepreneurs, 1911–1949* (Ithaca: SEAP, Cornell University, 2021).

38. *Hormat* literally means "respect," but in this context refers to customary social deference and etiquette.

39. Shiraishi also discusses this alignment of interests between the colonial government and the nascent nationalist movement in *An Age in Motion.*

40. Henk Schulte Nordholt, ed., *Outward Appearances: Dressing State and Society in Indonesia* (Leiden: KITLV Press, 1997).

41. Fridus Steijlen en Erik Willems, eds., *Met ons alles goed: brieven en films uit Nederlands-Indië van de familie Kuyck* (Zutphen: Walburg Pers, 2008), 124; Henk Schulte Nordholt, "Modernity and Cultural Citizenship in the Netherlands Indies: An Illustrated Hypothesis," *JSEAS* 42, no. 3 (October 2011): 454.

42. Bart Luttikhuis, "Negotiating Modernity: Europeanness in Late Colonial Indonesia, 1910–1942" (PhD diss., European University Institute, 2014), https://cadmus.eui.eu/handle/1814/33074.

43. Susie Protschky and Tom van den Berge, eds., *Modern Times in Southeast Asia, 1920s–1970s* (Leiden: Brill, 2018).

44. Frederick Cooper, *Colonialism in Question: Theory, Knowledge, History* (Berkeley: California University Press, 2005), 113–49.

45. Vincent Houben, "Representations of Modernity in Colonial Indonesia," in *Figurations of Modernity: Global and Local Representations in Comparative Perspective*, ed. Vincent Houben and Mona Schrempf (Frankfurt: Campus Verlag, 2008), 23–40.

46. Nobuto Yamamoto, *Censorship in Colonial Indonesia, 1901–1942* (Leiden: Brill, 2019).

47. Benedict Anderson, *Imagined Communities: Reflections on the Origin and Spread of Nationalism* (London: Verso, 1983), 120–23.

48. While the issue of mixed marriages has received scant attention, various studies have explored topics such as polygamy and concubinage. See Elsbeth Locher-Scholten, "Marriage, Morality and Modernity: The 1937 Debate on Monogamy," *Women and the Colonial State: Essays on Gender and Modernity in the Netherlands Indies, 1900–1942* (Amsterdam: Amsterdam University Press, 2000), 187–218; Elizabeth Martyn, *The Women's Movement in Post-Colonial Indonesia: Gender and Nation in a New Democracy* (New York: Routledge, 2005), 30–52; Cora Vreede-de Stuers, *The Indonesian Woman: Struggles and Achievements* (The Hague: Mouton, 1960).

49. Hans Pols, "Notes from Batavia, the Europeans' Graveyard: The Nineteenth-Century Debate on Acclimatization in the Dutch East Indies," *Journal of the History of Medicine and Allied Sciences* 67, no. 1 (2012): 120–48.

50. Elsbeth Locher-Scholten, "So Close and Yet So Far: The Ambivalence of Dutch Colonial Rhetoric on Javanese Servants in Indonesia, 1900–1942," in *Domesticating the Empire: Race, Gender, and Family Life in French and Dutch Colonialism*, ed. Julia Clancy-Smith and Frances Gouda (Charlottesville: University of Virginia Press, 1998), 131–53; Ann Laura Stoler, "Making Empire Respectable: The Politics of Race and Sexual Morality in 20th-Century Colonial Cultures," *American Ethnologist* 16, no. 4 (1989): 634–60; Ann Laura Stoler, *Carnal Knowledge and Imperial Power: Race and the Intimate in Colonial Rule* (Berkeley: University of California Press, 2002).

51. Freek Colombijn and Joost Coté, eds., *Cars, Conduits, and Kampongs: The Modernization of the Indonesian City, 1920–1960* (Leiden: Brill, 2015); Susie Protschky, ed., *Photography, Modernity, and the Governed in Late-Colonial Indonesia* (Amsterdam: Amsterdam University Press, 2015); Protschky and Van den Berge eds., *Modern Times in Southeast Asia*.

52. Yulia Nurliani Lukito, "Colonial Exhibition and a Laboratory of Modernity: Hybrid Architecture at Batavia's Pasar Gambir," *Indonesia* 100 (2015): 77–104; Joost Coté, "Staging Modernity: The Semarang International Colonial Exhibition, 1914," *Review of Indonesian and Malaysian Affairs* 40, no. 1 (2006): 1–44.

53. Henk Schulte Nordholt, "New Urban Middle Classes in Colonial Java: Children of the Colonial State and Ancestors of a Future Nation," BKI 173, no. 4 (2017): 439–41; Tom Hoogervorst and Henk Schulte Nordholt, "Urban Middle Classes in Colonial Java (1900–1942): Images and Language," BKI 173, no. 4 (2017): 424–74.

Chapter 1. Setting the Stage

1. Kartini, January 12, 1900, in *Letters of a Javanese Princess*, 29–47.

2. The term "Javanization" was first coined by Benedict Anderson in *Language and Power*, 133–34.

3. Van den Doel, *De stille macht*; Sutherland, *The Making of a Bureaucratic Elite*; Cees Fasseur, "Cornerstone and Stumbling Block: Racial Classification and the Late Colonial State in Indonesia," in *The Late Colonial State in Indonesia: Political and Economical Foundations of the Netherlands Indies, 1880–1942*, ed. Robert B. Cribb (Leiden: KITLV Press, 1994), 31–57; Stoler, *Carnal Knowledge*.

4. An important exception is Taylor, *The Social World of Batavia*.

5. A good example is the work of Bernard Cohn, *Colonialism and Its Forms of Knowledge*.

6. Taylor, *The Social World of Batavia*; Bosma and Raben, *Being "Dutch" in the Indies*.

7. Taylor, *The Social World of Batavia*, xvii–xxii and 33–77.

8. The third princely state was Mangkunagaran. In 1812, the British broke up Yogyakarta and created Pakualam as the fourth princely state.

9. M. C. Ricklefs, *Jogjakarta under Sultan Mangkubumi, 1749–1792: A History of the Division of Java* (London: Oxford University Press, 1974), 362–413; M. C. Ricklefs, *A History of Modern Indonesia since c. 1200* (Stanford, CA: Stanford University Press, 2001), 86–130; Pemberton, *On the Subject of "Java"*, 28–67.

10. Traditionally, Javanese states were divided administratively into regencies, or *kabupaten*, directed by a regency head, or bupati (in Dutch, *regentschap* and *regent*, respectively). In turn, regencies were divided into districts managed by district heads, or wedana. Village leadership was the third and lowest level of administration. This structure was preserved under the VOC and, later, Dutch colonialism.

11. Palmier, "The Javanese Nobility under the Dutch," 197–227; Sutherland, *The Making of a Bureaucratic Elite*, 1–18; Van Niel, *The Emergence of the Modern Indonesian Elite*, 1–29.

12. Jan Breman, *Mobilizing Labour*, 57–94.

13. Heather Sutherland, "Pangreh Pradja: Java's Indigenous Administrative Corps and its Role in the Last Decades of Dutch Colonial Rule" (PhD diss., Yale University, 1973) 41.

14. Wisseman Christie, "Rāja and Rāma," 21–35; Soemarsaid Moertono, *State and Statecraft*, 14–24; Anderson, *Language and Power*, 28.

15. Geertz, *Negara*, 120.

16. Taylor, *The Social World of Batavia*, xvii–xxii, 3–32, 39–42, and 56–67.

17. S. Kalff, "Javaansche poesaka," *Djåwå: Tijdschrift van het Java-Instituut*, 3 (1923), 151–58.

18. J. A. van der Chijs, *Nederlandsch-Indisch Plakaatboek, 1602–1811* 2 (Batavia: Landsdrukkerij, 1886), 111; 4 (1887), 239–44 and 333–536; Taylor, *Social World of Batavia*, 38–41 and 66–69; J. Groneman, "Javaansche rangen en pajoengs," *Tijdschrift van het Indisch Aardrijkskundig Genootschap*, no. 4 (1883), 1–13; J. Groneman, "Een en ander over den Javaanschen adel," *IG* 8, no. 2 (1886), 880–96.

19. Taylor, *The Social World of Batavia*, 39–42, 56–57, and 66–67.

20. This was part of a global trend. See C. A. Bayly, *The Birth of the Modern World, 1780–1914: Global Connections and Comparisons* (Malden: Blackwell Publishers, 2004).

21. "The Edict on Ceremonial and Etiquette of 28 July 1808" ("Reglement voor het ceremonieel, in acht te nemen door de residenten bij de hoven te Soerakarta en te Djokjokarta") can be found in J. A. van der Chijs, *Plakaatboek*, 15 (1896), 63–65.

22. Peter Carey, *The Power of Prophecy: Prince Dipanagara and the End of an Old Order in Java, 1785–1855* (Leiden: KITLV Press, 2007), 166–68.

23. Carey, *The Power of Prophecy*, 194–257.

24. Carey, *The Power of Prophecy*, 261–365.

25. The colonial civil service was known as the Administration of the Interior (*Binnenlands Bestuur* in Dutch).

26. Sutherland, *The Making of a Bureaucratic Elite*, 1–18; Van den Doel, *De stille macht*, 35–57; Palmier, "The Javanese Nobility under the Dutch," 197–227.

27. H. W. Daendels, *Staat der Nederlandsche Oostindische bezittingen onder het bestuur van den gouverneur-generaal Herman Willem Daendels in de Jaren 1808–1811* (The Hague: 1814), 94–99.

28. Van der Chijs, *Plakaatboek* 15 (1896), 63–65, 375–77.

29. Carey, *The Power of Prophecy*, 170; Peter Carey, *Babad Dipanagara: An Account of the Outbreak of the Java War, 1825–30: The Surakarta Court Version of the Babad Dipanagara with Translations into English and Indonesian-Malay* (Kuala Lumpur: Art Printing Works, 1981), 234–35.

30. Carey, *The Power of Prophecy*, 171; John Pemberton vividly described the politics of seating arrangements during the colonial encounter at the court of Surakarta. See *On the Subject of "Java"*, 56–57.

31. Carey, *The Power of Prophecy*, 194–257.

32. Carey, *The Power of Prophecy*, 261–365.

33. Daendels divided Java into administrative units headed by prefects. Under Raffles, the number of administrative provinces, now called residencies, were expanded and headed by residents. On Java's restoration to the Netherlands, Raffles's titles remained. Van den Doel, *De stille macht*, 37–40.

34. Van der Chijs, *Plakaatboek*, 15 (1896), 157–83, 292–301.

35. Governor General Daendels to the minister of commerce and colonial affairs, November 12, 1808, in S. van Deventer, *Bijdragen tot de kennis van het landelijk stelsel op Java, op last van zijne excellentie den minister van kolonien, J. D. Fransen van de Putte, eerste deel: De wording van het stelsel*, 1 (Zaltbommel: J. Noman en Zoon, 1865), 22.

36. B. Schrieke, *De inlandsche hoofden: rede in tegenwoordigheid van zijne excellentie den gouverneur-generaal van Nederlandsch-Indië uitgesproken bij de 4-jarige herdenking van de stichting der Rechtshoogeschool te Batavia, op 27 October 1928* (Weltevreden: Kolff, 1928).

37. Sutherland, *The Making of a Bureaucratic Elite*, 1–12; Van der Chijs, *Plakaatboek*, 15 (1896), 157–83.

38. Thomas Stamford Raffles, *The History of Java*, vol. 1 (London: John Murray, 1817), 309.

39. Raffles, *The History of Java*, vol. 1, 310.

40. Raffles, *The History of Java*, vol. 1, 309.

41. "Minute recorded by the Honourable Lieutenant-Governor of Java, on the 14th June 1813," in Thomas Stamford Raffles, *Substance of a minute recorded by the Honourable Thomas Stamford Raffles, Lieutenant-Governor of Java and its Dependencies, on the 11th February 1814; on the introduction of an improved system of internal management and the establishment of a land rental on the island of Java: to which are added several of the most interesting documents therein referred to* (London: Black, Parry, and Co., 1814), 253–78.

42. The Malay Peninsula was excluded from this agreement, and the resulting diplomatic tension was resolved with the Treaty of London of 1824. Raffles's disappointment in losing Java led him to establish Singapore in 1819.

43. Th. Stevens, "Van der Capellen's koloniale ambitie op Java: economisch beleid in een stagnerende conjunctuur 1816–1826" (Amsterdam: Historisch Seminarium van de Universiteit van Amsterdam, 1982).

44. Governor General G. A. G. P. baron van der Capellen to minister of public education, National Industry and Colonial Affairs Anton Reinhard Falck, 9 May 1820, *Tijdschrift voor Nederlandsch-Indië TNI*, 3, no. 1 (1865), 114–17.

45. Van der Capellen to Falck, May 9, 1820, in *TNI*, 3 (1865), 115.

46. *Staatsblad van Nederlandsch-Indië*, no. 22 (1820), 98–110.

47. *Staatsblad*, no. 13 (1824), 11–13; Sutherland, *The Making of a Bureaucratic Elite*.

48. *Staatsblad*, no. 22 (1820), 98–110.

49. Beautiful colored drawings of the payung hierarchies of Yogyakarta (ca. 1900), Surakarta (1869), and Mangkunegaran (1869) can be found in UBL, Special Collections, Collection KITLV, 37B42-37B148.

50. L. Th. Mayer, *Een blik in het Javaansche volksleven*, 2 (Leiden: Brill, 1897), 509–10; J. J. Verwijk, "Nota over de staatsie en het gevolg der Inlandsche ambtenaren in de gouvernementslanden op Java en Madoera," *TBB*, 17 (1899), 451–61; "Pajoengs of songsongs, adat en titels," *Het Koloniaal Weekblad*, 3, no. 33 (1903); J. Groneman, "Een pajoeng-kwestie," *TBB*, 25 (1903), 38–47; J. E. Jasper, "Staatsie, gevolg en songsongs van Inlandsche ambtenaren in de gouvernementslanden op Java en Madoera," *TBB*, 27, no. 1 (1904), 1–73.

51. Raffles, *A History of Java*, vol. 1, 308–12; P. J. Veth, *Java: geographisch, ethnologisch, historisch*, vol. 4 (Haarlem: De Erven F. Bohn, 1907), 367–68.

52. Carey, *The Power of Prophecy*, 588–89 and 617–55; Michael Adas, *Prophets of Rebellion: Millenarian Protest Movements against the European Colonial Order* (Chapel Hill: The University of North Carolina Press, 1979), 3–19, 93–99.

53. Carey, *Babad Dipanagara*, 234–35.

54. Carey, *The Power of Prophecy*, 588–89 and 617–55.

55. This is depicted in a manuscript image that shows Diponegoro seated on his horse accompanied by his gilded payung during the battle of Tegelrejo on July 20, 1825. Peter Carey, *Sisi lain Diponegoro: babad kedung kebo dan historiografi perang* (Jakarta: Gramedia, 2017); *Pandji Kuda Waneng Pati Klayan Klana Tunjung Seta*, 1860, D Or. 17, Collection KITLV, Special Collections, UBL.

56. Carey, *The Power of Prophecy*, 586; P. J. F. Louw, *De Java-Oorlog van 1825–1830*, vol. 2 (Batavia: Landsdrukkerij, 1897), 244.

57. "Gouvernements Besluit van den 21sten December 1827 No. 15," *TNI*, 1 (1865), 126.

58. Van der Capellen to Falck, May 9, 1820, *TNI*, 3 (1865), 115.

59. Anderson, *Language and Power*, 133–34.

60. "Advies van den Luitenant-Generaal Van Den Bosch over het stelsel van kolonisatie," in D. C. Steijn Parve, *Het koloniaal monopoliestelsel getoetst aan geschiedenis en staathuiskunde* (Zaltbommel: Joh. Noman en Zoon, 1851), 294–328; R. E. Elson, *Village Java under the Cultivation System, 1830–1870* (Sydney: Allen and Unwin, 1994); C. Fasseur, *The Politics of Colonial Exploitation: Java, the Dutch and the Cultivation System*, translated by R. E. Elson (Ithaca: SEAP, Cornell University Press, 1992).

61. C. W. Margadant, *Het Regeeringsreglement van Nederlandsch-Indië*, vol. 1–3 (Batavia: G. Kolff & Co., 1894–7); *Staatsblad*, no. 2 (1855).

62. Van den Bosch to Baud, January 31, 1831, in *Briefwisseling tussen J. van den Bosch en J. C. Baud, 1829–1832 en 1834–1836. Eerste deel: brieven van den Bosch* (Utrecht: Kemink en zoon N. V., 1956), 74.

63. Van den Bosch to Baud, June 4, 1831 and August 7, 1832, in *Briefwisseling*, vol. I, 93, and 158; J. van den Bosch, *Mijne verrigtingen in Indië: verslag van z. excellentie den Commissaris Generaal J. van den Bosch, over de jaren 1830, 1831, 1832, en 1833.* (Amsterdam: Frederik Muller, 1864), 398–402; Elson, *Village Java*, 179–84.

64. Heather Sutherland dubbed the rule of Daendels and Raffles the "nadir" of the bupati in *The Making of a Bureaucratic Elite*, 12–16; Elson, *Village Java*, 180–86; Van den Doel, *De stille macht*, 59–65; Palmier, "The Javanese Nobility under the Dutch," 202, 214–18.

65. Van Niel, *The Emergence of the Modern Indonesian Elite*, 26.

66. Kees Groeneboer, *Gateway to the West*; *Staatsblad*, no. 34 (1827), no. 109 (1827); Cees Fasseur, *De Indologen: ambtenaren voor de Oost 1825–1950* (Amsterdam: Aula, 2003), 25–28.

67. Cees Fasseur, "De taal is gans de Indisch ambtenaar. De taalopleiding van de bestuursambtenaren," in Kees Groeneboer (ed.), *Koloniale taalpolitiek in Oost en West: Nederlands-Indië, Suriname, Nederlandse Antillen en Aruba* (Amsterdam: Amsterdam University Press, 1997), 187–206.

68. J. C. Baud's report to King William I, June 28, 1842, in *Historische nota over het vraagstuk van de opleiding en benoembaarheid voor den administratieven dienst* (Batavia, Landsdrukkerij, 1900) 23. The English translation comes from Kees Groeneboer, *Gateway to the West*, 74.

69. Fasseur, *De Indologen*, 55–76, 90–97.

70. Sembah denotes worship, homage, or deference, but it also refers to the particular gesture of respect as described in the text. Jongkok refers to both static and active forms of crouching and was used interchangeably by contemporaries. When joined together, *sembah-jongkok* was used to signify the general culture of deference etiquette guiding social interactions and expressing social hierarchies. Anderson, *Language and Power*, 123–51 and 194–237. For Raffles's description, see Raffles, *A History of Java*, vol. I, 308–10.

71. "Geen Europeesche kangdjengs meer," *De Indiër*, I, no. 35 (June 18, 1914), 120.

72. Susie Protschky, "The Colonial Table: Food, Culture and Dutch Identity in Colonial Indonesia," *Australian Journal of Politics and History*, 54, no. 3 (2008), 346–57; Onghokham, *The Thugs, the Curtain Thief, and the Sugar Lord: Power, Politics, and Culture in Colonial Java* (Jakarta: Metafor Publishing, 2003), 311–22; D. C. M. Bauduin, *Het Indische leven* (The Hague: H. P. Leopold, 1941), 84–87; Louis Couperus, *The Hidden Force*, trans. E. M. Beekman (Amherst: University of Massachusetts Press, 1985), 101.

73. V. I. van de Wall, *Oude Hollandsche bouwkunst in Indonesië* (Antwerpen: De Sikkel, 1942); Cor Passchier, "Colonial Architecture in Indonesia: References and Developments," *The Past in the Present: Architecture in Indonesia*, ed. Peter J. M. Nas, 97–112.

74. Elson, *Village Java*, 84–85.

75. The hipped roof was an Austronesian (a language group covering most of maritime Southeast Asia and the Pacific) characteristic.

76. Ranked from least to most prestigious, the roof styles are known as *kampung*, *limasan*, and *joglo*.

77. Cor Passchier, "Colonial Architecture in Indonesia," 97–112; Van de Wall, *Oude Hollandsche*, 10–12 and 29–32; Huib Akihary, *Architectuur & stedebouw in Indonesië, 1870–1970* (Zutphen: De Walburg Pers, 1990), 14–15.

78. Passchier, "Colonial Architecture in Indonesia," 97–112; Abidin Kusno, "The Afterlife of the Empire Style: Indische Architectuur and Art Deco," *The Past in the Present*, 131–46.

79. Taylor, *The Social World of Batavia*, 52–77; Jean Gelman Taylor, "Costume and Gender in Colonial Java, 1800–1940," in *Outward Appearances,* ed. Henk Schulte Nordholt, 85–116; Inger McCabe Elliot, *Batik: Fabled Cloth of Java* (Singapore: Periplus Editions, 2004), 112–15.

80. McCabe Elliot, *Batik*, 36, 68–69; Taylor, "Costume and Gender," 91–94.

81. Harmen C. Veldhuisen, *Batik Belanda 1840–1940: Dutch Influence in Batik from Java, History and Stories* (Jakarta: PT. Gaya Favorit, 1993).

82. McCabe Elliot, *Batik*, 32; Dorine Bronkhorst and Esther Wils, *Tropenecht: Indische en Europese kleding in Nederlands-Indië* (The Hague: Stichting Tong, 1996).

83. Bart Luttikhuis, "Beyond Race: Constructions of 'Europeanness' in Late-Colonial Legal Practice in the Dutch East Indies, *European Review of History*, 20, no. 4 (2013), 539–58; Margadant, *Regeeringsreglement*; Fasseur, "Cornerstone and Stumbling Block," 31–57; A. van Marle, "De groep der Europeanen in Nederlands-Indie: iets over ontstaan en groei," *Indonesië*, 5 (1951–52), 97–99.

84. *Staatsblad*, no. 8 (1829, 21–30).

85. *Staatsblad*, no. 4 and 59 (1849), no. 26 (1851), no. 110 and 111 (1872).

86. Fasseur, *The Politics of Colonial Exploitation*, 117–19.

87. The declaration of the Agrarian and Sugar Laws in 1870 opened Java up for private enterprise. *Staatsblad*, no. 55 and 117 (1870). Elson, *Village Java*, 128–52.

88. This perception was popularized in Multatuli's influential novel, *Max Havelaar*, which was considered the nail in the coffin for the Cultivation System. The novel's negative view of the Javanese aristocracy deliberately overlooked the critical role played by Dutch officials, who suddenly acted as protectors of the colonized, at least rhetorically if not in reality. Multatuli, *Max Havelaar: Or, the Coffee Auctions of a Dutch Trading Company*, trans. Roy Edwards (New York: Penguin Books, 1987).

89. *Staatsblad*, no. 122, 123, and 125 (1867); Elson, *Village Java*, 148; Van den Doel, *De stille macht*, 107–56.

90. *Staatsblad*, no. 53 (1867).

91. Van den Doel, *De stille macht*, 80–104; Sutherland, *The Making of a Bureaucratic Elite*, 35–43.

92. Van Niel, *The Emergence of the Modern Indonesian Elite*, 23–29; J. A. A. van Doorn, *De laatste eeuw van Indie: ontwikkeling en ondergang van een koloniaal project*

(Amsterdam: Bert Bakker, 1994), 31–35; Liesbeth Hesselink, *Healers on the Colonial Market: Native Doctors and Midwives in the Dutch East Indies* (Leiden: KITLV Press, 2011).

93. Jasper, "Staatstie, gevolg en songsongs," 1–73; For pawnshop personnel, see *Staatsblad*, no. 393 (1906); Palmier, *Social Status and Power in Java*, 35; Liesbeth Hesselink, "The Unbearable Absence of Parasols: The Formidable Weight of a Colonial Java Status Symbol," *IIAS Newsletter*, no. 45 (2007), 26.

94. Van den Doel, *De stille macht*, 80–104.

95. George Murray Reith, *A Padre in Partibus: Being Notes and Impressions of a Brief Holiday Tour through Java, the Eastern Archipelago and Siam* (Singapore: Singapore and Straits Print. Office, 1897), 188–90.

96. Christiaan Snouck Hurgronje, "De Inlandsche bestuursambtenaren, vooral op Java," *De Gids*, 72 (1908), 220.

97. Benedict Anderson, *Mythology and the Tolerance of the Javanese* (Ithaca: SEAP, Cornell University Press, 1965); Sears, *Shadows of Empire*.

98. Schulte Nordholt, *The Spell of Power*, 7.

99. Corporal punishment, intimidation, and surveillance were intrinsic features of the Cultivation System. Official reports deliberately described peasant resistance—in the form of foot-dragging, flight, and sectarian withdrawal—as sporadic and small-scale as to not undercut the image of the docile Javanese. Breman, *Mobilizing Labour*, 267–70; Michael Adas, "From Footdragging to Flight." 64–86.

100. Kartini, January 12, 1900, 42.

Chapter 2. "Sweet Was the Dream, Bitter the Awakening"

1. Goenawan Mangoenkoesoemo, "De Javaan en zijn hormatgebruiken," *Java Bode* (May 22, 1905). The article also appeared in *Bintang Hindia*, 3, no. 14 (1905): 166.

2. Mangoenkoesoemo, "De Javaan en zijn hormatgebruiken."

3. Michael Adas, "Contested Hegemony: The Great War and the Afro-Asian Assault on the Civilizing Mission Ideology," *Journal of World History* 15, no. 1 (2004): 31–63; Locher-Scholten, *Ethiek in fragmenten*; Luttikhuis, "Negotiating Modernity," 1–32.

4. Van Niel, *The Emergence of the Modern Indonesian Elite*, 15–30; Hans Pols, *Nurturing Indonesia: Medicine and Decolonization in the Dutch East Indies* (Cambridge: Cambridge University Press, 2018), 1–20.

5. Goenawan Mangoenkoesoemo, "De geboorte van Boedi-Oetomo," in *Soembangsih: gedenkboek Boedi-Oetomo 1908 20 Mei 1918* (Amsterdam: Drukkerij J. Tjabring, 1918), 10.

6. D. A. Rinkes, "Oude en nieuwe stroomingen onder de bevolking," *Indisch Genootschap: Verslagen der Algemene Vergaderingen* (November 18, 1916): 55–78.

7. Scott, *Dominance and the Arts of Resistance*, 1–16.

8. Van Niel, *The Emergence of the Modern Indonesian Elite*, 46–72.

9. For a detailed study of these companies (among others) and their cultural significance in the history of empire, see Kris Alexanderson, *Subversive Seas: Anticolonial*

Networks across the Twentieth-Century Dutch Empire (Cambridge: Cambridge University Press, 2019).

10. Ravestijn and Kop (eds.), *For Profit and Prosperity*; Moon, *Technology and Ethical Idealism*; Herman Burgers, *De garoeda en de ooievaar: Indonesië van kolonie tot nationale staat* (Leiden: KITLV Press, 2011), 100–103. On technology and empire more generally, see Daniel R. Headrick, *The Tools of Empire: Technology and European Imperialism in the Nineteenth Century* (New York: Oxford University Press, 1981).

11. Elsbeth Locher-Scholten, "Summer Dresses and Canned Food: European Women and Western Lifestyles in the Indies, 1900–1942," in *Outward Appearances: Dressing State and Society in Indonesia*, ed. Henk Schulte Nordholt (Leiden: KITLV Press, 1997), 151–80.

12. J. A. A. van Doorn, *Indische Lessen: Nederland en de koloniale ervaring* (Amsterdam: Bert Bakker, 1995) 34.

13. Sysling, *Racial Science*; Gouda, *Dutch Culture Overseas*, 121–27.

14. Gouda, *Dutch Culture Overseas*, 149–54; Stoler, "Making Empire Respectable," 645–46. Christiaan Eijkman, *Over gezondheid en ziekte in heete gewesten* (Utrecht: J. van Druten, 1898).

15. Benedict Anderson referred to this as an idealized "Tropical Gothic" in *Imagined Communities*, 151.

16. Van Doorn, *De laatste eeuw van Indië*, 23–46; Burgers, *De garoeda en de ooievaar*, 100–103.

17. *Census of 1930 in the Netherlands Indies*, vol. 8 (Batavia: Landsdrukkerij, 1936) 84–86.

18. Van Marle, "De groep der Europeanen," 321.

19. Stoler, *Carnal Knowledge*, 79–161; Frances Gouda, "'Nyonyas' on the Colonial Divide: White Women in the Dutch East Indies, 1900–1942," *Gender & History* 5, no. 3 (1993): 318–42; Locher-Scholten, *Women and the Colonial State*, 19.

20. C. Th. van Deventer, "Een eereschuld," *De Gids* 63, no. 2 (1899): 205–57; P. Brooshooft, *De ethische koers in de koloniale politiek* (Amsterdam: J. H. de Bussy, 1901).

21. Locher-Scholten, *Ethiek in fragmenten*; Kuitenbrouwer, *The Netherlands and the Rise of Modern Imperialism*; H. L. Wesseling, "Bestond er een Nederlands imperialisme?" *Tijdschrift voor Geschiedenis* 99, no. 2 (1986): 214–25.

22. Alice L. Conklin, *A Mission to Civilize: The Republican Idea of Empire in France and West Africa, 1895–1930* (Stanford: Stanford University Press, 1997); Ballantyne and Burton, *Empires and the Reach of the Global*.

23. The vernacular press often referenced the French, Russian, and Filipino revolutions as models to emulate. For instance, see *Padjadjaran*, October 11, 1920, *Overzicht van de Inlandsche en Maleisisch-Chineesche Pers (IPO)*, no. 43 (1920). Others suggested that the Netherlands should follow the US example in the Philippines, see *Darmo Kondo*, May 3, 1919, *IPO*, no. 18 (1919). Anne Foster, *Projections of Power: The United States and Europe in Colonial Southeast Asia, 1919–1941* (Durham: Duke University Press, 2010).

24. P. H. Fromberg, *De Chineesche beweging op Java* (Amsterdam: Elsevier, 1911); P. Tjiook-Liem, *De rechtspositie der Chinezen*.

25. Van Dijk, *The Netherlands Indies and the Great War*, 19–90; Ahmat Adam, *The Vernacular Press*, 79–107; Van der Meer, "Igniting Change in Colonial Indonesia," 501–32.

26. For instance, in 1848 a school was established that trained scribes and administrators, followed in 1851 by a school for indigenous doctors (*dokter djawa*), in 1852 by a teacher training school, in 1879 by a school for "Native Heads" (*Hoofdenscholen*) for training prominent priyayi children to be administrators, and in 1893 by the First and Second Class Native Schools. Van Niel, *The Emergence of the Modern Indonesian Elite*, 15–30.

27. Van Niel, *The Emergence of the Modern Indonesian Elite*, 31–100.

28. Schulte Nordholt, "New Urban Middle Classes in Colonial Java," 439–41; Hoogervorst and Schulte Nordholt, "Urban Middle Classes in Colonial Java," 424–74.

29. Shiraishi, *An Age in Motion*," 26–27.

30. The most prominent associations with a predominantly culturally Javanese outlook were Boedi Oetomo (f. 1908), the Committee for Javanese Nationalism (f. 1919), and Taman Siswa (f. 1922). Those with a distinctly religious outlook were the Sarekat Islam (f. 1912), Muhammadiyah (f. 1912), and Nahdlatul Ulama (f. 1926). Those with an ideological basis were the Indische Partij (f. 1912), the Indische Sociaal-Democratische Vereenging (f. 1914), its successor Perserikatan Kommunis di Hindia (f. 1920), which changed its name to Partai Kommunis Indonesia in 1924. And finally, those with a secular perspective were the Indische Party (f. 1912) and Partai Nasional Indonesia (f. 1927). Elson, *The Idea of Indonesia*, 1–97.

31. William O'Malley, "Second Thoughts on Indonesian Nationalism," *Indonesia: Australian Perspectives* (1980): 601–13.

32. Anderson, *Language and Power*, 194–237; Raffles, *A History of Java*, vol. 1, 308–12.

33. Snouck Hurgronje to the Director of the European Administration of the Interior, April 20, 1904, in *Ambtelijke adviezen van C. Snouck Hurgronje 1889–1936*, vol. 1, ed. E. Gobée and C. Adriaanse (1957), 518–25; Sutherland, *The Making of a Bureaucratic Elite*, 24–25.

34. A. H. J. G. Walbeehm, "Het leven van den bestuursambtenaar in het binnenland," *Onze Koloniën* 1, no. 3 (1913).

35. Anderson, *Language and Power*, 131–32.

36. Hazeu to the Committee Mangajoe Basa Djawa, December 6, 1918, in Collection Hazeu, H 1083, no. 29, UBL.

37. Groeneboer, *Gateway to the West*, 6–7.

38. *Bijblad op het Staatsblad van Nederlandsch-Indië*, no. 6496 (1907).

39. Kartini to Mejuffrouw Zeehandelaar, January 12, 1900, in *Letters of a Javanese Princess*, 40–42.

40. "Nota betreffende de verhouding tusschen het Europeesch en het inlandsch bestuur," *IG* 11, no. 2 (1889): 1521–24.

41. Hadi Ningrat, "De achteruitgang van het prestige der inlandsche hoofden en de middelen om daarin verbetering te brengen," *TBB*, 17 (1899): 367–385.

42. Eckart [pseudonym of H. E. Steinmetz], *Indische brieven aan een staatsraad* (Haarlem: De Erven F. Bohn, 1888), 181–82.

43. Eckart, *Indische brieven*, 181–82.

44. Laffan, *The Makings of Indonesian Islam*, 190–208; Van den Doel, *De Stille Macht*, 181–82.

45. Snouck Hurgronje to the Director of Education, Religion, and Industry, September 10, 1896; Snouck Hurgronje to the Director of the Administration of the Interior, March 13, 1902; both in *Ambtelijke adviezen*, vol. 2, 1019–27.

46. Snouck Hurgronje to Governor General Roosenboom, August 16, 1903, in *Ambtelijke adviezen,* vol. 2, 1027–28.

47. *Bijblad*, no. 5946 (1904).

48. As president of the Diminished Welfare Committee, Steinmentz ensured that his view on the matter of hormat was included in its reports. Chair of the Welfare Committee Steinmetz to Governor General Idenburg, September 30, 1914, in *Onderzoek naar de Mindere Welvaart,* vol. 12, 1–5.

49. Snouck Hurgronje to the Director of the Administration of the Interior, May 26, 1904, *Ambtelijke adviezen* 2, 1028–35.

50. Van Heutsz was rewarded the highest office in Java for his pacification (brutal repression) of Aceh in northern Sumatra. The colonial campaign against the Acehnese lasted more than three decades (1873–1904) and was decided in part by Hurgronje's insights on Acehnese culture and society. Adrian Vickers, *A History of Modern Indonesia* (Cambridge: Cambridge University Press, 2005), 10–13.

51. *Bijblad*, no. 6118 (1905). The payung circular was dated November 3, 1904, but not published in the *Bijblad*.

52. Van Heutsz to the Minister of Colonial Affairs Idenburg, March 13, 1905, Collection A. W. F. Idenburg, inventory no. 129, HDC.

53. *Bijblad*, no. 6118 (1905).

54. *Bijblad*, no. 6118.

55. Snouck Hurgronje to the Director of the Administration of the Interior, April 20, 1904, *Ambtelijke adviezen* 1, 525.

56. See the editorial of M. van Geuns in *Soerabaiasch Handelsblad*, November 26, 1904.

57. See the editorial of T. Vierhout in *De Locomotief,* November 26, 1904.

58. Karel Wybrands, "Een idealist-practicus," *NNI,* November 30, 1904; "Hormat," *IG* 27, no. 1 (1905): 265–66.

59. "Nog even iets over de pajoengs," *NNI,* December 6, 1904; "De pajoeng," *NNI,* January 19 and 21, 1905. "Hormat," *IG,* 27, no. 1 (1905): 431–33.

60. Achmad Djajadiningrat, *Herinneringen van Pangeran Aria Achmad Djajadiningrat* (Batavia: Kolff, 1936), 224–26.

61. "Eens residenten afscheid aan zijn pajong," *NNI,* December 3, 1904.

62. "Eens residenten afscheid aan zijn pajong."

63. Idenburg to Van Heutsz, February 14, 1905, in Collection J. B. Van Heutsz, inventory no. 2, 2.21.008.79, NL-HaNA.

64. Idenburg succeeded Van Heutsz as governor general in 1909 and continued his struggle to implement a more ethical foundation of colonial authority. Van Heutsz to Idenburg, March 13, 1905, in Collection A. W. F. Idenburg, box 13, inventory no. 129, HDC.

65. Snouck Hurgronje to Van Heutsz, March 1, 1906, in *Ambtelijke adviezen*, vol. 2, 1037–38.

66. *Bijblad*, no. 6496 (1907).

67. *Bijblad*, no. 6496.

68. Karel Wybrands, "Regeerings-beleid en regeerings-organen." *NNI*, April 23, 1906; "Een tweede hormat-circulaire," *IG* 28, no. 2 (1906): 1101–2.

69. Henri Borel, "Ambtenaar," *WVI* 4, no. 14, July 28, 1907, 269–71; A. Muhlenfeld, "Iets over de naleving der voorschriften in bijblad 6061, 6118 en 6496," *TBB* 35 (1908), 33–39.

70. Carlo [pseudonym], "Indische indrukken XXIV," *WVI* 3, no. 14, July 29, 1906, 301–4.

71. Van Heutsz to the Director of the European Civil Service, January 20, 1909, in Collection Hazeu, H 1083, folder 17, no. 10, UBL. The abuses were reported in the *Bataviaasch Nieuwsblad*, December 30, 1908.

72. Like Javanese, the Sundanese language has distinct hierarchical levels.

73. Hazeu to Van Heutsz, March 11, 1909, in Collection Hazeu, H 1083, folder 17, no. 10, UBL.

74. *Bijblad*, no. 7029 (1910).

75. Gonggrijp to Van Heutsz, April 27, 1909, Collection Hazeu, H 1083, folder 17, no. 10, UBL.

76. Boissevain to Van Heutsz, April 30, 1909, in Collection Hazeu, H 1083, folder 17, no. 10, UBL.

77. *Pantjaran Warta*, January 18, 1912, *KT* 1 (1912): 229–30. Similar arguments can be found in *Pewarta Deli*, May 31, 1912, *KT* 1 (1912): 837–38 and *Medan Prijaji*, August 1, 1912, *KT*, 1 (1912): 1222.

78. *Bintang Soerabaja*, April 30, 1912.

79. Abdoel Rivai, "Bangsawan pikiran," *Bintang Hindia* 0, no. 1 (1902): 3–4; Abdoel Rivai, "Kaoem moeda," *Bintang Hindia* 3, no. 14 (1905): 159–61; Adam, *The Vernacular Press*, 138–40; Pols, *Nurturing Indonesia*, 21–45.

80. Goenawan Mangoenkoesoemo, "Iets over den Javaan en zijn hormatgebruiken," *Java Bode*, June 22, 1905.

81. Mangoenkoesoemo, "Iets over den Javaan en zijn hormatgebruiken."

82. Wongso [pseudonym], "Schetsen uit het Javaansche volksleven," *NNI*, June 5 and 6, 1905.

83. Goenawan Mangoenkoesoemo, "De tijden veranderen en wij met hen," *Java Bode*, June 23, 1905.

84. Mangoenkoesoemo, "De tijden veranderen en wij met hen."

85. Wongso, "Schetsen uit het Javaansche volksleven."

86. "De Javaan en zijn hormat-gebruiken," *Bintang Hindia* 3, no. 14 (1905): 166; "Nog eens: De Javaan en zijn hormat-gebruiken," *Bintang Hindia* 3, no. 15 and 16 (1905): 178 and 190–91. Rivai's commentary was published as introduction to these articles.

87. The *Bintang Hindia* was published between 1902 and 1907. By the end of 1904, it had a circulation of twenty-seven thousand, meaning its readership must have been even higher. Harry A. Poeze, "Early Indonesian Emancipation: Abdul Rivai, Van Heutz, and the Bintang Hindia," *BKI* 145, no. 1 (1989): 87–106; Adam, *The Vernacular Press*, 98–106; Nagazumi, *The Dawn of Indonesian Nationalism*, 26–65.

88. Rivai, "*Kaoem moeda*," 159–61.

89. "Kehormatan," *Bintang Hindia* 1, no. 4 (1903): 38–39; "Hormat," *Bintang Hindia* 1, no. 4 (1903): 39. Similar descriptive and uncritical publications can be found elsewhere before 1904. For instance, "Tjara Djawa dan hoeboengannja," *Taman Pengadjar*, October 15, 1899, 113–16. "Hormat," *Taman Pengadjar*, February 15, 1900, 225–26.

90. Kertowinoto, "Sembah dan jongkok," *Bintang Hindia* 3, no. 3 (1905): 38–39; Karno, "Hormat dan percaja," *Bintang Hindia* 3, no. 7 (1905): 75–77.

91. Ronggo, "Hormat," *Bintang Hindia* 3, no. 7 (1905): 74–75. For similar activist articles see "Adat roepa–roepa bangsa: memberi salam dan hal 'hormat circulair,'" *Taman Pengadjar*, January 15, 1905, 217–21; "Kemajoean bangsa Djawa," *Taman Pengadjar*, August 15, 1905, 55–61.

92. S., "Suka akan kehormatan," *Bintang Hindia* 4, no. 6 (1906): 200–204.

93. S., "Suka akan kehormatan," 200–204.

94. *Pemberita Betawi*, January 17, 1912, *KT* 1 (1912): 219.

95. *Sinar Djawa*, December 2, 1911, *KT* 1 (1911): 102.

96. *Pemberita Betawi*, March 31, 1913, *KT* 2 (1913): 1029.

97. Nagazumi, *The Dawn of Indonesian Nationalism*, 26–50. Kartodirdjo, *Pengantar Sejarah Indonesia baru*, 99–106. Adam, *The Vernacular Press*, 79–107. Van Niel, *The Emergence of the Modern Indonesian Elite*, 56–62.

98. Mangoekoesoemo, "De geboorte van Boedi-Oetomo," 9–14; Mangoenkoesoemo, "De Javaan en zijn hormatgebruiken."

99. Idenburg to Van Kol, July 7, 1913, in *De Opkomst van de nationalistische beweging in Nederlandsch-Indie: Een bronnenpublicatie*, ed. S. L. van der Wal (Groningen: J. B. Wolters, 1967), 297–98.

100. Hazeu to Van Heutsz, December 30, 1908, in Collection Hazeu, H 1083, no. 24, UBL.

Chapter 3. Disrupting the Colonial Performance

1. Descriptions of the encounter can be found in Advisor for Native Affairs G. A. J. Hazeu to Governor General A. W. F. Idenburg, August 18, 1913, in Collection Hazeu, H 1083, no. 29, UBL; Jaksa Raden Soemarsono to Resident H. Rijfsnijder, June 8, 1913,

Archive Ministerie van Koloniën: Openbaar Verbaal, 1901–1952, 2.10.36.04, 1076, Verbaal (Vb.) August 22, 1913, NL-HaNA.

2. P. H. Fromberg, "De Inlandsche beweging op Java," *De Gids* 78 (1914): 28–29.

3. Shiraishi, *An Age in Motion*, xi–xvi, 41–116.

4. L. W. C. van den Berg, *De Inlandsche rangen en titels op Java en Madoera* (Landsdrukkerij; Batavia, 1887).

5. Rijfsnijder to Idenburg, May 10, 1913, in Archive Ministerie van Koloniën: Geheim Archief, 1901–1940, 2.10.36.51, 153, Vb. August 9, 1913, B13, NL-HaNA; Heather Sutherland, "The Priyayi," *Indonesia* 19 (1975): 58.

6. On completion of his secondary education at the Gymnasium Willem III, Soemarsono enrolled in a three-year civil service training program known as the Afdeeling B at the same institution. After the first year, he opted out of his studies and began his civil service career. Graduation information was published in *NNI*, April 30, 1901, May 10, 1902, May 6, 1903, and May 8, 1905.

7. Hazeu to Idenburg, August 18, 1913, UBL.

8. Soemarsono to Rijfsnijder, June 8, 1913, NL-HaNA.

9. Soemarsono to Rijfsnijder, June 8, 1913, NL-HaNA.

10. Assistant Resident J. C. Bedding to Rijfsnijder, April 21, 1913 and May 13, 1913, in Koloniën: Geheim Archief, 2.10.36.51, 153, Vb. August 9, 1913, B13, NL-HaNA.

11. Soemarsono to Rijfsnijder, June 8, 1913, NL-HaNA.

12. Rijfsnijder to Idenburg, May 10 and 23, 1913; Bedding to Rijfsnijder, April 21, 1913, May 13 and 19, 1913, in Koloniën: Geheim Archief, 2.10.36.51, 153, Vb. August 9, 1913, B13, NL-HaNA. Soewardi Soerjaningrat, "Staat de regeering werkelijk sympathiek tegenover de S.I.?," *De Indiër* 1, no. 4 (November 13, 1913): 48.

13. Boedi Oetomo was founded on May 20, 1908.

14. Witness accounts of Kartakoesoema and Koesoemadipoera, May 29, 1913; Bedding to Rijfsnijder, June 1, 1913, in Koloniën: Openbaar Verbaal, 2.10.36.04, 1076, Vb. August 22, 1913, NL-HaNA.

15. "Gisting," *NNI*, June 2, 1913.

16. Bedding to Rijfsnijder, June 1, 1913, NL-HaNA.

17. Rijfsnijder to Idenburg, June 12, 1913; Idenburg to Rijfsnijder, June 17, 1913, Koloniën: Openbaar Verbaal, 2.10.36.04, 1076, Vb. August 22, 1913, NL-HaNA.

18. Idenburg to Minister of Colonial Affairs T. B. Pleyte, July 2, 1913; "Extract uit het register der besluiten van den Gouverneur-Generaal van Nederlandsch-Indië," June 30, 1913, in Koloniën: Geheim Archief, 2.10.36.51, 153, Vb. August 9, 1913, B13, NL-HaNA.

19. Soemarsono to Hazeu, July 28, 1913, in Collection Hazeu, H 1083, no. 29, UBL.

20. Soemarsono to Hazeu, July 28, 1913, NL-HaNA; Hazeu to Idenburg, July 11, 1913, in *De opkomst van de nationalistische beweging*, 299–301.

21. Soewardi Soerjaningrat, *Djika saja Nederlander,. . . / Als ik eens Nederlander was,. . .* (Bandung: Comité Boemipoetra, 1913).

22. Idenburg to Rijfsnijder, August 22, 1913, in Collection Hazeu, H 1083, no. 29, UBL.

23. Soemarsono to Hazeu, August 17, 1913, in Collection Hazeu, H 1083, no. 29, UBL.

24. Hazeu to Idenburg, August 18, 1913, in Collection Hazeu, H 1083, no. 29, UBL.

25. Bedding to Wirasaputra, July 7, 1913, in Collection Hazeu, H 1083, no. 29, UBL.

26. Soemarsono to Hazeu, August 17, 1913, UBL.

27. Soemarsono to Hazeu, August 17, 1913, UBL.

28. Hazeu to Idenburg, August 20, 1913, in Collection Hazeu, H 1083, no. 29, UBL.

29. Idenburg to Rijfsnijder, August 22, 1913; Idenburg to the Director of Department of Justice, August 22, 1922, in Collection Hazeu, H 1083, no. 29, UBL.

30. *Bijblad*, no. 7939 (1914).

31. In places the document's language was identical to that in Hazeu's correspondence about Soemarsono's case. "Nota bij de hormatcirculaire van 22 augustus 1913," in Collection Hazeu, H 1083, no. 57, UBL.

32. W. T. L. Boissevain, "Protestbeweging van de vereeniging van ambtenaren bij het binnenlandsch bestuur," *KT* 3, no. 1 (1914): 69–78; "De zevende hormat-circulaire en de uitlatingen van Dr. Rinkes," *KT* 3, no. 1 (1914): 365–67; Tertius, "Geef acht, B. B.!," *KT* 3, no. 1 (1914): 376–80; G. Th. Stibbe, "Nog een protest," *KT* 3, no. 1 (1914): 493–95.

33. Hazeu to Soemarsono, August 22, 1913, in Collection Hazeu, H 1083, no. 29, UBL.

34. Soemarsono to Hazeu, September 5, 1913, in Collection Hazeu, H 1083, no. 29, UBL.

35. The Purwakarta Sarekat Islam was legally recognized on April 20, 1915. For the deliberations leading up to this decision, see Rijfsnijder to Bedding, September 30, 1913; Bedding to Rijfsnijder, October 27, 1913; Rijfsnijder to Idenburg, November 4, 1913; Advisor for Native Affairs D. A. Rinkes to Idenburg, February 13, 1914; "Extract uit het register der besluiten van den Gouverneur-Generaal van Nederlansch-Indië, Buitenzorg, 20 april 1915, no. 43," in Koloniën: Openbaar Verbaal, 2.10.36.04, 1517, Vb. March 8, 1916, NL-HaNA.

36. Rinkes to Tjokjroaminoto, October 25, 1913, in *De opkomst van de nationalistische beweging*: 346–53.

37. *Oetoesan Hindia*, nos. 233–34 and 24, *Djawa Tengah*, no. 7, and *Kaoem Moeda*, no. 50–51, *KT* 3 (1913): 388, 519, 526, and 805. "Constitutievergadering S. I.," *De Indiër* 1 no. 28 (April 30, 1914): 31–32. *Bataviaasch Nieuwsblad*, March 19, 1914.

38. *Oetoesan Hindia*, no. 212, *KT* 4 (1914): 242.

39. *Pantjaran Warta*, no. 75, *KT* 3 (1913): 804–5; *Bescheiden betreffende de vereeniging "Sarekat Islam"* (Batavia: Landsdrukkerij, 1913), 21.

40. *Sarekat-Islam congres* (1916): 58; (1918): 65; (1919): 14–15 and 113–14.

41. Laffan, *Islamic Nationhood*, 77–102.

42. *Sarekat-Islam congres* (1916), 29–30. Two years later Tjokroaminoto repeated this message "The custom to crouch and present the sembah; maintaining these servile traditions keeps us small, makes us kindhearted; the feeling that we are servants of others persists." *Sarekat-Islam congres* (1919), 37–38.

43. Adam, *The Vernacular Press*; Mirjam Maters, *Van zachte wenk tot harde hand: persvrijheid en persbreidel in Nederlands-Indië, 1906–1942* (Hilversum: Uitgeverij Verloren, 1998).

44. Hendrik M. J. Maier, "Phew! Europeesche beschaving! Marco Kartodikromo's *Student Hidjo*," *Southeast Asian Studies* 34, no. 1 (June 1996): 184–210; Ahmat Adam,

"Radical Journalism and Press Persecution in Java: 1914–1918," *JEBAT* 20 (1992): 91–105; Shiraishi, *An Age in Motion*, 81–87.

45. *Pemberita Betawi*, no. 234, *Oetoesan Hindia*, no. 169, 176, and 180, and *Kaoem Moeda*, no. 287 and 288, *KT* 3 (1913): 87–88, 92–94, and 385.

46. "Siapa jang disediakan?," "Hormat," and "Boenga-rampai dari Zuid Bali," *Doenia Bergerak*, April 4, 1914, June 13, 1914, and August 29, 1914.

47. "Menghormati haroes dengan sepantasnja," *Doenia Bergerak*, May 16, 1914.

48. "Hormat circulaire," *Doenia Bergerak*, May 9, 1914.

49. "Siapa jang disediakan," *Doenia Bergerak*, April 4, 1914.

50. "Als ik eens regent was . . . ," *Doenia Bergerak*, April 25, 1914.

51. Vreede-De Stuers, *The Indonesian Woman*, 64–65.

52. *Oetoesan Hindia*, no. 180, *KT*, vol. 3 (1913) 92–94. A similar call to action can be found in Kartosiswojo, "Kamerdika'an," *Sinar Djawa*, April 8, 1914.

53. "Keloeh kesah," *Doenia Bergerak*, 20 June 1914.

54. For instance, see the following articles in *Doenia Bergerak*: "Hormat circulaire I" (July 11, 1914), "Hormat circulaire II" (July 11, 1914), "Dodok dan sembah?" (July 18, 1914), "Apakah ini boekan anti circulaire 2014" (August 1, 1914), "Hormat circulaire tiada di endahkan" (August 8, 1914), "Pengisap hormat circulaire" (August 20, 1914), and "B. B. contra pandhuis" (November 7, 1914).

55. "Onze kwaal," *Sinar Djawa*, April 28, 1914.

56. "Kemadjoean bangsa Djawa," *Sinar Djawa*, May 28, 1914.

57. "Pegawai O. R. ta'dapat kehormatan" and "Masih ada gila hormat," *Oetoesan Hindia*, June 10, 1914, and June 17, 1914.

58. "Hormat circulaire I," *Doenia Bergerak*, July 11, 1914. Kartosiswojo, "Kamerdika'an."

59. "Circulaire No. 2014," *Doenia Bergerak*, August 22, 1914.

60. "Circulaire No. 2014," *Doenia Bergerak*, October 31, 1914.

61. *Kaoem Moeda*, November 25, 1915.

62. Shiraishi, *An Age in Motion*.

63. "Extract uit het register der besluiten van den Gouverneur-Generaal van Nederlandsch-Indië, 23 september 1913," in Collection Hazeu, H 1083, no. 29, UBL; *NNI*, April 8, 1917, and August 27, 1917; *Bataviaasch Nieuwsblad*, August 10, 1917; July 27, 1918; August 26, 1919; *IG* 37, no. 2 (1915): 1631–33; *De Taak* 1, no. 23 and 28 (January 5 and February 9, 1918): 280 and 333.

64. *De Wederopbouw* 3, no. 2 (1920): 40–48; no. 3 (1920): 51–54 and 61–72; no. 4 (1920): 79–90; 4, no. 1 (1921): 13–20.

65. "De zevende hormat-circulaire en de uitlatingen van Dr. Rinkes," 365–67.

66. M. B. van der Jagt, "Ethische koers en bestuursambtenaar," *KT* 4, no. 2 (1915): 1191–215 and 1328–45.

67. Hazeu to J. P. van Limburg-Stirum, September 29, 1916, and November 30, 1916, in Collection Hazeu, H 1083, no. 67 and no. 70, UBL.

68. *Handelingen van den Volksraad* (June 24, 1918), 344.

69. Van der Jagt to the Resident of Kedu, March 1, 1918, in Collection Hazeu, H 1083, no. 70, UBL.

70. J. E. Stokvis, "Het B. B.," *De Taak* 2, no. 2 (Augustus 10, 1918, and September 7, 1918). M. B. van der Jagt, "B. B.," *De Taak* 2, no. 6 (September 7, 1918): 69–70.

71. *Handelingen* (November 14, 1918), 159–70.

72. *Handelingen* (November 14, 1918), 159–70 and 175–85.

73. *Handelingen* (November 15, 1918), 190–204.

74. Note by Hazeu titled "Optreden en mentaliteit v/d As.-Resident v.d. Jagt," in Collection Hazeu, H 1083, no. 17, UBL.

75. Hazeu to Van Limburg-Stirum, December 9, 1918, Collection Hazeu, H 1083, no. 70, UBL.

76. Locher-Scholten, *Ethiek in fragmenten*, 75–84.

77. *NNI*, April 8,1919, July 25, 1919, and September 23, 1919. Djajadiningrat Hoesein, "Dr. G. A. J. Hazeu," *De Taak*, no. 12 and 13 (October 18 and 25, 1919).

78. *Bintang Timoer*, December 8, 1926. *Neratja*, April 3, 1922, *IPO*, no. 15 (1922).

79. J. W. Meijer Ranneft, *De toekomst van het Binnenlandsch Bestuur*, 10.

80. Van den Doel, *De stille macht*, 376–87.

81. *Neratja*, November 18, 1918, and *Kaoem Moeda*, November 19, 1918, *IPO*, no. 47 (1918). *Neratja*, January 6, 1919, *IPO*, no. 2 (1919).

82. *Kaoem Moeda*, January 6, 1919, *IPO*, no. 2 (1919).

83. *Boedi Oetomo*, January 25, 1923, *IPO*, no. 5 (1923); *Sinar Hindia*, January 22 until 29, 1923, *IPO*, no. 5 (1923); *Hindia Baroe*, August 27 until September 2, 1925, *IPO*, no. 36 (1925); *Hindia Baroe*, August 27 until September 2, 1925, *IPO*, no. 36 (1925); *Bintang Timoer*, December 27, 1926.

84. Ruth McVey, *The Rise of Indonesian Communism* (Ithaca: Cornell University Press, 1965); Shiraishi, *An Age in Motion*, 339–42; Van den Doel, *De Stille Macht*, 387–94; Yamamoto, *Censorship in Colonial Indonesia*, 153–75.

85. Alexanderson, *Subversive Seas*, 168–208; Klaas Stutje, *Campaigning in Europe for a Free Indonesia: Indonesian Nationalists and the Worldwide Anticolonial Movement, 1917–1931* (Copenhagen: NIAS Press, 2019).

86. *Handelingen*, June 27, 1924, 460.

87. *NNI*, October 27, 1927.

88. Samuel Kalff, "Eerbewijzen in Indië," *Haagsch Maandblad* 8 (1927): 651.

89. *De Indische Courant*, March 28, 1927, and April 14, 1927. *NNI*, July 6, 1927, August 30, 1927, and November 30, 1930. *Soerabaiasch Handelsblad*, November 13, 1929.

90. *Handelingen* (June 12, 1927); *Handelingen* (July 1, 1927), 587.

91. *Handelingen* (July 15, 1927), 970.

92. *Handelingen* (July 15, 1927), 966.

93. *Handelingen* (June 20, 1928), 273.

94. *Handelingen* (June 15, 1929), 10.

95. *Handelingen* (August 6, 1929), 609–10.

96. *Indische Courant*, June 17, 1929. *Soerabaijasch Handelsblad*, June 19, 1929. *Bataviaasch Nieuwsblad*, June 19, 1929. *Handelingen*, July 18, 1928, 127–28.

97. *Handelingen* (July 26, 1929), 406.

98. *Handelingen* (July 18, 1929), 166–71. *Soerabaiasch Handelsblad*, September 4, 1929.

99. *Pertjatoeran*, July 6, 1929, and July 25, 1929. *Bahagia*, July 16, 1929.

100. *Handelingen* (July 16, 1929), 57–58, 80–82 and 92–93.

101. *Handelingen* (July 16, 1929), 137–44, 344–49, 379–82, and 658–63.

102. The circular can be found in *Bintang Timoer*, April 9, 1929. For further discussion, see *Bahagia*, May 16 and 17, 1929; *Bintang Timoer*, April 9, 1929, and September 7, 1929; *Onze Bode*, May 1929.

103. The hormat proposal of the Surabaya PPBB can be found in "Minta poenale santie," *Soeloeh Ra'jat Indonesia* 3, no. 38 (September 18, 1929): 577–78 and *Bintang Timoer*, September 7, 1929. For further context see "Sebabnja orang ta' soeka djadi prijaji!," *Soeloeh Ra'jat Indonesia* 3, no. 25 (June 19, 1929): 363–366; *Pemimpin*, August 1929.

104. The PPBB proposal can be found in *Bintang Timoer*, August 15, 1930.

105. *Handelingen* (August 7, 1930), 904; (August 17, 1930), 1081–84.

106. *Sipatahoenan*, January 20, 1930. *Handelingen* (August 4, 1932), 990–91; *Swara Publiek*, June 27, 1931.

107. Soetomo, "'Fahamnja' regent," *Soeloeh Ra'jat Indonesia* 3, no. 17 (April 24, 1929): 230–31; Soetomo, "Moeslihatnja regent," *Soeloeh Ra'jat Indonesia* 3, no. 18 (May 1, 1929): 246–47; Soetomo, "Sambat pada bawah-perintahnja," *Soeloeh Ra'jat Indonesia* 3, no. 20 (May 15, 1929): 290–91.

108. "Sembah dan jongkok," *Isteri* 1, no. 6–7 (October–November 1931); *Bintang Timoer*, May 18, 1931.

109. "Hormatstelsel antara goeroe dan pembasar," *Persatoean Goeroe*, September 15, 1930; Agus Suwignyo, "The Making of Politically Conscious Indonesian Teachers in Public Schools, 1930–42," *Southeast Asian Studies* 3, no. 1 (April 2014): 130.

110. The issue also reached the floor of the People's Council: *Handelingen* (August 12, 1931), 796, 861, 959, and 1081–84.

111. *Bintang Timoer*, September 28, 1931.

112. *Aksi*, October 8 and 13, 1931. Also see *Sedio Tomo*, September 16, 1931, and October 12, 1931; *Bintang Timoer*, October 16 and 17, 1931; *Persatoean Goeroe*, October 5, 1931; *Pemimpin*, August–September 1931.

113. *Darmo Kondo*, October 12, 21, 22, and 27, 1931; Also see *Aksi*, October 14, 1931.

114. Sastrawirja, "Moderne wellevendheid," *Djåwå* 11 (1931): 31–38; Hardjosoepoetro, "De oude gebruiken gewijzigd en in harmonie gebracht met de opvattingen van den tegenwoordigen tijd," *Djåwå* 11 (1931): 39–49.

115. The articles were published under the header "Sembah jongkok: Darmo Kondo contra Aksi," *Aksi*, October 15, 16, 17, and 21, 1931.

116. *Aksi*, October 17, 1931. For original reports of the incidents see *Bahagia*, January 11, 1929; *Sedio Tomo*, January 5, 1929.

117. *Aksi*, October 21, 1931.

118. For instance, see *Soeara Oemoem*, March 9, 1933; *Sipatahoenan*, February 8 and 9, 1934.

119. *Handelingen Volksraad* (August 5, 1935), 653; (July 9 and August 2 and 17, 1937), 101, 597, and 988; a similar argument was made by Representative Sorsodiprodjo (September 9, 1937), 1333.

120. Aksi, October 21, 1931.

Chapter 4. Contesting Sartorial Hierarchies

1. Raden Moehamad Enoch to Head Inspector Ten Damme, November 24, 1913; Enoch to Hazeu, December 1, 1913, in Collection Hazeu, H 1083, no. 29, UBL.

2. Ten Damme to Enoch, February 2, 1914, in Collection Hazeu, H 1083, no. 29, UBL.

3. See for instance, the rich contributions to the volume edited by Henk Schulte Nordholt, *Outward Appearances: Dressing State and Society in Indonesia* (Leiden: KITLV Press, 1997), especially Kees van Dijk, "Sarong, Jubbah, and Trousers: Appearance as a Means of Distinction and Discrimination," 39–84; Jean Gelman Taylor, "Costume and Gender in Colonial Java, 1800–1940," 85–116; Rudolf Mrázek, "Indonesian Dandy: The Politics of Clothes in the Late Colonial Period, 1893–1942," 117–47; Elsbeth Locher-Scholten, "Summer Dresses and Canned Food: European Women and Western Lifestyles in the Indies, 1900–1942," 151–80. See Jean Gelman Taylor, "Official Photography, Costume and the Indonesian Revolution," in *Women Creating Indonesia: The First Fifty Years*, ed. Jean Gelman Taylor (Clayton: Monash Asia Institute, 1997), 91–126; Jean Gelman Taylor, "Identity, Nation and Islam: A Dialogue about Men's and Women's Dress in Indonesia," in *The Politics of Dress in Asia and the Americas*, ed. Mina Roces and Louise Edwards (Brighton: Sussex Academic Press, 2007), 101–20; Dorine Bronkhorst and Esther Wils (eds.), *Tropenecht.*

4. Emma Tarlo, *Clothing Matters: Dress and Identity in India* (Chicago: University of Chicago Press, 1996), 8–9.

5. Elizabeth Wilson, *Adorned in Dreams: Fashion and Modernity* (Berkeley: University of California Press, 1987); 1–9; Alison Lurie, *The Language of Clothes* (New York: Random House, 1981), 1–31.

6. Fasseur, "Cornerstone and Stumbling Block," 31–57. Luttikhuis, "Beyond Race," 539–58.

7. *Staatsblad* no. 110 and 111 (1872).

8. Cohn, *Colonialism and its Forms of Knowledge*, 106–62. Rudolf Mrázek, "The Indonesian Dandy," 117–20.

9. *Staatsblad*, no. 22 (1820) and no. 13 (1824).

10. Taylor, "Costume and Gender," 103–5; Taylor, "Official Photography," 91–126; Taylor, "Identity, Nation, and Islam," 101–7.

11. This distinction between an occidental public sphere and an oriental private sphere can be traced back to the era of the VOC, when European men cohabitated with or married indigenous or Eurasian women, and local culture dominated in domestic spaces.

V. I. van de Wall, "Indische kleederdrachten," *D'Orient*, October 25, 1924; Taylor, *The Social World of Batavia*, 100.

12. Taylor, "Official Photography," 103; Veldhuizen, *Batik Belanda*.

13. Karel Wybrands, "Het naderend einde," *NNI*, October 5, 1916.

14. Bronkhorst and Wils, *Tropenecht*, 83; C. Vis-Janssen Van Raay, "De witte kleur bij de Inlandsche volken," *De Indische Verlofganger*, May 11, 1928; "De triomf van de witte jas," *NNI*, August 29, 1905; Alison Lurie, *The Language of Clothes*, 184–87.

15. Eric Tagliacozzo, *The Longest Journey: Southeast Asians and the Pilgrimage to Mecca* (Oxford: Oxford University Press, 2013); Kris Alexanderson, *Subversive Seas*, 135–67.

16. Advisor for Native Affairs Christiaan Snouck Hurgronje to the Governor General C. P. Hordijk, March 26, 1890, in *Ambtelijke adviezen*, vol. 1, 1318–23.

17. Natalie Mobini-Kesheh, *The Hadrami Awakening: Community and Identity in the Netherlands East Indies, 1900–1942* (Ithaca: SEAP, 1999).

18. Suzanne O'Brien, "Splitting Hairs: History and the Politics of Daily Life in Nineteenth-Century Japan," *The Journal of Modern Asian Studies* 67, no. 4 (2008): 1309–39.

19. Michael R. Godley, "The End of the Queue: Hair as Symbol in Chinese History," *East Asian History*, no. 8 (1994): 53–72.

20. Tjiook-Liem, *De rechtspositie der Chinezen*, 250–53.

21. The term "composite fashion" comes from Emma Tarlo's *Clothing Matters*, 42–55; "De evolutie der Javaansche kleeding," *De Sumatra Post*, April 4, 1912.

22. *Onderzoek naar de Mindere Welvaart*, vol. 9a (1907), 53–58.

23. Jean Gelman Taylor, "The Sewing-Machine in Colonial-Era Photographs: A Record from Dutch Indonesia," *Modern Asian Studies* 46, no. 1 (2012): 71–95.

24. Snouck Hurgronje to Governor General W. Rooseboom, December 25, 1900, in *Ambtelijke adviezen* 2, 1326–28.

25. *De Sumatra Post*, January 12 and October 2, 1900; *De Locomotief*, June 30, 1902; *NNI*, October 19, 1903, June 10, 1904, January 20, 1905, and March 1, 1905.

26. Snouck Hurgronje to Van Heutsz, June 12, 1905, in *Ambtelijke adviezen* 2, 1590.

27. Snouck Hurgronje to the Director of Education, Religion, and Industry, October 26, 1902, in *Ambtelijke adviezen* 2, 1041–45; Hesselink, *Healers on the Colonial Market*, 169–70; Pols, *Nurturing Indonesia*, 46–92.

28. Snouck Hurgronje to the Director of Education, October 26, 1902; *Bijblad*, no. 5941 (1904).

29. *Preanger Bode*, September 19, 1901, November 18, 1901, and April 2, 1902; *De Locomotief*, December 11, 1902; *Bataviaasch Nieuwsblad*, October 29, 1904, and November 10, 1904; *NNI*, June 10, 1904; *De Sumatra Post*, 18 February 1905.

30. Snouck Hurgronje to Van Heutsz, June 12, 1905.

31. *Bijblad*, no. 6241 (1906).

32. Moesa, "Kleeding en adat," *Bintang Hindia* 3, no. 10 (1905): 118–19.

33. Slamet, "Ingezonden," *Bintang Hindia* 5, no. 4 (1906): 46–47.

34. "Pakaian," *Bintang Hindia* 4, no. 2 (1906): 18–19; "Adat dan pakaian," *Bintang Hindia* 5, no. 4 (1907): 41–42; Pols, *Nurturing Indonesia*, 25–26.

35. "Mengapakah orang Jawa tiada membuang rambut panjang?," *Bintang Hindia* 4, no. 13 (1906): 171; "Apakah gunanya dibuang rambut panjang," *Bintang Hindia* 5, no. 4 (1907): 40–41.

36. "Ontwikkeling...van kleedij," *De Sumatra Post*, November 27, 1907.

37. "Teekenen," *De Indiër* 1, no. 29 (May 7, 1914): 46.

38. Arguments about employing dress as a means of curtailing traditional deference had been published since the turn of the century, but it was not until 1913 that the issue received explicit government support in the form of the hormat circular. *Bintang Soerabaja*, December 29, 1911, *KT* 1 (1911) 96; Van Dijk, "Sarong, Jubbah, and Trousers," 39–84; Mrázek, "Indonesian Dandy," 117–47; Locher-Scholten, "Summer Dresses and Canned Food," 151–80.

39. *Bintang Soerabaja*, April 30, 1913, *KT* 2 (1913), 1202; Korver, *Sarekat Islam*, 52.

40. "Tweede Sarekat-Islam rapport van Dr. Rinkes, dd. 30 November 1915," in Collection Hazeu 1083, no. 35, UBL; Korver, *Sarekat Islam*, 52.

41. *Pemberita Betawi*, November 30, 1913, *KT* 3 (1913) 382; "Pakean tjara Europa," *Sinar Djawa*, February 11, 1914; *Kaoem Moeda*, January 31, 1914; Soewardi Soerjaningrat, "Javanen in Europeesche kleeding," *De Indiër* (February 5, 1914), 191–92; "Inlandsche onderwijzers en de westersche kleederdracht," *De Sumatra Post*, February 13, 1914.

42. "Pakean tjara Europa," *Sinar Djawa*, February 26, 1914; *Pemberita Betawi*, October 30, 1913, *KT* 3 (1913) 222; "Pengsiap hormat circulaire," *Doenia Bergerak*, August 29, 1914; "Fourneeren Evolutie pakaian Europa," *Sinar Djawa*, June 5, 1914; Tjipto Mangoenkoesoemo, "Het "prestige" in gevaar," *De Indiër* 1 (December 4, 1913), 82.

43. Soewardi Soerjaningrat, "Europeesche kleeding," *De Indiër* 1, no. 15 (January 29, 1914): 180.

44. "Lagi lagi hal pakeian," *Sinar Djawa*, January 20, 1914.

45. "Tjerita hal pakaian," *Oetoesan Hindia*, January 13, 1914.

46. Maier, "Phew? Europeesche Beschaving," 184–210; Adam, "Radical Journalism," 91–105.

47. "Hormat Circulaire," *Doenia Bergerak*, May 9, 1914.

48. "Nina boeboek," *Doenia Bergerak*, March 28, 1914.

49. *Pemberita Betawi*, September 30, 1913, *KT* 3 (1913): 87–88.

50. "Pakaian Europa," *Oetoesan Hindia*, April 15, 1914.

51. *Kaoem Moeda*, May 1, 1915.

52. *Oetoesan Hindia*, January 7, 1920.

53. Marco Kartodikromo, "Pakaian Europa," *Doenia Bergerak*, October 17, 1914.

54. "Chef yang main gila," *Doenia Bergerak*, May 23, 1914.

55. "Anti-sepatoe," *Doenia Bergerak*, May 7, 1914.

56. Bunga-rampai dari Zuid-Bali," *Doenia Bergerak*, August 29, 1914; "Sepakat mendjadi koeat," *Doenia Bergerak*, April 25, 1914; "Apakah ini boekan anti circulaire no. 2014?," *Doenia Bergerak*, July 18, 1914; "Berpakaian tjara Europa," *Doenia Bergerak*, November 28, 1914.

57. "Sedikit voorstel tentang pakaian," *Oetoesan Hindia*, May 16, 1914.

58. Henk Schutte Nordholt, "The State on the Skin: Clothes, Shoes, and Neatness in (Colonial) Indonesia," *Asian Studies Review* 21, no. 1 (1997) 22.

59. Soetatmo Soeriokoesoemo, "Taal en kleeding," *De Indiër* 1, (November 12, 1914): 9–11.

60. Farabi Fakih, "Conservative Corporatist: Nationalist Thoughts of Aristocrats: The Ideas of Soetatmo Soeriokoesoemo and Noto Soeroto," *BKI* 168, no. 4 (2012): 420–44; Hans van Miert, *Een koel hoofd en een warm hart: nationalisme, Javanisme en jeugdbeweging in Nederlands-Indië, 1918–1930* (Amsterdam: De Bataafsche Leeuw, 1995); Takashi Shiraishi, "The Disputes between Tjipto Mangoenkoesoemo and Soetatmo Soeriokoesoemo: Satria vs Pandita," *Indonesia* 32 (1981): 93–108.

61. Soewardi Soerjaningrat, "Onze nationale kleeding," *De Indiër* 1, no. 37 (July 2, 1914): 136.

62. Soewardi Soerjaningrat, "Onze nationale kleeding," 138.

63. *Hindia Dipa*, November 21 and December 5, 1921, *IPO*, no. 1 (1922). *Darmo Kondo*, May 24, 1922 and June 3, 1922, *IPO*, no. 25 (1922).

64. Adas, "Contested Hegemony," 31–63; Streets-Salter, *World War One*, 88–110.

65. Pols, *Nurturing Indonesia*, 80–91; Van Miert, *Een Koel Hoofd*.

66. "Prijsvraag," *Djawa* 3, no. 2 (1923): 92.

67. *Bundels met gegevens BG I, No 2; prysvraag kleeding en woning Java Instituut*, Special Collections, UBL.

68. The winning essay was significantly edited for publication and can be found in *Djawa*'s archives. Roesalam Dwidjadisastra, "De Europeesche kleederdracht voor Inlanders," *Djawa* 4, no. 2 (1924): 101–4; *BG I, No 2*, UBL.

69. Taylor, "Official Photography," 94–100.

70. *Neratja*, November 2, 1920, *IPO*, no. 45 (1920); *Oetoesan Melajoe*, April 28, 1920, *IPO*, no. 20 (1920); *Sinar Hindia*, January 12, 1921, *IPO*, no. 3 (1921).

71. Taylor, "Official Photography," 94–100; Vreede-De Stuers, *The Indonesian Woman*.

72. Taylor, "Costume and Gender," 109; Luttikhuis, "Negotiating Modernity," 171–206; Kenji Tsuchiya, "The Taman Siswa Movement—Its Early Eight Years and Javanese Background," *Journal of Southeast Asian Studies* 6, no. 2 (1975): 164–77.

73. Groeneboer, *Gateway to the West*, 497–98.

74. "Teekenen," 46.

75. *Panggoegah*, August 1, 1921, *IPO*, no. 22 (1921).

76. Soeriokoesoemo, "Taal en kleeding," 9–11.

77. *Panggoegah*, September 10 and 20, 1921, *IPO*, no. 39 (1921).

78. Dwidjadisastra, "De Europeesche kleederdracht voor Inlanders," 104.

79. Taylor, "Official Photography," 91–126.

80. *Kaoem Moeda*, February 6, 1922, *IPO*, no. 7 (1922); *Pertjatoeran*, June 23 and 27, 1925, *IPO*, no. 29 (1925); *Pantjadjania*, May 21, 1926, *IPO*, no. 24 (1926); *Sedijo Tomo*, September 21 and 26, 1927, *IPO*, no. 40 (1927).

81. *Djawa Tengah*, January 5, 1920, *IPO*, no. 6 (1920).

82. *Sri Djojobojo*, April 28, 1924, *IPO*, no. 23 (1924).

83. *Sinar Hindia*, November 30, 1918, *IPO*, no. 48 (1918); *Kaoem Moeda*, May 10, 1919, *IPO*, no. 19 (1919).

84. Mrázek, "Indonesian Dandy," 121.

85. Ann Laura Stoler, "Sexual Affronts and Racial Frontiers: European Identities and the Cultural Politics of Exclusion in Colonial Southeast Asia," *Comparative Studies in Society and History* 34, no. 3 (1992): 514–51.

86. Tarlo, *Clothing Matters*, 33–42.

87. Wybrands, "Het naderend einde."

88. Patricia Spyer, "The Tooth of Time, or Taking a Look at the 'Look' of Clothing in Late Nineteenth-Century Aru," in *Border Fetishisms: Material Objects in Unstable Spaces*, ed. Patricia Spyer (New York: Routledge, 1998), 150–82; Mrázek, "Indonesian Dandy," 132; "Inlanders in Europ. kleederdracht," *NNI*, June 25, 1919.

89. *Handelingen* (November 15, 1918), 200–201.

90. Van der Jagt, "Ethische koers en bestuursambtenaar," 1203–4.

91. "Vooruitgang," *NNI*, June 14, 1916.

92. Locher-Scholten, "Summer Dresses and Canned Food," 158–61; Taylor, "Costume and Gender," 101–5; Bronkhorst and Wils, *Tropenecht*, 28–43; Vilan van de Loo, "Tobben in Indië: wijze vriendinnen adviseren Hollandse vrouwen," *Indische Letteren* 9, no. 2 (July 1994): 66–80.

93. Bas Veth, *Het leven in Nederlandsch-Indië* (The Hague: P. N. Van Kampen & Zoon, 1900), 25–27.

94. Koopman, *Het paradijs der vrouwen: tegenschrift op Veth's "Leven in Indië"* (The Hague: N. Veenstra, 1900), 16–17.

95. J. M. J. Catenius-van der Meijden, *Ons huis in Indië: handboek bij de keuze, de inrichting, de bewoning en de verzorging van het huis met bijgebouwen en erf, naar de eischen der hygiëne, benevens raadgevingen en wenken op huishoudelijk gebied* (Semarang: Masman & Stronk, 1908).

96. Maurits Wagenvoort, *Nederlandsch-Indische menschen en dingen* (Amsterdam: H. J. W. Becht, 1910).

97. Henri Borel, "Wat in Indië verdwijnt," *Het Vaderland*, October 19, 1920.

98. Borel, "Wat in Indië verdwijnt."

99. Van de Wall, "Indische kleederdrachten"; D. C. M. Bauduin, *Het Indische leven* (The Hague: H. P. Leopold, 1927), 12–18; Jo van Ammers-Kuller, *Wat ik zag in Indië* (Amsterdam: J. M. Meulenhof, 1939), 87.

100. Locher-Scholten, "Summer Dresses and Canned Food," 160; Taylor, "Costume and Gender," 105–8; Bronkhorst and Wils, *Tropenecht*, x, 28–43; Veldhuisen, *Batik Belanda*, 128–29.

101. "Lain doeloe! Lain sekarang!," *De Reflector*, July 14, 1917.

102. "Het hooglied van de sarong kabaai," *De Reflector*, November 9, 1918. For other examples: "De sarong," *Het Indische Leven*, May 28, 1921, 810–11. "Uit mijn Boudoir: De sarong-kabaja," *De Zweep*, February 4, 1922.

103. Locher-Scholten, "Summer Dresses and Canned Food," 161–75; "Winkelbezoek," *De Reflector*, January 8, 1916. "Modern Bandoeng," *Het Indische Leven*, October 11, 1919, 151; "Een bezoek aan au Palais des Modes," *Het Indische Leven*, December 6, 1919, 308; "De installatie van het nieuwe warenhuis 'Adler,'" *D'Oriënt*, October 15, 1927.

104. *D'Oriënt*, February 13, 1926.

105. Barlow, Tani E., Uta G. Poiger, Priti Ramamurthy, Lynn M. Thomas, and Alys Eve Weinbaum, "The Modern Girl around the World: A Research Agenda and Preliminary Findings," *Gender & History* 17, no. 2 (2005): 245–94.

106. *D'Oriënt*, August 24, 1929; September 28, 1929; April 19, 1930.

107. B. van Helsdingen-Schroevers, *De Europeesche vrouw in Indië* (Baarn: Hollandia-Drukkeriy, 1914) 22–45.

108. Gouda, *Dutch Culture Overseas*; Taylor, *The Social World of Batavia*; Stoler, "Making Empire Respectable," 634–60.

109. "Vrouwen met kort haar," *D'Oriënt*, March 12, 1927.

110. "Haar 'A la ninon' en het moderne jonge meisje," *D'Oriënt*, May 24, 1924.

111. "De Mode: Sportweek," *De Reflector*, April 21, 1917.

112. "Het 'moderne' meisje," *De Zweep*, January 21, 1922. "Kort of lang haar: is kort haar blijvend?," *D'Oriënt*, January 15, 1927. "Rookende vrouwen", *D'Oriënt*, March 19, 1927.

113. Barlow, "The Modern Girl around the World," 245–94.

114. "Kleeding-Excessen," *De Indische Courant*, October 8, 1927.

115. "Batavia bij avond en nacht: dwars door Chinatown," *De Revue*, July 2, 1921; "Film en werkelijkheid: het prestige der vrouw," *De Indische Courant*, October 31, 1925.

116. "Bioscoop-gevaar," *NNI*, May 1, 1919.

117. "Het westersche prestige," *NNI*, February 25, 1929; "Westersch prestige en de bioscoop," *De Sumatra Post*, August 9, 1932; Locher-Scholten, "Summer Dresses and Canned Food," 165–75; Bronkhorst and Wils, *Tropenecht*, 112–41.

118. Pols, *Nurturing Indonesia*, 82–92; Van Miert, *Een koel hoofd en een warm hart*.

119. The Indonesian National Association (Perserikatan Nasional Indonesia) was renamed the Indonesian National Party (Partai Nasional Indonesia) in 1928. The acronym, PNI, remained the same.

120. Anderson, *Imagined Communities*.

121. Elson, *The Idea of Indonesia*, 64–72.

122. *Darmo Kondo*, August 14, 1930, *IPO*, no. 34 (1930).

123. "A-la Indonesia, bagaimana?," *Bintang Timoer*, August 16, 1930.

124. "Nasionalisme... dioejoeng "petji"!," *Bintang Timoer*, August 23, 1930.

125. Wilson, *Adorned in Dreams*, 14; Schutte Nordholt, "The State on the Skin," 22–23; Mrázek, "Indonesian Dandy," 137–39.

126. "Pakaian nasional," *Bintang Timoer*, May 8, 9, 11, 12, 13, and 15, 1931.

127. *Darmo Kondo*, October 14, 1930, *IPO*, no. 43 (1930).

128. Achmad Sukarno and Cindy Adams, *Sukarno: An Autobiography as Told to Cindy Adams* (New York: Bobbs-Merill, 1965): 51.

129. KITLV Digital Image Library, Image Code 3725, UBL.

130. "Pakaian nasional I," *Bintang Timoer*, May 8, 1931.

131. "Nasionalisme ... dioejoeng "petji"!," *Bintang Timoer*, Augustus 23, 1930.

132. For a good selection of clothing advertisements: *Oetoesan Hindia*, December 6, 1920; *Kemadjoean Hindia*, April 28, 1923; *Bahagia*, June 4, 1929; *Aksi*, June 29, 1931.

133. "Pakaian pantalon," *Bahagia*, June 3, 1929.

134. *Bintang Timoer*, September 17, 1931.

135. *Bintang Timoer*, January 11, 1929.

136. "Pakaian nasional I," *Bintang Timoer*, May 8, 1931.

137. *Bahagia*, November 26, 1931, and March 21, 1933.

138. *Radio*, July 27, 1929, *IPO*, no. 32 (1929).

139. "Koerang 'aibkah?," *Pembela Islam*, no. 23 (April 1931): 2–4.

140. *Sedio Tomo*, August 24 and 25, 1931, *IPO*, no. 36 (1931).

141. *Djanget*, December 21, 1928, *IPO*, no. 1 (1929).

142. "Pakaian kebesaran asli," *Soera 'Aisjijah* 3, no. 8–12 (January–May 1929): 7.

143. Vreede-De Stuers, 89–99; Martyn, *The Women's Movement*, 30–51.

144. "Pakaian nasional," *Bintang Timoer*, May 8, 9, 11, 12, 13, and 15, 1931; "Mode," *Isteri* 1, no. 6–7 (October–November 1931).

145. Sukarno and Adams, Sukarno, 80–81; Taylor, "Official Photography," 119–120.

Chapter 5. East Is East and West Is West

1. "Student Hidjo" appeared as a serial in *Sinar Hindia* in 1918. It was published as a novel the following year. Marco Kartodikromo, *Student Hidjo* (Semarang: Masman en Stroink, 1919).

2. Interestingly, the rest of the poem contradicts the meaning of Kipling's infamous first line, emphasizing that people from different backgrounds can be equals.

3. *D'Oriënt*, September 6, 1924.

4. *Indonesia Raja*, April 3, 1929, *IPO*, no. 15 (1929).

5. *Sin Po*, March 2, 1931, *IPO*, no. 13 (1931).

6. Annemarie De Knecht-van Eekelen, "The Debate about Acclimatization in the Dutch East Indies (1840–1860)," *Medical History*, no. 20 (2000): 70–85; Pols, "Notes from Batavia," 120–48.

7. Pols, "Notes from Batavia," 121–22 and 135–38.

8. Cornelis Swaving, "Iets over den invloed van het klimaat dezer gewesten op den Europeaan," *Natuur-en Geneeskundig Archief voor Neerlands-Indië* 1 (1844): 86–87; Cornelis Swaving, "De invloed van Java's klimaat op den gezonden Europeaan en gezondheidsregelen voor den nieuw uitgekomene," *Indisch Archief* 1 (1849): 161–80.

9. For an overview on acclimatization and scientists in colonial Indonesia, see Goss, *The Floracrats*, 36–59.

10. Carl Waitz, *Onderrigtingen en voorschriften, om de gewone ziekten van Europeanen in heete gewesten te ontgaan, en zich aldaar spoedig aan het klimaat te gewennen, bijzonder met betrekking tot Nederlandsch Indië* (Amsterdam: Sulpke, 1829); Pols, "Notes from Batavia," 128–31.

11. For more pessimistic perspectives on the issue of acclimatization see Franz Junghuhn, "De gematigde en koude streken van Java, met de aldaar voorkomende warme bronnen: uit een natuur-aardrijks-en geneeskundig oogpunt beschouwd, als stellende een middel daar ter voorkoming en genezing van die ziekten, waaraan Europeanen, ten gevolge van hun lang verblijf in heete luchtstreken, gewoonlijk lijden," *TNI* 4, no. 2 (1842): 81–82.

12. This is in contrast to British, French, and American colonies, where fears of racial degeneration came to dominate the debate on acclimatization much earlier, see Dane Kennedy, "The Perils of the Midday Sun: Climatic Anxieties in the Colonial Tropics," in *Imperialism and the Natural World*, ed. John Mackenzie (Manchester: Manchester University Press, 1990) 118–40; Eric T. Jennings, *Curing the Colonizers: Hydrotherapy, Climatology, and French Colonial Spas* (Durham and London: Duke University Press, 2006); Warwick Anderson, *Colonial Pathologies: American Tropical Medicine, Race, and Hygiene in the Philippines* (Durham: Duke University Press, 2006).

13. L. H. Verwey, *De acclimatatie van Nederlanders in Indië, en van Indiërs in Nederland* (The Hague: P. J. Kraft, 1863); C. L. van der Burg, *Persoonlijke gezondheidsleer voor Europeanen die naar Nederlandsch-Indië gaan of daar wonen* (Amsterdam: J. H. de Bussy, 1895).

14. Christiaan Eijkman, "Vergelijkend onderzoek van de physische warmteregeling bij den Europeeschen en den Maleischen tropenbewoner," *Geneeskundig Tijdschrift voor Nederlandsch-Indië* 34 (1894): 544–80.

15. Eijkman, *Over gezondheid en ziekte*, 20.

16. J. H. F. Kohlbrugge, "Climatologie en tropische ziekten," *TNI* 4 (1900): 119–24; J. H. F. Kohlbrugge, *Blikken in het zieleleven van den Javaan en zijner overheerschers* (Leiden: Brill, 1907) 47–52 and 90–101.

17. Michael Adas, *Machines as the Measure of Men: Science, Technology, and Ideologies of Western Dominance* (Ithaca: Cornell University Press, 1989), 307–16.

18. Gouda, *Dutch Culture Overseas*, 118–56; Sysling, *Racial Science*, 1–24.

19. Kohlbrugge, *Blikken in het zieleleven*, 111–12.

20. Kohlbrugge preferred the term "metamorphoses" over degeneration, but from his argumentation it is clear that he meant degeneration. This was not lost on his contemporaries. Kohlbrugge, *Blikken in het zieleleven*, 109–14 and 128. See the criticism of Christiaan Snouck Hurgronje, "Blikken in het zielenleven der Javaan?," *De Gids* 72 (1908): 423–47.

21. Kohlbrugge, *Blikken in het zieleleven*, 90.

22. Carlo [pseud.], "Indische indrukken," *WVI*, March 11, 1906. Also see R. Broersma, "Java's Kolonisatie en de Wetenschap," *WVI*, January 24, 1909.

23. *Onderzoek naar de Mindere Welvaart, vol. XII*, 6–22.

24. Kohlbrugge, *Blikken in het zieleleven*, 128; J. H. F. Kohlbrugge, "The Influence of a Tropical Climate on Europeans," *The Eugenics Review* 3, no. 1 (1911): 25–36.

25. This popular proverb derived from Goethe's *Wahlverwandschaften* (1809): "Es wandelt niemand ungestraft unter Palmen." For instance, see Corax [pseud.], "Indrukken van den dag XXIV," *WVI*, July 28, 1907.

26. Anna Crozier, "What Was Tropical about Tropical Neurasthenia? The Utility of the Diagnosis in the Management of British East Africa." *Journal of the History of Medicine and Allied Sciences* 64, no. 4 (2009): 518–48.

27. Anna Greenwood, "The Strange History of Tropical Neurasthenia," *The Psychologist* 24, no. 3 (2011): 226–27.

28. F. H. G. van Loon, "Het zenuwlijden der blanken in de tropen," *Geneeskundig Tijdschrift voor Nederlandsch-Indië* 67 (1927): 435–78; F. H. G. van Loon, "Wie is geschikt voor de tropen?," *KT* 19 (1930): 1–25.

29. "Sanatogen: A Scientific Investigation of Its Alleged Action on the Recuperating Powers of the Blood," *Journal of the American Medical Association* 63, no. 13, (1914): 1127–29.

30. Sanatogen's impressive advertising campaign lasted roughly from 1910 to 1930. For a very small selection of its diverse advertisements, see *NNI*, June 9 and November 5, 1910; January 5, 1911; July 5 and September 26, 1912; April 28, 1913; April 2, 1928.

31. *De Indische Courant*, June 16, 1926.

32. Van der Burg, *Persoonlijke zezondheidsleer*, 153; A. H. Nijland, *Hygiënische wenken voor het leven in Nederlandsch-Indië* (Leiden: S. C. van Doesburgh, 1921), 35; E. H. Hermans, *Gezondheidsleer voor Nederlandsch-Indië: een boek voor ieder die naar Indië gaat, of daar woont* (Amsterdam: J. M. Meulenhoff, 1925), 33–43.

33. G. J. Nieuwenhuis, *Lichamelijk opvoeding in Indië* (Weltevreden: Vereeniging Nederlandsch-Indisch Onderwijs Kongres, 1918); "Sport en succes in het leven," *De Reflector*, December 25, 1915; "Iets over lichamelijke opvoeding," *Het Indische Leven*, December 2, 1922; "Sport in Netherland India," *Tourism in Netherland India* 7, no. 6 (1932).

34. Jennings, *Curing the Colonizers*, 1–7.

35. Anderson, *Colonial Pathologies*, 1–12.

36. Locher-Scholten, "So Close and Yet So Far," 131–53.

37. Gouda, "Nyonyas on the Colonial Divide," 318–42.

38. "Het Kind en de Baboe," *WVI*, October 5, 1919, 366.

39. Ofoei [pseud.], "Indische Penkrassen XXI," *WVI*, February 5, 1911; "Het Baboeïsme en de Pest," *Bijblad van het WVI voor Dames*, June 11, 1911; "Het Kind en de Baboe," *WVI*, October 5, 1919.

40. Frances Gouda, "Good Mothers, Medeas, or Jezebels: Feminine Imagery in Colonial and Anticolonial Rhetoric in the Dutch East Indies, 1900–1942," in *Domesticating the Empire*, 236–54.

41. Ofoei [pseud.], "Indische penkrassen XXI," *WVI* 7, no. 42 (1911): 701–2.

42. Van Helsdingen-Schoevers, *De Europeesche vrouw in Indië*, 25–26.

43. Ofoei [pseud.], "Indische Penkrassen XXIX," *WVI* 8, no. 6 (1911): 126–28.

44. The Quaker Oats advertisement campaign in the colonial press was modern, intelligent, and appealing. For instance, see the numerous advertisements in the weekly *D'Oriënt* 4, no. 36 and 49 (1925); 5, no. 10, 40, 44, and 48 (1926); 6, no. 4, 5, 11, 13, 14, and 16 (1927); 8, no. 1, 3, 4 (1928); 17, no. 14 (1938).

45. Locher-Scholten, "Summer Dresses and Canned Food," 151–80.

46. M. Buijsman, "Tarwe in Indië," *Algemeen Landbouwweekblad voor Nederlandsch-Indië* 2, no. 6 (1917).

47. On the difficulty of disentangling identities in India, see Ashis Nandy, *The Intimate Enemy: Loss and Recovery of Self under Colonialism* (New Delhi: Oxford University Press, 1988).

48. Schulte Nordholt, "Modernity and Cultural Citizenship," 435–57; Hoogervorst and Schulte Nordholt, "Urban Middle Classes in Colonial Java," 442–74.

49. Laffan, *Islamic Nationhood*, 47–76 and 165–69; Kartodirdjo, *Pengantar sejarah Indonesia baru* 2, 106–11; Korver, *Sarekat Islam*, 5–13; M. C. Ricklefs, *Polarizing Javanese Society: Islamic and Other Visions, c. 1830–1930* (Honolulu: University of Hawaii Press, 2007), 214–50; Noer, *The Modernist Muslim Movement*, 1–29; Formichi, *Islam and the Making of the Nation*, 1–14.

50. *Sinar Hindia*, November 30, 1918, *IPO*, no. 48 (1918); *Neratja*, December 13, 1920 and May 28, 1921; Adas, "Contested Hegemony," 49–55.

51. *Hindia Dipa*, September 5, 1921.

52. Ki Hadjar Dewantara, "Some Aspects of National Education and the Taman Siswa Institute of Jogjakarta," *Indonesia* 4 (1967): 152.

53. "De Theosophie en Boedi-Oetomo," *IG* 31, no. 1 (1909): 534–35; "Toestanden in de Vorstenlanden," *IG* 34, no. 1 (1912): 797–800.

54. S. S. J. Ratu Langie, *Serikat Islam* (Baarn: Hollandia, 1913), 20.

55. Korver, *Sarekat Islam*: 49–78.

56. J. F. H. A. Later, "De Inlandsche beweging," *IG* 38, no. 2 (1916): 922.

57. *Sinar Djawa*, no. 172, *KT* 3 (1913): 1398.

58. Jiří Jákl, "An Unholy Brew: Alcohol in Pre-Islamic Java," *The Newsletter*, no. 77 (2017).

59. Ricklefs, *Polarizing Javanese society*, 254; Pemberton, *On the Subject of "Java"*, 68–101.

60. *Bintang Soerabaja*, May 31, 1912, *KT* 1 (1912): 833–34; A. H. J. G. Walbeehm, "Een drankverbod voor Nederlandsch-Indië," *Indisch Genootschap* (January 16, 1912): 119–47.

61. *Oetoesan Hindia*, July 2, 1915, *KT* 4 (1915): 1393; *Pemberita Betawi*, October 1, 1916, *KT* 5 (1916): 213.

62. Ardjoena [pseud.], "Ook dat nog," *De Indiër* 1, no. 6 (1913): 65–66.

63. *Bintang Soerabaja*, no. 154, *KT* 2 (1913): 1485–86.

64. Hazeu to Van Heutsz, 30 December 1908, in Collection Hazeu, H 1083, no. 24, UBL; Tjipto Mangoenkoesoemo, "De Indische Regeering moet zich schamen," *De Indiër* 1, no. 11 (1914): 130; Rush, *Opium to Java*; Siddhartha Chandra, "What the Numbers Really Tell Us about the Decline of the Opium Regie," *Indonesia* 70 (2000): 101–23.

65. Tjipto Mangoenkoesoemo, "Het Binnenlandsch Bestuur," *De Indiër* 2, no. 154 (1918).

66. "Wat het Oosten van het Westen noodig heeft," *De Indiër* 1, no. 18 (1914): 205–6.

67. "Hal dansah," *Isteri* 1, no. 4 (August 1929).

68. "Lagi hal dansah," *Isteri* 1, no. 6 (October 1929).

69. *Oetoesan Hindia*, January 13, 1921, *IPO*, no. 3 (1921); *Kaoem Moeda*, February 11, 1922; Vreede-de Stuers, *The Indonesian Woman*; Martyn, *The Woman's Movement in Post-Colonial Indonesia*, 30–51.

70. Ricklefs, *Polarizing Javanese Society*, 251–57.

71. Stoler, *Carnal Knowledge*, 1–139; Gouda, "Nyonyas on the Colonial Divide," 318–42; Locher-Scholten, *Women and the Colonial State*, 187–218; Hanneke Ming, "Barracks-Concubinage in the Indies, 1887–1920," *Indonesia* 35 (1983): 65–93; Betty de Hart, "'De verwerpelijkste van alle gemengde huwelijken': De gemengde huwelijken regeling Nederlands-Indie 1898 en de rijkswet op het Nederlanderschap 1892 vergeleken," *Gaan & staan. Jaarboek voor de vrouwengeschiedenis* 21 (Amsterdam: Stichting Beheer IISG, 2001): 60–81.

72. Taylor, *The Social World of Batavia*, 14–16.

73. Van Marle, "De groep der Europeanen," 97–121, 314–41, and 481–507; Reggie Baay, *De njai: het concubinaat in Nederlands-Indië* (Amsterdam: Athenaeum-Polak & Van Gennep, 2008).

74. Taylor, *The Social World of Batavia*, 15–17; Stoler, "Making Empire Respectable," 634–60.

75. Eckart, *Indische brieven*; Adelante [pseud.], "Concubinaat bij de ambtenaren van het binnenlandsch bestuur in Nederlandsch-Indië," *TNI* 2 (1898): 304–14 and 610–17; J. H. F. Kohlbrugge, "Prostitutie in Nederlandsch Indië," *Indisch Genootschap* (February 19, 1901): 17–36; R. A. Kern, "De kontroleurs en 't concubinaat," *TBB* 28 (1905): 250–52.

76. Ming, "Barracks-Concubinage," 65–93. Stoler, *Carnal Knowledge*.

77. Wagenvoort, *Nederlandsch-Indische menschen en dingen*, 90–95; Van Helsdingen-Schoevers, *De Europeesche vrouw in Indië*, 6–8.

78. Van Marle, "De groep der Europeanen," 322–23.

79. Van Marle, "De groep der Europeanen," 314–41.

80. J. A. Nederburgh, *Gemengde huwelijken: Staatsblad 1898 no. 15: officieele bescheiden met eenige aanteekeningen* (Batavia, 1899), 9–21; Betty de Hart, "'De verwerpelijkste van alle gemengde huwelijken'," 60–81.

81. Van Marle, "De groep der Europeanen," 491; *Pantjaran Warta*, no. 258, 259, and 265, *KT* 3 (1913): 225; "Als de Sarekat Islam naar Deli komt," *De Telegraaf,* July 1, 1913.

82. Korver, *Sarekat Islam*, 49–78.

83. Pedro [pseudonym], "Sikapnya bangsa Europa terhadap pada perempoean Boemipoetera," *Kemadjoean Hindia*, June 5, 1923; Sally White, "The Case of Nyi Anah: Concubinage, Marriage and Reformist Islam in Late Colonial Dutch East Indies," *Review of Indonesian and Malaysian Affairs* 38, no. 1 (2004): 87–98.

84. *Kawan Kita Jang Toeloes*, February 7, 1919, *IPO*, no. 7 (1919); *Poesaka*, June 2, 1919, *IPO*, no. 23 (1919); *Djawi Hiswara*, November 19, 1919, *IPO*, no. 48 (1919).

85. Ki Wiroloekito, "Gemengde huwelijken," *De Vrouw in Indië*, May 1, 1915.

86. "Een niet alledaagsche verloving," *Algemeen Handelsblad*, June 8, 1915.

87. *Sinar Djawa*, no. 134, *KT* 4 (1915): 1238–39.

88. "Een opzienbarende verloving," *Bataviaasch Nieuwsblad*, April 27, 1915.

89. For more examples, see *Kaoem Moeda*, no. 228, *KT* 5 (1916): 86; *Neratja*, September 7–9, 1920, *IPO*, no. 37 (1920); *Oetoesan Hindia*, September 8, 1920, *IPO*, no. 37 (1920); *Oetoesan Hindia*, November 22, 1920, *IPO*, no. 48 (1920); *Oetoesan Hindia*, December 12 until 19, 1922, *IPO*, no. 51 (1922); *De Sumatra Post*, November 13, 1915; "Gemengde huwelijken," *IG* 38, no. 2 (1916): 979–80.

90. "Kawin dengan lain bangsa (gemengd huwelijk)," *Perempoean Bergerak*, December 16, 1919.

91. "Doenia Istri," *Padjadjaran*, October 25, 1920.

92. Vreede-de Stuers, *The Indonesian Woman*, 61–74; *Pemberita Betawi*, no. 283, *KT* 2 (1912): 595; *Poesaka*, June 2, 1919, *IPO*, no. 23 (1919).

93. *Oetoesan Hindia*, November 22, 1920, *IPO*, no. 48 (1920); *Boedi Oetomo*, December 3, 1920, *IPO*, no. 49 (1920).

94. *Sinar Pasoendan*, March 22, 1919, *IPO*, no. 12 (1919). A similar advertisement can be found in *Darmo Kondo*, March 15, 1928, *IPO*, no. 12 (1928).

95. Part of the study committee's letter as well as Sam Ratu Langie's response can be found in "Bespreking over gemengde huwelijken in de vergadering der Indische Vereeniging op 30 Juni 1915," *Indische Vereeniging: Voordrachten en Mededeelingen*, no. 10 (1916): 56–59.

96. "Bespreking over gemengde huwelijken," 59–73.

97. Examples of Indonesian men with a European spouse are discussed in Van Marle, "De groep der Europeanen," 336.

98. *Boedi Oetomo*, December 3, 1920, *IPO*, no. 49 (1920); *Warta Hindia*, December 18, 1924, *IPO*, no. 1 (1925).

99. *Oetoesan Hindia*, January 8, 1919, *IPO*, no. 2 (1919); *Kawan Kita Jang Toeloes*, February 7, 1919, *IPO*, no. 7 (1919); *Neratja*, June 16, 1919, *IPO*, no. 25 (1919).

100. Kartodikromo, *Student Hidjo*.

101. Abdoel Moeis, *Salah Asoehan* (Weltevreden: Balai Poestaka, 1928); Keith Foulcher, "Biography, History and the Indonesian Novel: Reading Salah Asuhan," *BKI* 161, no. 2/3 (2005): 247–68.

102. Habib St. Maharadja, *Nasib* (Batavia: Balai Poestaka, 1932); A. L. V. L. van der Linden, *De Europeaan in de Maleische literatuur* (Meppel: B. ten Brink, 1937): 433–52.

103. John Ingleson, "Sutomo, the Indonesian Study Club and Organised Labour in Late Colonial Surabaya," *JSEAS* 39, no. 1 (2008): 31–57.

104. Paul W. van der Veur, *Towards a Glorious Indonesia: Reminiscences and Observations of Dr. Soetomo* (Athens: Ohio University Center for Southeast Asian Studies, 1987), 91; *Neratja*, January 7, 1919, *IPO*, no. 2 (1919).

105. *Bintang Mataram*, December 20, 1930, *IPO*, no. 2 (1913); *Swara Publiek*, December 27, 1930, *IPO*, no. 2 (1931); *Oetoesan Sumatra*, January 30, 1931, *IPO*, no. 7 (1931); *Bintang Mataram*, January 30, 1931, *IPO*, no. 7 (1931); *Darmokondo*, February 14, 1931, *IPO*, no. 8 (1931).

106. *Oetoesan Soematra*, January 22, 1931, *IPO*, no. 5 (1931).

107. *Soeara Indonesia*, January 5–15, 1931, *IPO*, no. 4 (1931).

108. *Darmokondo,* January 24, 1931, *IPO,* no. 4 (1931); *Nan Sing,* January 16, 1931, *IPO,* no. 4 (1931).

109. Paul W. van der Veur, Towards a Glorious Indonesia, 99.

Chapter 6. Staging Colonial Modernity

1. "Naar de Soerabajasche jaarmarkt-tentoonstelling," *WVI,* June 16, 1907.

2. Coté, "Staging Modernity," 1–44.

3. M. I. Cohen, *Inventing the Performing Arts: Modernity and Tradition in Colonial Indonesia* (Honolulu: University of Hawai'i Press, 2016), 83–101.

4. Nurliani Lukito, *Exhibiting Modernity,* 17–68.

5. Joost Coté, "'To See is to Know': The Pedagogy of the Colonial Exhibition, Semarang, 1914," *Paedagogica Historica* 36, no. 1 (2000): 340–66; Coté, "Staging Modernity," 1–44.

6. For the world's fairs, see Marieke Bloembergen, *Colonial Spectacles: The Netherlands and the Dutch East Indies at the World Exhibitions, 1880–1931* (Singapore: Singapore University Press, 2006); P. A. Morton, *Hybrid Modernities: Architecture and Representation at the 1931 Colonial Exposition, Paris* (Cambridge: MIT Press, 2003); R. W. Rydell, *All the World's a Fair: Visions of Empire at American International Expositions, 1876–1916* (Chicago: University of Chicago Press, 1987).

7. Locher-Scholten, *Ethiek in fragmenten,* 176–208; Van Doorn, *De laatste eeuw van Indië;* Houben, "Representations of Modernity," 23–40.

8. Schulte Northolt, "New Urban Middle Classes in Colonial Java," 439–41; Schulte Northolt and Hoogevorst, "New Urban Middle Classes in Colonial Java," 442–74; Dafna Ruppin, "The Emergence of a Modern Audience for Cinema in Colonial Java," *BKI,* Vol. 173, no. 4 (2017) 475–502.

9. Van Niel, *The Emergence of the Modern Indonesian Elite;* Schulte Nordholt, "Modernity and Cultural Citizenship," 435–57; Takashi Shiraishi, *An Age in Motion,* 27–40.

10. Houben, "Representations of Modernity," 25.

11. For non-Indonesian examples: George Dutton, "Advertising, Modernity, and Consumer Culture in Colonial Vietnam," in *The Reinvention of Distinction: Modernity and the Middle Class in Urban Vietnam,* ed. V. Nguyen-Marshall, L. B. W. Drummond, and D. Bélanger (New York: Springer, 2012), 21–42; Mark Liechty, *Suitably Modern: Making Middle-Class Culture in a New Consumer Society* (Princeton: Princeton University Press, 2003), 1–7; Sanjay Joshi, *Fractured Modernity: Making of a Middle Class in Colonial North India* (New Delhi: Oxford University Press, 2001), 1–22.

12. J. H. Abendanon, *Rapport van den directeur van onderwijs, eeredienst en nijverheid betreffende de maatregelen in het belang van de Inlandsche nijverheid op Java en Madoera in verband met de door het moederland voor dit doel beschikbaar te stellen fondsen* (Batavia: Landsdrukkerij, 1904) vol. 1, 48–50 and vol. 2, 247–55.

13. *Onderzoek naar de Mindere Welvaart,* vol. 6a, 12–14 and 146–48; vol. 9, 56–57.

14. Abendanon, *Rapport,* 12–13, 217.

15. C. M. Pleyte, *Verslag nopens de Pasar-Gambir: Gehouden op het Koningsplein te Weltevreden van 18 Augustus–2 September 1906* (Batavia: Landsdrukkerij, 1907), 10.

16. J. E. Jasper, *Verslag van de eerste tentoonstelling-jaarmarkt te Soerabaja.* (Batavia: Landsdrukkerij, 1906).

17. Susie Protschky, *Photographic Subjects: Monarchy and Visual Culture in Colonial Indonesia* (Manchester: Manchester University Press, 2019); Bloembergen, *Colonial Spectacles,* 246–55; Cohen, *Inventing the Performing Arts,* 84–86; V. I. van de Wall, "Pasar Gambir voor Honderd Jaren," *D'Oriënt* 3, no. 35 (1924).

18. M. A. J. Kelling, "Het jaarbeurswezen in Nederlandsch-Indië," *Koloniale Studiën* 9, no. 2 (1925): 212–15; "34 jaren bij het Binnenlandsch Bestuur," *Soerabaiasch Handelsblad,* June 8, 1929.

19. J. E. Jasper, *Verslag van de vierde tentoonstelling-jaarmarkt te Soerabaja* (Batavia: Landsdrukkerij, 1909); Pleyte, *Verslag nopens de Pasar-Gambir*; "De jaarmarkt," *Bataviaasch Nieuwsblad,* August 27, 1906; "De Pasar Gambir," *NNI,* August 26, 1907.

20. Bloembergen, *Colonial Spectacles,* 223–25.

21. Abendanon, *Rapport,* vol. 1, 14, and 23; *Onderzoek naar de Mindere Welvaart,* vol. 9a, 53–58.

22. Jasper, *Verslag van de vierde tentoonstelling-jaarmarkt.*

23. Kelling, "Het jaarbeurswezen in Nederlandsch-Indië," 210–12; Van Dijk, *The Netherlands Indies and the Great War.*

24. G. J. Dijkerman, "Het jaarmarktwezen in Nederlandsch-Indië," *Koloniale Studiën* 11, no. 2 (1927): 121–52; Kelling, "Het jaarbeurswezen in Nederlandsch-Indië," 210–42.

25. *Jaarverslag Nederlandsch-Indische jaarbeurs te Bandoeng* (Tegal: De Boer, 1929–1933); S. A. Reitsma, "Bandoeng en de jaarbeurs," *D'Oriënt* 6, no. 26 (1927); "Openingsrede Ten Damme, 17-9-1922," *De Jaarbeurs,* January 15, 1922.

26. "De jaarmarkt," *Indische Courant,* July 28, 1923; *Programma van de Soerabaiasche jaarmarkt Vereeniging* (Surabaya, 1924–1931).

27. Kelling, "Het jaarbeurswezen in Nederlandsch-Indië," 226–39; "Jaarbeurs en jaarmarkt," *Indische Courant,* June 29, 1923; "De verhouding tusschen de Nederl. Ind. Jaarbeurs-Vereeniging te Bandoeng en de Jaarmarkt-Vereeniging te Soerabaia," *De Jaarbeurs,* April 15, 1923.

28. "Bevordering van het jaarmarktwezen in Indië," *Indische Courant,* March 29, 1928.

29. Lukito, *Exhibiting Modernity,* 17–68; Susie Protschky, *Photographic Subjects,* 87.

30. "Dertig jaar in Indië in drie minuten," *Bataviaasch Nieuwsblad,* June 11, 1937.

31. A. E. Simon Thomas, *De importeur, de pasar gambir, jaarbeurs, pasar malem en jaarmarkten* (Soerabaia: Hahn, 1928), 1–4; A. E. Simon Thomas, *Een en ander over de plaats der jaarmarkten in de Indische maatchappij: Prae-advies uitgebracht op de jaarvergadering der Vereeniging tot bevordering van het jaarmarktwezen in Nederlandsch-Indië, gehouden te Soerabaja op 13 October 1929* (Weltevreden: Emmink, 1929), 1–17.

32. *Programma van den Pasar Gambir* (Batavia: Pasar Gambir Comité, 1922–1933). For instance, see "Pasar Gambir 1925," *Pandji Poestaka*, August 25, 1925; "Pasar Gambir 1936," *Pandji Poestaka*, August 28, 1936.

33. "De Luna Park Czar van het Oosten," *D'Oriënt*, September 24, 1938; *Pewarta Deli*, May 21, 1929, *IPO*, no. 22 (1929).

34. *Programma van den Pasar Gambir* (1923–1933).

35. Van der Meer, "Performing Colonial Modernity," 503–38.

36. Simon Thomas, *Een en ander over de plaats der jaarmarkten*, 7–8.

37. *Indisch Verslag 1931*, 221–22.

38. *Programma van den Pasar Gambir* (1923–1933); *Jaarverslag Nederlandsch-Indische jaarbeurs* (1929–1933).

39. *Indisch Verslag* (1931–1937).

40. "Inlandsche kunstnijverheid," *D'Oriënt*, August 30, 1924; "De Indische kunstnijverheid op den Pasar Gambir," *D'Oriënt*, September 5, 1925.

41. *Programma van den Pasar Gambir* (1923–1933).

42. M. A. J. Kelling, "De eerste hygiëne-tentoonstelling in Nederlandsch-Indië," *D'Oriënt*, vol. 6, no. 26 (1927).

43. Kelling, "De eerste hygiëne-tentoonstelling," 63.

44. Kelling, "De eerste hygiëne-tentoonstelling," 63.

45. "Pemboekaan Pasar Gambir," *Pandji Poestaka*, September 1, 1931 and September 8, 1931; *Programma van den Pasar Gambir* (1923–1933).

46. Simon Thomas, *De importeur*, 9.

47. Dijkerman, "Het jaarmarktwezen in Nederlandsch-Indië," 127–32.

48. Simon Thomas, *Een en ander over de plaats der jaarmarkten*, 9–11. "De jaarmarkt," *De Indische Courant*, October 12, 1927; "Hoe anderen den Pasar Gambir zien," *NNI*, September 7, 1929.

49. H. Cox, *The Global Cigarette: Origins and Evolution of British American Tobacco, 1880–1945* (New York: Oxford University Press, 2000), 279–83.

50. These percentages are rough indications based on *Programma van den Pasar Gambir* (1925–1927).

51. *Programma van den Pasar Gambir* (1923–1933).

52. Simon Thomas, *Een en ander over de plaats der jaarmarkten*, 17.

53. "Pasar Gambir," *Pandji Poestaka*, August 30, 1929.

54. "Eerste Ned: Indische reclame tentoonstelling," *D'Oriënt*, September 5, 1925.

55. Dutton, "Advertising, Modernity, and Consumer Culture," 21–42; Liechty, *Suitably Modern*, 6–7.

56. Simon Thomas, *Een en ander over de plaats der jaarmarkten*, 7–11.

57. The currency in the Netherlands Indies was known as the Netherlands Indies Guilder (fl.). *Programma van den Pasar Gambir* (1925).

58. J. E. Jasper, *Verslag van de eerste Semarangsche jaarmarkt-tentoonstelling, 1908* (Batavia: Landsdrukkerij, 1911).

59. "Sambil laloe," *Hindia Baroe*, May 25, 1925; "Wit Java," *Hindia Baroe*, June 15, 1925.

60. "Pasar Gambir," *Pandji Poestaka*, August 30, 1929.

61. "Pasar Gambir 1930," *Pandji Poestaka*, September 5, 1930; "Berdjalan-djalan kekota bamboe: Pasar Gambir," *Pandji Poestaka*, July 30, 1937.

62. Lukito, *Exhibiting Modernity*, 17–68.

63. "Electrische Lichtreclame," *D'Oriënt*, September 4, 1926.

64. F. van der Kooi to A. A. Cense, in Collection A. A. Cense, D OR. 545–305, UBL; "Pasar Gambir," *Pandji Poestaka*, 29 July 1932.

65. See graphs in Van der Meer, "Performing Colonial Modernity," 524–25.

66. At provincial fairs, the proportion of indigenous visitors was even larger than in the major cities. For instance, of the 134,993 visitors to Pekalongan's 1924 pasar malam, only 2 percent was European and 8 percent Foreign Oriental, while 90 percent was indigenous. J. E. Jasper, *De organisatie van een jaarmarkt-tentoonstelling: De 2e te Pekalongan* (Tegal: De Boer, 1924).

67. "Pasar Gambir ke-12," *Pandji Poestaka*, September 6, 1932.

68. "Pasar Gambir te Batavia," *Algemeen Handelsblad*, September 17, 1935.

69. *Pandji Poestaka*, September 1, 1933.

70. See graph in Van der Meer, "Performing Colonial Modernity," 524–25.

71. "Rempah-Ratus: Pasar Gambir," *Pandji Poestaka*, July 30, 1937.

72. Schulte Northolt and Hoogevorst, "Urban Middle Classes in Colonial Java," 442–74; Schulte Nordholt, "Modernity and Cultural Citizenship in the Netherlands Indies," 435–57.

73. Dutton, "Advertising, Modernity, and Consumer Culture in Colonial Vietnam," 21–42; Liechty, *Suitably Modern*, 6–7.

74. *Bahagia*, April 3, 1930, *IPO*, no. 15 (1930).

75. Dijkerman, "Het jaarmarktwezen in Nederlandsch-Indië," 127.

76. Hardjo Soë, "Omong kosong: pemandangan tentang Pasar Gambir," *Pandji Poestaka* 16, no. 70/72 (1938).

77. Hardjo Soë, "Omong kosong: Pasar Gambir," *Pandji Poestaka* 13, no. 70 (1935).

78. Hardjo Soë, "Omong kosong: Pasar Gambir di Betawi," *Pandji Poestaka* 14, no. 71 (1936).

79. Taylor, "Costume and Gender," 85–116; Taylor, "Identity, Nation and Islam," 101–120.

80. Hardjo Soë, "Omong kosong: Pasar Gambir."

81. *Persatoean Indonesia*, June 1, 1929, *IPO*, no. 23 (1929); "Tentoonstelling kolonial di Paris," *Persatoean Indonesia* 4, no. 5, October 7, 1931.

82. "Pertjoendjoekkan bangsa manoesia," *Bintang Timoer*, June 29, 1929; *Darmo Kondo*, May 17–18, 1929, *IPO*, no. 21 (1929).

83. "Het jaarmarktwezen," *Timboel*, August 15, 1928.

84. For a similar critique "Javaansche cultuurbeweging: Een passer derma," *Djawa*, no. 4 (1925).

85. *Bendee*, September 19 and 26, 1928, *IPO*, no. 40 (1928); *Djanget*, October 1, 1928, *IPO*, no. 41 (1928); *Sedijo Tomo*, July 27, 1929, *IPO*, no. 31 (1929).

86. What makes *Pandji Poestaka* such an interesting source is its continuous publication over a long period of time (1922–1945), which offers scholars the opportunity to trace and compare reporting over time.

87. Hardjo Soë, "Omong kosong: Pasar Gambir di Betawi."

88. Hardjo Soë, "Omong kosong: Pasar Gambir." Hardjo Soë, "Omong kosong: pemandangan Pasar Gambir," *Pandji Poestaka* 15, no. 75 (1937).

89. "Pasar Gambir," *Pandji Poestaka*, August 28, 1924.

90. *Sedijo Tomo*, September 10, 1928, *IPO*, no. 8 (1928); *Fadjar Asia*, September 15, 1928, *IPO*, no. 8 (1928); *Kristen Djawi*, no. 26, *IPO*, no. 44 (1929).

91. "Pasar-pasar Malem bikin mlarat pada ra'jat," *De Samenwerking*, September 7, 1929; *De Samenwerking*, March 15, 1930.

92. "Pasar-pasar Malem bikin mlarat pada ra'jat I," *De Samenwerking*, October 26, 1929.

93. "Pasar-pasar Malem bikin mlarat pada ra'jat I."

94. "Pasar-pasar Malem bikin mlarat pada ra'jat II," *Samenwerking*, November 2, 1929; "Soerat Terboeka: Passar Malem dan Pendjoedian," *Samenwerking*, September 13, 1930; "Doenia handel dan pasar Malam," *Samenwerking*, November 29, 1930.

95. *Sinar Hindia*, November 30, 1918, *IPO*, no. 48 (1918); *Neratja*, December 13, 1920, *IPO*, no. 51 (1920).

96. Taylor, "Costume and Gender," 85–116; Taylor, "Identity, Nation and Islam," 101–120.

97. *Oetoesan Hindia*, January 13, 1921, *IPO*, no. 3 (1921); *Kaoem Moeda*, February 6, 1922, *IPO*, no. 7 (1922).

98. Vreede-de Stuers, *The Indonesian Woman*, 91.

99. Taylor, "Identity, Nation and Islam," 101–120.

100. *Kaoem Moeda*, April 7, 1924, *IPO*, no. 16 (1924).

101. "Berdjalan-djalan ke Pasar Gambir," *Pandji Poestaka*, September 4, 1924.

102. *Pantjadjania*, May 21, 1926, *IPO*, no. 24 (1926).

103. Hardjo Soë, "Omong kosong: pemandangan Pasar Gambir."

104. *Djawa Tengah*, January 5, 1920, *IPO*, no. 6 (1920).

105. *Boedi Oetomo*, January 19, 1921, *IPO*, no. 4 (1921); *Persamaan*, August 20, 1924, *IPO*, no. 36 (1924).

106. Hardjo Soë, "Omong kosong: pemandangan dalam Pasar Gambir," *Pandji Poestaka* 13, no. 72 (1935).

107. *Darmo Kondo*, January 28, 1925, *IPO*, no. 6 (1925).

108. "Sambil laloe," *Hindia Baroe*, May 25, 1925.

109. "Ketel nasional," *Bintang Timoer*, April 8–13, 1931; "Batik kita dan lurik kita," *Aksi*, June 25, 1931.

110. The original proposal for organization of a pasar malam derma came from Gondokoesoemo, appointed treasurer of the organizing committee. The periodical of the Indonesian Study Club, *Soeloeh Ra'jat Indonesia* (Torch of the Indonesian People), published a special issue to reflect on the first fair. "Nomor Pasar-Malem 31 Mei–9 Juni," *Soeloeh Ra'jat Indonesia* 4 (1930).

111. "Nomor Pasar-Malem 31 Mei–9 Juni," 1–2.

112. Vreede-de Stuers, *The Indonesian Woman*, 61–74.

113. "Nomor Pasar-Malem 31 Mei–9 Juni," front page and page 4.

114. Cohen, *Inventing the Performing Arts*.

115. Nomor Pasar-Malem 31 Mei–9 Juni," 7.

116. Elson, *The Idea of Indonesia*, 39–72; Nomor Pasar-Malem 31 Mei–9 Juni," 3. "Teekende feiten," *Bataviaasch Nieuwsblad*, June 5, 1931.

117. "Pasar Malem derma nasional," *Swara Oemoem*, May 23 and 26, 1931; "Pasar Malem derma nasional ka 2," *Swara Oemoem*, May 27, 28, and 30, 1931 and June 1, 1931.

118. The financial results can be found in "Nomor Pasar-Malem 31 Mei–9 Juni," 12–13.

119. *Sedio Tomo*, June 19 and 20, 1930, *IPO*, no. 26 (1930); *Bintang Timoer*, June 12, 1930, *IPO*, no. 25 (1930).

120. The objective was to organize the *Pasar Malam Nasional* annually, but both for economic reasons (the crisis years) and political reasons (discord with the nationalist movement) it only opened it gates five times: in 1930–1933 and in 1937.

121. Compare Joshi, *Fractured Modernity*, 1–22.

122. Steijlen en Willems, Met ons alles goed, 124.

Epilogue. Pawnshops as Stages of the Colonial Performance of Power

1. *De Zweep*, January 15, 1922.

2. *Staatsblad*, no. 393 (1906).

3. "Keloeh kesah," *Doenia Bergerak*, June 20, 1914, 9–10; "B. B. contra pandhuis," *Doenia Bergerak*, November 7, 1914, 8–9.

4. *Oetoesan Hindia*, March 26, 1919.

5. *Oetoesan Hindia*, April 3, 1919.

6. G. A. J. Hazeu to R. A. Kern, September 21, 1922, in Collection Kern, H 797, no. 291, UBL.

7. R. A. Kern to D. Fock, January 23, 1922 and March 16, 1922, in Collection Kern, H 797, no. 291, UBL; Akira Nagazumi, "The Pawnshop Strikes of 1922 and the Indonesian Political Parties," *Archipel* 8 (1974): 187–206; *Een en ander naar aanleiding van de staking bij den Pandhuisdienst* (Yogyakarta: H. Bruning, 1922).

8. *NNI*, March 18, 1920.

9. *NNI*, February 4, 1920. *Het Indische Leven*, August 7, 1920 and April 24, 1926.

10. "Djanganlah sampai loepa daratan!," *Pandji Poestaka*, January 31, 1940.

11. John Pemberton, On the Subject of "Java," 1–27.

BIBLIOGRAPHY

Archival Collections

Historical Documentation Center for Dutch Protestantism, Amsterdam,
    The Netherlands (HDC)
    Collection A. W. F. Idenburg, Inventory no. 129
Leiden University Library, Special Collections, The Netherlands (UBL)
    Collection R. A. Kern, H 797
    Collection G. A. J. Hazeu, H 1083
    Collection A. A. Cense, D OR. 545–305
    Collection KITLV
Nationaal Archief, Den Haag, (National Archives, The Hague,
    The Netherlands) (NL-HaNA)
    Archive Ministerie van Koloniën: Geheim Archief, 1901–1940, 2.10.36.51
    Archive Ministerie van Koloniën: Openbaar Verbaal, 1901–1952, 2.10.36.04
    Collection J. B. van Heutsz, 1882–1935, 2.21.008.79

Newspapers and Periodicals

Aksi
Algemeen Handelsblad
Bahagia
Bataviaasch Nieuwsblad
Bintang Hindia
Bintang Timoer
D'Oriënt
Darmo Kondo
De Gids
De Indiër
De Indische Courant
De Indische Gids
De Indische Verlofganger
De Jaarbeurs
De Locomotief
De Preanger Bode
De Reflector

De Revue
De Sumatra Post
De Taak
De Telegraaf
De Wederopbouw
De Zweep
Djåwå
Doenia Bergerak
Geneeskundig
    Tijdschrift voor
    Nederlandsch-Indië
Haagsch Maandblad
Het Indische Leven
Het Koloniaal Weekblad
Het Nieuws van
    den Dag voor
    Nederlandsch-Indië

Hindia Baroe
Hindia Dipa
Hindia Poetra
Indologenblad
Isteri
Java Bode
Kaoem Moeda
Kemadjoean Hindia
Koloniaal Tijdschrift
Koloniale Studiën
Oetoesan Hindia
Onze Bode
Onze Koloniën
Padjadjaran
Pandji Poestaka
Pembela Islam
Pemimpin

Perempoean Bergerak
Persatoean Goeroe
Persatoean Indonesia
Samenwerking
Sedio Tomo
Sinar Djawa
Sinar Hindia
Sipatahoenan
Soeara Aisjijah

Soeloeh Ra' jat Indonesia
Soerabajasch Handelsblad
Swara Oemoem
Taman Pengadjar
Tijdschrift voor het
   Binnenlandsch Bestuur
Tijdschrift voor
   Nederlandsch-Indië
Timboel

Tourism in the
   Netherlands East Indies
Verslagen der Algemeene
   Vergaderingen van het
   Indisch Genootschap
Weekblad voor Indië

Published Primary Sources

Abendanon, J. H. *Rapport van den directeur van onderwijs, eeredienst en nijverheid betreffende de maatregelen in het belang van de Inlandsche nijverheid op Java en Madoera in verband met de door het moederland voor dit doel beschikbaar te stellen fondsen.* 2 vols. Batavia: Landsdrukkerij, 1904.

Ammers-Küller, Jo van. *Wat ik zag in Indië.* Amsterdam: Meulenhoff, 1939.

Ardjoena [Pseud.]. "Ook dat nog." *De Indiër* 1, no. 6 (November 27, 1913): 65–66.

Bauduin, D. C. M. *Het Indische leven.* The Hague: H. P. Leopold, 1927.

Beckman Lapré, F. O. M. *Een en ander naar aanleiding van de staking bij den Pandhuisdienst.* Yogyakarta: H. Bruning, 1922.

Berg, L. W. C. van den. *De Inlandsche rangen en titels op Java en Madoera.* Batavia: Landsdrukkerij, 1887.

Bescheiden betreffende de vereeniging "Sarekat Islam." Batavia: Landsdrukkerij, 1913.

"Bespreking over gemengde huwelijken in de vergadering der Indische Vereeniging Op 30 Juni 1915." *Indische Vereeniging: Voordrachten en Mededeelingen*, no. 10 (1916): 56–59.

Bijblad op het Staatsblad van Nederlandsch-Indië. Batavia: Landsdrukkerij, 1857.

Boissevain, W. T. L. "Protestbeweging van de Vereeniging van Ambtenaren bij het Binnenlandsch Bestuur." *KT* 3, no. 1 (1914): 69–78.

Borel, Henri. "Ambtenaar." *WVI* 4, no. 14 (July 28, 1907): 269–71.

———. "Wat in Indië verdwijnt." *Het Vaderland*, October 19, 1920.

Bosch, Johannes van den. *Mijne verrigtingen in Indië verslag van z. excellentie den commissaris generaal J. van den Bosch, over de jaren 1830, 1831, 1832 en 1833.* Amsterdam: F. Muller, 1864.

Briefwisseling tussen J. van den Bosch en J. C. Baud, 1829–1832 en 1834–1836. Eerste deel: brieven van den Bosch. Utrecht: Kemink, 1956.

Brooshooft, P. *De ethische koers in de koloniale politiek.* Amsterdam: J. H. de Bussy, 1901.

Burg, C. L. van der. *Persoonlijke gezondheidsleer voor Europeanen, die naar Nederlandsch-Indië gaan of daar wonen.* Amsterdam: J. H. de Bussy, 1895.

Carlo [pseud.]. "Indische indrukken XXIV." *WVI* 3, no. 14 (July 29, 1906): 301–4.

Catenius-van der Meijden, J. M. J. *Ons huis in Indië: handboek bij de keuze, de inrichting, de bewoning en de verzorging van het huis met bijgebouwen en erf, naar de eischen der hygiëne, benevens raadgevingen en wenken op huishoudelijk gebied.* Semarang: Masman & Stroink, 1908.

Census of 1930 in Netherlands India. Vol. 8. Batavia: Landsdrukkerij, 1936.

Chijs, J. A. van der. *Nederlandsch-Indisch Plakaatboek, 1602–1811.* 17 vols. Batavia: Landsdrukkerij, 1885.

Couperus, Louis. *The Hidden Force.* Translated by E. M. Beekman. Amherst: University of Massachusetts Press, 1985.

Daendels, Herman Willem. *Staat der Nederlandsche Oostindische bezittingen onder het bestuur van den gouverneur-generaal Herman Willem Daendels in de Jaren 1808–1811.* The Hague, 1814.

Deventer, C. Th. van. "Een eereschuld." *De Gids* 63, no. 2 (1899): 205–57.

Deventer, S. van. *Bijdragen tot de kennis van het landelijk stelsel op Java op last van zijne excellentie den minister van kolonien, J. D. Fransen van de Putte, eerste deel: de wording van het stelsel,* 1. Zalt-Bommel: J. Noman en Zoon, 1866.

Dewantara, Ki Hadjar [previously Soewardi Soerjaningrat]. "Some Aspects of National Education and the Taman Siswa Institute of Jogjakarta." *Indonesia,* no. 4 (1967): 150–68.

Dijkerman, G. J. "Het jaarmarktwezen in Nederlandsch-Indië." *Koloniale Studiën* 11, no. 2 (1927): 121–52.

Djajadiningrat, Achmad. "De positie van de regenten op Java en Madoera in het huidige bestuursstelsel." *Verslagen der Vergaderingen van het Indisch Genootschap* (November 15, 1929): 83–104.

———. *Herinneringen van Pangeran Aria Achmad Djajadiningrat.* Amsterdam: G. Kolff, 1936.

Djajadiningrat, Hoesein. "Dr. G. A. J. Hazeu." *De Taak* 3, no. 12 and 13 (n.d.): 13, 18, and 25 October 1919.

Dwidjadisastra, Roesalam. "De Europeesche kleederdracht voor inlanders." *Djâwâ: Tijdschrift van Het Java-Instituut* 4, no. 2 (1924): 101–4.

Eckart [Pseudonym for H. E. Steinmetz]. *Indische brieven aan een staatsraad.* Haarlem: Erven F. Bohn, 1888.

Eijkman, Christiaan. *Over gezondheid en ziekte in heete gewesten.* Utrecht: J. van Druten, 1898.

———. "Vergelijkend onderzoek van de physische warmteregeling bij den Europeeschen en den Maleischen tropenbewoner." *Geneeskundig Tijdschrift voor Nederlandsch-Indië* 34 (1894): 544–80.

Fromberg, P. H. *De Chineesche beweging op Java.* Amsterdam: Elsevier, 1911.

———. "De Inlandsche beweging op Java." *De Gids* 78 (1914): 23–44.

Gobée, E., and C. Adriaanse, eds. *Ambtelijke adviezen van C. Snouck-Hurgronje, 1889–1936.* The Hague: M. Nijhoff, 1957.

Groneman, J. "Een en ander over den Javaanschen adel." *IG* 8, no. 2 (1886): 880–96.

———. "Een pajoeng-kwestie." *TBB* 25 (1903): 38–47.

———. "Javaansche rangen en pajoengs." *Tijdschrift van het Indisch Aardrijkskundig Genootschap*, no. 2 (1883): 1–13.

Habib St. Maharadja. *Nasib*. Batavia: Balai Poestaka, 1932.

Hadi Ningrat. "De achteruitgang van het prestige der Inlandsche hoofden en de middelen om daarin verbetering te brengen." *TBB* 17 (1899): 367–85.

Handelingen van Den Volksraad. Batavia: Volksraad van Nederlandsch-Indië, 1918.

Hardjo Soë [Pseud.]. "Omong kosong: Pasar Gambir." *Pandji Poestaka* 13, no. 70 (1935).

———. "Omong kosong: Pasar Gambir di Betawi." *Pandji Poestaka* 14, no. 71 (1936).

———. "Omong kosong: pemandangan dalam Paar Gambir." *Pandji Poestaka* 13, no. 72 (1935).

———. "Omong kosong: pemandangan Pasar Gambir." *Pandji Poestaka* 15, no. 75 (1937).

———. "Omong kosong: pemandangan tentang Pasar Gambir." *Pandji Poestaka* 16, no. 70/72 (1938).

Hardjosoepoetro. "De oude gebruiken gewijzigd en in harmonie gebracht met de opvattingen van den tegenwoordigen tijd." *Djåwå* 11 (1931): 39–49.

Helsdingen-Schoevers, B. van. *De Europeesche vrouw in Indië*. Baarn: Hollandia, 1914.

Hermans, E. H. *Gezondheidsleer voor Nederlandsch-Indië: Een boek voor ieder die naar Indië gaat, of daar woont*. Amsterdam: J. M. Meulenhoff, 1925.

Historische nota over het vraagstuk van de opleiding en benoembaarheid voor den administratieven dienst in Nederlandsch-Indië. Batavia: Landsdrukkerij, 1900.

Indisch Verslag. The Hague: Landsdrukkerij, 1931.

Jaarverslag Nederlandsch-Indische jaarbeurs te Bandoeng. Tegal: De Boer, 1929–1933.

Jagt, M. B. van der. "B. B." *De Taak* 2, no. 6 (September 7, 1918).

———. "Ethische koers en bestuursambtenaar." *KT* 4, no. 2 (1915): 1191–1215 and 1328–45.

Jasper, J. E. *De organisatie van een jaarmarkt-tentoonstelling: de 2e te Pekalongan*. Tegal: De Boer, 1924.

———. "Staatstie, gevolg en songsongs van Inlandsche ambtenaren in de gouvernementslanden op Java en Madoera." *Extra bijlage van het TBB* 27, no. 1 (1904): 1–73.

———. *Verslag van de eerste Semarangsche jaarmarkt-tentoonstelling, 1908*. Batavia: Landsdrukkerij, 1911.

———. *Verslag van de eerste tentoonstelling-jaarmarkt te Soerabaja*. Batavia: Landsdrukkerij, 1906.

———. *Verslag van de vierde tentoonstelling-jaarmarkt te Soerabaja*. Batavia: Landsdrukkerij, 1909.

Junghuhn, Franz. "De gematigde en koude streken van Java, met de aldaar voorkomende warme bronnen: uit een natuur-aardrijks-en geneeskundig oogpunt beschouwd, als stellende een middel daar ter voorkoming en genezing van die ziekten, waaraan Europeanen, ten gevolge van hun lang verblijf in heete luchtstreken, gewoonlijk lijden." *Tijdschrift Voor Neerland's Indië* 4, no. 2 (1842): 81–121.

Kalff, S. "Eerbewijzen in Indië." *Haagsch Maandblad* 8 (1927): 651.

———. "Javaansche poesaka." *Djåwå: Tijdschrift van Het Java-Instituut* 3 (1923): 151–58.

Karno. "Hormat dan percaja." *Bintang Hindia* 3, no. 7 (1905): 75–77.

Kartodikromo, Marco. "Pakaian Europa." *Doenia Bergerak*, October 17, 1914.

———. "Pakaian Europa." *Doenia Bergerak*, October 17, 1914.

———. *Student Hidjo*. Semarang: Masman en Stroink, 1919.

Kartosiswojo. "Kamerdika'an." *Sinar Djawa*, April 8, 1914.

Kelling, M. A. J. "Het jaarbeurswezen in Nederlandsch-Indië." *Koloniale Studiën* 9, no. 2 (1925): 210–42.

———. "De eerste hygiëne-tentoonstelling in Nederlandsch-Indië." *D'Oriënt* 6, no. 26 (1927).

Kern, R. A. "De kontroleurs en 't concubinaat." *TBB* 28 (1905): 250–52.

Kertowinoto. "Sembah dan jongkok." *Bintang Hindia* 3, no. 3 (1905): 38–39.

Ki Wiroloekito. "Gemengde huwelijken." *De Vrouw in Indië*, May 1, 1915.

Kohlbrugge, J. H. F. *Blikken in het zieleleven van den Javaan en zijner overheerschers.* Leiden: Brill, 1907.

———. "Climatologie en tropische ziekten." *TNI* 4 (1900): 119–24.

———. "Prostitutie in Nederlandsch Indië." *Verslagen der Vergaderingen van het Indisch Genootschap* (February 19, 1901): 17–36.

———. "The Influence of a Tropical Climate on Europeans." *The Eugenics Review* 3, no. 1 (1911): 25–36.

Koopman. *Het paradijs der vrouwen: tegenschrift op Veth's "Leven in Indië."* The Hague: N. Veenstra, 1901.

Later, J. F. H. A. "De Inlandsche beweging." *IG* 38, no. 2 (1916): 922.

Linden, A. L. V. L. van der. *De Europeaan in de Maleische literatuur.* Meppel: B. ten Brink, 1937.

Loon, F. H. G. van. "Het zenuwlijden der blanken in de tropen." *Geneeskundig Tijdschrift voor Nederlandsch-Indië* 67 (1927): 435–78.

———. "Wie Is geschikt voor de tropen?" *KT* 19 (1930): 1–25.

Louw, P. J. F. *De Java-Oorlog van 1825–1830.* Vol. 2. Batavia: Landsdrukkerij, 1897.

Mangoenkoesoemo, Goenawan. "De Javaan en zijn hormatgebruiken." *Bintang Hindia* 3, no. 14 (1905): 166.

———. "De Javaan en zijn hormatgebruiken." *Java Bode*, May 22, 1905.

———. "Iets over den Javaan en zijn hormatgebruiken." *Java Bode*, June 22, 1905.

———. "De tijden veranderen en wij met hen." *Java Bode*, June 23, 1905.

———. "Nog eens: De Javaan en zijn hormat-gebruiken." *Bintang Hindia* 3, no. 15 (1905): 178 and 190–91.

———. "De geboorte van Boedi-Oetomo." In *Soembangsih: gedenkboek Boedi-Oetomo 1908 20 Mei 1918*, 9–16. Amsterdam: Drukkerij J. Tjabring, 1918.

Mangoenkoesoemo, Tjipto. "De Indische regeering moet zich schamen." *De Indiër* 1, no. 11 (January 1, 1914): 130.

———. "Het Binnenlandsch Bestuur." *De Indiër* 2, no. 154 (n.d.): 3 July 1918.

———. "Het 'prestige' in gevaar." *De Indiër* 1 (December 4, 1913): 82.

Margadant, C. W. *Het Regeeringsreglement van Nederlandsch-Indië.* 3 vols. Batavia: Kolff, 1894.

Mayer, L. Th. *Een blik in het Javaansche volksleven*. Leiden: Brill, 1897.

Meijer Ranneft, J. W. *De toekomst van het Binnenlandsch Bestuur*. Buitenzorg: Archipel Drukkerij, 1922.

Moeis, Abdoel. *Salah Asoehan*. Weltevreden: Balai Poestaka, 1928.

Moesa. "Kleeding en adat." *Bintang Hindia* 3, no. 10 (1905): 118–19.

Muhlenfeld, A. "Iets over de naleving der voorschriften in Bijblad 6061, 6118 en 6496." *TBB* 35 (1908): 33–39.

Multatuli [Pseudonym for Eduard Douwes Dekker]. *Max Havelaar: Or, the Coffee Auctions of a Dutch Trading Company*. Translated by Roy Edwards. New York: Penguin Books, 1987.

Nederburgh, J. A. *Gemengde huwelijken. Staatsblad 1898 no. 158: officiele bescheiden met eenige aanteekeningen*. Batavia, 1899.

Nieuwenhuis, G. J. *Lichamelijke opvoeding in Indië*. Weltevreden: Vereeniging Nederlandsch-Indisch Onderwijs Kongres, 1918.

Nijland, A. H. *Hygiënische wenken voor het leven in Nederlandsch-Indië*. Leiden: S. C. van Doesburgh, 1921.

"Nomor Pasar-Malem 31 Mei–9 Juni." *Soeloeh Ra' jat Indonesia* 4 (1930).

Onderzoek naar de Mindere Welvaart der Inlandsche Bevolking op Java en Madoera. 14 vols. Batavia: Landsdrukkerij, 1905.

Overzicht van de Inlandsche en Maleisisch-Chineesche Pers. Weltevreden: Drukkerij Volkslectuur, 1917–1940.

Parvé, D. C. Steijn. *Het koloniaal monopoliestelsel getoetst aan geschiedenis en staatshuishoudkunde*. Zaltbommel: Joh. Noman en Zoon, 1851.

Pedro [pseud.]. "Sikapnya bangsa Europa terhadap pada perempoean Boemipoetera." *Kemadjoean Hindia*, June 5, 1923.

Pleyte, C. M., ed. *Verslag nopens de Pasar-Gambir: Gehouden op het Koningsplein te Weltevreden van 28 Augustus–2 September 1906*. Batavia: Landsdrukkerij, 1907.

Programma van de Soerabaiasche Jaarmarkt Vereeniging. Surabaya, 1924.

Programma van Den Pasar Gambir. Batavia: Pasar Gambir Comité, 1922.

Raffles, Thomas Stamford. *Substance of a Minute Recorded by the Honourable Thomas Stamford Raffles, Lieutenant-Governor of Java and Its Dependencies, on the 11th February 1814 on the Introduction of an Improved System of Internal Management and the Establishment of a Land Rental on the Island of Java: To Which Are Added Several of the Most Interesting Documents Therein Referred To*. London: Black, Parry, and Co., 1814.

———. *The History of Java*. 2 vols. London: Allen, 1817.

Ratu Langie, S. S. J. *Serikat Islam*. Baarn: Hollandia, 1913.

Reith, G. M. *A Padre in Partibus: Being Notes and Impressions of a Brief Holiday Tour through Java, the Eastern Archipelago and Siam*. Singapore: Singapore and Straits Print. Office, 1897.

Reitsma, S.A. "Bandoeng en de jaarbeurs." *D'Oriënt* 6, no. 26 (1927).

Rinkes, D. A. "Oude en nieuwe stroomingen onder de bevolking." *Verslagen der Algemeene Vergaderingen van het Indisch Genootschap* (November 18, 1916): 55–78.

Rivai, Abdoel. "Bangsawan pikiran." *Bintang Hindia* 0, no. 1 (1902): 3–4.

——. "Kaoem moeda." *Bintang Hindia* 3, no. 14 (1905): 159–61.

Ronggo. "Hormat." *Bintang Hindia* 3, no. 7 (1905): 74–75.

S. "Suka akan kehormatan." *Bintang Hindia* 4, no. 6 (1906): 200–204.

"Sanatogen: A Scientific Investigation of Its Alleged Action on the Recuperating Powers of the Blood." *Journal of the American Medical Association* 63, no. 13 (1914): 1127–29.

Sarekat-Islam congres: (1e nationaal congres), 17–24 juni 1916 te Bandoeng. Batavia: Landsdrukkerij, 1916.

Sarekat-Islam congres (2e nationaal congres) 20–27 oktober 1917 te Batavia. Batavia: Landsdrukkerij, 1918.

Sarekat-Islam congres (3e nationaal congres) 29 september–6 oktober 1918 te Soerabaja. Batavia: Landsdrukkerij, 1919.

Sastrawirja. "Moderne wellevendheid." *Djåwå* 11 (1931): 31–38.

Schrieke, B. *De Inlandsche hoofden: rede, in tegenwoordigheid van zijne excellentie den gouverneur-generaal van Nederlandsch-Indië uitgesproken bij de 4-jarige herdenking van de stichting der Rechtshoogeschool te Batavia, op 27 October 1928.* Weltevreden: Kolff, 1928.

Simon Thomas, A. E. *De importeur, de Pasar Gambir, jaarbeurs, pasar malem en jaarmarkten.* Surabaya: Hahn, 1928.

——. *Een en ander over de plaats der jaarmarkten in de Indische maatchappij: Prae-advies uitgebracht op de jaarvergadering der vereeniging tot bevordering van het jaarmarktwezen in Nederlandsch-Indië, gehouden te Soerabaja op 13 October 1929.* Weltevreden: Emmink, 1929.

Slamet. "Ingezonden." *Bintang Hindia* 5, no. 4 (1906): 46–47.

Snouck Hurgronje, Christiaan. "Blikken in het zielenleven der Javaan?" *De Gids* 72 (1908): 423–47.

——. "De Inlandsche bestuursambtenaren, vooral op Java." *De Gids* 72 (1908): 211–34.

Soembangsih: gedenkboek Boedi-Oetomo 1908 20 Mei 1918. Amsterdam: Drukkerij J. Tjabring, 1918.

Soetatmo, Soeriokoesoemo. "Taal en kleeding." *De Indiër* 2, no. 3 (November 12, 1914): 9–11.

Soetomo. "'Fahamnja' regent." *Soeloeh Ra'jat Indonesia* 3, no. 17 (April 24, 1929): 230–31.

——. "Moeslihatnja regent." *Soeloeh Ra'jat Indonesia* 3, no. 18 (May 1, 1929): 246–47.

——. "Sambat pada bawah-perintahnja." *Soeloeh Ra'jat Indonesia* 3, no. 20 (May 15, 1929): 290–91.

Soewardi Soerjaningrat. *Djika saja Nederlander,… / Als ik eens Nederlander was,…* Bandung: Comité Boemipoetra, 1913.

——. "Europeesche kleeding." *De Indiër* 1, no. 15 (1914): 180.

——. "Javanen in Europeesche kleeding." *De Indiër* 1, no. 16 (1914): 191–92.

——. "Onze nationale kleeding." *De Indiër* 1, no. 37 (1914): 134–38.

——. "Staat de regeering werkelijk sympathiek tegenover de S.I.?" *De Indiër* 1, no. 4 (November 13, 1913): 48.

Staatsblad van Nederlandsch-Indië. Batavia: Landsdrukkerij, 1816.

Stibbe, G. Th. "Nog een protest." *KT* 3, no. 1 (1914): 493–95.

Stokvis, J. E. "Het B. B." *De Taak,* August 10, 1918.

Swaving, Cornelis. "De invloed van Java's klimaat op den gezonden Europeaan en gezondheidsregelen voor den nieuw uitgekomene." *Indisch Archief* 1 (1849): 161–80.

———. "Iets over den invloed van het klimaat dezer gewesten op den Europeaan."
Natuur-En Geneeskundig Archief voor Neerland's-Indië 1 (1844): 81–115.

Tertius [Pseud.]. "Geeft acht, B. B.!" *KT* 3, no. 1 (1914): 376–80.

Verwey, L. H. *De acclimatatie van Nederlanders in Indië, en van Indiërs in Nederland.*
The Hague: Kraft, 1863.

Verwijk, J. J. "Nota over de staatsie en het gevolg der Inlandsche ambtenaren in de
gouvernementslanden Op Java en Madoera." *TBB* 17 (1899): 451–61.

Veth, Bas. *Het leven in Nederlandsch-Indië.* Amsterdam: P. N. Van Kampen &
Zoon, 1900.

Veth, P. J. *Java: geographisch, ethnologisch, historisch.* Vol. 4. Haarlem: De Erven F.
Bohn, 1907.

Wagenvoort, Maurits. *Nederlandsch-Indische menschen en dingen.* Amsterdam: H. J.
W. Becht, 1910.

Waitz, Carl. *Onderrigtingen en voorschriften, om de gewone ziekten van Europeanen in
heete gewesten te ontgaan, en zich aldaar spoedig aan het klimaat te gewennen, bijzonder met betrekking tot Nederlandsch Indië.* Amsterdam: Sulpke, 1829.

Wal, S. L. van der, ed. *De opkomst van de nationalistische beweging in
Nederlands-Indië: Een bronnenpublikatie.* Groningen: J. B. Wolters, 1967.

Walbeehm, A. H. J. G. "Een drankverbod voor Nederlandsch-Indië." *Verslagen der
Vergaderingen van het Indisch Genootschap* (January 16, 1912): 119–47.

———. "Het leven van den bestuursambtenaar in het binnenland." *Onze Koloniën* 1,
no. 3 (1913).

Wall, V. I. van de. "Indische kleederdrachten." *D'Oriënt,* October 25, 1924.

———. *Oude Hollandsche bouwkunst in Indonesië.* Antwerpen: De Sikkel, 1942.

Wongso [Pseud.]. "Schetsen uit het Javaansche volksleven." *NNI,* June 5 and
July 4, 1905.

Wybrands, Karel. "Een idealist-practicus." *NNI,* November 30, 1904.

———. "Regeerings-beleid en regeerings-organen." *NNI,* April 23, 1906.

Published Secondary Sources

Adam, Ahmat B. "Radical Journalism and Press Persecution in Java: 1914–1918." *Jebat*
20 (1992): 91–105.

———. *The Vernacular Press and the Emergence of Modern Indonesian Consciousness
(1855–1913).* Ithaca: SEAP, Cornell University Press, 1995.

Adamson, Walter L. *Hegemony and Revolution: A Study of Antonio Gramsci's Political
and Cultural Theory.* Berkeley: University of California Press, 1980.

Adas, Michael. "Contested Hegemony: The Great War and the Afro-Asian Assault on the Civilizing Mission Ideology." *JWH* 15, no. 1 (2004): 31–63.

———. "From Avoidance to Confrontation: Peasant Protest in Precolonial and Colonial Southeast Asia." *Comparative Studies in Society and History* 23, no. 2 (1981): 217–47.

———. "From Footdragging to Flight: The Evasive History of Peasant Avoidance Protest in South and South-East Asia." *Journal of Peasant Studies* 13, no. 2 (1986): 64–86.

———. *Machines as the Measure of Men: Science, Technology, and Ideologies of Western Dominance.* Ithaca: Cornell University Press, 1989.

———. *Prophets of Rebellion: Millenarian Protest Movements against the European Colonial Order.* Chapel Hill: University of North Carolina Press, 1979.

Akihary, Huib. *Architectuur & stedebouw in Indonesië, 1870–1970.* Zutphen: De Walburg Pers, 1990.

Alexanderson, Kris. *Subversive Seas: Anticolonial Networks across the Twentieth-Century Dutch Empire.* Cambridge: Cambridge University Press, 2019.

Anderson, Benedict R. O'G. *Imagined Communities: Reflections on the Origin and Spread of Nationalism.* London: Verso, 1983.

———. *Language and Power: Exploring Political Cultures in Indonesia.* Ithaca: Cornell University Press, 1990.

———. *Mythology and the Tolerance of the Javanese.* Ithaca: SEAP, Cornell University Press, 1965.

Anderson, Perry. "The Antinomies of Antonio Gramsci." *New Left Review* 1, no. 100 (1976): 5–78.

Anderson, Warwick. *Colonial Pathologies: American Tropical Medicine, Race, and Hygiene in the Philippines.* Durham: Duke University Press, 2006.

Arnold, David. "Gramsci and Peasant Subalternity in India." *Journal of Peasant Studies* 11, no. 4 (1984): 155–77.

Baay, Reggie. *De njai: het concubinaat in Nederlands-Indië.* Amsterdam: Athenaeum-Polak & Van Gennep, 2008.

Ballantyne, Tony, and Antoinette M. Burton. *Empires and the Reach of the Global, 1870–1945.* Cambridge: Belknap Press of Harvard University Press, 2014.

Barlow, Tani E., Madeleine Yue Dong, Uta G. Poiger, Priti Ramamurthy, Lynn M. Thomas, and Alys Eve Weinbaum. "The Modern Girl around the World: A Research Agenda and Preliminary Findings." *Gender & History* 17, no. 2 (2005): 245–94.

Bayly, C. A. *The Birth of the Modern World, 1780–1914: Global Connections and Comparisons.* Malden: Blackwell Publishers, 2004.

Bloembergen, Marieke. *Colonial Spectacles: The Netherlands and the Dutch East Indies at the World Exhibitions, 1880–1931.* Singapore: Singapore University Press, 2006.

Bloembergen, Marieke, and Remco Raben, eds. *Het koloniale beschavingsoffensief: wegen naar het nieuwe Indië, 1890–1950.* Leiden: KITLV Press, 2009.

Blussé, Leonard. *Strange Company: Chinese Settlers, Mestizo Women and the Dutch in VOC Batavia.* Dordrecht: Foris Publications, 1986.

Bosma, Ulbe, and Remco Raben. *Being "Dutch" in the Indies: A History of Creolisation and Empire, 1500–1920.* Singapore: National University of Singapore Press, 2008.

Breman, Jan. *Mobilizing Labour for the Global Coffee Market: Profits from an Unfree Work Regime in Colonial Java*. Amsterdam: Amsterdam University Press, 2015.

Bronkhorst, Dorine, and Esther Wils. *Tropenecht: Indische en Europese kleding in Nederlands-Indië*. The Hague: Stichting Tong, 1996.

Burgers, Herman. *De garoeda en de ooievaar: Indonesië van kolonie tot nationale staat*. Leiden: KITLV Press, 2011.

Carey, Peter. *Babad Dipanagara: An Account of the Outbreak of the Java War, 1825–30: The Surakarta Court Version of the Babad Dipanagara with Translations into English and Indonesian-Malay*. Kuala Lumpur: Art Printing Works, 1981.

———. *Sisi lain Diponegoro: Babad Kedung Kebo dan Historiografi perang Jawa*. Jakarta: Gramedia, 2018.

———. *The Power of Prophecy: Prince Dipanagara and the End of an Old Order in Java, 1785–1855*. Leiden: KITLV Press, 2007.

Chandra, Siddhartha. "What the Numbers Really Tell Us about the Decline of the Opium Regie." *Indonesia*, no. 70 (October 2000): 101–23.

Cohen, M. I. *Inventing the Performing Arts: Modernity and Tradition in Colonial Indonesia*. Honolulu: University of Hawai'i Press, 2016.

Cohn, Bernard S. *Colonialism and Its Forms of Knowledge: The British in India*. Princeton: Princeton University Press, 1996.

Colombijn, Freek, and Joost Coté, eds. *Cars, Conduits, and Kampongs: The Modernization of the Indonesian City, 1920–1960*. Leiden: Brill, 2015.

Conklin, Alice L. *A Mission to Civilize: The Republican Idea of Empire in France and West Africa, 1895–1930*. Stanford: Stanford University Press, 1997.

Cooper, Frederick. *Colonialism in Question: Theory, Knowledge, History*. Berkeley: University of California Press, 2005.

Coté, Joost J. P. "Staging Modernity: The Semarang International Colonial Exhibition, 1914." *Review of Indonesian and Malaysian Affairs* 40, no. 1 (2006): 1–44.

———. "'To See Is to Know': The Pedagogy of the Colonial Exhibition, Semarang, 1914." *Paedagogica Historica* 36, no. 1 (2000): 340–66.

Cox, Howard. *The Global Cigarette: Origins and Evolution of British American Tobacco, 1880–1945*. New York: Oxford University Press, 2000.

Cribb, R. B., ed. *The Late Colonial State in Indonesia: Political and Economic Foundations of the Netherlands Indies, 1880–1942*. Leiden: KITLV Press, 1994.

Crozier, Anna. "What Was Tropical about Tropical Neurasthenia? The Utility of the Diagnosis in the Management of British East Africa." *Journal of the History of Medicine and Allied Sciences* 64, no. 4 (2009): 518–48.

Dijk, Kees van. "Sarong, Jubbah, and Trousers: Appearance as a Means of Distinction and Discrimination." In *Outward Appearances: Dressing State and Society in Indonesia*, 38–84. Edited by Henk Schulte Nordholt. Leiden: KITLV Press, 1997.

———. *The Netherlands Indies and the Great War 1914–1918*. Leiden: KITLV Press, 2007.

Doel, H. W. van den. *De stille macht: het Europese binnenlands bestuur op Java en Madoera, 1808–1942*. Amsterdam: Bert Bakker, 1994.

Doorn, J. A. A. van. *De laatste eeuw van Indië: ontwikkeling en ondergang van een koloniaal project*. Amsterdam: Bert Bakker, 1994.

———. *Indische lessen: Nederland en de koloniale ervaring*. Amsterdam: Bert Bakker, 1995.

Dutton, George. "Advertising, Modernity, and Consumer Culture in Colonial Vietnam." In *The Reinvention of Distinction: Modernity and the Middle Class in Urban Vietnam*, 21–42. Edited by V. Nguyen-Marshall, L. B. W. Drummond, and D. Bélanger. New York: Springer, 2012.

Elliot, Inger McCabe. *Batik: Fabled Cloth of Java*. New York: Clarkson N. Potter, 1984.

Elson, R. E. *The Idea of Indonesia: A History*. New York: Cambridge University Press, 2008.

———. *Village Java under the Cultivation System, 1830–1870*. Sydney: Allen and Unwin, 1994.

Engels, Dagmar, and Shula Marks, eds. *Contesting Colonial Hegemony: State and Society in Africa and India*. New York: British Academic Press, 1994.

Fakih, Farabi. "Conservative Corporatist: Nationalist Thoughts of Aristocrats: The Ideas of Soetatmo Soeriokoesoemo and Noto Soeroto." *BKI* 168, no. 4 (2012): 420–44.

Fasseur, C. "Cornerstone and Stumbling Block: Racial Classification and the Late Colonial State in Indonesia." In *The Late Colonial State in Indonesia: Political and Economic Foundations of the Netherlands Indies, 1880–1942*, 31–57. Edited by Robert B. Cribb. Leiden: KITLV Press, 1994.

———. *De Indologen: ambtenaren voor de Oost 1825–1950*. Amsterdam: Aula, 2003.

———. "De taal is gans de Indisch ambtenaar. De taalopleiding van de bestuursambtenaren." In *Koloniale taalpolitiek in Oost en West: Nederlands-Indië, Suriname, Nederlandse Antillen en Aruba*, 187–206. Edited by Kees Groeneboer. Amsterdam: Amsterdam University Press, 1997.

———. *The Politics of Colonial Exploitation: Java, the Dutch, and the Cultivation System*. Translated by R. E. Elson. Ithaca: SEAP, Cornell University Press, 1992.

Formichi, Chiara. "Indonesian Readings of Turkish History, 1890s to 1940s." In *From Anatolia to Aceh: Ottomans, Turks, and Southeast Asia*, 241–60. Edited by A. C. S. Peacock and Annabel Teh Gallop. Oxford: Oxford University Press, 2015.

———. *Islam and the Making of the Nation: Kartosuwiryo and Political Islam in Twentieth-Century Indonesia*. Leiden: KITLV Press, 2012.

Foster, Anne. *Projections of Power: The United States and Europe in Colonial Southeast Asia, 1919–1941*. Durham: Duke University Press, 2010.

Foulcher, Keith. "Biography, History and the Indonesian Novel: Reading Salah Asuhan." *BKI* 161, no. 2/3 (2005): 247–68.

Geertz, Clifford. *Negara: The Theatre State in Nineteenth-Century Bali*. Princeton: Princeton University Press, 1980.

Godley, Michael R. "The End of the Queue: Hair as Symbol in Chinese History." *East Asian History*, no. 8 (1994): 53–72.

Goss, Andrew. *The Floracrats: State-Sponsored Science and the Failure of the Enlightenment in Indonesia*. Madison: University of Wisconsin Press, 2011.

Gouda, Frances. *Dutch Culture Overseas: Colonial Practice in the Netherlands Indies, 1900–1942*. Amsterdam: Amsterdam University Press, 1995.

———. "Good Mothers, Medeas, or Jezebels: Feminine Imagery in Colonial and Anticolonial Rhetoric in the Dutch East Indies, 1900–1942." In *Domesticating the Empire: Race, Gender, and Family Life in French and Dutch Colonialism*, 236–54. Edited by Julia Clancy-Smith and Frances Gouda. Charlottesville: University of Virginia Press, 1998.

———. "'Nyonyas' on the Colonial Divide: White Women in the Dutch East Indies, 1900–1942." *Gender & History* 5, no. 3 (1993): 318–42.

Gramsci, Antonio. *Selections from the Prison Notebooks of Antonio Gramsci*. Translated by Quintin Hoare and Geoffrey Nowell-Smith. New York: International Publishers, 1972.

Greenwood, Anna. "The Strange History of Tropical Neurasthenia." *Psychologist* 24, no. 3 (2011): 226–27.

Groeneboer, Kees. *Gateway to the West: The Dutch Language in Colonial Indonesia, 1600–1950*. Amsterdam: Amsterdam University Press, 1998.

Guha, Ranajit. *Dominance without Hegemony: History and Power in Colonial India*. Cambridge: Harvard University Press, 1997.

Haedrick, Daniel R. *The Tools of Empire: Technology and European Imperialism in the Nineteenth Century*. New York: Oxford University Press, 1981.

Hall, Stuart. "Gramsci's Relevance for the Study of Race and Ethnicity." *Journal of Commonwealth Inquiry* 10, no. 5 (1986): 5–27.

Hart, Betty de. "'De verwerpelijkste van alle gemengde huwelijken': de gemengde huwelijken regeling Nederlands-Indië 1898 en de rijkswet op het Nederlanderschap 1892 vergeleken." In *Gaan & staan: jaarboek voor de vrouwengeschiedenis*, 60–81. Edited by Carolien Bouw. Amsterdam: Stichting Beheer IISG, 2001.

Haynes, Douglas, and Gyan Prakash. *Contesting Power: Resistance and Everyday Social Relations in South Asia*. Berkeley: University of California Press, 1992.

Hesselink, Liesbeth. *Healers on the Colonial Market: Native Doctors and Midwives in the Dutch East Indies*. Leiden: KITLV Press, 2011.

———. "The Unbearable Absence of Parasols: The Formidable Weight of a Colonial Java Status Symbol." *International Institute for Asian Studies Newsletter*, no. 45 (2007): 26.

Hoogervorst, Tom, and Henk Schulte Nordholt. "Urban Middle Classes in Colonial Java (1900–1942): Images and Language." *BKI* 173, no. 4 (2017): 424–74.

Hoogervorst, Tom G. *Language Ungoverned: Indonesia's Chinese Print Entrepreneurs, 1911–1949*. Ithaca: SEAP, Cornell University Press, 2021.

Houben, Vincent. "Representations of Modernity in Colonial Indonesia." In *Figurations of Modernity: Global and Local Representations in Comparative Perspective*, 23–40. Edited by Vincent Houben and Mona Schrempf. Frankfurt: Campus Verlag, 2008.

Ingleson, John. "Sutomo, the Indonesian Study Club and Organised Labour in Late Colonial Surabaya." *JSEAS* 39, no. 1 (2008): 31–57.

Jákl, Jiří. "An Unholy Brew: Alcohol in Pre-Islamic Java." *The Newsletter*, no. 77 (2017).

Jennings, Eric T. *Curing the Colonizers: Hydrotherapy, Climatology, and French Colonial Spas.* Durham: Duke University Press, 2006.

Jones, Steve. *Antonio Gramsci.* London; New York: Routledge, 2006.

Joshi, Sanjay. *Fractured Modernity: Making of a Middle Class in Colonial North India.* New Delhi: Oxford University Press, 2001.

Kartini, Raden Adjeng. *Letters of a Javanese Princess.* Translated by Agnes Louise Symmers. Kuala Lumpur: Oxford University Press, 1976.

——. *The Complete Kartini: The Collected Works of R. A. Kartini.* Translated by Joost J. P. Coté. Clayton: Monash University Publishing, 2013.

Kartodirdjo, Sartono. *Pengantar sejarah Indonesia baru: sejarah pergerakan nasional dari kolonialisme sampai nasionalisme.* Vol. 2. Jakarta: Gramedia Pustaka Utama, 1992.

Kennedy, Dane. "The Perils of the Midday Sun: Climatic Anxieties in the Colonial Tropics." In *Imperialism and the Natural World*, 118–40. Edited by John MacKenzie. Manchester: Manchester University Press, 1990.

Knecht-van Eekelen, A. de. "The Debate about Acclimatization in the Dutch East Indies (1840–1860)." *Medical History*, no. 20 (2000): 70–85.

Korver, A. P. E. *Sarekat Islam, 1912–1916: opkomst, bloei en structuur van Indonesië's eerste massabeweging.* Amsterdam: Historisch Seminarium van de Universiteit van Amsterdam, 1982.

Kuitenbrouwer, Maarten. *The Netherlands and the Rise of Modern Imperialism: Colonies and Foreign Policy, 1870–1902.* New York: St. Martin's Press, 1991.

Kusno, Abidin. "The Afterlife of the Empire Style: Indische Architectuur and Art Deco." In *Past in the Present: Architecture in Indonesia*, 131–46. Edited by P. Nas. Leiden: KITLV Press, 2007.

Laffan, Michael Francis. *Islamic Nationhood and Colonial Indonesia: The Umma Below the Winds.* New York: Routledge, 2003.

——. *The Makings of Indonesian Islam: Orientalism and the Narration of a Sufi Past.* Princeton: Princeton University Press, 2011.

Lears, Jackson. "The Concept of Cultural Hegemony: Problems and Possibilities." *The American Historical Review* 90, no. 3 (1985): 567–93.

Liechty, Mark. *Suitably Modern: Making Middle-Class Culture in a New Consumer Society.* Princeton: Princeton University Press, 2003.

Locher-Scholten, Elsbeth. *Ethiek in fragmenten: vijf studies over koloniaal denken en doen van Nederlanders in de Indonesische Archipel 1877–1942.* Utrecht: HES Publishers, 1981.

——. "Marriage, Morality and Modernity: The 1937 Debate on Monogomy." In *Women and the Colonial State: Essays on Gender and Modernity in the Netherlands Indies, 1900–1942*, 187–218. Amsterdam: Amsterdam University Press, 2000.

——. "So Close and Yet So Far: The Ambivalence of Dutch Colonial Rhetoric on Javanese Servants in Indonesia, 1900–1942." In *Domesticating the Empire: Race,*

Gender, and Family Life in French and Dutch Colonialism, 131–53. Edited by
Julia Clancy-Smith and Frances Gouda. Charlottesville: University of Virginia
Press, 1998.

———. "Summer Dresses and Canned Food: European Women and Western Lifestyles
in the Indies, 1900–1942." In *Outward Appearances: Dressing State and Society in
Indonesia*, 151–80. Edited by Henk Schulte Nordholt. Leiden: KITLV Press, 1997.

———. *Women and the Colonial State: Essays on Gender and Modernity in the Netherlands Indies, 1900–1942*. Amsterdam: Amsterdam University Press, 2000.

Loo, Vilan van de. "Tobben in Indië: wijze vriendinnen adviseren Hollandse vrouwen." *Indische letteren* 9, no. 2 (July 1994): 66–80.

Lukito, Yulia Nurliani. "Colonial Exhibition and a Laboratory of Modernity: Hybrid
Architecture at Batavia's Pasar Gambir." *Indonesia* 100 (2015): 77–104.

———. *Exhibiting Modernity and Indonesian Vernacular Architecture: Hybrid Architecture at Pasar Gambir of Batavia, the 1931 Paris International Colonial Exhibition
and Taman Mini Indonesia Indah*. Wiesbaden: Springer VS, 2016.

Lurie, Alison. *The Language of Clothes*. New York: Random House, 1981.

Luttikhuis, Bart. "Beyond Race: Constructions of 'Europeanness' in Late-Colonial
Legal Practice in the Dutch East Indies." *European Review of History* 20, no. 4
(2013): 539–58.

———. "Negotiating Modernity: Europeanness in Late Colonial Indonesia, 1910–
1942." PhD diss., European University Institute, 2014. https://cadmus.eui.eu/
handle/1814/33074.

Luttikhuis, Bart, and Arnout H. C. van der Meer. "1913 in Indonesian History: Demanding Equality, Changing Mentality." *TRaNS: Trans-Regional and-National
Studies of Southeast Asia* 8, no. 2 (2020): 115–33.

———. "New Turning Points in Southeast Asian History: Re-Writing Southeast Asian
Chronologies from Within." *TRaNS: Trans-Regional and-National Studies of
Southeast Asia*, 8, no. 2 (2020): 81–83.

Maier, Hendrik M. J. "Phew! Europeesche Beschaving: Marco Kartodikromo's 'Student Hidjo.'" *Southeast Asian Studies* 34, no. 1 (1996): 184–210.

Marle, A. van. "De groep der Europeanen in Nederlands-Indië: iets over ontstaan en
groei." *Indonesië* 5 (1951): 97–121, 314–41, and 481–507.

Martyn, Elizabeth. *The Women's Movement in Post-Colonial Indonesia: Gender and
Nation in a New Democracy*. New York: Routledge, 2005.

Maters, Mirjam. *Van zachte wenk tot harde hand: persvrijheid en persbreidel in
Nederlands-Indië, 1906–1942*. Hilversum: Verloren, 1998.

McVey, Ruth. *The Rise of Indonesian Communism*. Ithaca: Cornell University
Press, 1965.

Meer, Arnout H. C. van der. "Igniting Change in Colonial Indonesia: Soemarsono's
Contestation of Colonial Hegemony in a Global Context." *JWH* 30, no. 4 (October 30, 2019): 501–32.

———. "Performing Colonial Modernity: Fairs, Consumerism, and the Emergence of
the Indonesian Middle Classes." *BKI* 173, no. 4 (2017): 503–38.

——. "Rituals and Power: Cross-Cultural Exchange and the Contestation of Colonial Hegemony in Indonesia." In *Cross-Cultural Exchange and the Colonial Imaginary: Global Encounters via Southeast Asia*, 75–103. Edited by Hazel Hahn. Singapore: National University of Singapore Press, 2019.

Miert, Hans van. *Een koel hoofd en een warm hart: nationalisme, Javanisme en jeugdbeweging in Nederlands-Indië, 1918–1930*. Amsterdam: De Bataafsche Leeuw, 1995.

Ming, Hanneke. "Barracks-Concubinage in the Indies, 1887–1920." *Indonesia* 35 (1983): 65–93.

Mobini-Kesheh, Natalie. *The Hadrami Awakening: Community and Identity in the Netherlands East Indies, 1900–1942*. Ithaca: SEAP, Cornell University Press, 1999.

Moertono, Soemarsaid. *State and Statecraft in Old Java: A Study of the Later Mataram Period, 16th to 19th Century*. Ithaca: SEAP, Cornell University Press, 1968.

Moon, Suzanne. *Technology and Ethical Idealism: A History of Development in the Netherlands East Indies*. Leiden: CNWS Publications, 2007.

Moor, Jaap de. "The Recruitment of Indonesian Soldiers for the Dutch Colonial Army, c. 1700–1950." In *Guardians of Empire: The Armed Forces of the Colonial Powers c. 1700–1964*, 53–69. Edited by David Killingray and David Omissi. Manchester: Manchester University Press, 1999.

Morton, P. A. *Hybrid Modernities: Architecture and Representation at the 1931 Colonial Exposition, Paris*. Cambridge: MIT Press, 2003.

Mrázek, Rudolf. *Engineers of Happy Land: Technology and Nationalism in a Colony*. Princeton: Princeton University Press, 2002.

——. "Indonesian Dandy: The Politics of Clothes in the Late Colonial Period, 1893–1942." In *Outward Appearances: Dressing State and Society in Indonesia*, 117–47. Edited by Henk Schulte Nordholt. Leiden: KITLV Press, 1997.

Nagazumi, Akira. *The Dawn of Indonesian Nationalism: The Early Years of the Budi Utomo, 1908–1918*. Tokyo: Institute of Developing Economies, 1972.

——. "The Pawnshop Strikes of 1922 and the Indonesian Political Parties." *Archipel: Études Interdisciplinaires Sur Le Monde Insulindien Archipel*, no. 8 (1974): 187–206.

Nandy, Ashis. *The Intimate Enemy: Loss and Recovery of Self under Colonialism*. New Delhi: Oxford University Press, 1988.

Newbury, C. W. "Patrons, Clients, and Empire: The Subordination of Indigenous Hierarchies in Asia and Africa." *JWH* 11, no. 2 (2000): 227–63.

Niel, Robert van. *The Emergence of the Modern Indonesian Elite*. The Hague: W. van Hoeve, 1960.

Noer, Deliar. *The Modernist Muslim Movement in Indonesia, 1900–1942*. Kuala Lumpur: Oxford University Press, 1973.

O'Brien, Suzanne G. "Splitting Hairs: History and the Politics of Daily Life in Nineteenth-Century Japan." *The Journal of Asian Studies* 67, no. 4 (2008): 1309–39.

O'Malley, William. "Second Thoughts on Indonesian Nationalism." In *Indonesia: Australian Perspectives*, 601–13. Edited by James J. Fox. Canberra: National University Press, 1980.

Onghokham. *The Thugs, the Curtain Thief, and the Sugar Lord: Power, Politics, and Culture in Colonial Java*. Jakarta: Metafor Publishing, 2003.

Osterhammel, Jürgen. *The Transformation of the World: A Global History of the Nineteenth Century*. Princeton: Princeton University Press, 2015.

Palmier, Leslie H. *Social Status and Power in Java*. London: University of London, Athlone Press, 1960.

———. "The Javanese Nobility under the Dutch." *Comparative Studies in Society and History* 2, no. 2 (1960): 197–227.

Passchier, Cor. "Colonial Architecture in Indonesia: References and Developments." In *Past in the Present: Architecture in Indonesia*, 97–112. Edited by Peter J. M. Nas. Leiden: KITLV Press, 2007.

Pemberton, John. *On the Subject of "Java."* Ithaca: Cornell University Press, 1994.

Poeze, Harry A. "Early Indonesian Emancipation: Abdul Rivai, Van Heutz, and the Bintang Hindia." *BKI* 145, no. 1 (1989): 87–106.

Pols, Hans. "Notes from Batavia, the Europeans' Graveyard: The Nineteenth-Century Debate on Acclimatization in the Dutch East Indies." *Journal of the History of Medicine and Allied Sciences* 67, no. 1 (2012): 120–48.

———. *Nurturing Indonesia: Medicine and Decolonization in the Dutch East Indies*. Cambridge: Cambridge University Press, 2018.

Protschky, Susie. *Photographic Subjects: Monarchy and Visual Culture in Colonial Indonesia*. Manchester: Manchester University Press, 2019.

———, ed. *Photography, Modernity, and the Governed in Late-Colonial Indonesia*. Amsterdam: Amsterdam University Press, 2015.

———. "The Colonial Table: Food, Culture and Dutch Identity in Colonial Indonesia." *Australian Journal of Politics and History* 54, no. 3 (2008): 346–57.

Protschky, Susie, and Tom van den Berge, eds. *Modern Times in Southeast Asia, 1920s–1970s*. Leiden: Brill, 2018.

Raben, Remco. "Ethnic Disorder in VOC Asia: A Plea for Eccentric Reading." *BMGN – Low Countries Historical Review* 134, no. 2 (2019): 1115–28.

Rambe, Safrizal. *Sarekat Islam pelopor nasionalisme Indonesia, 1905–1942*. Jakarta: Yayasan Kebangkitan Insan Cendekia, 2008.

Ravensbergen, Sanne. "Courtrooms of Conflict: Criminal Law, Local Elites and Legal Pluralities in Colonial Java." PhD diss., Leiden University, 2018. http://hdl.handle.net/1887/61039.

Ravesteijn, Wim, and Jan Kop, eds. *For Profit and Prosperity: The Contribution Made by Dutch Engineers to Public Works in Indonesia, 1800–2000*. Leiden: KITLV Press, 2008.

Ricklefs, M. C. *A History of Modern Indonesia since c. 1200*. Stanford: Stanford University Press, 2001.

———. *Jogjakarta under Sultan Mangkubumi, 1749–1792: A History of the Division of Java*. London: Oxford University Press, 1974.

———. *Polarizing Javanese Society: Islamic and Other Visions, c. 1830–1930*. Honolulu: University of Hawai'i Press, 2007.

Rooy, Piet de, Ann Laura Stoler, and Jan Breman, eds. *Imperial Monkey Business: Racial Supremacy in Social Darwinist Theory and Colonial Practice*. Amsterdam: VU University Press, 1990.

Rupin, Dafna. "The Emergence of a Modern Audience for Cinema in Colonial Java." *BKI* 173, no. 4 (2017): 475–502.

Rush, James R. *Opium to Java: Revenue Farming and Chinese Enterprise in Colonial Indonesia, 1860–1910*. Ithaca: Cornell University Press, 1990.

Rydell, R. W. *All the World's a Fair: Visions of Empire at American International Expositions, 1876–1916*. Chicago: University of Chicago Press, 1987.

Schulte Nordholt, Henk. "Modernity and Cultural Citizenship in the Netherlands Indies: An Illustrated Hypothesis." *JSEAS* 42, no. 3 (2011): 435–57.

———. "New Urban Middle Classes in Colonial Java: Children of the Colonial State and Ancestors of a Future Nation." *BKI* 173, no. 4 (2017): 439–41.

———, ed. *Outward Appearances: Dressing State and Society in Indonesia*. Leiden: KITLV Press, 1997.

———. *Spell of Power: A History of Balinese Politics, 1650–1940*. Leiden: KITLV Press, 1996.

———. "The State on the Skin: Clothes, Shoes, and Neatness in (Colonial) Indonesia." *Asian Studies Review* 21, no. 1 (1997): 19–39.

Scott, James C. *Domination and the Arts of Resistance: Hidden Transcripts*. New Haven: Yale University Press, 1990.

———. *Weapons of the Weak: Everyday Forms of Peasant Resistance*. New Haven: Yale University Press, 1987.

Sears, Laurie J. *Shadows of Empire: Colonial Discourse and Javanese Tales*. Durham: Duke University Press, 1996.

Shiraishi, Takashi. *An Age in Motion: Popular Radicalism in Java, 1912–1926*. Ithaca: Cornell University Press, 1990.

———. "The Disputes between Tjipto Mangoenkoesoemo and Soetatmo Soeriokoesoemo: Satria vs. Pandita." *Indonesia* 32 (1981): 93–108.

Spyer, Patricia, ed. "The Tooth of Time, or Taking a Look at the 'Look' of Clothing in Late Nineteenth-Century Aru." In *Border Fetishisms: Material Objects in Unstable Spaces*, 150–82. New York: Routledge, 1998.

Steijlen, Fridus, and Erik Willems, eds. *Met ons alles goed: brieven en films uit Nederlands-Indië van de familie Kuyck*. Zutphen: Walburg Pers, 2008.

Stevens, Th. "Van der Capellen's koloniale ambitie op Java: economisch beleid in een stagnerende conjunctuur, 1816–1826." Amsterdam: Historisch Seminarium van de Universiteit van Amsterdam, 1982.

Stoett, F. A. *Nederlandsche spreekwoorden, spreekwijzen, uitdrukkingen en gezegden*. Zutphen: W. J. Thieme & Cie, 1923.

Stoler, Ann Laura. *Along the Archival Grain: Epistemic Anxieties and Colonial Common Sense*. Princeton: Princeton University Press, 2009.

———. *Carnal Knowledge and Imperial Power: Race and the Intimate in Colonial Rule*. Berkeley: University of California Press, 2002.

——. "Making Empire Respectable: The Politics of Race and Sexual Morality in 20th-Century Colonial Cultures." *American Ethnologist* 16, no. 4 (1989): 634–60.

——. "Sexual Affronts and Racial Frontiers: European Identities and the Cultural Politics of Exclusion." *Comparative Studies in Society and History* 34, no. 3 (1992): 514.

Streets-Salter, Heather. *World War One in Southeast Asia*. West Nyack, New York: Cambridge University Press, 2017.

Stutje, Klaas. *Campaigning in Europe for a Free Indonesia: Indonesian Nationalists and the Worldwide Anticolonial Movement, 1917–1931*. Copenhagen: Nordic Institute of Asian Studies Press, 2019.

Sukarno, Achmad and Cindy Adams. *Sukarno: An Autobiography as Told to Cindy Adams*. New York: Bobbs-Merrill, 1965.

Sutherland, Heather. "Pangreh Pradja: Java's Indigenous Administrative Corps and Its Role in the Last Decades of Dutch Colonial Rule." Phd Diss., Yale University, 1973.

——. *The Making of a Bureaucratic Elite: The Colonial Transformation of the Javanese Priyayi*. Singapore: Heinemann Educational Books, 1979.

——. "The Priyayi." *Indonesia* 19 (1975): 57–77.

Suwignyo, Agus. "The Making of Politically Conscious Indonesian Teachers in Public Schools, 1930–42." *Southeast Asian Studies* 3, no. 1 (2014): 119–49.

Sysling, Fenneke. *Racial Science and Human Diversity in Colonial Indonesia*. Singapore: National University of Singapore Press, 2016.

Tagliacozzo, Eric. "The Indies and the World: State Building, Promise, and Decay at a Transnational Moment, 1910." *BKI* 166, no. 2–3 (2010): 270–92.

——. *The Longest Journey: Southeast Asians and the Pilgrimage to Mecca*, 2013.

Tarlo, Emma. *Clothing Matters: Dress and Identity in India*. Chicago: University of Chicago Press, 1996.

Taylor, Jean Gelman. "Costume and Gender in Colonial Java, 1800–1940." In *Outward Appearances: Dressing State and Society in Indonesia*, 85–116. Edited by Henk Schulte Nordholt. Leiden: KITLV Press, 1997.

——. "Identity, Nation and Islam: A Dialogue about Men's and Women's Dress in Indonesia." In *The Politics of Dress in Asia and the Americas*, 101–20. Edited by Mina Roces and Louise P. Edwards. Brighton: Sussex Academic Press, 2007.

——. "Official Photography, Costume and the Indonesian Revolution." In *Women Creating Indonesia: The First Fifty Years*, 91–126. Edited by Jean Gelman Taylor. Clayton: Monash Asia Institute, 1997.

——. "The Sewing-Machine in Colonial-Era Photographs: A Record from Dutch Indonesia." *Modern Asian Studies* 46, no. 1 (2012): 71–95.

——. *The Social World of Batavia: Europeans and Eurasians in Colonial Indonesia*. Madison: University of Wisconsin Press, 1983.

Tjiook-Liem, Patricia. *De rechtspositie der Chinezen in Nederlands-Indië 1848–1942: wetgevingsbeleid tussen beginsel en belang*. Amsterdam: Leiden University Press, 2009.

Tsuchiya, Kenji. "The Taman Siswa Movement—Its Early Eight Years and Javanese Background." *JSEAS* 6, no. 2 (1975): 164–77.

Veldhuisen, Harmen. *Batik Belanda, 1840–1940: Dutch Influence in Batik from Java, History and Stories.* Jakarta: Gaya Favorit, 1993.

Veur, Paul W. van der. *Toward a Glorious Indonesia: Reminiscences and Observations of Dr. Soetomo.* Athens: Ohio University Center for Southeast Asian Studies, 1987.

Vickers, Adrian. *A History of Modern Indonesia.* Cambridge: Cambridge University Press, 2005.

Vreede-de Stuers, Cora. *The Indonesian Woman: Struggles and Achievements.* The Hague: Mouton, 1960.

Wedema, Steven. *"Ethiek" und Macht: die niederländisch-indische Kolonialverwaltung und indonesische Emanzipationsbestrebungen 1901–1927.* Stuttgart: F. Steiner, 1998.

Wesseling, H. L. "Bestond er een Nederlands imperialisme?" *Tijdschrift Voor Geschiedenis* 99, no. 2 (1986): 214–25.

White, Sally. "The Case of Nyi Anah: Concubinage, Marriage and Reformist Islam in Late Colonial Dutch East Indies." *Review of Indonesian and Malaysian Affairs* 38, no. 1 (2004): 87–98.

Williams, Raymond. *Marxism and Literature.* Oxford: Oxford University Press, 1977.

Wilson, Elizabeth. *Adorned in Dreams: Fashion and Modernity.* Berkeley: University of California Press, 1987.

Wisseman Christie, Jan. "Rāja and Rāma: The Classical State in Early Java." In *Centers, Symbols, and Hierarchies: Essays of the Classical States of Southeast Asia*, 21–35. Edited by Lorraine Gesick and Michael Aung-Thwin. New Haven: Yale University Southeast Asia Studies Monographs, 1983.

Wolters, O. W. *History, Culture, and Region in Southeast Asian Perspectives.* Ithaca: SEAP, Cornell University Press, 1999.

Yamamoto, Nobuto. Censorship in Colonial Indonesia, 1901–1942. Leiden: Brill, 2019.

INDEX

Page numbers followed by *f* refer to figures.

CPSIA information can be obtained
at www.ICGtesting.com
Printed in the USA
LVHW110400240822
726751LV00003B/107